Eilís Quinn

Montréal
& Québec City

Introducing Montréal

Cities like Montréal don't happen very often. By day, it bubbles with Eurocharm and North American pizzazz. After dark, its nightlife sizzles with creativity and abandon. It's the city of a hundred nations, all lured by Montréal's intoxicating mix of Gallic tradition and joie de vivre rubbing up against North American innovation and optimism. It's one of the most fascinating urban cultures in the world – and we've barely even started.

It may seem strange that it all works so well, but it does. French, English, immigrants from all over the world…somehow it all sticks together despite the occasional frictions and flare-ups. Perhaps it's all the great food, cutting-edge culture and enduring thirst for wine that keeps the whole machine humming. Whatever it is, every Montrealer knows deep down that despite the problems the city may have, it is the epicenter of fabulousness and fun in all of Canada.

The frighteningly delicious mix of influences has turned the city into a 24-hour cultural and culinary all-you-can-eat banquet. Montréal, the cultural chameleon, has a kaleidoscope of identities: Latin capital of the north, culinary paradise, hub of hipdom, mosaic of cultures, Paris without the jet lag, to name but a few. And now the international accolades are flooding in, for everything from its culinary prowess and foodie culture to its indie music scene. Its film industry is on fire and everyone from the city's artists to actors are getting international acclaim.

Nor has Montréal's cultural pull gone unnoticed by the powerful shapers of the city's future. Montréal may never compete economically with Toronto, but when it comes to the arts, the glory days for this city lie ahead. However, the city's greatest asset is its laid-back attitude and how Montrealers manage to be sophisticated, friendly and tolerant of visitors as well as of each other. The result is a bubbling economy and a city sparkling with more energy and mischief than ever before.

Perhaps the most rewarding way to explore it all is to just throw yourself into the mix and let the crowds carry you along. No matter what you do, certainly you'll end your stay with one overwhelming desire: to return.

1 *Montréal International Jazz Festival (p57)* **2** *Montréal's Divers/Cité Festival (p23)* **3** *Coffee drinkers on rue St-Denis, Montréal* **4** *Gourmet paradise at Montréal's Marché Atwater (p125)*

Previous Pages (left) *Montréal's autumn foliage in full bloom* **(right)** *King Sunshine, Denis Alix Montréal International Jazz festival (p57)*

1 Creative lighting at Olive + Gourmando, Montréal (p127) 2 People-watching sculpture outside Kilo cafe, The Village, Montréal (p135) **3** Terrace on rue de la Commune, Old Montréal (p72)

5

1 *Icicles at Montréal's McGill University (p91)* **2** *Visionary urban art around rue St-Denis Montréal* **3** *Culinary delights at Montréal's Marché Atwate (p125)*

1 Coffee break, Little Italy (p161), Montréal 2 Berry heaven at Montréal's Marché Jean-Talon (p125) 3 Drummers gather at Parc du Mont-Royal, Montréal, every Sunday for 'Tam-Tam Jam' concerts (p149)

1 *Street mural on rue St-Denis, Montréal* **2** *Montréal's architectural masterpiece, The Biosphère, on Île Ste-Hélène, is a showcase for environmental education (p82)* **3** *Bench sculpture on ave McGill College, Montréal* **4** *Fountain outside the vibrant Palais des Congrès, Montréal (p87)*

1 *Rue Crescent is a popular dining and clubbing area in Downtown Montréal* **2** *Skating at Parc du Bassin Bonsecours in Montréal's Old Port (p170)* **3** *Basilique Notre-Dame, Old Montréal (p73)*

Calèche ride in Old Montréal (p71) **2** *Montréal International Jazz Festival, Place des Arts (p57)* **3** *Casino de Montréal in Parc Jean-Drapeau (p166)*

1 *Street artists near Place d'Armes, Québec City* 2 *View over the Cathedral of the Holy Trinity (p223) to the St Lawrence River, Québec City* 3 *Québec City's JA Moisan Epicier, the oldest grocery store in North America (p248)*

1 Street musician on Place Royale, Québec City 2 The toboggan slide near Québec City's historic landmark Château Frontenac (p253)

1 Rotunda on the Terrasse Dufferin boardwalk overlooking the St Lawrence River
2 Old Lower Town, Québec City (p224) **3** Bluegrass musicians in Québec City

1 Capture the breathtaking scenery at Lac Supérieur, Mont Tremblant (p259) 2 Ski trail through village at the base of Mont Tremblant

Next Page Château Frontenac on Québec City's waterfront (p253)

Contents

Published by Lonely Planet Publications Pty Ltd
ABN 36 005 607 983

Australia Head Office, Locked Bag 1, Footscray,
Victoria 3011, ☎ 03 8379 8000, fax 03 8379 8111,
talk2us@lonelyplanet.com.au

USA 150 Linden St, Oakland, CA 94607,
☎ 510 893 8555, toll free 800 275 8555,
fax 510 893 8572, info@lonelyplanet.com

UK 72–82 Rosebery Ave, Clerkenwell, London,
EC1R 4RW, ☎ 020 7841 9000, fax 020 7841 9001,
go@lonelyplanet.co.uk

The Author

Eilís Quinn

While other kids in Vancouver were playing with trucks and dolls, Eilís was playing with foreign-language dictionaries and verb books. She spent decades flailing around the world looking for her linguistic *coup de foudre* (love) and finally found it with Québec French when she landed in Montréal in 1994. She then went on to earn language degrees in Russian, Chinese and German and studied at universities in Sichuan, Moscow, Kassel and Hanover. Despite all that, something about Montréal kept drawing her back no matter how hard she tried to leave – a world without Daniel Bélanger, Jean Leloup and films starring Pascale Bussiéres and Luc Picard, is one Eilís just didn't want to live in. Realizing she went a little overboard on the language BAs, she added journalism into the mix. She went on to work as a reporter in newsrooms across Canada and in New York City until her career finally brought her back to Montréal for good. She's manned the hatches at both the *Montréal Gazette* and later as a reporter/editor in the Montréal bureau of the *Canadian Press* newswire service. These days, when she's not on the road for Lonely Planet, she calls a gorgeous little apartment in the city's Ville-Marie borough home. She's been based in Montréal full time since 2003.

Eilís' Top Montréal Day

I couldn't imagine living in Montréal without my bicycle to whisk me all over the city. There's nothing quite like starting the day off with a latte at Café L'Esperanza (p143) followed by an aimless roam around Mile End to soak up the atmosphere. Next, I dash into Fairmount Bagel (p143) for a couple of the poppy-seed variety, hop on my bike and head to Parc Jean-Drapeau (p81) to whiz around the Circuit Gilles-Villeneuve. From there, I mount the island's bike route. Hugging the island's edges, you see waves from the St Lawrence River trying to claw their way up onto land as well as beautiful views of the Montréal skyline. After that, I take the bike path back to the Old Port (p79) swinging into Restaurant Holder (p128) for the fab foie-gras salad and a glass of wine before heading over to the Belgo (p182) building to peruse all the great new artists showing in the galleries and seeing what's up at the Musée d'Art Contemporain de Montréal (p89). I head up rue St-Denis after that, and make my weekly pilgrimage to Librairie Michel Fortin (p186) to see what new language tapes or books they've got in. Working my way up to ave Laurier's Middle Eastern café Byblos (p140), I vicariously travel through my new books as I nosh on Iranian purées and eavesdrop on conversations around me. Next, it's back on my bike to microbrasserie Dieu du Ciel (p155) to sample their chocolate-, smoke- and coffee-flavored brews. As always, I'll plan to hit Les Deux Pierrots (p152) or Boîte à Maurice (p153) afterwards, but likely won't make it. In Montréal, there's so much on offer it's impossible to take it all in.

LONELY PLANET AUTHORS

Why is our travel information the best in the world? It's simple: our authors are independent, dedicated travelers. They don't research using just the internet or phone, and they don't take freebies in exchange for positive coverage. They travel widely, to all the popular spots and off the beaten track. They personally visit thousands of hotels, restaurants, cafés, bars, galleries, palaces, museums and more – and they take pride in getting all the details right, and telling it how it is. For more, see the authors section on lonelyplanet.com.

PHOTOGRAPHER
RAY LASKOWITZ

For Ray, working in Montréal was similar to living and working in his home town of New Orleans. Both cities have a remarkable French-based culture. Making travel-friendly images in the dead of winter proved to be challenging even though Ray has been photographing all manner of subjects for 28 years. He lists making travel images among his favorite work.

City Life

City Life

MONTRÉAL TODAY

It's thrilling to see Montréal shine these days in a way it hasn't shone in decades. Sometimes it feels like it's in the midst of a giant coming-out party – only this time getting attention for being a sizzling, classy, cultured city instead of for linguistic struggles. Montréal is known these days more for its eating and music and culture scenes than the politics of separatism.

Heavyweights of American culture have christened the city's music scene as the next big thing; in March 2006 the New York City–based *Gourmet* magazine devoted an entire issue to the city's foodie culture; and Montrealer Denys Arcand won the Foreign Film Oscar in 2004 for *Les Invasions Barbares*, reminding the world there's a vibrant French-language film industry right here in North America.

Montréal also hosted world-class events including what may have been the most attractive ever World Aquatic Championships in 2005 and the first ever World Outgames, an Olympics-like sporting event that drew gay, straight and transgendered athletes from countries all over the world and had 100,000 people a night partying for two weeks straight in downtown streets.

Elsewhere, Old Montréal has been revamped from depressing tourist trap to one of the most fashionable addresses in communications and media, while sweeping redevelopment has molded the Old Port into a gleaming tourist attraction. Once-battered shops along downtown's rue Ste-Catherine are also starting to shine again with renewed vigor.

Loft conversions are becoming de rigueur for the hip yuppies of the Plateau and beyond, giving poor areas a new lease of life. The Village has emerged from nowhere to become a mainstream bastion of alternative living that, like the rest of the city, is safe and open to all.

Tired yet?

Even for locals it's taken some getting used to. It seems like it's only now, with the separatist flames turned down, that the curtain on the rest of the city has come off. Visitors who remember the fire-and-brimstone separatism speeches in the 1990s and all-around linguistic tensions will be sur-

LOWDOWN	
Population 3.5 million (Greater Montréal)	
Time zone Eastern Time (GMT − 5 hours)	
3-star room $130	
Favorite spectator sport after hockey Canadian Football League football	
Cup of coffee $1.50	
A Montrealer's average income $28,258	
Metro/bus ticket $2.50	
Percentage of Montrealers who say they know both English and French 57%	
Essential drink Microbrew $5	
No-no Don't ask a Québécois if they speak 'proper French'	

Take a stroll down rue Ste-Catherine Est through the Village (p94)

prised to hear the most fiery political conversations these days revolve around inept garbage and snow removal. And this from a metropolis that only a decade ago was literally shrinking under its troubles, a time when asking for directions in English on the Plateau would get you a look that could shoot daggers.

The transformation hasn't been without hiccups, however. Everything from Montréal's near loss of the Grand Prix to the mediocre performance of the Canadiens ice-hockey team and the loss of the Montréal Expos baseball team in 2005 has shaken the city's confidence. And though the economy is humming, the strong Canadian dollar has been having an impact on everything from tourism to the local film industry.

The language wars may be dormant, but everyone in the city knows it doesn't take much to inflame them on either side and Montrealers are wringing as much as possible out of these boom days in the meantime, leaving the city with a tangible live-for-the-day abandon that's contagious.

CITY CALENDAR

If Montréal is throwing a festival somewhere, do yourself a favor and just go. Nobody does parties like this city does and even locals book their holiday time according to the festival calendar – not so they can get out of town, but so they can stay, immerse themselves and soak up every last minute of it. They don't call it the City of Festivals for nothing. Summer is the unrivalled king with monster jazz and comedy festivals fighting for space with multiday events devoted to dance, drama, African culture, cinema or even punk music. Entire blocks are closed to traffic and stages are set up for free concerts and film screenings – leaving plenty of room in the streets for the party. Public holidays are also usually marked with massive downtown parades and raucous concerts. Winter events tend to have less out-of-town visitors but Montrealers themselves are out in droves. See p273 for public holiday listings.

JANUARY
LA FÊTE DES NEIGES

☎ 872-6120; www.fetedesneiges.com; Île Ste-Hélène, Parc Jean-Drapeau

Montréal's Snow Festival features some ice-sculpting contests, dog-sled races, snow games and costumed characters like mascot polar bear Boule de Neige. It's held over three consecutive weekends in late January and early February.

FEBRUARY
MONTRÉAL EN LUMIÈRE

☎ 288-9955, 888-477-9955; www.montreal highlights.com

Created to help locals shake off the late-winter doldrums, the Montréal Highlights Festival is a kind of wintry Mardi Gras with most events taking place downtown. There are classical music and dance performances, exhibitions, fireworks, celebrity chefs

and weirdly wonderful events like a 5km race through the Underground City (p86).

MARCH
ST PATRICK'S DAY PARADE

☎ 932-0512; www.montrealirishparade.com

Rue Ste-Catherine turns shamrock-green during this monster event. Hundreds of thousands of Montrealers turn out annually for the 40-plus marching bands and floats on the second Sunday in March.

MONTRÉAL FASHION WEEK

☎ 876-1499; www.mfw.ca

This twice-yearly fashion event (March for the winter/fall collections and October for the spring/summer collections) is closed to the general public, but is worth noting for the excitement it generates around local fashion and the festivities that spill over into local bars afterwards. Venues change regularly.

APRIL
BLUE METROPOLIS – MONTRÉAL INTERNATIONAL LITERARY FESTIVAL
☎ 932-1112; www.blue-met-bleu.com
This festival brings together 200-plus writers from all over the globe for five days of literary events in English, French, Spanish and other languages in the first week of April.

MAY
BIENNALE DE MONTRÉAL
☎ 288-0881; www.ciac.ca
This awesome biennial event showcases the best and the brashest on the Canadian art scene including conferences and seminars on contemporary art. Upcoming dates are May 10 to July 8, 2007.

FESTIVAL TRANSAMÉRIQUES
☎ 842-0704; www.fta.qc.ca
Formerly known as *the* cutting-edge drama showcase *Festival de Théâtre des Amériques*, this new festival is casting a wider net, promising to show off everything that is new and exciting in drama, dance and art. It takes place in late May to early June in venues all over town.

MONTRÉAL BEER FESTIVAL
☎ 722-9640; www.festivalmondialbiere.qc.ca
Quaff brews from around the globe inside the old Windsor Station. The five-day event starts late May/early June.

JUNE
TOUR DE L'ÎLE
☎ 521-8356; www.velo.qc.ca; Île Ste-Hélène & Downtown
Also known as the Montréal Bikefest, the Tour draws 30,000 enthusiasts for a 50km spin around the Island of Montréal and a big party in the city afterwards. It's staged on the first Saturday in June, with pre-registration.

NUIT BLANCHE SUR TABLEAU NOIR
☎ 522-3797; www.tableaunoir.com
Ave du Mont-Royal becomes an artist's canvas on the second weekend in June when the street comes alive with music, various workshops and children's activities.

FORMULA ONE GRAND PRIX
☎ 350-0000; www.grandprix.ca; Île Notre-Dame in Parc Jean-Drapeau
Sometime in mid- to late June, the world's flashiest drivers, crews and entourages converge on the Circuit Gilles-Villeneuve for North America's biggest Formula One event.

ST-AMBROISE MONTRÉAL FRINGE FESTIVAL
☎ 849-3378; www.montrealfringe.ca
An off-Broadway-style theater and repertory festival of new local and international talent, with dancing, music and the ever-popular drag races (as in drag *queen* races). Held over 10 days from mid-June.

LOTO-QUÉBEC INTERNATIONAL FIREWORKS COMPETITION
☎ 397-2000; www.internationaldesfeuxloto -quebec.com
Thousands camp out on rooftops and on the Jacques-Cartier Bridge for the planet's hottest pyrotechnics contest accompanied by dramatic musical scores. The 10 shows last 30 minutes each and are held on Saturday nights and a few Wednesday nights from late June to the end of July.

OFF-FESTIVAL DE JAZZ
☎ 570-0722; www.lofffestivaldejazz.com
The alternative jazz fest presents around 50 shows in several downtown venues to showcase young new talent. It's held over 10 days in late June and early July.

JULY
SHAKESPEARE IN THE PARK
☎ 931-2644; www.shakespeareinthepark.ca
Families spread out on blankets for performances of the bard's best plays at park stages around town on weekends, usually throughout July and August.

MONTRÉAL INTERNATIONAL JAZZ FESTIVAL
☎ 523–3378, 888-515-0515; www.montreal jazzfest.com
With over 400 concerts and nearly two million visitors every year, North America's hippest music fest just gets bigger and better with world music, rock and even

pop music sharing the program with jazz legends and upstarts. Hundreds of brand-name musicians hit the halls and outdoor stages, and dozens of concerts are given for free over 13 days from late June to mid-July (p57).

FESTIVAL INTERNATIONAL NUITS D'AFRIQUE

☎ 499-9239; www.festivalnuitsdafrique.com
Celebrates the cultures of Africa and the Caribbean with more than 500 artists from 20-plus countries, with workshops, exotic cuisine and an African market. Held at Place Émilie-Gamelin and several clubs and halls for 10 days in mid-July.

JUST FOR LAUGHS

☎ 845-3155, 888-244-3155; www.hahaha.com; Quartier Latin
More than 650 artists perform in over 1000 shows at this comedy festival which runs for two weeks in mid-July. Past events have featured Jason Alexander of *Seinfeld* fame, Craig Ferguson, John Cleese and Margaret Cho.

FANTASIA

www.fantasiafestival.com
An unabashed love-fest for devotees of international fantasy, action and horror films; Japanese anime geeks are drawn out in droves. Local genre films are also screened during this 18-day festival held in mid-July.

DIVERS/CITÉ

☎ 285-4011; www.diverscite.org
Montréal's Gay Pride is *the* event on the Village calendar, drawing more than a million people, even in slow years. The streets around the Place Émilie-Gamelin pulse with dancing, art exhibits, concerts and parades. It's held over one week starting in late July.

MONTRÉAL INTERNATIONAL DRAGON BOAT RACE

☎ 866-7001; www.montrealdragonboat.com
Rowing teams from all over the world compete in Chinese Dragon Boats on Île Notre-Dame, punctuated by entertainment and gastronomic events. Held over one weekend in late July.

AUGUST
LES FRANCOFOLIES

☎ 876-8989; www.francofolies.com
The annual musical showcase of international French-language music and theater spotlights today's biggest stars, and those on the rise, in 200-plus shows and free outdoor presentations during 10 days around mid-August.

MONTRÉAL WORLD FILM FESTIVAL

☎ 848-3883; www.ffm-montreal.org
One of the most prestigious film events in Canada, attracting 400,000 visitors to screenings from 70 countries. The stars come out, as well as the directors, producers and writers of the big screen. It's held over 10 days in late August and early September.

NASCAR: BUSCH SERIES EVENT

www.nascar.com; Parc Jean-Drapeau's Île Notre-Dame; ⊙ Aug 4, 2007; Ⓜ Jean-Drapeau
The Champ Car Series that usually took place here in August got the boot in 2006 to make way for a NASCAR Busch Series Event on the 2007 calendar. The Champ Car series never really took off in Montréal but many say it never had a chance coming so soon on the heels of June's star-studded, megawatt Formula 1 event. There's high hopes NASCAR may break through however, and if all goes well in 2007, there's talk of making it a permanent Montréal event. They'll be a Grand-Am series race on August 3, 2007 too.

TOP FIVE UNUSUAL FESTIVALS

- Manifestation Internationale Vidéo et Art Électronique (p24) – for making cutting-edge art mediums accessible
- Montréal Beer Festival (opposite) – self-explanatory
- Fantasia (left) – where else can you see a Hideo Nakata and a Satoshi Kon film in the same day, along with dozens of people as obsessed with them as you are?
- Montréal International Dragon Boat Race (left) – because the city's Chinese community shines alongside it
- Nuit Blanche sur Tableau Noir (opposite) – have you ever *seen* dozens of artists slapping down masterworks in a major street before?!

SEPTEMBER

MAGIC OF LANTERNS

☎ 872-1400; www.ville.montreal.qc.ca/jardin/en
/propos/lanternes.htm; Jardin Botanique
The Jardin Botanique extends its hours
into the night and lights up hundreds of
Chinese lanterns all over the park. Locals
swamp this popular event, running from
early September to late October.

MANIFESTATION INTERNATIONALE VIDÉO ET ART ÉLECTRONIQUE

☎ 393-3937; www.champlibre.com
Every two years, this event showcases
interactive video and electronic art at some
super-cool city location. Fantastic niche
event that still manages to draw everyone
from families with small children to retirees.
The next edition runs from September 23
to October 5, 2008.

OCTOBER

FESTIVAL DU NOUVEAU CINÉMA DE MONTRÉAL

☎ 282-0004; www.nouveaucinema.ca
This festival highlights who is up-and-
coming in feature films, documentaries,
experimental shorts, videos, narrative
features and electronic art forms during 10
days in early October.

BLACK & BLUE FESTIVAL

☎ 875-7026; www.bbcm.org
One of the biggest gay events in the Village, with major dance parties, cultural and
art shows as well as a killer mega-party
in the Olympic Stadium, all in the second
week of October.

Meet Victor, the official mascot of the Just for Laughs Festival (p23)

DECEMBER

CHRISTMAS AT THE JARDIN BOTANIQUE

☎ 872-1400; www2.ville.montreal.qc.ca/jardin
'Tis the season at the Jardin Botanique.
The main greenhouse becomes a fairyland
of poinsettia Christmas trees and fanciful
chandeliers made of plants. Activities in
past years have included storytelling for
kids, or choirs. It's open the entire month of
December.

THE FINAL FRONTIERS

The city's legendary boul St-Laurent (referred to by locals as 'the Main') traditionally served as Montréal's linguistic
divider: francophones hung out east of the street and anglophones to the west, while immigrants occupied a kind of
buffer zone in between. You can still sense the geographic division today: conversations along rue St-Denis in the Latin
Quarter are almost exclusively in French, while conversations in English dominate the bars of western downtown. The
trendy bars along boul St-Laurent are often frequented by second-generation immigrants, who readily mix French and
English with a minority language like Italian or Arabic.

Young Montrealers, however, will tell you that these old neighborhood lines are no longer significant in their
lives. While a francophone or anglophone Montrealer might frequent a local restaurant, video store or grocery,
they go to school or work in other parts of town and after dark head out to trendy neighborhoods like the Plateau
for fun.

CULTURE

Montrealers have one foot in Europe and the other in North America, giving the city a complex local culture. However, many locals have difficulty explaining it themselves, so they certainly don't expect foreigners to be able to make sense of it all. Instead, travelers are warmly embraced here and locals are usually more than game to show newcomers the ropes.

IDENTITY

To outsiders Montréal is often defined by its French and English characteristics, before they discover the city is so much more than that – it's been shaped as much by its Italian, Greek, Haitian, Jewish, Portuguese and Lebanese communities (and immigrants from dozens of other countries) as by the French and English.

City Life

CULTURE

HOT CONVERSATION TOPICS

- Montréal's monster potholes – why can't City Hall fix them?
- The québécois film industry – always hot, films made here are smashing box-office records left, right and centre, something that even English Canada is taking notice of.
- The Canadiens' new coach and re-jigged lineup – will things finally turn around for them?
- Your municipal taxes – they've increased by how much?!? Real-estate prices have soared across town, and property reevaluations have condo and homeowners worried breathless as they watch taxes jump by up to 47%.
- The city got the 2006 Outgames and the 2005 World Aquatic Championships – is a permanent spot on the NASCAR calendar next?

These days the typical Montrealer embraces all the identities that make up the city – the nationalist St Jean-Baptiste society invites non-francophone groups to participate in the Fête Nationale, while anglophones have accepted French as the day-to-day language of Québec society, along with the realization that it's not the end of the world. Don't be surprised to see two Montreal anglophones meeting for the first time socially, serving each other in a boutique or restaurant, and seeing them speak in French to each other without even realizing it, before switching back to their mother tongue.

Check the neighborhoods in and around the Plateau and Mile End to the north for some of the best experiences Montréal has to offer. On any given summer evening, streets around the Portuguese church in the Plateau may be closed off for a religious procession, while in Mile End a family of Hasidic Jews will be making their way to the synagogue. Italians now form the third-largest group in Montréal at more than 230,000, or more than 10% of the population, creating a vibrant Little Italy centered on the north of boul St-Laurent.

Not too long ago, if Montréal was in the news or fighting with Ottawa, it was French-English struggles at the core. But these days, the city and Québec's distinctness are being expressed in much more pronounced ways by their position on social issues and policies than through language issues – Québec's cornerstone universal day-care program charges parents just $7 a day and is unique in the country, for example. When demonstrations were held throughout the world protesting the US invasion of Iraq, over 100,000 Montrealers took to the streets – more than all the other demonstrations in Canada put together (the next biggest was 20,000 protesters in Vancouver).

Compared to the rest of Canada, Quebecers are the staunchest supporters for gun control and environmental initiatives like the Kyoto accord, and they're the most opposed to the Canadian military's involvement in Afghanistan. Montrealers under 40 are also some of the least likely to marry, and anecdotally at least, more likely to be living together and raising children in common-law relationships.

The city is not without its thorny issues, however. There's a critical shortage of family doctors – meaning many Montrealers have no primary-care physician – and a law requiring parents to send their children to French public schools, unless they themselves were educated in English, is controversial as many families, including francophone ones, would prefer to educate their children in English.

And, for a reason nobody has been able to adequately explain, Québec has the highest suicide rates in Canada with about 1,300 people killing themselves province-wide each year. A poll conducted in 2006 suggesting that 42% of Quebecers felt that suicide was an 'acceptable' act made headlines across the country.

LOCAL VOICES: FACES OF MONTRÉAL

Pascale Prinsen-Geerligs, Calèche Driver

This Laurentians native was born on October 3, 1975 and moved to Montréal in 1993. She studied film at Concordia University and worked on shot-in-Montréal Hollywood productions, but these days her average work shift has her hitching up her horse at the stables at 9am; by 10am she's out taking fares in Old Montréal until her shift ends 10 hours later. Pascale has been ferrying travelers through Old Montréal on calèches – horse-drawn carriages – on and off since 1999.

Calèche driver is an unusual job. How did you get into it?
By accident. I had no previous experience with horses. I was riding my bike with my father along the Lachine Canal, saw the [calèche] stables and got interested in the animals. I ended up taking courses at l'Institut de tourisme et d'hôtellerie du Québec [ITHQ-Québec Tourism and Hotel Institute]. We learned the history of Montréal and things like that.

What's the most frequent question travelers ask?
How much snow do you get in winter? We learned that in school but I still don't know what to tell them. They're also always asking about language stuff and are surprised we speak such good English here.

What's the best part of your job?
Working with the horses and my colleagues – they're a colorful bunch.

The worst?
The traffic, pollution and noise.

What's Old Montréal's best-kept secret?
The islands at Parc Jean-Drapeau. They're actually not really part of Old Montréal, but there's a ferry that leaves for them from the Old Port that I don't think a lot of people really know about, even locals.

What's your typical day off like?
I go to Atwater or Jean Talon Market to do my grocery shopping. I clean house, do yoga, go to the library – normal stuff.

What's your favorite Montréal movie?
The Score – I worked on that film as a production assistant. I'm not saying it's the best movie ever, but it was shot in Montréal, the story takes place in Montréal, and in the movie Robert De Niro lives in Montréal.

Favorite Montréal singer or musician?
Martha Wainwright, Rufus's sister. She's a Montrealer even though she lives in New York City now. I've been downhill skiing with her. The music's off-tempo and I like the lyrics.

Religion

One of the first things you'll notice in Montréal are the church steeples commanding the skyline of almost every neighborhood. It's not by chance – the Roman Catholic Church was the driving force behind the development of Québec society for centuries and it's hard to overstate the church's influence on the destiny of the province. Before 1960 they had as much a say in running the state as the politicians did (both officially and un-officially), until the church's stranglehold on society was thrown off during the Quiet Revolution (p62). The vast majority of Quebecers and 63% of Montrealers are Catholic, but the active church-going population has dropped to only 20% from roughly 85% in the 1950s.

Dwindling numbers of parishioners have left most congregations in financial crisis and churches are being sold off across the province. Though legislation is being discussed to curtail such sales it looks to be a tough sell – of the 285 churches on the Island of Montréal alone, about a third are expected to be sold or demolished within the next 10 years.

Many Catholic Montrealers born after the Quiet Revolution are publicly dismissive of religion, but behind closed doors, there is often a strong sentimental attachment to the church, and services are flooded at traditional times, like Easter and Christmas celebrations.

The majority of religious English-speaking Montrealers are Protestant (Anglicans, Presbyterians and members of the United Church of Canada). About 5% of residents are Jewish, and another 5% Muslim.

LIFESTYLE

How to define a typical Montrealer? At first glance – impossible! Head to any downtown street and you'll see immigrants chatting with French-speaking Quebecers while nearby, old-moneyed Westmounters wait in line behind Mile End hipsters. High-powered entrepreneurs chow down at Schwartz's, talking in French next to frustrated fiction writers complaining in English over their medium-fats.

You cannot class Montrealers by their jobs, where they are from or what language they speak, but when it comes to their attitude to life…wow, that's where it gets fun. Whether they want to make it big in the arts capital of French Canada or build a business empire from here all the way to Toronto, you can be sure that typical Montrealers will be working to live instead of living to work, definitively proving that old cliché is around for a reason.

A true Montrealer steals away for a wet lunch at the local bistro at least once a week. They'll talk with equal gusto (or disdain) about the most recent movie blockbuster from France before launching into a critique of the latest American cinematic hit. They talk up their neighborhoods with unabashed swagger, touting the shops and street life as the city's best kept secrets while dishing on local restaurants as if they were all Toqué!. Art really matters, and Montrealers can reel off the biographies of local authors and musicians as if they were family members, and Montrealers are as likely to arrive at business meetings on bicycle as they are on foot, and won't even bother to hide their casque or helmet hair – they manage to look perfectly stylish anyway.

It may all sound too good to be true, but just wait until you get here, and find out for yourself.

CATHOLICS HANG CURSE WORDS ON CHURCHES

The French spoken in Québec has a character all its own (p34) and swear words are no exception. While English curses tend to centre on the…uh…bodily functions or carnal side of human behavior, Quebecers' swear words center on the objects used in church services, a legacy of the church's centuries-long dominance.

The words are untranslatable, but let's just say where an English speaker might yell 'fuck', a Quebecer will unleash 'tabarnac' (from tabernacle). Where you might say shit, a Quebecer will cry 'sacrament' (from sacrament). And if it's really, really bad, just pray you're never on the receiving end of a killer combo like the lethal 'hostie de câlisse de tabarnac!' (rough translation: 'host in the chalice in the tabernacle!'). English speakers do NOT try this at home.

Now that you're oriented, imagine if such curse words were pasted all over your city, hanging on places of worship, and that the churches themselves wanted them there. Welcome to Montréal summer 2006 and possibly the church's most creative ever fundraising campaign.

In an effort to get people buzzing about church, huge signs appeared all over the city, like this: 'Tabernacle: a small cupboard closed with a key that sits in the middle of the altar and contains the ciborium.'

To say the signs caused locals to do a double take would be an understatement, and reactions were wildly mixed. Many people were offended, while others supported the campaign saying it would get people to think about swearing less. Whatever the long-term results may be, the short-term effects were dramatic. It got people buzzing about the church again and donations flooded in.

While it's good for visitors to know these words so you can understand what the motorists and cyclists are yelling at you when you innocently try to cross the street, don't bother trying to master the words yourselves. No English speaker or foreigner (even those from other French-speaking countries) seems able to nail them. As one francophone Québécoise said, 'No matter how good their French is, they never get the swearwords right. They always use "câlisse" when it should be "tabarnac" or "hostie" when it should be "sacrament." It just sounds bad.'

Women

Québec women attained the right to vote only in 1940, about two decades behind the rest of Canada; Thérèse Casgrain, a leading Québec feminist and activist of the postwar era, was the first woman to become a Québec minister. The feminist movement in Canada emerged in the 1960s in line with the international trend, and the Montréal Women's Liberation Movement was founded in 1969. Québec outlawed any discrimination against women in 1975.

Québec women today enjoy virtual social equality and are as likely as men to initiate contact with the opposite sex. It's a different story in the workplace, however, where relatively few women hold positions in senior management. Salaries continues to lag well behind men's in medicine or administration, and despite the province's overall social progressiveness, women are still vastly underrepresented in provincial politics. Only one in five Quebecers earning over $100,000 a year is a woman.

Gay & Lesbian Montréal

Canada's most romantic metropolis doesn't just tolerate alternative lifestyles – it hardly even bats an eyelash at them. Gay and lesbian marriage has been legal in Québec since 2004, and in many neighborhoods two woman or men walking down the street and holding hands rarely gets a second look. The great thing about the city's scene is the gay **Village** (p94), with its cafés, restaurants, sleek bars, galleries, sex shops and B&Bs, and – above all – its irrepressible sense of fun and openness. Here, no one cares if you speak English or French, what color you are, how you dress or who you sleep with. In fact, the appeal of mega-events like **Divers/Cité** (p22) is now mainstream, and some shows attract as many straights as gays.

Montréal hosted the first ever World Outgames in 2006, a sporting event for gay, lesbian and transgendered athletes, and the Village was the epicenter of festivities. There was some controversy that venues weren't as full as they should have been but it hardly mattered. The Village partied as if its life depended on it and rue Ste-Catherine turned into a kind of giant 24-hour, open-air discothéque, as rainbow pride flags fluttered along every side street.

FOOD

Montréal's dining scene is marked by dazzling variety and quality, and brash chefs who attack their creations with innovative gusto. Life in Montréal revolves around food and it's as much about satisfying your sensual fantasies as it is about nourishment.

There are well over 5000 restaurants in Montréal, offering classic French cuisine, hearty québécois fare and a huge variety of ethnic restaurants from 80-odd nationalities. Today's haute cuisine is as likely to be conjured up by talented young Italian, Japanese or British chefs as graduates from the Académie Culinaire du Québec.

Montrealers can enjoy an enormous variety of locally produced ingredients and delicacies: raw cheeses, foie gras, game and maple syrup, to name a few. The outdoor markets carry exotic foodstuffs that weren't available even a decade ago, alongside the tasty pro-

---

DEFENSE DE FUMER

Québec's long-feared smoking ban came into effect on May 31, 2006, forbidding smoking in bars, restaurants and indoor public places. Bar owners are trying to get an injunction to suspend the law, saying business is down and 520 jobs have been lost province-wide. However, despite Québec regularly posting the highest smoking rates in Canada, Montrealers have been sucking it up without a whimper. It's even created some interesting, very social, street life on the main drags as clubbers and pub-crawlers gather outside chatting with each other on smoke breaks. For the moment, smoking is still permitted on restaurant terraces, but there are rumblings about that coming to an end, too.

Hotels must limit their smoking rooms to a maximum of 40% of available accommodation, though many smaller hotels have taken the initiative to make their businesses smoke free altogether. Fines for first-time infractions are $87 for individuals who light up where they shouldn't and over $400 for businesses that allow it.

duce from local farms. Residents will argue heatedly over which places serve the best of anything – chewy bagels, espresso, comfort soup, fluffy omelet or creamy cakes.

Montréal smoked meat and bagels, of course, have a formidable reputation that stretches across the country and is a constant source of friendly rivalry with New Yorkers over which city has the best of each.

WHEN IN MONTRÉAL...

Montrealers are generally a pretty relaxed bunch, but you'll make yourself more popular if you observe a few simple rules.

Dos

- Start off in French no matter what. It's polite to begin your queries in shops, restaurants and public places with *'Est-ce que vous parlez anglais?'* ('Do you speak English?'), rather than launching straight into English. You might be addressed with *'Bonjourhello'* to suss out your own language preference.
- When walking into a small shop or *dépanneur* (convenience store), say *'Bonjour'* when you arrive and *'Merci, bonjour'* when you leave.
- As in France, it's customary among French Quebecers who know each other to exchange *bises* (kisses) as a greeting (men do this occasionally, too). While two to three kisses on each cheek are typical in France, the usual ritual in Québec is one glancing peck on each cheek. Any more will get you weird looks.
- Act as if you are interested in something other than the Plateau. Yes, you should still go there, and yes it has tons of cool stuff, but this neighborhood dominates everything from film locations to real estate and Montrealers who don't live there are sick of it. Get curious about Mile End instead.
- See a Québec film and buy at least one CD before you arrive – instant ice-breaker!
- If invited to someone's home or party, bring some sort of gift such as good wine.

Don'ts

- If invited to someone's home or party, do not – under any circumstances – bring a $10 bottle from the local dépanneur, no matter how desperate you are. This is NOT real wine (see p31).
- Don't address the topic of Québec separatism with anyone under 40 the first time you meet them – unless you want to be seen as hopelessly square. Whether you're speaking to a separatist or a federalist, the subject these days is deemed *tired* to the extreme and an unforgivable bore on social occasions.
- Don't talk about Montréal's 'hot' music scene – locals figure *NYT* and *Spin* got it all wrong anyway and still haven't forgiven them for leaving all the cool francophone bands out of the articles.
- Don't address waiters as *'garçon'*, which means 'boy' and is considered rude. Say *'Excusez madame/mademoiselle/ monsieur'*

29

Traditional Cuisine

Traditional québécois cuisine is classic comfort food, heavy and centered on meat dishes. The fact that the ingredients are basic is said to be a historical legacy, as French settlers only had access to limited produce.

A québécois meal tends to be a hearty, cholesterol-filled affair and might include stews with potatoes, carrots or turnips; game (caribou, duck, wild boar); or *tourtière* (meat pie). A favorite staple is *poutine* (see Top Five Poutine p142). To appease your sweet-tooth, order *pudding chômeur* (literally, 'pudding for the unemployed'), a kind of sponge cake doused in a gooey brown-sugar sauce.

LOCAL VOICES: FACES OF MONTREAL

Normand Laprise, Chef and co-owner of Toqué!

Don't call Normand Laprise a 'star chef' – he says he doesn't believe in such a thing and hates the term with a passion. But the truth is, it's hard to describe the buzz his name evokes on the North American food scene in any other way. Born near Québec City on March 24, 1961, he's cooked all over the world from California and Europe to Asia and Australia. Most memorably, he had a 14-month dream run at New York City's brilliant but now defunct Cena restaurant, where he garnered rave reviews from everyone who mattered, including three stars from the *New York Times*. These days you'll find him at the helm of **Toqué!** (p132), arguably the most coveted dining experience in town.

You're known for favoring Québec produce and local producers. Where does that passion come from?
I grew up on a farm, so everything was fresh from the milk to the meat. When I was doing a cooking apprenticeship I saw frozen food for the first time and it was a complete shock to me – I had just never seen anything like it. Later, I apprenticed at **Marie Clarisse** (p237) in Québec City. It's all fresh fish there and what was served depended on what was in the market that day. Working there was one of two major turning points of my career.

What was the other one?
I went to France for another cooking apprenticeship and was so thrilled about the new cooking techniques I would be exposed to, I could hardly wait. But those things I barely noticed – it was all the exquisite products supplied by the small producers that caught my eye. They were impeccable. The quality was evident just by looking at them.

There's been an explosion of *produits du terroir* (p140). Do you consider yourself part of all that?
Ah, this *produits du terroir*. This is what everybody is talking about now, isn't it? But what is it really? I don't know. Everybody talks about it but nobody seems able to define it. If it means using local produce, then yes, we could say so. But the difference is I've been doing this for 15 years, I'm doing it now, and I'll be doing it 15 years from now whether it's in fashion or not.

What makes Montréal such a standout city for dining?
There's a wonderful quality-price relationship here. It's also so multiethnic – the dining scene is influenced with new ideas. But it's also because Montrealers are gourmands. For them, eating out is not just a meal, it's an experience. In other places like New York, yes, people love good food but dinner is something to fit in between a cocktail party and a late business meeting or a show. Here, dining out itself is the event and Montrealers will spend 2½ to 3½ hours – or even the whole night – at a restaurant.

What's a typical workday like for you?
We get here at around 11am. We start preparing for the day; farmers and producers are stopping by; we plan the menus around what produce we have. After work we all go out for a drink. I have to keep up with all my chefs – they keep me young.

What's your favorite québécois comfort food?
I ate so much of it when I was growing up on the farm that I don't think I really have one now. I've had so much *tourtiére* in my life already. Enough! It was good but I've had my fill.

Other classic Québécois dishes include *tourtière*, a meat pie usually made with pork and another meat like beef or veal along with celery and onions, and *pâté chinois*, a kind of shepherd's pie with a layer of beef or pork, a layer of creamed corn and a layer of mashed potatoes that is jazzed up through family variations – like a fourth layer sprinkled with cheddar or parmesan cheese. Should you desire to tackle your own *tourtière* at home, pick up the cookbook *A Taste of Québec* by Julian Armstrong.

Quebecois pea soup is the yellow variety (ie not the green split-pea soup you'll find elsewhere in Canada) and is usually packed with ham or another type of pork.

Baked beans are another fixture of traditional cuisine – even at breakfast Quebecers inhale them with a gusto that can leave visitors queasy.

Montréal smoked meat and bagels are legendary the world over. Different altogether from pastrami, smoked meat is sold all over town, but few delicatessens come close to Schwartz's (p138), the uncrowned king of curers. Bagels also enjoy a wide, if not cult, following (see p145).

There's a drool-inducing choice of French food in the city, with bistros and brassieres of all types and price ranges (see Eating p124). Many of them incorporate the best of Québec's produce and market ingredients (see boxed text *produits du terroir* p140), and you'll find everything from no-nonsense French food to experimental takes on the classics.

Drinks

In Montréal a dark, strong espresso is king, preferred by most to the weaker drip variety. Locally produced microbrew beers are most locals' first choice, with Boréale, St-Ambroise and Belle Gueule sold widely in pubs and nightclubs.

Wine is sold in SAQs outlets (liquor stores) and you'll find Californian, French, Italian, Chilean and Australian wines. However, because SAQs are government-controlled, you won't find the same variety here as you would in Paris or New York. Wine is also sold in supermarkets and *dépanneurs* but beware – this is not the real stuff, but is a mix of concentrate from bulk wines shipped from overseas that has water added to it once it arrives in Québec.

The Québec wine industry is centered in the Eastern Townships. The industry is young, but fun to try out and definitely worth exploring if only for the adventure. Ice wines like the one from L'Orpailleur are, however, starting to be taken seriously, and regularly show up on wine lists all over town (see p262).

HELPFUL PHRASES

A table for two, please.
Une table pour deux, s'il vous plaît.

Do you have a menu in English?
Est-ce que vous avez un menu en anglais?

What's the specialty here?
Quelle est la spécialité ici?

I'd like the dish of the day.
Je voudrais avoir le plat du jour.

I'd like the set menu.
Je vais prendre la table d'hôte.

I'm a vegetarian.
Je suis végétarien/végétarienne. (m/f)

I'd like to order the...
Je voudrais commander...

The bill, please.
L'addition, s'il vous plaît.

I don't eat...
Je ne mange pas de...

    meat   *viande*
    fish   *poisson*
    seafood   *fruits de mer*

Could you recommend something?
Est-ce que vous pouvez recommander quelque chose?

I'd like to reserve a table.
J'aimerais réserver une table.

I'd like a local specialty.
J'aimerais une spécialité régionale.

Is service included in the bill?
Est-ce que le service est inclu?
(If you are in a classy, expensive restaurant)
Est-ce que le pourboire est inclu?
*(If you are anywhere else but the above
ie bistros, cafés etc)*

The only people who will find themselves frustrated in Montréal on the beverage front are tea drinkers. While coffee drinkers quaff a silken espresso or a sensuously presented cappuccino enveloped in copious foam, tea drinkers more often than not, can do little but look on enviously while they try to content themselves with lukewarm water, a cold cup to pour it in and a teabag slapped on a saucer nearby.

CULINARY PASSIONS

iharrison – 25 Jan 2006
Montréal is the love child of Old World charisma and the cultural mosaic sensibility of North America. The result is a city huge on taste, sophistication and culinary pleasures. Residents have a proud maniacal obsession with food and drink.

(blu.list) v. to recommend
a travel experience.
www.lonelyplanet.com/bluelist

BLUELIST.

FASHION

One of the things visitors first notice here is how well people are dressed – and it's not just the women that stop traffic. The navy suit reigns supreme in the rest of Canada and only in Montréal do men sport business suits that get double takes – wearing chic, sober shades, like an olive-green suit with a lavender tie, that their counter parts in Vancouver, Toronto or even New York wouldn't dream of touching.

It's not that the locals are all gorgeous – but they do know how to dress. Whether artists, students or entrepreneurs, it seems like everybody knows the look they're going for and pulls it off flawlessly. Label watchers put it down to the perfect fusion of European and American fashion – there's the daringness and willingness to experiment from Paris, but with a kind of American practicality that makes people chose what's right for them and not what's just of the moment. Probably most of all, Montrealers have a love of culture and an enjoyment of life that feeds right into its garments. In short, they just have fun with clothes and are happy to flaunt it.

Québec fashion magazines like *Clin d'Oeil*, *Lou Lou* and *Elle Québec* are excellent places to check out for exciting new boutiques and up-and-coming Québec designers.

After Los Angeles and New York, Montréal is the third-largest garment-making city in North America, and its fashion industry has annual sales of $4 billion to the USA.

SPORTS

Hockey is the 'national religion' of Quebecers, and their allegiance to the Montréal Canadiens is legendary. Nicknamed the 'Habs' for the early French settlers 'Les Habitants,' the Canadiens are the most successful hockey team ever with 24 Stanley Cups, the North American hockey championship trophy to their credit. Over the past decade, however, some doubtful trades, a lack of leadership and players' strikes have been blamed for the Canadiens' choppy performance on the ice. Happily, there's been a turnaround of late: the team made the Stanley Cup playoffs in 2006 and Guy Carbonneau has taken over as head coach, keeping hope alive for legions of fans.

Baseball is another story: in 2004, after years of uncertainty, the city lost its team, the Montréal Expos, to Washington D.C. Although the Expos had problems filling the Olympic Stadium (p98), attending the season opener game was a Montréal tradition, filling the venue to capacity. The move has definitely left a hole in the hearts of the city's sports fans.

The Formula One Grand Prix (p175) race was in danger of being cancelled in 2004 because of Canada's new ban on tobacco sponsorship for sporting events. In a controversial move, the government agreed to fork out $12 million to compensate for the lost revenue, keeping the event in Montréal for the meantime. There's also talk about bringing NASCAR to Montréal permanently. Despite concerns about the lack of a proper oval track, and how weather may affect the scheduling of a regular event in the longterm, a race has been confirmed for August 4, 2007. If it goes well, Montréal may nab a spot on the racing calendar for good.

But there's good news, too. Following their revival in the mid-1990s, the Montréal Alouettes, in the Canadian Football League, have been the unlikely stars of the pro-sports circuit. After their 2002 Grey Cup victory, tens of thousands of ecstatic fans lined rue Ste-Catherine for a banner-waving parade, the likes of which hadn't been seen since the Habs' heyday.

Local soccer is also enjoying a new lease of life. The Montréal Impact team, relaunched in 2002, averages 11,000 spectators a game and is getting a brand-new $15-million soccer stadium and complex to be built near the Olympic Stadium. The new facility will seat around 13,000 and could be finished as early as fall 2007.

MEDIA

Montréal is the seat of Québec's French-language media companies and has four big TV networks (p45). New-media firms like Discreet Logic and **Softimage** (p42) are renowned for their special effects, and the Cité du Multimédia center in Old Montréal is an incubator for start-ups.

The daily *Montreal Gazette* (www.montrealgazette.com) is the major English-language daily newspaper, with coverage of national affairs, politics and the arts. The big French dailies are the federalist *La Presse* (www.cyberpresse.ca) and the separatist-leaning *Le Devoir* (www.ledevoir.com).

Le Journal de Montréal is *the* city's wild and rollicking tabloid, replete with sensational headlines and photos. Though much derided, the *Journal* does the brashest undercover and investigative reporting in town and has the city's biggest daily circulation.

Four free entertainment mags appear every Thursday: *Mirror* (www.montrealmirror.com) and *Hour* (www.hour.ca) in English; *Ici* (www.ici.ca) and *Voir* (www.voir.ca) in French. They focus on entertainment, culture and local events with some great features and columns.

Canada's only truly national papers are the left-leaning Toronto *Globe and Mail* and the right-leaning *National Post*. *The Walrus* is a Canadian *New Yorker/Atlantic Monthly* style magazine, with tremendous writing and musings from the country's intellectual heavyweights.

Though thin and a bit of a snore in general, Canada's weekly news magazine *Maclean's* is full of high-quality writing and still holds a certain amount of clout with its special issues. *L'actualité* is Québec's monthly news magazine and though it suffers from some of the same snore-syndrome as *Maclean's*, when it gets creative on Québec issues – like with its *100 words to understand Québec* edition – it does a bang-up job.

The glossy, illustrated *Canadian Geographic* carries excellent articles and photography like its sister US monthly *National Geographic*. The Canadian Broadcasting Corporation's site (montreal.cbc.ca) is an excellent source for current affairs.

E-zines and blogs proliferate in this growing cyber-hub. For a survey of the country's news and media links, see www.canada.com. The *Web Citylog* (via www.montreal.com) routes to a discerning choice of stories from various electronic media. *Maisonneuve* (www.maisonneuve.org) is a sophisticated general-interest magazine with a good e-zine.

MONTRÉAL CHIC

Montréal Fashion Week (p21) used to be a purely Canadian affair, but nowadays is filled with as many buyers from around the world as local fashion writers. For the public, the most exciting event is the Montréal Fashion and Design Festival, a free, outdoor fashion show where you can see Québécois, Canadian and international designers show off their collections outdoors, usually on stages set up on ave McGill College. The event corresponds with the Formula 1 Grand Prix.

It's been said that Montréal fashion boutiques have the right styles but the wrong country, ie the local market is limited. But in recent years that's changed. The ultra-classy men's boutique **Kamkyl** (p180) sells to an international clientele including boutiques in London, Belgium and Japan, while Montrealer Siphay Southidara, known as YSO (ee-sew), is one of Canada's most exciting designers and has an eponymous label (the moniker YSO is derived from the last letter of his first name and the first two of his last name – it's easier for Canadians to pronounce).

After immigrating to Canada from Laos in 1979, YSO attended fashion school in Montréal and later apprenticed with designer Marie Saint-Pierre. Heaps of awards followed, and by 1996 he was making samples for designer Tod Lynn and designing costumes for U2's Bono. Later he made the costumes for the Cirque du Soleil's show *Alegria* and presented to catwalks in Montréal and Toronto. You can find his creations at **Parasuco Jeans** (p184) and the **U&I boutique** (p187).

Georges Lévesque is another designer making waves – he's designed stage costumes for Céline Dion and Québec singing superstar Diane Dufresne. You can check out his designs at **Scandale** (p184).

LANGUAGE

French is the official language of Québec and French Quebecers are passionate about it, seeing their language as the last line of defense against Anglo-Saxon culture. What makes Montréal unique in the province is the interface of English and French – a mix responsible for the city's dynamism as well as the root of many of its conflicts.

Until the 1970s it was the English minority (few of whom spoke French) who ran the businesses, held positions of power and accumulated wealth in Québec; a French Quebecer who would go into a downtown store couldn't get service in his or her own language more often than not.

But as Québec's separatist movement arose, the Canadian government passed laws in 1969 that required all federal services and public signs to appear in both languages. The separatists took things further and demanded the primacy of French in Québec, which was affirmed by the Parti Québécois with the passage of Bill 101 in 1977 (see below). Though there was much hand wringing, the fact is that Bill 101 probably saved the French language from dying out in North America. If you're at a party with five anglophones and one francophone these days, chances are everyone will be speaking French, something that would have been rare 10 years ago.

These days Montrealers with French as their mother tongue number 928, 905, and native English speakers 300,580. Fifty-seven per cent of Montrealers from a variety of backgrounds speak both official languages.

Québec settlers were relatively cut off from France once they arrived in the New World, so the French you hear today in the province, known colloquially as Québécois, developed more or less independently from what was going on in France. The result is a rich local vocabulary, with its own idioms and sayings, and words used in everyday speech that haven't been spoken in France since the 1800s.

Accents vary widely across the province, but all are characterized by a delicious twang and rhythmic bounce unique to Québec French, and the addition of the word *là* repeated from one to three times at the end of each spoken sentence.

The French spoken in Montréal most closely resembles that of France and will be easiest for French speakers from elsewhere to understand.

To francophone Quebecers, the French spoken in France sounds desperately posh. To people from France, the French spoken in Québec sounds terribly old-fashioned, quaint and at times unintelligible – an attitude that ruffles feathers here in an instant as it's found to be condescending.

Quebecers learn standard French in school, hear standard French on newscasts and grow up on movies and music from France, so if you speak standard French, locals will have no problem understanding you – it's you understanding them that will be the problem. Remember, even when French-language québécois movies are shown in France, they are shown with *French* subtitles.

Young Montrealers today are less concerned about language issues, so visitors shouldn't worry too much. Most residents grew up speaking both languages, and people you meet in daily life – store owners, waiters, bus drivers – switch effortlessly between French and English.

SIGNS OF PRIDE

Québec's French Language Charter, the (in)famous Bill 101, asserts the primacy of French on public signs across the province. Stop signs in Québec read 'ARRÊT,' a word that actually means a stop for buses or trains (even in France, the red hexagonal signs read 'STOP'), apostrophes had to be removed from storefronts like Ogilvy's in the 1980s to comply with French usage, and English is allowed on signage provided it's no more than half the size of the French lettering. Perhaps most comical of all is the acronym PFK (Poulet Frit Kentucky) for a leading fast-food chain – even communist China still allows signs for KFC (Kentucky Fried Chicken).

The law is vigorously enforced by language police who roam the province with tape measures (yes – for real!) and hand out fines to shopkeepers if a door says 'Push' more prominently than '*Poussez*'. These days, most Quebecers take it all in their stride, and the comical language tussles between businesses and the language police that were such regular features of evening newscasts and phone-in shows have all but disappeared in recent years.

ECONOMY & COSTS

Montréal is Canada's second economic center after Toronto – growth has been above the national average, reaching 3% to 4% in the past few years. Montrealers who recall the 1990s recession are pinching themselves to wake up, but the new prosperity is very real. You can see it in the many new boutique hotels, the glam shops along rue Ste-Catherine and the number of affluent people under 30 buying condos.

Every upswing, of course, has a downside: real-estate prices and rents have soared, and the Plateau has become so expensive that many residents can't afford to buy their own homes. Finding a place to rent is devilishly difficult; the vacancy rate is ridiculously low in popular districts like the Plateau. All the same, living costs are very reasonable compared to other big cities. You can still rent a two-bedroom apartment for around $800 per month, cheap compared to New York City or London.

Montréal accounts for almost two-thirds of the province's income, and big-ticket manufacturers include defense, aerospace, telecommunications and information technology. With its four universities Montréal is the biggest center of academic research in Canada. The city has also blossomed in the new media and related services for the movie industry – Hollywood shoots alone earn Montréal about $1 billion every year. There's also a large financial sector, a screen-based stock exchange and a bevy of international banks in the downtown skyscrapers. The Old Port and docking facilities on the St Lawrence Seaway make Montréal an important transport center.

Québec's high taxes put the city at a competitive disadvantage though, and salaries tend to lag behind those in Toronto or the USA. At the same time the abundance of relatively cheap, qualified personnel increasingly makes Montréal a lucrative place to do business.

> ## HOW MUCH?
>
> *Montreal Gazette* newspaper: 75¢
> Pint of beer: $5
> Ticket to major museum: $10 per adult
> Liter of unleaded gas: $1
> T-shirt: $20
> Three-course meal with wine/beer: $35
> Cinema ticket: $10-12
> Taxi per km: $1.30
> Club cover charge on a Friday: $7-10
> Hour-long, horse-drawn carriage tour: $75

Coffee and newspaper at Marché Jean-Talon

GOVERNMENT & POLITICS

For decades Québec politics was dominated by the question: are you separatist or federalist? But since Quebecers voted out the Parti Québécois in the 2003 provincial elections, the entire province has been given a reprieve. These days Québec spends its time clashing with the federal government over respecting the Kyoto accord, fiscal imbalance, toughening gun control and protesting the Canadian military's mission in Afghanistan rather than language and separation issues.

Québec's premier is Sherbrooke-born Jean Charest, elected on an ambitious platform of better health care, better education, tax cuts, and a leaner, less-interventionist government. However, he's had a rocky ride – his decision to raise the price of Québec's cornerstone $5-a-day day-care program to $7 unleashed a torrent of demonstrations, and tens of thousands of Montrealers have flooded the streets during his premiership to protest cuts to the public service and contracting out to the private sector. That's a bizarre twist, since those were the very things he ran on.

Montréal's moderate mayor, Gérald Tremblay, is something of a Teflon man. He has enjoyed healthy approval ratings since his 2001 election and was easily reelected in 2005 obtaining 53% of the vote. Among other feathers in his cap, he is credited with saving the 2005 World Aquatic Championships with a zero-hour flight to Europe after it was withdrawn from Montréal because of a lack of funding guarantees. He is also remembered for stopping a mugging in 2003 when he saw a student being attacked by robbers near McGill University. However, his new mandate got off to a rocky start. Though he pledged no tax hikes during his 2005 campaign, his first municipal budget – a scant month or so after his reelection – included tax hikes, and lots of them. Citywide uproar and mass condemnation followed him until he withdrew the budget and went back to the drawing board.

ENVIRONMENT

Montréal is a healthy place to live – so salubrious, in fact, that it routinely ranks in the top 20 places to live on the planet, according to the UN.

Air quality is generally good and the waters of the St Lawrence have benefited from strict environmental laws. Some practices, however, remain behind the times: salting of icy winter roads fouls the soil and groundwater despite the availability of substitutes; recycled waste is picked up, but unsorted; household water is unmetered; Québec's subsidized electricity is cheap and thus easy to waste.

And high taxes at the pump don't stop Quebecers from driving gas-guzzlers.

MONTRÉAL'S MEGACITY

The idea as such was simple: one city, one administration, one urban development plan, and lots of saved tax revenues. So in 2001 the Parti Québécois – when it was still in power at the National Assembly, the province's parliament – put into motion a plan to merge towns across the province into megacities. This included the 28 towns and municipalities on the Island of Montréal being turned into a megacity of 1.8 million people.

The thing is, no referendum was held, and many communities, both anglophone and francophone, felt they'd been bushwhacked. The boroughs across the island that replaced the municipalities could no longer decide how local tax dollars were spent, and there were complaints that public services like snow removal, libraries, garbage pick up and the ambulance service had deteriorated. Many felt their small towns had been better run.

When Jean Charest was campaigning for election in 2003, he promised Quebecers, including Montrealers, that their municipalities could opt out of the megacity. Charest won the election, kicked the PQ out of office and referendums were held. In Montréal fifteen of the former municipalities, mostly in the island's west including upper-class Westmount, did opt out. However, they will have fewer powers than they did before the forced mergers and taxes will likely be raised to cover the cost of demerging.

The new City of Montréal population is 1.58 million.

CLIMATE

Even the earliest European explorers were surprised by Montréal's seasonal extremes. Temperatures of -20°C to -6°C are typical in January and February and snaps down to -40°C can occur. While Montréal winters of past have enjoyed a notoriously frigid reputation, the truth is in recent years they've not been so bad. Snowy and cold? Yes. But other than a few glacial weeks, the rest of the season rarely strays beyond a moderate, 'can-still-play-outside' kind of winter temperature. Parking meters are set back so snow ploughs can clear sidewalks

LOCAL VOICES: FACES OF MONTRÉAL

Benoît Labonté, Mayor of Ville-Marie Borough & Member of Montréal's Arts and Heritage Committee

Born December 28, 1959 in Lachute, Québec, Benoît Labonté came to study political science in Montréal at age 17. After years in the private sector, he's now mayor of Montréal's most bustling borough, where the mother load of the city's tourist magnets, including Old Montréal, are located. He's held office since January 2006.

What's the most frequent complaint you get from citizens?
Here in Ville-Marie we've got 75,000 residents, but around 500,000 Montrealers come here each day for work, culture or to study along with 14 million tourists a year. Downtown is alive but some residents want more quiet and complain about noise and traffic. I think we're fortunate in Montréal, though. In most North American cities, downtown is just for business and nobody actually lives there. Here we have a 'living downtown' that's very animated.

We hear and see politicians being lambasted all the time. Do Montrealers ever let you know when you're doing something right?
Surprisingly, yes. Recently it's about garbage. It's no secret we had a problem here, but our new program for fixing it seems to be working. Merchants and citizens have told us they're pleased with the improvement. I was really surprised to hear from them but I think it's because of the ease of internet and email these days.

Where do you bring friends who've never been to Montréal before?
The Old Town and then in the summer to all the festivals – there's always such good spirit and a good mood, and visitors are fascinated by it. At the 2006 World Outgames we had 100,000 people partying in the streets every night for two weeks and had no problems. What other city in North America could say that?

What's your favorite québécois movie?
Le Déclin de l'Empire Américain. But for someone coming to Montréal and wanting to understand us a bit, I'd recommend *Bon Cop, Bad Cop*, a comedy, about [anglophone and francophone] cultural differences – people can see it and quickly understand what the situation is here.

What's your favorite Montréal band or singer?
The Montréal Symphony Orchestra with [musical director] Kent Nagano – they're one of the top 10 in the world, and that's not just me saying it. They have an edge, like Montréal, being in touch with both North American and European flavors and styles. Kent Nagano is American but he worked in Germany so I think he's probably one of the best people to understand that. Of course I like Jean Leloup (now Jean Leclerc p55) and Pierre Lapointe, but I mostly just listen to them on the radio. I like new music but I'm not a specialist.

Montréal's independent music scene is booming now and getting all kinds of attention. You're on Montréal's Arts and Heritage Committee – ever have someone lean over excitedly in a business meeting and ask if you've actually met Arcade Fire or Simple Plan?
Nobody's asked me yet and no, I've never met them, but I'd like to because I'm very curious about this phenomenon. It's very important for us and it captures what the new Montréal is all about – a lot of highly integrated influences from all over the world creating vibrant culture. Montréal's not the only city in the world with so many cultures but it's definitely one of the most successfully integrated examples of it.

as well as roads – it also means the ploughs can swoop down on unsuspecting pedestrians, forcing them into the roads or into the snow banks. BEWARE!

The warm seasons are short but delightful. First buds appear in late April and blossoms appear in mid-May for a couple of weeks. Summer arrives late. Early June can still be chilly; in brutal, steamy July an air conditioner becomes a major asset. Highs of 25°C or 30°C are common from mid-July to late August. Come September the mercury drops sharply in the evenings, but Indian summers are common in early October.

THE LAND

Montréal occupies an island on the north shore of the St Lawrence River. Officially known as the Island of Montréal, it's bordered on all sides by rivers rather than great expanses of lakes or oceans, meaning the barriers are more psychological than physical. The city proper, lying on a disjointed collection of plateaus and hills shaped by glaciers eons ago, has an area of 158 sq km, but greater Montréal now encompasses the entire island and several towns on the south bank of the St Lawrence.

The north-south streets of Old Montréal and downtown cross several ridges that challenge some pedestrians. Pleasantly green residential areas around the fringes of Mont Royal can throw up precipitous inclines and sharp curves. Bicyclists will find the riverside paths a breeze but face a series of hurdles as they head north into the Plateau.

Montréal overlooks rich, rolling farmland along the St Lawrence Valley, but the river has shaped the lives of Quebecers more than any other factor: two-thirds of the province's people live along its banks, and almost everyone draws river water for drinking.

The Laurentian Mountains (Laurentides in French) to the northeast are part of the Canadian Shield – the world's oldest mountain range formed more than three billion years ago. It provided the rough-hewn granite you see in Montréal buildings today.

GREEN MONTRÉAL

Some 8% of the city's territory is protected green space, and the abundance of leafy parks, bicycle paths and outdoor recreation options keeps the residents in tune with nature.

For a terrific list of the city's parks, check out www.montreal.com/parks/index.html.

Every third resident takes the metro, helping to curb auto emissions. New bicycle lanes have been laid downtown and in Old Montréal; the network of trails is constantly expanding, converting erstwhile commuters from four to two wheels. Fourteen kilometers of new bike paths are in the works, along with 448 new bike racks.

City Hall is pledging to reduce greenhouse gas emissions by 20% by 2012, three times more than what's required by the Kyoto protocol.

Cycling at Parc LaFontaine, along one of Montréal's many bike paths

LOCAL VOICES: FACES OF MONTRÉAL

Karim Benzaïd, musician & facilitator at an immigrant integration centre

When Karim Benzaïd was 18, he moved to Montreal with his family and later founded the world music collective Syncop in 2001 (he was born January 28, 1978 in Algeria). Musicians of North African and Québécois backgrounds fill out the line up, churning out North African musical styles like *rai* and *choui* tinged with hip-hop and reggae – a mix that won them first place at Les Francouvertes musical festival in 2003. Their second CD *Contes à Rebours* was released in 2007.

When he's not in the studio or touring the country with the band, you'll find Benzaïd teaching Québec culture, history and French conversation at La Francisation des Immigrants à l'École de Français, an immigrant integration program at Université de Montréal.

How did you get into music?
Honestly? Because in primary school the music teacher was the only one who didn't yell at us all the time. When my family moved from Algeria to Tunisia (before coming to Montréal), I started getting in touch with my *rai* roots and at the same time started listening to [French rap artists] IAM and other hip-hop music from France. Music's been part of my life ever since.

Why Montréal?
It's the only francophone city in today's world that works – anything is possible here and there aren't the barriers to immigrants here like there are in France or other places in Europe. I can honestly say that since I've arrived here I've never experienced any kind of hostility. Not once.

Do the immigrants you work with find it difficult to adjust to life in Montréal?
It's always difficult wherever you immigrate to. There are professional qualifications to redo, French to learn, jobs to find. But Montréal is very multicultural, very eclectic and very welcoming. There's no norm that characterizes people here so you can fit in wherever you want to.

What defines a real Montrealer?
Just a person who's here because they chose to be.

What's the world music scene like in Montréal?
New. There's not many francophone bands like us doing world music in Québec. It's just in the last two or three years that they're playing our songs on radio, or asking for us on TV. I'm curious to see what the scene will be like in another 10 years.

What's great about being an artist in this city?
French culture is so present everywhere in everyday life. A francophone artist here has a whole industry from print to broadcast to support them. That's why musicians in Québec can sell 200,000 copies of their albums even if there are only seven million francophones. It's not at all the same in English Canada, where culture is oriented to what's going on in the US and they need to move there to be successful.

Which Montréal-based musicians do you admire?
I could go on forever about this... The old Bottine Souriante CDs for the music; Les Cowboys Fringants and Loco Locass for the lyrics; and Jean Leloup (now Jean Leclerc p55) for his crazy eclecticism, his melodies. You listen to his lyrics and you ask yourself 'How? How did he come up with that?' It's phenomenal.

What's your favorite québécois movie?
La Grande Séduction is unbeatable, by far the best film I've ever seen. In my [immigration and integration] courses I teach a session on Québec film. My students are Chinese, Persians from Iran, Latin Americans, and they all love it – its humor and intelligence are international.

DEPRESSED? HOW ABOUT A MÉTRO RIDE?

A ride on the city's aging subway fleet is enough to make any Montrealer depressed – breakdowns and delays are frequent and some locals have given up on it altogether. The métro started running in 1966 and many of the cars being used today date from the early 1970s. An ambitious plan is underway to replace around 350 subway cars between 2010 and 2012, but in the meantime planners have come up with something to take the edge off – replacing white fluorescent lighting in métro cars with full-spectrum lighting, the same kind of light used to treat people with Seasonal Effectiveness Disorder. It's said such lighting mimics sunlight and so has a positive effect on people's mood and metabolism. The first three-dozen cars with the new lighting were in place by mid-2006, and several more outfitted with the full-spectrum treatment are being put into action each month.

URBAN PLANNING & DEVELOPMENT

Since the 1960s the government has spent billions in developing tourist attractions and infrastructure in Montréal. Recently, a number of exciting projects have been realized or are in the works. The 33,000-square-meter **Bibliothèque et Archives Nationales du Québec** (Library and National Archives of Québec; p95) opened in the Latin Quarter to huge success in 2005, with a record number of Montrealers flocking to the building each day.

The government is investing millions of dollars on the Main – phase II of this project will see $25 million spent on the most popular part of the strip between rue Sherbrooke and ave du Mont-Royal, and should be finished by December 2007. Sidewalks will be widened, dozens of trees planted and dozens of street lights added to this part of the strip, which also houses the trendiest restaurants and hippest bars. Rue Notre-Dame, a two-laned nightmare pocked with potholes that's nonetheless an important artery into Old Montréal, is also slated for modernization, including expansion to four lanes.

Also exciting is the proposed Maison de l'Image et de la Photographie (House of Image and Photography), a $12- to $15-million project near the Place des Arts, to be opened in 2009.

Arts & Architecture

Arts & Architecture

Montréal is the undisputed centre of the French-language entertainment universe in North America and the cultural mecca of Québec. It is ground zero for everything from Québec's monster film and music industry to visual and dramatic arts and book publishing. Actors, directors and writers flock to this Hollywood of Québec from all over the province with dreams of making it big in the movies or on TV. Québec artists don't typically look for recognition from France, English Canada or the United States. Though they may want it at some point, they don't need it to survive – the market for them here is insatiable and they have a whole industry behind them.

Québec films reign at the box office, Québec bands dominate the music charts. (see Music chapter, p54). There are countless TV shows and glossy entertainment and gossip magazines chronicling the careers of French-speaking musicians and movie stars from Québec. Every triumph, failure and sneeze is dutifully reported and Quebecers consume news about them voraciously. The Jutras, named after pioneer filmmaker Claude Jutra, are the equivalent to the Oscars, and the Félix awards, named for singer-songwriter Félix Leclerc, are equivalent to the Grammys. There are also awards for theater, comedy and TV and all of the awards shows are followed more closely by Quebecers than their English counterparts.

Montrealers more than any other Canadians crave art that reflects the life they see unfolding around them. This has made Montréal one of the most vibrant and one-of-a-kind cultural scenes on the planet. For visitors, exploring it can be one of the most exciting and fascinating sides of a trip to Montréal. There are world class ballet companies, museums, eclectic theater – from Molière to the latest in fringe – art museums of distinction and a catalogue of sophisticated galleries. Whether you are a theater lover, art collector or dance aficionado there is something for you in this city.

CINEMA

To say the Québec film industry is booming would be the gross understatement of the decade. Québec films regularly steamroll over their foreign (including Hollywood) competition and are smashing box-office records in the province that would have been unimaginable even a few years ago.

Les Boys, about the shenanigans of an amateur hockey team, is the province's most successful movie franchise ever. When *Les Boys 3* was released in Québec the same weekend as the smash *Titanic* was crushing its competition all over the world, *Les Boys* sold almost as many tickets throughout its run as director James Cameron's film was. Stars of *Les Boys* still remember calls from Hollywood executives asking 'What the fuck is going on up there and what the fuck is *Les Boys*?'

More recently, *Bon Cop, Bad Cop* (2006) a bilingual comedy about a French-speaking Québec cop forced to work with a detective from Ontario became a runaway hit across the province, breaking just about every Québec cinema record there is, shutting out international hit films like *Pirates of the Caribbean: Dead Man's Chest* from the number one spot.

Quebecers' appetite for stories about their lives and the people around them is

> ### TOP FIVE MUSEUMS
> - Musée d'Art Contemporain (p89) – a sophisticated playground of contemporary art
> - Musée des Beaux-Arts (p92) – the giant of the art scene
> - Centre d'Histoire de Montréal (p73) – for creative temporary exhibitions on the city's recent history
> - Musée McCord (p92) – Canadian history front and centre
> - Musée d'Archéologie Pointe-à-Callière (p76) – time capsule of Montréal's humble beginnings

Mural detail on Rue St Denis

insatiable. It's an enthusiasm some outsiders have difficulty understanding. Québécois films are often full of odd pacing, silences and cultural references that newcomers to the province can have trouble interpreting. For Quebecers however, it doesn't matter how rough a film is around the edges. Leaving the cinema with them you'll notice they talk much more about the film's themes and ideas and the relation to their own lives than they do about whether it was successfully executed or visually exciting.

Animation and multimedia technologies became a Montréal specialty following the success of Softimage, a company founded by special-effects guru Daniel Langlois. Creator of some of the first 3-D animation software, Softimage masterminded the special effects used in Hollywood blockbusters like *Jurassic Park, The Mask, Godzilla* and *Titanic.*

The foundations of Québec cinema were laid in the 1930s when Maurice Proulx, a pioneer documentary filmmaker, charted the colonization of the gold-rich Abitibi region in northwestern Québec. It was only in the 1960s that directors were inspired by the likes of Frederico Fellini or Jean-Luc Godard to experiment, though the subject of most films remained the countryside and rural life. The 1970s were another watershed moment when erotically charged movies sent the province a-twitter. The most representative works of this era were Claude Jutra's *Mon Oncle Antoine* and *La Vraie Nature de Bernadette* by Gilles Carle.

Montréal finally burst onto the international scene in the 1980s with a new generation of directors like Denys Arcand (p44), Louis Archambault, Michel Brault and Charles Binamé. Films are produced in French but dubbing and subtitling have made them accessible to a wider audience.

Montréal is also a massive draw for foreign film shoots. The old town which can double for Europe and the skyscrapers that can double for just about anywhere in North America has made it a popular back drop for film crews. However 2006 was a difficult year for the local industry, the strong Canadian dollar made shooting in Montréal less attractive and labor strife between technical unions also had a negative impact. But by the end of 2006, it appeared things were picking up again.

FILM REVIEWS

All names listed here refer to the director of the film.

Bon Cop, Bad Cop by Érik Canuel (2006) – when a dead body shows up on the Ontario/Québec border, a corrupt Montréal cop and an uptight Toronto cop are assigned together to find the killer. This film crushed every box office record in the province from biggest opening weekend to highest grossing Québec film ever.

C.R.A.Z.Y. by Jean-Marc Vallée (2005) – Québec went crazy (sorry!) for this film of a young Montrealer growing up gay. It swept the 2006 Genie Awards (the Canadian Oscars). Despite real charm and a killer soundtrack, this film doesn't quite live up to the media frenzy that surrounded it. You should still see it however, if only so you're not the only person in the province who didn't.

Eldorado by Charles Binamé (1995) – no other film before or since has captured the spirit of urban life in Montréal for young people the way this one did and still does over 10 years later. Montréal's rhythms and moods pulse in every frame and this remains the coolest and one of the most relevant films ever about the city and the people in it. It stars Pascale Bussières, James Hyndman, Pascale Montpetit and nightclub Foufounes Électriques.

L'Ange de Goudron (Tar Angel) by Denis Chouinard (2001) – an almost-too-sad-to-watch story about an immigrant Algerian family in Montréal. The father dreams of Canadian citizenship and does everything he can to fit into Canadian society, while his son does everything he can not to. With pacing and structural problems, the film never fully realizes its potential but there are so few films about the immigrant experience in Québec, it resonated strongly in multicultural Montréal anyway.

Les Invasions Barbares (The Barbarian Invasions) by Denys Arcand (2003) – the sequel to 1986's *The Decline of the American Empire,* an estranged family is brought together by the hedonistic, ex-radical father's losing battle with cancer. In 2004 it won the Oscar for best foreign film, Canada's first ever in this category.

L'Audition by Luc Picard (2005) – directed and acted by one of Québec's most respected actors and scored by Daniel Bélanger, one of the province's most respected singer-songwriters. This film is about a hit man in Montréal who wants to leave it all behind and become an actor and is one of the best pieces of storytelling released in 2005.

Octobre by Pierre Falardeau (1994) – Falardeau's separatist politics are well-known and this film, the dramatization of the FLQ crisis based on the book by FLQ cell member Francis Simard, was embroiled in controversy for the director's sympathetic portrayal of the terrorists. Oddly, Falardeau ends up making viewers feel most sympathy for the terror cell's victim. Serge Houde gives a wrenching performance as kidnapped labour minister Pierre Laporte who was later murdered by the cell. The scene when he overhears the government of which he was part refuse to negotiate for his life will be seared in your memory long after the film is over.

QUÉBEC'S MASTER FILMMAKER

No director portrays modern Québec with a sharper eye than Montréal's own Denys Arcand. His themes are universal enough to strike a chord with international audiences: modern sex in *The Decline of the American Empire,* religion in *Jésus of Montréal,* and most recently, death in the brilliant tragicomedy *The Barbarian Invasions* (2003). The *Invasions* casts a satirical light on Québec's creaking healthcare system, the demise of the sexual revolution and the failed ideologies of the 1960s. Many of its misfit-intellectual characters are based on Arcand's own professorial friends.

Born in 1941 near Québec City, Arcand studied history in Montréal and landed a job at the National Film Board making movies for Expo '67. The young director was a keen supporter of francophone rights and the Quiet Revolution, but became deeply disillusioned with Québec politics in the 1970s. He then trained his lens on the establishment in documentaries like *Le Confort et l'Indifférence,* a scathing critique of Québec's first referendum on sovereignty in 1980. *Réjeanne Padovani,* a political thriller, ends with a body being entombed in the fresh concrete of a Montréal freeway.

So far Arcand has been able to resist Hollywood's siren calls. After scoring a big hit with *Decline* (winner of eight 'Genies,' the Canadian Oscars, in 1986), a big US studio asked for a remake of the film in English. Arcand politely refused, and a few years later actor Meg Ryan lobbied for him to direct *Sleepless in Seattle.* But the Quebecer didn't like the script – and rejected a million-dollar offer.

Arcand's best films are inextricably tied to French Canada. This may explain why his only English-language films to date – *Love and Human Remains* (1993) and *Stardom* (2000) – failed to ignite audiences. Arcand himself admits his characters may be too Gallic to work in any language but French.

His next film *L'Âge des Ténèbres,* about a government bureaucrat who escapes into a fantasy world, may be out by the time you read this.

TELEVISION

While on any given night English Canada will be tuned into imported shows from the United States, Québec airwaves are devoted almost entirely to homegrown content with the odd program, movie from France or dubbed-American offering thrown into the mix.

The biggest presence province-wide is Radio-Canada, the French service of the Canadian Broadcasting Corporation. Radio-Canada, and French stations Télé-Québec, TVA and Télévision Quatre-Saisons dish up a varied diet of drama, news, comedy and sport that is tuned into by millions of Quebecers and enjoy a popularity and status unimaginable for English-language programs.

The most enduring genre is the *téléroman,* a cross between a soap opera and prime-time drama. But runaway hit of the day is Radio-Canada's *Tout le Monde en Parle* (Everybody is Talking About It), a rollicking current affairs show hosted by comedian Guy A Lepage. It's controversial, snappy and the first stop for anyone doing anything in Québec's public arena from politicians and actors, to war heroes and wacko psychiatrists. The province literally grinds to a halt on Sunday nights, as two million Quebecers (almost one third of the entire population of the province!) tune in to find out what people will be talking about in newspapers and airwaves for the rest of the week.

Private stations serving English-language viewers in Montréal include CFCF/CTV, the first private TV station in Québec (1961). Its 6pm news broadcast is the city's most watched in that language. Competitor Global TV runs news and a breakfast talk show. Global's multilingual station CH Montréal serves the city's ethnic communities with broadcasts in 15 languages every month.

THEATER

Canada was a desert for playwrights in the early 1960s when a group of disgruntled writers formed the Playwrights' Workshop Montréal, which revolutionized the way plays were staged. An important drama center, the workshop has been the key to developing contemporary work and new writers for the Canadian stage. Its pioneers included playwrights such as Dan Daniels, Aviva Ravel, Walter Massey, Justice Rinfret and Guy Beaulne, many of whom are active on Montréal's theater scene today.

Founded in 1968, the **Centaur Theater** (p162) is Québec's premier English-language stage for drama. Initially its programming was contemporary-international, eg Miller, Brecht and Pinter. When a second stage for experimental theater was added in the 1970s, the Centaur set about developing English-speaking playwrights such as David Fennario, whose satirical *On the Job* was considered a breakthrough production for the company. Fennario's *Balconville* in 1980 (p48) brought critical acclaim as well as an international tour.

Today the Centaur is considered one of Canada's leading theaters. Works by its playwrights appear in collaborations with other theaters in Canada as well as the USA and Ireland. Recently the Centaur produced *Mambo Italiano* by Montréal playwright Steve Galluccio, and the play's incredible success led to a film version released in 2003 (p43).

Modern theatrical dance in Canada developed in tandem with the drama scene. **Les Grands Ballets Canadiens'** (p165) modern staging of *Carmina Burana* for Expo '67, followed by the 1970 rock ballet adaptation of The Who's *Tommy,* gave the company two of its greatest hits. Together with ballet companies in Winnipeg and Toronto, and the professional schools they spawned, the LGBC helped to form the bedrock of Canadian professional dance and drama.

Québec's fabulously successful **Cirque du Soleil** (p46) set new artistic boundaries by combining dance, theater and circus in a single power-packed show.

Michel Tremblay's plays with people speaking in their own dialects changed the way Quebecers felt about their language. And in 2006 Montréal star director and francophone playwright Wajdi Mouawad whose plays have received raves in France and Québec and who led the Théâtre de Quat'Sous from 2000 to 2004, was appointed as the artistic director for the National Arts Centre's French theater in Ottawa.

DANCE

Montréal's dance scene crackles with innovation. Virtually every year a new miniseries, dance festival or performing-arts troupe emerges to wow the audiences in wild and unpredictable ways. Hundreds of performers and dozens of companies are based in the city and there's an excellent choice of venues for interpreters to strut their stuff.

Several major companies established the city's reputation in the 1980s as an international dance mecca. **Les Grand Ballets Canadiens** (p165) attracts the biggest audiences with evergreens such as *Carmen* and *The Nutcracker*. O Vertigo, MC2 Extase, La La La Human Steps, Fondation Jean-Pierre Perraeault and **Les Ballets Jazz de Montréal** (see opposite) are troupes of international standing. Initially they all struggled but operate today with annual budgets running into the millions of dollars.

A new breed of independent dancer-choreographers has emerged over the past few years. These all-round talents tend to work outside the bounds of formal troupes to diversify and explore a broader spectrum of traditions.

Venezuela-born José Navas is one of the most exciting soloists working today he and also works as choreographer of Compagnie Flak. Dance fans who saw his extraordinary *One Night Only* ten years ago still talk about it when they get together.

Montréal-born Margaret Gillis is a modern dancer of international renown and combines performing, teaching and choreography all over the world. Recently, she choreographed two solos for the Cirque du Soleil's *LOVE* which premiered in Las Vegas in June 2006. She usually does at least one performance in Montréal per year. Check www.margiegillis .org for details.

Transatlantique Montréal Manifestation de Danse Comtemporaine (www.trans atlantiquemontreal.com) is a relatively new week-long contemporary dance festival held at the end of September focusing on new creations by Québécois, Canadian and international performers.

RAGS TO RICHES CIRCUS STYLE: CIRQUE DU SOLEIL

The real life story of Guy Laliberté is one of the great Canadian entertainment stories and almost as dramatic as one of the performances his company is so well-known for.

Born in Québec City in 1959, he spent his youth basking in the kind of hobbies other people label as weird – stilts, fire breathing and accordion playing. But that all changed when he got together with a group of like-minded friends that became the first incarnation of Cirque du Soleil (Circus of the Sun).

Their big break came with the 450th anniversary of Jacques Cartier's arrival in New France in 1984 and has snowballed ever since and now the difficult-to-describe performances are riots of dance, acrobatics, music and elements that defy categorization but are just mind-blowing to watch.

Though the no-animals, no-speaking rules have remained true to their roots, these days there is no stereotypical Cirque performer who might be hired.

Fulltime Cirque scouts comb the world including Eastern Europe and remote parts of China, searching for new performers, tricks and skills to add to their shows. Cirque scouts are also regular fixtures at the Olympic Games where as soon as the competition is over, they burn up the phones with offers to gymnasts, swimmers and any other charismatic amateur athlete who catches their eyes.

Laliberté's productions also regularly include guest performers and artistic contributions.

Most recently, Montréal dance icon Margie Gillis choreographed two solos for *LOVE*, the Beatles inspired Cirque production in Las Vegas. Designer Thierry Mugler created the erotically charged costumes for *Zumanity*, which included metal underwear and latex coats chosen as much for their suggestive connotations as for the sounds they made on stage.

One of the best examples of pushing the creative limits was the mega-production *O* which took place in a 25-foot deep pool filled with 1.5 million gallons of water. An underwater crew was submerged in the pool for the entire 90-minute performance to catch divers, give them hits of oxygen (about 30 liters a night for each performer) and direct them out of the pool.

So Laliberté, the performer who once busked for change is now a billionaire entertainment mogul whose world empire keeps expanding and there are already plans in the works for a permanent production in Tokyo amongst other locations.

BALLET YES, BUT IS IT JAZZ?

You notice it right away, the sizzling dynamics and awesome precision of the dancers. Though the faces may have changed during the company's three decades, physical exhilaration remains the trademark of Les Ballets Jazz de Montréal. Its repertoire has switched from finger-snapping, pelvis-twisting routines to hot-cold contemporary reflections, but its dancers still test the limits with inexhaustible energy.

When the BJM was founded in 1972, the company performed only to jazz music. With artistic director Louis Robitaille's arrival in the late 1990s, its repertoire became more eclectic, both in music and choreography. Today, the company goes by the moniker BJM Danse and while the director acknowledges the company's jazz roots he stresses that his dancers – all of whom are classically trained – need to perform in a fusion of styles. 'Dance isn't one thing anymore. To stay in one direction will kill the company,' says Robitaille. BJM Danse showcases its interpreters' talents, while encouraging works of cutting-edge choreographers such as Jiri Kylian and William Forsythe. Success on the international stage has silenced the critics who once griped that the troupe had strayed from its jazz roots. Vancouverite Crystal Pite, who previously worked for the Ballett Frankfurt, has been their resident choreographer since 2001 and the company is getting some of the best reviews of its career.

Because it performs before audiences all over the world, BJM Danse has learned to tailor its repertoire to varied tastes. Robitaille notes that in the USA, Asia and much of Canada, spectators like to be entertained, while in Montréal the audience is 'very connected and prefers the avant-garde.'

Notable troupes include Danièle Desnoyers' Le Carré des Lombes, Sylvain Érnard Danse, Benoît Lachambre's Par b.l.eux and MAPS (run by Suzanne Miller and Allan Paivio).

Danse Danse, put on by Productions Loma, packs its season with international talent at high-profile venues. Tangente plays four-night runs nearly every weekend with performances by emerging and established artists. Agora de la Danse (p165) serves local, midsized companies and choreographers. Finally, Studio 303 fills its agenda with experimental artists and choreographers who present short works and improvisation in the Vernissage Danse series.

LITERATURE

Montréal proudly calls itself the world's foremost cradle of French-language writers, after Paris. But the city also boasts intimate links to many English-language writers of repute.

On the English side, Montréal's most famous literary son is Nobel Prize-winner Saul Bellow. Born in the town of Lachine near Montréal in 1915, Bellow moved with his family to Chicago when he was 10 years old, but wrote about the city in his classic novel *Herzog* (1964). Montréal was a recurring nostalgic theme for the book's grumpy middle-aged hero, Herzog.

Caustic, quick-witted and prolific, Mordecai Richler was the 'grumpy old man' of Montréal literature in the latter part of the 20th century. Richler grew up in the working-class Jewish district in Mile End and for better or worse remained the most distinctive voice in anglophone Montréal until his passing in 2001. Most of his novels focus on Montréal and its wild and wonderful characters.

Self-imposed exile also fell to Mavis Gallant, an émigré to France whose witty, bittersweet novels wove in her native Montréal. Gallant won many prizes and wrote short stories that graced the pages of the *New Yorker*.

On the French side, Québec writers who are widely read in English include Anne Hébert, Marie-Claire Blais, Hubert Aquin, Christian Mistral and Dany Laferrière, whose first book *Comment Faire l'Amour avec un Nègre sans se Fatiguer* (the book was released in English as *How to Make Love to a Negro*) a wild and witty look at race relations in Canada

TOP FIVE MONTRÉAL FICTION

- *Les Aurores Montréales* by Monique Proulx
- *A Full Moon in Summer* by Michel Tremblay
- *Bonheur d'Occasion* (The Tin Flute) by Gabrielle Roy
- Any book set in Montréal by Kathy Reichs
- *The Apprenticeship of Duddy Kravitz* by Mordecai Richler

was eventually made into a film whose screenplay was nominated for a Genie award. For stories about everyday life on the Plateau, try Michel Tremblay's short stories.

As for literary trends in the province, many of today's buzz-inducing young writers are immigrants from other French-speaking countries writing about conflicts back home. Lebanese-born Rawi Hage moved to Montréal in 1991 and his first novel *De Niro's Game* about life in Beirut was nominated for the 2006 Scotiabank Giller Prize, Canada's highest literary award. Elsewhere, Quebecers never seem to get enough of historical novels, and bookshelves are groaning with fiction set in the province's past.

Writers' groups can be contacted via spoken-word venues like the Yellow Door (p153). A literary festival, **Blue Metropolis** (p22), brings together more than 200 writers for five days of literary events in early April.

BOOK REVIEWS

A Full Moon in Summer by Michel Tremblay (2001) – eleven Montrealers recount their stories of love, piecing together the landscape of an affair and tracing the slopes between intoxicating highs and heartbreaking lows.

The Apprenticeship of Duddy Kravitz by Mordecai Richler (1959) – A rough young hustler becomes obsessed with buying land as his ticket out of the Plateau ghetto; the character type has entered Montréal parlance. Richler won an Oscar nomination for the classic 1974 movie made from the book.

Around the Mountain by Hugh Hood (1967) – this collection of 12 Montréal narratives is a documentary-fantasy portrait of its people and ambience in the heady days of Expo '67, from the misadventures of a convivial soldier to the fruitless efforts of an angelic messenger.

Les Aurores Montréales by Monique Proulx (1996) – a genius collection of short stories with Montréal starring as its inhabitants fumble through life in the city. Everyone who loves Montréal, rough edges and all, needs to read this book.

Book of Longing by Leonard Cohen (2006) – Cohen's most recent collection of poetry and drawings.

Bonheur d'Occasion (The Tin Flute) by Gabrielle Roy (1947) – the tragic ironies of WWII provide an escape from the claustrophobic poverty of the Depression in working-class Montréal. This gritty urban novel became a million-copies-seller and was made into a film.

Briser le Silence by Nathalie Simard and Michel Vastel (2005) – superstar producer and musical svengali Guy Cloutier took Nathalie Simard under his wing as a child and made her, along with her brother René, two of Québec's major singing stars of the 1980s. He also

Getting lost in a book, Downtown Montréal

TOP FIVE NONFICTION BOOKS

- *A Short History of Quebec* (1993, revised 2002) by John A Dickinson and Brian Young. Social and economic portrait of Québec from the pre-European period to modern constitutional struggles.
- *City Unique: Montreal Days and Nights in the 1940s and '50s* (1996) by William Weintraub. Engaging tales of Montréal's twilight period as Sin City and an exploration of its historic districts.
- *The Road to Now: A History of Blacks in Montreal* (1997) by Dorothy Williams. A terrific and rare look at a little known aspect of the city's history and the black experience in New France.
- *Canadiens Legends: Montreal's Hockey Heroes* (2004) by Mike Leonetti. Wonderful profiles and pics on some of the key players that made this team an NHL legend. Whether you're a sports fan or not, Les Canadiens and the mythology around them is an important part of the city's 20th century cultural history.
- *The Illustrated History of Canada* (2002) edited by Craig Brown. Several historians contributed to this well-crafted work with fascinating prints, maps and sketches.

sexually abused Nathalie from the time she was 11. When she pressed charges it rocked the province's entertainment industry to its core. This is her autobiography, a heartbreaking and searing portrait of the dark side of Québec's star system.

Dance With Desire by Irving Layton (2002) – chosen from across the span of this Montréal poet's long career, these poems feed on the excesses, embarrassments and foolishness of unstifled love.

Deadly Decisions by Kathy Reichs (1999) – this celebrated American crime novelist, like her heroine Temperance Brennan, is a forensic anthropologist who divides her time between Montréal and North Carolina where she's a university professor. She bases about half her crime stories in Montréal. The dead bodies are most important but her keen observation of the city's people and culture absolutely shines in this book whether she's talking about local hotdogs or Montréal winters.

L'Hiver de Force by Réjean Ducharme (2002) – two lovers in a Montréal apartment seek escape from daily life through a variety of means from TV and chansons to alcohol and drugs in a critique of 1970s Québec (in French). The author is one of Québec's major writers and recluses.

The Hockey Sweater by Roch Carrier (1979) – due to a mail-order mix-up a child is forced to wear a Toronto Maple Leafs sweater in a small Québec town teeming with Montréal Canadiens fans. A wise parable of the friction between Québec's French and English populations of the era.

Oh Canada! Oh Quebec! Requiem for a Divided Country by Mordecai Richler (1992) – Montréal-born Richler's scathing critique of Québec's independence movement set off a furor among Canadian politicians – one member of parliament even called for the book to be banned. You need to read it for the impact it once had, not because it's the reality today.

VISUAL ARTS

The municipal visual-arts scene is livelier than ever, thanks to generous support from the Québec government but also to the arrival of new media as a serious art form.

PAINTING

Québec's lush forests and icy winter landscapes have been inspiring landscape artists since the 19th century. Horatio Walker was known for his sentimental interpretations of Québec farm life such as *Oxen Drinking* (1899). Marc-Aurèle Fortin (1880–1972) became famous for his watercolors of Québec countryside, notably the treescapes of the Laurentian Mountains and Charlevoix. His portraits of majestic elms along Montréal avenues can be viewed in the eponymous museum in **Old Montréal** (p76).

William Brymner influenced an entire generation of painters as director of the Art Association of Montréal in the early 20th century. His forte was delicate human figures, interiors and landscapes in the glowing colors of romantic classicism. One of his pupils was Clarence Gagnon, who produced subtle snowscapes and dazzling autumn scenes. Other key artists of the period included Adrien Hébert and Robert Pilot, usually identified by their snowy portraits of Montréal and Québec City.

In the 1940s the modern era of Canadian painting was ushered in by three leading figures: Paul-Émile Borduas, John Lyman and Alfred Pellan, who all worked closely together in Montréal. Borduas developed a radical style of surrealism that came to be identified with an alternative group called the 'Automatistes.'

In 1948 Borduas drafted the manifest *Refus Global* (Global Refusal), which rejected the values of traditional landscape painting in favor of abstract art. The highly controversial document endorsed personal freedoms of expression while attacking state repressions and the dominant place of the church in Québec.

The most prolific of the Automatistes was Jean-Paul Riopelle (1923–2002). Though initially a surrealist, Riopelle soon produced softer abstracts called 'grand mosaics' – paintings created with a spatula and colors juxtaposed like a landscape viewed from an airplane. In the 1980s he abandoned conventional painting to work with aerosol sprays. His most renowned paintings are on permanent display at Montréal's **Musée d'Art Contemporain** (p89) and the **Musée National des Beaux-Arts du Québec** (p221) in Québec City.

Abstract painting has been an exciting field to follow in the past few years in Montréal. François Lacasse is a master in manipulating acrylic into new depths that evoke a strong sense of virtuality without the aid of computers. And lithograph artists like Elmyna Bouchard and Francine Simonin are getting attention throughout Canada and abroad.

> ## TOP FIVE GALLERIES
> - Galeries d'Art Contemporain du Belgo (p182) – five floors of some of the most exciting contemporary art, design and architecture
> - Parisian Laundry (p184) – no gallery shows off big canvases better than this place, the building alone is reason enough to visit
> - Galerie St-Dizier (p180) – beautiful space at the forefront of the avant-garde
> - Galerie Orange (p180) – contemporary art and some of the best openings in town
> - Galerie de Bellefeuille (p188) – leading ambassador of Canadian creations abroad

PHOTOGRAPHY & NEW MEDIA

Québec's strong visual traditions owe much to documentary photography. Montréal's first master photographer was William Notman, who rose to international fame for his portraits, landscapes and urban subjects in the late 19th century. **Musée McCord** (p92) has a permanent collection of his works.

Documentary photography has fed a strong tradition of Québec photo art since the late 1960s. Most recently, Emmanuelle Léonard took a novel approach by having dozens of people from different walks of life photograph their workplaces themselves; the views of each worker's environment were quite different from what the viewer expected.

The work of photographer-artist Alain Paiement, by contrast, redefines space through spectacular images of urban spaces. For one project Paiement shot the floor area of an apartment house and joined the images into one huge composition. Small ruptures in the picture pointed out the image's structural impossibility.

Nicolas Baier uses computers and digital photography to take inventory of the world around him. Baier takes many pictures of a space and, on an abstract collage principle, cuts and reorganizes them so that parts of the surface represent different moments in time. In one work an image of the artist's bedroom was rearranged in this disconcerting fashion.

Montréal's many new media studios testify to the multimedia revolution that has taken place over the past decade. Kooky machines and organic sounds are the trademarks of Jean-Paul Gauthier, whose work has been shown at Montréal's **Musée des Beaux-Arts** (p92). His 'instruments' are tubes and pipes, air compressors, radio interference and sheet metal that produce percussive sounds; in one installation, large springs scratch over rotating mirrors to a soundtrack of shrill cries.

ARCHITECTURE

Montréal's split personality is nowhere more obvious than in its architecture, a beguiling mix of cozy European warmth and North American pizzazz. Lovingly preserved Victorian mansions and stately Beaux Arts monuments rub shoulders with the sleek lines of modern skyscrapers, lending Montréal's urban landscape a creative, eclectic sophistication all of its own. Sometimes one building even straddles the divide: the **Centre Canadien d'Architecture** (p84) integrates a graceful historical greystone right into its contemporary facade.

Other important buildings were meant to break with the past. Place Ville-Marie, a multitowered complex built in the late 1950s, revolutionized urban architecture in Montréal and was the starting point for the **underground city** (p86). Since then, architects have explored new forms such as the **Habitat '67** (p83), a controversial apartment building designed by Montréal architect Moshe Safdie when he was only 23. Located on a promontory off the Old Port, the structure resembles a child's scattered building blocks. The **Biosphère** (p82) wears a skin made of spherical mesh, while the **Casino de Montréal** (p83) cleverly merges two of the most far-out pavilions of Expo '67.

> ## TOP FIVE ARCHITECTURAL THRILLS
>
> - Basilique Notre-Dame (p73) – enduring Gothic symbol of Catholic power
> - Casino de Montréal (p83) – cross between a spaceship and an airport terminal
> - Oratoire St-Joseph (p105) – Renaissance monument to a monk's resolve
> - Bibliothèque et Archives Nationales du Québec (p95) – brilliant example of contemporary architecture made with people in mind
> - Olympic Stadium (p98) – like a Triffid attacking a giant turtle

Those heady days are back: Montréal's economic revival has sparked a construction boom. Not since the 1976 Olympic Games has the city seen such an explosion of large-scale projects, some of which are designed to repair defects in the urban fabric. One of the largest redevelopment projects in Canada was Montréal's $200-million convention center **Palais des Congrès** (p87) and its adjacent squares. Dubbed the Quartier International, this new minidistrict unites Downtown and Old Montréal by concealing an ugly sunken expressway.

Residential architecture and street gardens, Latin Quarter

CANADA'S STAR ARCHITECT MOSHE SAFDIE

Born in Haifa, Israel in 1938, Moshe Safdie graduated from McGill University's architecture program in 1961 and became almost an instant star. He was only 23 when asked to design Habitat '67 (p83) which was actually based on his university thesis. Now based in Boston, Safdie has crafted a stellar career gravitating towards high-profile projects where he can unleash innovative buildings with just the right dash of controversy to get people talking about them.

Most notably, Safdie designed the $56-million, 4000-square-meter Holocaust Memorial in Jerusalem, Israel which opened in 2005. He also designed Ottawa's National Gallery of Canada which opened in 1988 with its trade mark soaring glass front and the Roman colosseum-like Vancouver Library Square.

Most recently, Safdie's design for the Jepson Center for the Arts in Savannah, Georgia, has provoked intense debate, with critics lambasting the imposing structure of glass and stone for 'intruding' into the area's historic character while fans praise its vision towards the future.

Safdie was made a companion of the Order of Canada in 2005, Canada's highest civilian honor.

For many visitors, the weathered greystones, such as the old stone buildings along rue St-Paul, offer the strongest images of Old Montréal. The style emerged under the French regime in Québec (1608–1763), based on the Norman and Breton houses with wide, shallow fronts, stuccoed stone and a steep roof punctuated by dormer windows. But the locals soon adapted the blueprint to Montréal's harsh winters, making the roof less steep, adding basements and extending the eaves over the walls for extra snow protection.

From the 19th century, architects tapped any number of retro styles: classical (**Bank of Montréal**, p73), Gothic (**Basilique Notre-Dame**, p73) or Italian renaissance (**Royal Bank**, p78), to name a few. As Montréal boomed in the 1920s, a handful of famous architects like Edward Maxwell, George Ross and Robert MacDonald left their mark on handsome towers in Old Montréal and Downtown. French Second Empire style continued to be favored for comfortable francophone homes and some public buildings like the **Hôtel de Ville** (City Hall; p75).

Montréal also boasts the largest collection of Victorian row houses in all of North America. Numerous examples can be viewed in the Plateau such as along rue St-Denis north of rue Cherrier, or ave Laval north of Carré St-Louis. Visitors are inevitably charmed by their brightly painted wrought-iron staircases, which wind up the outside of duplexes and triplexes. They evolved for three important reasons: taxes – a staircase outside allowed each floor to count as a separate dwelling, so the city could hike property taxes; fuel costs – an internal staircase wastes heat as warm air rises through the stairwell; space – the 1st and 2nd floors were roomier without an internal staircase.

Music

Music

Montréal is all about the music these days. There's such a laboratory of musical experiences and styles going on that whether you're into jazz or punk, classical music or folk, just exploring the city's music scene could keep you busy for your whole trip.

There are dozens of large and medium-sized venues and theaters that regularly host concerts. The best concert venue of all is downtown Montréal during the monster International Jazz Festival (see boxed text p57) when the city core is sealed off to traffic and becomes a kind of giant open-air concert venue where the whole city comes to party. The event draws two million people to Montréal each year.

These days there's also another kind of musical tourism going on because of the commercial and critical success of independent bands like Arcade Fire and the Dears as well as the mass punk-pop of Simple Plan in the United States and beyond. It's put a spotlight on the city's musical scene and talented bands are making everyone wonder, 'Why didn't we notice this before?' After the scene was touted in the *New York Times* and *Spin* magazine, the music and entertainment press in town have reported seeing a mini boom in non–Jazz Fest 'musical tourism.' Visitors are coming just to take in Montréal's clubs and gigs hoping they'll come across the next big thing before everybody else does and be able to say they saw Group XYZ at a little club in Montréal way-back-when.

However, the accolades were not without criticism. The music scene in Montréal has been vibrant, creative and adventurous in everything from folk to rock since the Quiet Revolution. With Québec's huge music industry behind them (also see Arts chapter p42) Québec's French-language singers, bands and other musicians regularly sell hundreds of thousands of albums a year, but because they're sold to other Quebecers instead of English-speaking North Americans, no one has sat up to take notice.

When the North American press ignored that part of the scene, which makes up the lion's share of what goes on in Montréal, a lot of people were irritated.

Montréal International Jazz Festival

Though there's huge respect in the music scene for independent bands like the Dears and the others of their ilk who are getting so much attention, the reality is, go into any bar or club on boul St-Laurent or in Mile End these days and more often than not, people will be sitting around talking about the new albums by Malajube or Les Breastfeeders (see below), not Simple Plan or Arcade Fire. And absolutely nothing will break the ice faster with a Quebecer than knowing who Les Colocs or Jean Leloup is.

ROCK & POP

To say that Montréal's popular-music scene is diverse is a gross understatement. The music guide in the alternative weekly *Montreal Mirror* lists more than 260 active bands that embrace anything and everything from electropop, hip-hop and glam rock to Celtic folk, indie punk and yéyé. Oh, and you can't forget roots, ambient, grunge or rockabilly.

Québec's best-known recording artist is Céline Dion. Born in Charlemagne some

TOP FIVE NEW CDS

- The Dears *Gang of Losers*, 2006
- Malajube *Trompe-L'oeil*, 2006
- Les Breastfeeders *Les Matins de Grands Soirs*, 2006
- Arcade Fire *Funeral*, 2005
- Mononc' Serge & Anonymus *L'Académie du Massacre*, 2003

30km east of downtown Montréal, Dion was a megastar in Québec and France long before she won a Grammy for 'My Heart Will Go On' from the movie *Titanic*. In 1983 she became the first Canadian to get a gold record in France.

Genius management from husband/music svengali René Angélil spared Céline much criticism of 'selling out' when she started to work on an English-language career. By alternating English and French-language releases, she's kept both her English and Québec fan bases happy for decades.

On the rock scene, Arcade Fire is definitely the group of the moment. Their eclectic folk/rock/indie sound and manic ensemble of instruments made them critics' darlings since their first CD *Funeral* was released in 2004 and made top 10 lists all over the US and UK. Many Montrealers who saw their early shows at the old Corona Theatre in Montréal's St-Henri/Pointe-St-Charles neighborhood remember them as some of the best live shows ever. The group is highly respected not just because of their music but because they were able to sell over 500,000 copies of *Funeral* around the world without a major label, buzz being fuelled mainly through the internet.

While Dion and Arcade Fire are the best known Québec musicians internationally, within the province there's only one artist that can claim iconic status – Jean Leloup.

Born in Québec City in 1961, Leloup (The Wolf) grew up in Africa, mainly in Algeria, before coming back to Québec with his parents at age 15. His music career was kick-started by a win at the 1983 Festival International de la Chanson de Granby (www.ficg.qc.ca, a festival devoted to discovering new francophone talent) but it wasn't until the release of his second album *L'amour est sans Pitié* (1990) that the province (and Europe and Japan)

TOP FIVE INDEPENDENT CD/RECORD SHOPS

Montréal's zany independent record shops (used and new) are a great way to impress your friends with your taste and myriad resources. Ave Mont-Royal and boul St-Laurent are the best places to explore to see if anything new has opened up. You'll surely find that pirated Nirvana or late-1960s *Recorded at Playboy Mansion* jazz album here. The listing below is just a sampling of what's on offer.

- Au Tourne-Livre (Map pp316–17; ☎ 598-8580; 707 ave du Mont-Royal Est; Ⓜ Mont-Royal)
- Les Disques Beatnick (Map pp316–17; ☎ 842-0664; 3770 rue St-Denis; Ⓜ Sherbrooke)
- Marché du Disque (Map pp316–17; ☎ 526-3757; 793 ave du Mont-Royal Est; Ⓜ Mont-Royal)
- CD Esoterik (Map pp310–11; ☎ 937-5192, 1841-C Ste-Catherine Ouest; Ⓜ Guy-Concordia)
- Inbeat Records (Map pp310–11; ☎ 499-2063; 3841 boul St-Laurent; Ⓜ Sherbrooke)

went mental for him. The CD spawned one hit after another and pretty much every music fan between the ages of 20 and 50 in Québec has it. The album's mega hit single '1990' is regularly played in bars and clubs even now, almost 20 years later.

In 2003, Leloup said fame was getting too much for him and (figuratively – don't worry) announced he was killing off Jean Leloup and never wanted to have to sing his 'Leloup' songs again. His retirement didn't last long and he released *Mexico* in 2006 but is now only recording and performing under 'Jean Leclerc,' his legal name.

Les Colocs is one of the most influential Québec bands of the last 20 years. Known for its outrageous and energetic live shows, its lyrics in particular resonated with music fans, touching on everything from alienation to poverty and social problems in Québec. Band singer Dédé Fortin committed suicide in 2000 and was grieved by the whole province and the band broke up soon afterward. However, music fans of all ages still talk about it in the present tense today, like it never went away. Former Coloc, Mononc' Serge is still recording and performing. A committed Québec separatist, his raging brand of folk rock deals mostly with Québec's struggles and frustrations with Canada.

On the pop front, singer-songwriter Daniel Bélanger's moody, atmospheric albums and mesmerizing lyrics have been seducing the province's music fans since the 1990s.

Up-and-coming bands and singers to keep an eye out for when you're in town are indie-rock band Malajube, eclectic singer Ariane Moffatt and Les Breastfeeders, whose infectious mix of '60s rock-styled pop punk have made them one of the best live shows in all of Montréal.

To find out more, MusiquePlus is Québec's all-music-video channel. To find out what's up and coming in indie francophone music, the Université de Montréal's radio station CISM 89.3FM is excellent and the frequency is available in most parts of Montréal.

RAP & HIP-HOP

Montréal's rap scene has not really taken off the way other scenes have. Loco Locass is the most popular hip-hop group in the province today and its popularity crosses over genre lines. Its lyrics are highly political and touch on subjects like Québec independence, anger at the Canadian political system and frustration with Québec's place in it. Many visitors, and even English Canadians, have difficultly understanding the 'whys' behind the separatist movement but if you can read some French and get your hands on one of Loco Locass' CDs, like its 2006 *Amour Oral,* you will get good insight into the phenomenon whether you agree with it or not.

JAZZ

Outside the frenetic weeks of the International Jazz Festival, the contemporary scene in Montréal bubbles away in a few designated clubs and cafés. During the day musicians might teach at McGill University's music school – or play for sidewalk donations.

In the 1940s and '50s, Montréal was one of the most important venues for jazz music in North America. It produced a number of major jazz musicians, like pianist Oscar Peterson and trumpeter Maynard Ferguson. The secret of its success? Montréal was one of the most open cities on the continent, a town where the committed hedonist could find just about anything. The scene went into decline in the late 1950s but revived after the premiere of the Jazz Festival in 1980.

Peterson, who grew up dirt-poor in a southwestern Montréal suburb, has dazzled audiences with his keyboard pyrotechnics for the best part of seven decades. He's never been particularly concerned about fame or commercial success. 'I don't do something because I think it will sell 30 million albums,' Peterson says. 'I couldn't care less. If it sells one, it sells one.'

The city's other grand pianist, Oliver Jones, was already in his fifties when he was discovered by the jazz world. He had studied with Oscar Peterson's sister Daisy and the influence can be heard in his sound. Since the 1980s he has established himself as a major mainstream player with impressive technique and a hard-swinging style.

HOT, HIP & COOL – MONTRÉAL'S JAZZ FESTIVAL

In a city that loves festivals the Montréal International Jazz Festival is the mother of them all. It started as the pipe dream of a young local music producer, Alain Simard, who tried to sell his idea to the government and corporate sponsors, with little success.

'I was saying that one day this festival would bring thousands of American tourists to Montréal,' Simard says. 'They really made fun of me.'

The first event in 1979 drew 12,000 visitors. Simard had to finance three years of festivals with his own money, but from the beginning there were quality headliners like Ray Charles, Ella Fitzgerald and Pat Metheny. The festival was judged as hip thanks to its laid-back atmosphere, quality acts and free street concerts, and in 1989 it moved from the Quartier Latin to its current home at the Place des Arts.

Now it's the single biggest tourist event in Québec, attracting nearly two million visitors to 400 concerts – and many say it's the best jazz festival on the planet. Miles Davis, Herbie Hancock, Al Jarreau, Sonny Rollins, Wayne Shorter, Al Dimeola, John Scofield and Jack DeJohnette are but a few giants who have graced the podia over the years. More and more though, you'll find music of every style under the sun: blues, Latin, reggae, Cajun, Dixieland, world and even pop.

Some people lament this change somewhat (see boxed text p58) but festival goers are voting with their feet and the number of visitors just keeps going up each year.

The magic of the festival's success is its inclusiveness. Go to any of the free outdoor shows on any given night and you may see punks next to seniors next to an immigrant couple from China next to a Sikh family all grooving together at the same gig.

Practicalities

Info Jazz Bell (☎ 871-1881 or 888-515-0515; www.montrealjazzfest.com) provides events details, free festival programs and maps at kiosks around the **Place des Arts** (Map pp310-11). Most concerts are held in the halls or on outdoor stages; several downtown blocks are closed to traffic. The music starts around noon and lasts until late evening when the clubs take over.

Tickets go on sale in mid-May and are available from the **Places des Arts box office** (☎ 842-2112; www.pdarts .com) and **Admission** (☎ 790-1245; www.admission.com). The biggest acts cost $80 and up but some very good concerts may be on offer for just a few bucks. Free concerts are held daily from noon to 8pm.

Pay parking garages at the **Complexe Desjardins** (Map pp310–11; ☎ 845-4636) and Place des Arts fill up quickly; take the métro to avoid hassle and traffic. Hotels raise their prices by as much as 50% and early booking is essential. Lawn chairs, bicycles, dogs and your own alcohol aren't allowed – but there's plenty of seating on the steps of the Place des Arts and plenty of beer and food sold from the concession tents that dot the festival grounds.

Pharoah Sanders, Montréal International Jazz Festival

HOT HIP & COOL PART II: BEHIND THE SCENES

The Montréal International Jazz Festival is not so much a festival as a feeling: hip tunes, blazing sun, cool players and a kind of magical connection between two people, the Musician and the Fan.

The Musician: Vic Vogel

Born in 1935, Vogel grew up on the Plateau and has been playing piano since he was five. He's racked up gold and platinum records his entire career including the musical arrangement he did for the opening ceremonies of the 1976 Olympic Games in Montréal. A pianist and arranger, he's collaborated with the best of the best including Maynard Ferguson, Eartha Kitt, Dizzy Gillespie, Ann Margaret, Paul Anka and Sammy Davies Jr. He's also played every jazz fest since the beginning. The 2006 event had just wrapped up when we caught up with him at Else's (p157), one of his favorite watering holes. He was enjoying a late morning beer before heading off to a gig in New York City.

What was the jazz scene in Montréal like when you started?
'It was the pop music of the day and Montréal was wall-to-wall in it. You had clubs all over the place. Not like now [grunts].'

And these days?
'Too many musicians are playing it safe. They're not telling me a story. And they won't join the union [musicians' guild]. I don't like that.'

Do you remember the first time you heard they were starting up a jazz fest?
'I heard this young-punk booking agent Alain Simard was starting something up. I was doing Big Band and I told him we'd charge $2 and sell the place out. He laughed. We did. Right off the bat.'

Did you ever think the Jazz Fest would get this big?
'Jazz fest? Elvis Costello is playing it now. You want me to call it a jazz fest? Let's just call it entertainment.'

What about Montréal, what's the best way for hard-core jazz fans who don't know the city to suss out the scene?
'Don't read the music critics. What do they know? Talk to the musicians to find out what's going on. Go look for a rehearsal somewhere. Don't be lazy. Get out the phone book and call Local 406 [the musicians' guild], they'll tell you what's going on.'

You do gigs all over the world. What do you miss most about Montréal when you're gone?
'It's the friendliest city in the world and it has the most beautiful women. That and Schwartz's. (Vogel smiles for first time during entire interview.) Medium fat.'

The Fan: Melvin Fossett

Melvin Fossett is about as hardcore a Jazz Fest fan as you can find. This Baltimore, Maryland resident from the United States is a lifelong jazz fan and came to the Montréal festival for the first time in 2000 when he was 60 years old. He and the same group of friends have been coming back religiously every single year since. It's an event he calls 'Jazz Heaven.' Now a certified festival veteran, we caught up with Fossett on the last night of the 2006 event where he had some words of wisdom to pass on to fellow jazz freaks about how best to take it all in.

Fossett's Top Five:
- Plan ahead. 'Peruse your Jazz Fest program before you get up here. You have to buy your tickets in advance. Things sell out quickly. You don't want to get disappointed.'
- Pace yourself. 'My first time I came here I tried to do and see everything and I was running around all the time. It's not humanly possible, just don't try.'
- Learn French. 'I bought some teach-yourself-French CDs in 2005 to listen to them in the car. I come up to Québec each year so I thought, "Why not learn the language?" People are so great I want to make the effort.'
- Go for the late-night jam sessions. 'They're my favorite part. Just don't stay up all night at them. You need to get some rest for the next day.'
- Get off the festival grounds once in a while. 'There's so many great restaurants and cafés to try in Montréal, the town is so friendly. The city and the people somehow help you enjoy the jazz more.'

Singer, pianist and knockout blond Diana Krall enjoys mass appeal without sacrificing her bop and swing roots. In 1993 she launched her career on Montréal's Justin Time record label, and has since gone on to become the top-selling jazz vocalist. Her 1998 album *When I Look Into Your Eyes* earned a Grammy and spent a full year at the top of the Billboard jazz chart.

Originally from New York City, singer Ranee Lee is known for her virtuosity that spans silky ballads, swing standards and raw blues tunes. She has performed with many jazz notables and is a respected teacher on the McGill University music faculty.

The Vic Vogel Big Band, directed by pianist and arranger Vogel (see boxed text opposite), performs razor-sharp arrangements in the Duke Ellington mould. Hard bop drummer and band leader Bernard Primeau was one of Canada's most famous bandleaders and was known for picking young, talented players from obscurity. He died in 2006.

CLASSICAL

The backbone of Montréal's classical music scene is the Orchestre Symphonique de Montréal. The OSM was the first Canadian orchestra to achieve platinum (500,000 records sold) on its 1984 recording of Ravel's 'Boléro'. Since then it has won a host of awards including two Grammys and 12 Junos, the Canadian music industry award. The OSM has made 88 recordings with leading record labels like Decca and CBS.

In recent years, however, the symphony has stumbled, finding itself in the papers more for its real-life dramas than its music. Morale at the symphony was trashed after clashes between former musical director Charles Dutoit and the musicians union led to Dutoit's explosive resignation in 2002, and an acrimonious 2005 strike took five months to resolve.

But the symphony is poised for a major turnaround. In 2006 star American conductor Kent Nagano came on board as musical director. It's hard to overstate the rabid excitement his arrival has created around the symphony. His first performance with the orchestra was broadcast on a giant movie screen outside the symphony's home at Place des Arts (p89) and the performance had people alternately crying or cheering as if he was Mick Jagger.

The smaller Orchestre Métropolitain du Grand Montréal is a showcase of young Québec talent and as such is staffed by graduates from the province's conservatories. The director is Yannick Nézet-Séguin, a Montrealer and among the youngest to lead a major orchestra in Canada. Its regular cycle of Mahler symphonies is a particular treat for classical-music buffs.

OPERA

Over the past 25 years the Opéra de Montréal has become a giant on the North American landscape. It has staged over 600 performances of 76 operas and collaborated with numerous international companies. Many great names have graced its stages including Québec's own Leila Chalfoun, Lyne Fortin, Suzie LeBlanc and André Turp, alongside a considerable array of Canadian and international talent. The opera stages six new operas every season including classics like *Le Nozze di Figaro* and *The Magic Flute*.

Locally, new operas are not created but in 1989, the Opéra de Montréal won a Félix (Québec music award like the Grammys) for the most popular production of the season for *Nelligan* – an opera created in Québec about the life of poet Émile Nelligan (see boxed text p74) by André Gagnon; Michel Tremblay did the libretto.

FOLK

English-language folk singers are few and far between in Québec – apart from Leonard Cohen. Best known as a pop icon and novelist of the 1960s Cohen remains one of the world's most eclectic folk artists. The romantic despair in his compositions recalls the style of Jacques Brel. A second burst of major creativity occurred in the 1980s when Cohen's dry, gravelly baritone could be heard on albums such as *Various Positions* (1984), a treatise on lovers' relationships, and the sleek *I'm Your Man* (1988), which suddenly made him hip again to younger audiences. The aging bard can be heard at the annual Leonard Cohen Event every spring in Montréal.

TOP FIVE CLASSIC MUST-HAVE QUÉBEC ALBUMS

- Jean Leloup *Le Dôme*, 1996. We know, we know. *L'amour est sans Pitié* (1990) is considered *the* album. We're picking *Le Dôme* anyway – monster songwriting, killer hooks, Leloup at his mind-blowing best on every single track.
- Les Colocs *Les Colocs*, 1993. The song 'Passe-moé la puck' alone would be reason enough to add this CD to your collection, but this, their first disc, is also full of everything that made them so unique: social criticism, manic energy and a wicked sense of fun.
- Daniel Bélanger *Quatre saisons dans le désordre*, 1996. Bélanger draws you into his world so deeply on this one you never want to leave.
- Céline Dion *On ne change pas*, 2005. This CD is a collection of her French-language hits drawn from her entire career. Whatever you may think of her, no matter how kitsch the song, she makes you believe she's feeling every single emotion she sings about the way no one else has ever felt it before.
- Pierre Lapointe *La forêt des Mal-Aimés*, 2006. Yeah, 2006. But sometimes something is so good, everyone just knows.

CHANSON

It's hard to understand music in Québec without understanding what they call chanson, no matter how difficult it may seem to penetrate for non-French speakers at the beginning. While France has a long tradition of this type of French folk music, where a focus on lyric and poetry takes precedence over the music itself, in Québec the chanson has historically been tied in with politics and identity in a profound way. With the Duplessis-era Québec stifling any real creative production, Quebecers were tuned into only what was coming out of France like Edith Piaf or Charles Aznavour.

The social upheaval of the Quiet Revolution (p62) changed all that, when a generation of musicians took up their guitars, sung in Québécois and penned deeply personal lyrics about life in Québec and often independence.

Gilles Vigneault is synonymous with the chanson *Gens du pays* (People of the Country), a favorite on nationalist occasions. Vigneault has painted a portrait of the province in over 100 chanson recordings. Other leading chansonniers include Félix Leclerc, Raymond Lévesque, Claude Léveillé, Richard Desjardins and veteran Jean-Pierre Ferland.

As for new artists, chansonnier Pierre Lapointe is *the* musical sensation in Québec and one of the most exciting and original musicians to come out this decade. Born in Lac St-Jean, Québec, he's been showered with prizes and adulation for his music from Montréal to France and back again.

You can hear chanson in *boîtes à chanson,* clubs where this type of music is played. Try not to leave Montréal or Québec City without taking in at least one show. Because the songs are so much a part of Québécois culture every francophone knows the lyrics by heart. Once the shows start the place erupts like a punk concert with everyone singing along at the top of their lungs. Dancing on table tops is not uncommon. If it's your first time you'll never forget it. Two *boîtes à chansons* in Montréal are the fabulous **Les Deux Pierrots** (p152) and **Boîte à Maurice** (p153).

History

History

Montréal's history is a fascinating story of sparkling successes followed by dramatic downs. Over the centuries the city has swung from the proverbial economic/political centre-of-the-Canadian universe, only to see-saw back into a kind of national backwater. The city's evolution has been anything but smooth, usually involving two steps forward and one step back.

THE RECENT PAST

Canada's most important decision after WWII was to create a welfare state. Ottawa intended to concentrate federal power by keeping control over key taxation and social programs in all provinces. It was at this crucial juncture that Québec's nationalists seized their chance to launch their state within a state.

QUIET REVOLUTION

In 1960 the nationalist Liberal Party won control of the Québec assembly and passed sweeping measures that would shake Canada to its very foundations. In the first stage of this Quiet Revolution, the assembly vastly expanded Québec's public sector and nationalized the provincial hydroelectric companies.

Suddenly francophones – who had long been denied equal rights in the private sector – were able to work in French and develop their skills in white-collar positions. Still, progress wasn't swift enough for radical nationalists (see The Separatist Movement, opposite), and by the mid-1960s they claimed Québec independence was the only way to ensure francophone rights.

To head off clashes with Québec's increasingly separatist leaders, Prime Minister Pierre Trudeau proposed two key measures in 1969: Canada was to be made fully bilingual to give francophones equal access to national institutions; and the constitution was to be amended to guarantee francophone rights. Ottawa then pumped cash into French-English projects which, nonetheless, failed to convince francophones that French would become the primary language of work in Québec.

In 1976 this lingering discontent helped to elect René Lévesque and his Parti Québécois, committed to the goal of independence for the province. The following year the Québec assembly passed Bill 101, which not only made French the sole official language of Québec, but also stipulated that all immigrants enroll their children in French-language schools. The trickle of anglophone refugees turned into a flood. Alliance Québec, an English rights group, estimates that between 300,000 and 400,000 anglos left Québec during that period.

THE ALMOST-DISTINCT SOCIETY

The Quiet Revolution heightened tensions not only in Québec but across Canada. After their re-election in 1980, federal Liberals, led by Pierre Trudeau, sold most Quebecers on the idea of greater rights through constitutional change, helping to defeat a referendum on Québec sovereignty the same year by a comfortable margin. Québec premier Robert Bourassa then agreed to a constitution-led solution – but only if Québec was recognized as a 'distinct society' with special rights.

In 1987 the federal Conservative Party was in power and Prime Minister Brian Mulroney unveiled an accord that met most of Québec's demands. To take effect, the Meech

TIMELINE	1642	1760
	French mission Ville-Marie founded	British troops take Montréal from the French

62

Lake Accord needed ratification by all 10 provinces and both houses of parliament by 1990. Dissenting premiers in three provinces eventually pledged their support, but incredibly the accord collapsed when a single member of Manitoba's legislature refused to sign.

The failure of the Meech Lake Accord triggered a major political crisis in Québec. The separatists blamed English-speaking Canada for its demise, and Mulroney and Bourassa subsequently drafted the Charlottetown Accord, a new, expanded accord. But the separatists picked it apart, and in October 1992 the second version was trounced in Québec and five other provinces. The rejection sealed the fate of Mulroney, who stepped down as prime minister the following year, and of Bourassa, who left political life a broken man.

REFERENDUM & REBIRTH

In the early 1990s Montréal was wracked by political uncertainty and economic decline. No one disputed that the city was ailing. The symptoms were everywhere: corporate offices closed down and moved their headquarters to other parts of Canada, shuttered shops lined downtown streets, and derelict factories and refineries rusted on the perimeter. Relations between anglophones and francophones, meanwhile, plumbed new depths after Québec was denied a special status in Canada.

THE SEPARATIST MOVEMENT

In 1960 the Rassemblement pour l'Indépendance Nationale (Rally for National Independence, or RIN) was founded in Montréal with the aim of Québec separation from Canada. This was the beginning of the Quiet Revolution that eventually gave French Quebecers more sway in industry and politics and ultimately established the primacy of the French language.

The Front de Libération du Québec (FLQ), a radical nationalist group committed to overthrowing 'medieval Catholicism and capitalist oppression' through revolution, was founded in 1963. Initially the FLQ attacked military targets and other symbols of federal power but soon became involved in labor disputes. In the mid-1960s the FLQ claimed responsibility for a spate of bombings.

In October 1970 the FLQ kidnapped Québec's labour minister Pierre Laporte and a British trade official in an attempt to force the independence issue. Prime Minister Pierre Trudeau declared a state of emergency and called in the army to protect government officials. The next day Laporte's body was found in the trunk of a car. The murder discredited the FLQ in the eyes of many erstwhile supporters. By December the crisis had passed. In the years that followed, the FLQ effectively ceased to exist as a political movement.

While support for Québec independence still hovers around 30% to 45% in the polls, there's little appetite at the moment for another referendum on separation from Canada – the economy is on the upswing these days and real-estate prices surged across the province after Jean Charest of the federalist Liberal Party was elected Québec premier in the spring of 2003.

The future of the separatist movement, however, is never predictable. The impassioned separatists who came of age during the heady days of the Quiet Revolution are getting older now, and a critical mass of rah-rah separatists from the younger generation hasn't yet emerged to take their place – a phenomenon leaving some to speculate that the demographic window on separatism may be closing for good.

However, the Parti Québécois election of the 1966-born, photogenic and openly gay André Boisclair as their leader in 2005, over the 1949-born Pauline Marois – despite her experience as vice-premier and cabinet minister in almost every single government portfolio including finance, health and education – was widely interpreted as a concrete attempt to draw youth to the cause. Boisclair has promised to hold another referendum 'as soon as possible' if he's elected premier in the next provincial election, although he comes with plenty of baggage and admitted using cocaine while a provincial cabinet minister in the late 1990s. Despite this, some feel he may take the next election given Charest's unpopularity (see above), but it doesn't take much to inflame passions on either side when it comes to Québec separatism, so stay tuned. Charest doesn't have to go to the polls until 2008 so has time to turn his party's fortunes around.

1832	1844
Montréal incorporated as a city	Montréal becomes capital of United Province of Canada

The victory of the separatist Parti Québécois in the 1994 provincial elections signaled the arrival of another crisis. Support for an independent Québec rekindled, and a referendum on sovereignty was called the following year. While it first appeared the referendum would fail by a significant margin, the outcome was a real cliff-hanger: Quebecers decided by 52,000 votes – a razor-thin majority of less than 1% – to stay part of Canada. In Montréal, where the bulk of Québec's anglophones and immigrants live, more than two-thirds voted against sovereignty, causing Parti Québécois leader Jacques Parizeau to (in)famously declare that 'money and the ethnic vote' had robbed Québec of its independence.

In the aftermath of the vote, the locomotives of the Quiet Revolution – economic inferiority and linguistic insecurity among francophones – ran out of steam. Exhausted by decades of separatist wrangling, most Montrealers put aside their differences and went back to work.

Oddly enough, a natural disaster played a key role in bringing the communities together. In 1998 a freak ice storm – some blame extra-moist El Niño winds, others blame global warming – broke power masts like matchsticks across the province, leaving over three million people without power and key services in the middle of a Montréal winter. Some people endured weeks without electricity and heat but regional and political differences were forgotten as money, clothing and offers of personal help poured into the stricken areas. Montrealers recount those dark days with a touch of mutual respect.

As the political climate brightened, Montréal began to emerge from a fundamental reshaping of the local economy. The city experienced a burst of activity as sectors like software, aerospace, telecommunications and pharmaceuticals replaced rustbelt industries like textiles and refining. Québec's moderate wages became an asset to manufacturers seeking qualified, affordable labor, and foreign investment began to flow more freely. Tax dollars were used to recast Montréal as a new-media hub, encouraging dozens of multimedia firms to settle in the Old Port area.

The upshot is a city transformed and brimming with self-confidence. Rue Ste-Catherine teems with trendy boutiques and department stores; Old Montréal buzzes with fancy hotels and restaurants; once-empty warehouses around town have been converted to chic apartments and offices. The Plateau has become one of North America's hippest neighborhoods.

Montréal's renewed vigor has lured back some of the anglophones who'd left in the 1980s and '90s. Language conflicts have slipped into the background because most young Montrealers are at least bilingual, and for the first time there are more homeowners than renters and property prices have soared. Montrealers here in the early 90s remember renting Plateau apartments with balcony views of Parc LaFontaine for only $250 while the same apartment wouldn't rent for less than $700 these days.

Québec flag flies over the dome of Marché Bonsecours in Old Montréal

1852	1867
Great Fire destroys much of Old Montréal	Canadian Confederation

IRISH IN MONTRÉAL

The Irish have been streaming into Montréal since the founding of New France, but they came in floods between 1815 and 1860, driven from Ireland by the Potato Famine. Catholic like the French settlers, the Irish easily assimilated into québécois society. Today a phenomenal 45% of Quebecers have Irish ancestry somewhere in their family tree, though many of them don't even know it. Several québécois family names are a legacy of this era of immigration, when French Catholic priests in Québec City registered settler's names phonetically upon arrival. So, an 'O'Reilly' in Ireland ended up living as a 'Riel' in the colony. Other names from this period still encountered today include 'Aubrey' or 'Aubry', from 'O'Brinnan' or 'O'Brennan', and 'Mainguy' from 'McGee'. In Montréal, most of these immigrants settled in Griffintown, then an industrial hub near the Lachine Canal. The first St Patrick's Day parade in the city was held in 1824 and has run every year since; it's now one of the city's biggest events. For some terrific reads on the Irish community, check out *The Shamrock and the Shield: An Oral History of the Irish in Montreal* by Patricia Burns and *The Untold Story: The Irish in Canada* (1988), edited by Robert O'Driscoll and Lorna Reynolds.

Condo-talk and real-estate conversations unheard of before are now *de rigueur* everywhere from downtown restaurants to Mile End cafés.

Though less divisive than in times past, contemporary Québec faces thorny issues in areas like civil rights of minorities, administration and the welfare state: English-language education is denied to many families and Montréal's new island-wide administration is under severe strain. Jean Charest's Liberals successfully knocked the separatist Parti Québécois out of office in 2003 but the federalist party has had a rocky ride since then and has been the target of dozens of demonstrations by workers for wanting to cut public-sector jobs, hiking day-care prices from $5 to $7 and pruning Québec's bloated bureaucracy.

FROM THE BEGINNING

The Island of Montréal was long inhabited by the St Lawrence Iroquois, one of the tribes who formed the Five Nations Confederacy of Iroquois. In 1535 French explorer Jacques Cartier visited the Iroquois village of Hochelaga (Place of the Beaver) on the slopes of Mont Royal, but by the time Samuel de Champlain founded Québec City in 1608, the settlement had vanished. In 1642 Paul de Chomedey de Maisonneuve founded the first permanent mission despite fierce resistance by the Iroquois. Intended as a base for converting aboriginal people to Christianity, this settlement quickly became a major hub of the fur trade. Québec City became the capital of the French colony Nouvelle-France, while Montréal's *voyageurs* (trappers) established a network of trading posts into the hinterland. After the British conquest of Montréal in 1760, Scottish fur traders consolidated their power by founding the North West Company.

The American army seized Montréal during the American Revolution (1763–1783) and set up headquarters at **Château Ramezay** (p74). But even the formidable negotiating skills of Benjamin Franklin failed to convince French Quebecers to join their cause, and seven months later the revolutionaries decided they'd had enough and fled empty-handed.

INDUSTRIAL REVOLUTION

In the early 19th century Montréal's fortunes dimmed as the fur trade shifted north to the Hudson Bay. However, a new class of international merchants and financiers soon emerged, founding the **Bank of Montréal** (p73) and investing in shipping as well as a new railway network. Tens of thousands of Irish immigrants came to work on the railways and in the factories, mills and breweries that sprang up along the **Canal de Lachine** (p108). Canada's industrial revolution was born, with the English clearly in control.

1976	1980
Summer Olympics held in Montréal	First Québec referendum rejects separation from Canada

The Canadian Confederation of 1867 gave Quebecers a degree of control over their social and economic affairs and acknowledged French as an official language. French Canadians living in the rural areas flowed into the city to seek work and regained the majority. At this lofty point in time, Montréal was Canada's premier railway center, financial hub and manufacturing powerhouse. The Canadian Pacific Railway opened its head office there in the 1880s, and Canadian grain bound for Europe was shipped through the port.

In the latter half of the century, a wave of immigrants from Italy, Spain, Germany, Eastern Europe and Russia gave Montréal a cosmopolitan flair that would remain unique in the province. By 1914 the metropolitan population exceeded half-a-million residents, of whom more than 10% were neither British nor French.

WAR, DEPRESSION & NATIONALISM

The peace that existed between the French and English ran aground after the outbreak of WWI. Many thousands of French Quebecers signed up for military service until Ontario passed a law in 1915 restricting the use of French in its schools. When Ottawa introduced the draft in 1917, French-Canadian nationalists condemned it as a plot to reduce the francophone population. The conscription issue resurfaced in WWII, with 80% of francophones rejecting the draft and nearly as many English-speaking Canadians voting yes.

During the Prohibition era Montréal found a new calling as 'Sin City', as hordes of free-spending, pleasure-seeking Americans flooded over the border in search of booze, brothels and betting houses. But with the Great Depression the economic inferiority of French Canadians became clearer than ever.

Québec's nationalists turned inward with proposals to create co-operatives, nationalize the anglophone power companies and promote French-Canadian goods. Led by the right-wing, ruralist, ultraconservative Maurice Duplessis, the new Union Nationale party took advantage of the nationalist awakening to win provincial power in the 1936 elections. The party's influence would retard Québec's industrial and social progress until Duplessis died in 1959.

GRAND PROJECTS

By the early 1950s the infrastructure of Montréal, by now with a million-plus inhabitants, badly needed an overhaul. Mayor Jean Drapeau drew up a grand blueprint that would radically alter the face of the city, including the metro, a skyscraper-filled downtown and an **underground city** (p86). The harbor was extended for the opening of the St Lawrence Seaway.

Along the way Drapeau set about ridding Montréal of its 'Sin City' image by cleaning up the shadier districts. His most colorful nemesis was Lili St-Cyr, the Minnesota-born stripper whose affairs with high-ranking politicians, sports stars and thugs were as legendary in the postwar era as her bathtub performances.

The face of Montréal changed dramatically during the 1960s as a forest of skyscrapers shot up. Private developers replaced creaking Victorian-era structures with landmark buildings such as Place Bonaventure, a modern hotel-shopping complex, and the **Place des Arts** (p89) performing-arts center. The focus of downtown shifted from Old Montréal to Ville-Marie, where the first passages of the underground city took shape. The skyscraper at Place Ville-Marie was the most important skyscraper in Montréal throughout the 1960s and for decades afterwards.

Around 1960 Montréal lost its status as Canada's economic capital to Toronto. But new expressways were laid out and the métro was finished in time for Expo '67 – the 1967 World's Fair – a runaway success that attracted 50 million visitors. It was the defining moment of Montréal as a metropolis, and Mayor Drapeau was encouraged to launch the city's candidacy for the 1976 Olympics. A snazzy stadium complex was built for the event, but unlike the highly successful Expo '67, it was completed late and amassed a mountain of debt (see p97).

2003	2005
100,000 Montrealers march to protest a war in Iraq, the biggest demonstration in the nation; Canada legalizes same-sex marriage	Montrealer Michaëlle Jean installed as 27th Governor General of Canada, the Queen's representative in Canada

Sights

Sights

Montréal's charm doesn't lie so much in its 'official' attractions as in the wonderfully relaxed atmosphere of the place. Sure, the city is packed with must-see sights, but in the end it's the neighborhoods that visitors return home talking about. Locals are fiercely proud of their stomping grounds, and each area of the city is fueled with unique energy, food culture and interminable charm. To get a real taste of how Montrealers live, work and party, make room for rewarding hours in the ambience-rich residential districts. Eavesdrop on local artists in a Mile End café, fall in step with active types in Parc Jean-Drapeau, or bask solo in the old-world grandeur of Outremont.

There is a fitting French verb that sums up the perfect method of experiencing it all: *flâner*, meaning to stroll (or on public signs, to loiter). Montrealers are dedicated *flâneurs*, and breaks are definitely allowed – there's no reason to grab a burger and run when they can savor a beef bourguignon and

ESSENTIAL MONTRÉAL

- Old Port (p79) – street music on a balmy summer evening, ice skating by the St Lawrence River in winter
- Mile End (p102) – for its diversity, ethnic restaurants and palpable sense of community
- Parc Jean-Drapeau (p81) – filled with hidden treasures; museums, swimming facilities and the awesome Circuit Gilles-Villeneuve for bike rides or inline skating
- Plateau du Mont-Royal (p98) – explore the one-of-a-kind shopping and admire the architecture
- Parc du Mont Royal (p103) – the views! The greenery! Feel like you are on top of the whole city, all urban stress left way down in the streets below

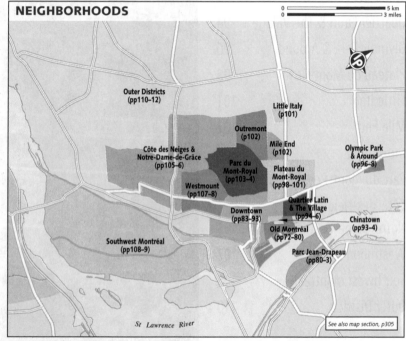

NEIGHBORHOODS

0 — 5 km
0 — 3 miles

Outer Districts (pp110–12)

Little Italy (p101)

Outremont (p102)

Mile End (p102)

Olympic Park & Around (pp96–8)

Côte des Neiges & Notre-Dame-de-Grâce (pp105–6)

Parc du Mont-Royal (pp103–4)

Plateau du Mont-Royal (pp98–101)

Westmount (pp107–8)

Downtown (pp83–93)

Quartier Latin & The Village (pp94–6)

Chinatown (pp93–4)

Old Montréal (pp72–80)

Southwest Montréal (pp108–9)

Parc Jean-Drapeau (pp80–3)

St Lawrence River

See also map section, p305

ponder the world from a café terrace. They take to the streets *en masse* at any time of year, whether they're packing the terraces on rue St-Denis at the first sign of spring, surging into downtown's arteries for the summer festivals, walking through crisp autumn leaves in Parc du Mont Royal, or toting cross-country skis and skates to the city's outdoor rinks and ski trails.

ITINERARIES

Two Days
A walking tour of Old Montréal (p72) is a great way to start your adventure. You can visit Basilique Notre-Dame (p73), have lunch at La Gargotte (p128), then explore the Old Port (p79), before hopping on the ferry to Parc Jean-Drapeau (p81) to explore its two islands.

On day two get to know downtown Montréal starting at the Musée des Beaux-Arts (p92). Have lunch at Les Chenêts (p132) before working your way east. For shopping and a look at what this darned underground city (p86) is all about head along rue Ste-Catherine (p89). Keep moseying east and by evening you'll be in the Gay Village just as things are getting going. Take in a show at Mado Cabaret (p160) then settle down in the tiny, bustling Mozza (p135) for a delicious pasta dinner.

Four Days
Same as for two days, adding two days to explore the city's neighborhoods. Start day three at the Olympic Stadium with an ascent of Montréal Tower (p98) and some blossom-sniffing at the Jardin Botanique (p97). Nip in later to the Chateâu Dufresne (p97) for a peek at how upper-class Montrealers used to live.

On day four, take in the atmosphere on the Plateau du Mont-Royal (p98), lingering along ave Mont-Royal or rue St-Denis for shopping and a pick of terrific restaurants and terraces. Relax at the end of the day with beers at Barouf (p156).

One Week
Begin day five by taking in the Oratoire St-Joseph (p105), then go for a bike ride along the Canal de Lachine (p108), where you can explore some of the further-flung museums and areas of the city. After getting an unforgettable dose of Montréal, spend days six and seven in Québec City, the stunning provincial capital, and follow the two-day tour (p216) in that city.

MONTRÉAL FOR CHILDREN
Summer or winter, rain or shine, there's always plenty of cool stuff for kids to do
- Biodôme (p96) – a giant indoor zoo with forest, river and marine habitats
- Biosphère (p82) – hands-on and multimedia exhibits about water, water everywhere
- Jardin Botanique (p97) – Chinese and Japanese gardens, greenhouses and an arboretum for romping
- Centre des Sciences de Montréal (p80) – technological wonders, unusual games and an IMAX cinema
- Insectarium (p97) – discover a bug's world and a splendid butterfly house
- Labyrinth (p79) – amazing maze with obstacles, traps and play zones
- La Ronde (p82) – chills and thrills galore at Québec's largest amusement park
- Montréal Planetarium (p86) – quarks, black holes and celestial shows
- Musée Ferroviaire Canadien (p111) – stationary, moving, new, old…trains galore that thrill adults as much as children
- Musée Stewart (p82) – the cannon displays and guides in period costumes are no-fail kid-pleasers
- Old Port (p79) – hop into a paddle boat or mini-train for a grand tour
- Parc Nature du Cap St-Jacques (p111) – nature park with trails, a beach, a sugar shack and a working farm

ORGANIZED TOURS
Bicycling
LA MAISON DES CYCLISTES Map p122
☎ 521-8356, 800-567-8356; 1251 rue Rachel Est;
🕙 8:30am-6pm Mon-Fri, 10am-6pm Sat & Sun;
Ⓜ Mont-Royal

This place offers a range of guided bicycling tours of Montréal for groups of five to 20 people. There's also a **travel agency** (ext 361) on site, completely devoted to bike trips, both in Montréal's countryside and abroad. The shop has a good selection of guidebooks and maps for cyclists and bikes for rent.

VÉLO-TOUR Map pp308-9
☎ 259-7272; www.velomontreal.com; 3880 rue Rachel Est; 🕙 9am-6pm Mon-Wed, 9am-7pm Thu & Fri, 10am-4pm Sat, noon-4pm Sun; Ⓜ Pie IX

Among many other services, this all-in-one bicycle shop was offering five guided tours ranging from three-hour routes exploring the Plateau and ave Mont-Royal to six-hour jaunts taking in the Lachine Canal and Parc Jean-Drapeau. They've been suspended but you can buy a booklet of five self-guided tours for $5.

TOP FIVE MONTRÉAL LANDMARKS
- Montréal Tower (p98) – rise above it all in the Olympic Park
- Bibliothèque et Archives Nationales du Québec (p95) – much-loved intellectual and cultural heart of the city
- Oratoire St-Joseph (p105) – grand testimony to one priest's devotion
- Place Ville-Marie (p93) – cruciform tower with swirling beacons
- Farine Five Roses Sign (p79) – neon icon of wheaty proportions

Boat
AML CRUISES Map p314
☎ 842-3871, 800-563-4643; www.croisieresaml.com; Quai King-Edward; 1½hr tour adult/child $25/12; 🕙 11:30am, 2pm & 4pm; Ⓜ Champ-de-Mars

These 1½-hour river tours in a glassed-in sightseeing boat take in the Old Port, Île Ste-Hélène (Map p319) and Îles de Boucherville (Map pp306–7). Other options include night cruises with a band, dancing and a gourmet dinner. Early and late cruises are in high season only.

Rollerblade or grab a pedicab in Montréal's Old Port

WHAT'S FREE

It's easy to spend a fortune but, as they say, some of the best things in life are free. Here are some suggestions:
- Soaking up the atmosphere in Old Montréal (p72) and the Old Port (p79).
- Listening to weeks and weeks of free music at the summer music festivals (p21).
- Wandering along rue St-Denis (p100) and boul St-Laurent (p99), day or night.
- Riding a bike along the Circuit Gilles-Villeneuve in Parc Jean-Drapeau (p81).
- Taking in the wonderful public art all over town.
- Admiring the big-city panorama from Parc du Mont Royal (p104).
- Catching a Tam-Tam concert (p149) or two at the George-Étienne-Cartier monument in Parc du Mont Royal (Map p122).
- Cycling along the Canal de Lachine (p108).
- Loitering on the observation deck over the St Lawrence Seaway (p112).
- Squinting at fireworks displays on weekends in summer (p22).

LE BATEAU MOUCHE Map p314
☎ 849-9952, 800-361-9952; Quai Jacques-Cartier; 1hr tour adult/child $18/10, 90min tour adult/child $24/10; ⊙ 1hr tour 10am, 1:30pm, 3pm & 4:30pm, 90min tour 11:30am mid-May–mid-Oct; Ⓜ Champ-de-Mars

This comfortable, climate-controlled sightseeing boat with a glass roof offers narrated cruises of the Old Port and Parc Jean-Drapeau. Dinner cruises of 3½ hours are also available. Phone ahead for reservations and make sure you board the vessel 15 minutes before departure.

L'ÉCLUSIER Map pp310-11
☎ 846-0428, 866-846-0448; Marché Atwater; 2hr tour adult/child $17/10; ⊙ call for times; Ⓜ Lionel-Groulx

Take a cruise of the Canal de Lachine aboard this sightseeing boat with a slidable glass top. A Parks Canada interpreter brings to life the canal's industrial and commercial history and you visit an archeological site. The two-hour round trip begins at the canal dock near the pedestrian footbridge just south of Atwater Market and goes all the way to the Old Port locks. Other tours include brunch or dinner cruises.

Bus

GRAY LINE Map pp310-11
☎ 934-1222; www.grayline.com; Centre Infotouriste, 1001 Square Dorchester; tram tour adult/child $36/30; ⊙ 10am & 1pm year-round, plus extra departures May-Oct; Ⓜ Peel

Montréal's biggest tour operator offers a wide variety of circuits on comfortable

pseudo-trolleys. The Montréal tram tour lasts three hours and takes in dozens of sights including Basilique Notre-Dame, Oratoire St-Joseph and the residential districts. Longer trips include Parc des Îles and the Laurentian Mountains north of Montréal.

IMPÉRIAL AUTOCAR Map pp310-11
☎ 871-4733; Centre Infotouriste, 1001 Square Dorchester; 3hr tour adult/child $35/18; ⊙ call for times; Ⓜ Peel

Climb on board a climate-controlled coach for stops throughout Old Montréal with a half-hour tour of Basilique Notre-Dame, time on Île Notre-Dame (with its casino and La Ronde amusement park) and visits to Olympic Park, Oratoire St Joseph and Parc du Mont Royal. Another hop-on, hop-off tour aboard a double-decker bus can be spread over two days. Buses leave hourly from 11am to 4pm and cost $31/16 per adult/child. Tours run less frequently in the off-season.

Calèche

Horse-drawn carriages are one of the post popular (and romantic!) ways to see downtown; they leave from Place d'Armes (Map p314). A half-hour ride is $45, one hour is $75.

Walking

The *Heritage's Great Calendar*, which lists walking tours of the city, and the *Discover Old Montreal* illustrated walking guide ($6) are both available from the Infotouriste on Square Dorchester and the Old Montréal tourist office.

GUIDATOUR

☎ 844-4021, 800-363-4021; www.guidatour.qc.ca; 477 rue St-François-Xavier; adult/child/student $15/7/13; ⏰ 11am & 1:30pm late Jun-Oct, weekends only late May–mid-Jun & Oct 7-15

The experienced bilingual guides of Guida tour paint a picture of Old Montréal's eventful history with anecdotes and legends. Tours depart from **Basilique Notre-Dame** (opposite); tickets go on sale at the basilica gift shop 15 minutes before departure.

HERITAGE MONTRÉAL Map pp310-11

☎ 286-2662; www.heritagemontreal.qc.ca; 100 rue Sherbrooke Est; admission varies; ⏰ Sat & Sun mid-May–mid-Oct

This independent, nonprofit organization is charged with the preservation of Montréal's heritage – urban, architectural and social. Its qualified guides conduct a series of architecture-based tours, focusing on a different neighborhood every week. The departure point varies and reservations are essential. The library will also open on a weekday afternoon by appointment.

OLD MONTRÉAL GHOST WALK

Map p314

☎ 868-0303; www.phvm.qc.ca; adult/child/student $16/7/12; ⏰ 8:30pm Wed-Sun Jul-Aug, 8:30pm Sat Jun, Sep & Oct

Gives evening tours tracing historic crimes and legends, led by guides in period costume (read: hard-up local actors). The walks may sound hokey but are actually a lot of fun. Tours leave from the **Jacques Cartier Information Booth** (Map p314), where you can buy tickets on tour nights from 6:30pm to 8:30pm.

OLD MONTRÉAL

Eating p126; Shopping p179; Sleeping p192

Most visitors to the city begin their trips in Vieux-Montréal, drawn by its beautiful churches, the historical punch of its old buildings, the winding cobblestone alleys, and terrific museums telling the story of French and British settlement in Canada.

Ville-Marie, the settlement that was to become Montréal, was established here as a base to convert aboriginals to Christianity. It has gone through numerous incarnations since, from hub of the fur trade to financial giant of Canada to kitschy tourist trap to the trendy 'it' neighborhood of today. Award-winning eateries have slowly overtaken the shoddy, overpriced restaurants serving mediocre food that were so much a feature of the Old Town even a decade ago. Boutique hotels now occupy some of the most stunning old buildings, media and communications companies have set up shop on the main drags, and the area's lofts are some of the priciest (and most coveted) real estate in town.

Vieux-Montréal hums with energy year-round, with summertime drawing street performers and hordes of visitors to the Old Port, and wintertime warranting atmospheric *calèche* rides, hours of browsing in shops or still more hours lingering over a decadent meal.

Orientation

Old Montréal lies just south of downtown. The focal points are the old market square, Place Jacques-Cartier, mecca of performance artists and tourist eateries; and Place d'Armes, home of the imposing Basilique Notre-Dame. The narrow rue St-Paul, the old main street, teems with art galleries, shops and eateries; the bigger, busier rue Notre-Dame runs parallel and to the north. On the bank of the St Lawrence, the broad concourse of the Old Port is lined with green parkland and cafés along rue de la Commune.

The Old Montréal tourist office is at the river end of Place Jacques-Cartier.

TOP FIVE SIGHTS IN OLD MONTRÉAL

- Basilique Notre-Dame (opposite) – magnificent carvings, kooky lighting
- Marché Bonsecours (p75) – wander the shops in this historic building
- Château Ramezay (p74) – opulent mansion that ruined a doting governor
- Musée d'Archéologie Pointe-à-Callière (p76) – crawl down (literally) into Montréal's distant past
- Old Port (p79) – ice-skating in winter, performers, paddle boats and recreation in summer

BANK OF MONTRÉAL Map p314

☎ 877-7373; 119 rue St-Jacques; ⏱ 9am-5pm
Mon-Fri; Ⓜ Place-d'Armes

Modeled after the Pantheon in Rome, the
grand colonnaded edifice of Canada's
oldest chartered bank, built in 1847, dominates the north side of Place D'Armes (p76)
and is still a working bank. The imposing
interior has 32 marble columns and a
coffered 20m ceiling in Italian Renaissance
style over a long row of tellers behind glass
partitions. The helmeted marble lady is
Patria, representing a minor Roman god
of patriotism to honor the war dead. Take
a closer look at the pediment above the
entrance: a sailor in the scene represents
commerce, and a settler depicts agriculture.
A money museum inside the bank has a replica
of a cashier's window, old banknotes and
an account of early banking in Canada.

BASILIQUE NOTRE-DAME Map p314

☎ 842-2925; 110 rue Notre-Dame Ouest; adult/
child $4/2; ⏱ 8am-4:30pm Mon-Sat, 12:30-4:15pm
Sun, extended in summer, tours hourly Jul-Sep;
Ⓜ Place-d'Armes

One of Montréal's most enduring symbols,
the basilica occupies a site rich with three
centuries of history. Besides religious
services, the weddings and funerals of the
city's well-known and well-heeled regularly
take place here. Its most recent claim to
fame was the baptism of Céline Dion's son
in July 2001. Contrary to some tourist tales
the basilica is *not* modeled on Notre-Dame
cathedral in Paris.

The Sulpicians had an ever growing
congregation and no one in the soon-to-be
Canadian colonies schooled in neo-Gothic
architecture. So they commissioned James
O'Donnell, a New York architect and Irish
Protestant, to design what would be the
largest church north of Mexico. Such was
O'Donnell's dedication to the project that
he converted to Catholicism so he could
have his funeral in the basilica. Today, he's
buried in the basement under the gift shop.

Opened in 1829, the basilica has a spectacular interior with a forest of ornate wood
pillars and carvings made entirely by hand
(and constructed without the aid of a single
nail). Gilt stars shine from the ceiling vaults
and the altar is backlit in heavenlike blues.
The massive Casavant organ with 5772
pipes is a thrill to hear, particularly at the
famous Christmas concerts; the church bell,

lonelyplanet.com

TRANSPORTATION IN OLD MONTRÉAL

Métro Square-Victoria, Place-d'Armes or Champ-
de-Mars.

Bus 14 runs along rue Notre-Dame in Old Montréal
between rue Berri and boul St-Laurent; 55 stops on
boul St-Laurent.

Parking The best bet is the big paid parking lot at
the Quai d'Horloge.

the Gros Bourdon, is the largest on the continent. Stained-glass windows, which depict
scenes from Montréal's history rather than
the usual biblical stories, was the brainchild
of the Sulpicians who wanted to teach the
mostly illiterate French-Canadians about
the founding of the colony. The Musée de la
Basilique (Map p314) at the rear of the basilica has a collection of religious artifacts.

The Chapelle du Sacré Coeur (Sacred Heart
Chapel; Map p314) located behind the
main hall is nicknamed the Wedding
Chapel. It's so popular that couples might
have to wait two years to tie the knot. The
curious mix of styles emerged after a 1978
fire, when the chapel was rebuilt with a
brass altar with abstract-modern motifs.

An evening sound and light display (adult/
child $10/5; ⏱ 6:30pm Tue-Thu, 6:30pm &
8:30pm Fri, 7pm & 8:30pm Sat) uses cutting-edge technology to tell the story of
the church and the city.

CENTRE DE COMMERCE MONDIAL DE MONTRÉAL map p314

393 rue St-Jacques; Ⓜ Square-Victoria

This shopping-cum-office complex is
wedged into one side of the Nordheimer
Building (1888), which is in turn part of the
posh Intercontinental Montréal Hotel (p193). The
indoor plaza is bathed in soft light from the
atrium; a reflecting pool features a statue
of sea goddess Amphritite gushing water
from her mouth. Close to the hotel entrance is a chunk of the Berlin Wall given to
Montréal for its 350th anniversary.

CENTRE D'HISTOIRE DE MONTRÉAL
Map p314

☎ 872-3207; 335 Place d'Youville; adult/child
$4.50/3; ⏱ 10am-5pm Tue-Sun; Ⓜ Square-Victoria

Housed in a handsome old fire hall on Place
d'Youville, the Montréal History Centre has

Sights

OLD MONTRÉAL

300-plus artifacts that illustrate the city's eventful past with the aid of models and videos. It also does wonderful temporary exhibits like the recent 'Swinging Nights in Montréal, the history of the city's jazz scene. Old films on reels (from the National Film Board) are shown throughout the day in a period living room, bringing to life the Prohibition era or a 1950s Christmas on rue Ste-Catherine.

CHAPELLE NOTRE-DAME-DE-BONSECOURS Map p314

☎ 282-8670; www.marguerite-bourgeoys.com; 400 rue St-Paul Est; chapel free, museum adult/ student & senior $6/4; ◷ 10am-5:30pm Tue-Sun May-Oct, 11am-3:30pm Tue-Sun Nov–mid-Jan & March-April; Ⓜ Champ-de-Mars

Known as the Sailors' Church, this enchanting chapel derives its name from the sailors who left behind votive lamps in the shape of ships in thanksgiving for safe passage. The restored interior has inspirational paintings of the Virgin Mary, stained-glass windows depicting stations of her life and a variety of icons including a recumbent statue of Marguerite Bourgeoys. The exterior has been remodeled so many times

that little of the original remains; a large statue of the Virgin Mary crowned with an aureole of stars graces the roof of the double-bell tower.

In the attached **Musée Marguerite-Bourgeoys** (Map p314), vignettes tell the story of Montréal's first teacher and the founder of the Congregation of Notre-Dame order of nuns. The crypt has artifacts dating back 2000 years and foundations of the original chapel from 1773. Climb the 292 steps to the observation tower for a fabulous view of the Old Port; it's a great spot for the kids.

CHÂTEAU RAMEZAY Map p314

☎ 861-3708; www.chateauramezay.qc.ca; 280 rue Notre-Dame Est; adult/child $8/4; ◷ 10am-6pm May 1–Thanksgiving, 10am-4:30pm Tue-Sun rest of the year; Ⓜ Champ-de-Mars

A home of French governors in the early 18th century, this mansion is one of the finest examples from the *ancien régime*. It was built for the 11th governor, Claude de Ramezay, and includes 15 interconnecting rooms with a ballroom of mirrors and mahogany galore. Ramezay went broke trying to maintain it. American generals used it as a headquarters during the revo-

---

MONTRÉAL'S TURN-OF-THE-CENTURY LITERARY BAD BOY

Émile Nelligan (1879–1941) is one of Québec's literary icons, a star like Oscar Wilde or Lord Byron whose mix of talent and tragedy keeps them in the public consciousness long after their era is over. A poetic genius, Nelligan created most of his famous works by the age of 20 before being committed and spending the rest of his life in mental institutions.

Born in Montréal of an Irish father and a québécoise mother, his bohemian traits were in evidence from the time he was a teenager. He sailed in and out of school to the dismay of his parents and seemed interested in little other than romantic poetry. After submitting two samples of his work, he was accepted by the l'École Littéraire de Montréal (Literary School of Montréal); public readings followed and his poems exploring love and loneliness were regularly published in French-language magazines around Montréal. Nelligan had always marched to a different drummer but by the time 1899 rolled around, it was apparent his problems were more than just those of a temperamental artist and there was something seriously wrong.

His father had him committed to a mental institution that year. Though he tried briefly to rejoin society in 1925 he was back in care within days. What was wrong with him? Historians who've examined his hospital records believe he may have suffered from schizophrenia.

Though there has been both a movie and play about his life and he was immortalized in a painting by master Québec painter Jean-Paul Lemieux, there is scandalously still no museum devoted to his work or life. Hunting his ghost around town is the best you'll be able to do. The **Château Ramezay** (above) is where l'École Littéraire de Montréal used to meet and where Nelligan's poems were first read in public. Nelligan lived in a house on the west side of **Carré St-Louis** (St Louis Square; Map p122). It is now a private home but there is a plaque on the wall outside marking it. The square is also the setting for the famous Lemieux painting. Further along, **St Patrick's Cathedral** (p88) is where Nelligan was baptized; there's a plaque at the back commemorating this event, along with a plaque devoted to Montréal's other famous Irishman, D'Arcy McGee.

Not much for one of the province's famous sons and the anchor of its 20th-century literary canon is it? Ministère de la Culture, Heritage Canada, where are you when we need you?

lution, and Benjamin Franklin stayed here attempting (and failing) to convince the Canadians to join the cause. In 1903 turrets were added to give the 'château' its fanciful French look.

The building is now a repository of Québec history with a collection of 20,000 objects including valuable Canadian art and furniture. The **Governor's Garden** in the rear re-creates a horticultural garden from the 18th century including many original varieties of fruit trees and vegetables.

COURS LE ROYER Map p314
Ⓜ **Place-d'Armes**
Montréal's first ever hospital was founded here by Jeanne Mance in 1644. Later on, a huge commercial complex was built here, leaving several beautiful 19th-century warehouses behind. The buildings caught the eyes of developers in the 1970s and were converted into apartments and offices. Today, the buildings line this quiet pedestrian mall pocked with lush greenery.

HÔTEL DE VILLE Map p314
☎ 872-3355; 275 rue Notre-Dame Est; ☽ 8am-5pm Mon-Fri, free tours 10am-4pm late Jun–mid-Aug; Ⓜ **Champ-de-Mars**
Montréal's City Hall is a gorgeous building built between 1872 and 1878. Far from being a hum-drum administrative centre, it's actually steeped in local lore. Most famously, it's where French leader Charles de Gaulle

Marché Bonsecours

took to the balcony in 1967 and yelled to the crowds outside *'Vive le Québec libre!'* ('Long live a free Québec!'). Those four words fueled the fires of québécois separatism and strained relations with Ottawa for years.

Earlier in the century, city hall was the site of a vicious fire in 1922 spawning a famous story of how the mayor fought the flames to retrieve precious documents. Only the building's walls were salvageable, so they were incorporated into the new building constructed between 1923 and 1926, which was based on the city hall in Tours, France.

Peer into the **Great Hall of Honor** for some scenes of rural Québec and busts of Jacques Viger, the first French-speaking mayor (1833–36), and Peter McGill, the first English-speaking mayor (184042). The chambers of the current mayor Gérald Tremblay are adjacent to the Great Hall.

LIEU HISTORIQUE DE SIR GEORGE-ÉTIENNE-CARTIER Map p314
☎ 283-2282; www.parkscanada.gc.ca/cartier; 458 rue Notre-Dame Est; adult/child/senior $4/2/3.50; ☽ 10am-6pm Jun-Aug, 10am-noon & 1-5pm Sep-Dec & Apr-May, closed Jan-Mar
The Sir George Étienne-Cartier National Historic Site consists of two historic houses owned by the Cartier family. One residence explains the life of Sir George-Étienne, one of the founders of the Canadian Confederation, and the changes that society saw in his lifetime. The other house is a faithful reconstruction of his home during the Victorian era. Staff in period costume run guided tours throughout the day and hold dramatic presentations on etiquette and a servant's life. In season the program includes a Victorian Christmas.

MARCHÉ BONSECOURS Map p314
☎ 872-7730; 350 rue St-Paul Est; ☽ 10am-6pm Jan-March, 10am-6pm Sat-Wed, 10am-9pm Thu & Fri April-Jun & Labor Day–Dec, 10am-9pm Mon-Sat, 10am-6pm Sun Jul–Labor Day; Ⓜ **Champ-de-Mars**
Opened in 1847, this sprawling neoclassical building has been everything from a farmers market to a concert theatre to a brief stint as city hall (1852–1878). It's also where the government of United Canada retreated to, so as to continue the legislative session after the parliament buildings nearby were burned down by an angry anglo mob in 1849.

The marché was reopened in 1992 as a gallery for shops selling arts and crafts, leather goods and garments. Though spectacular outside, renovations have left the inside with all the character and warmth of an airport terminal. Don't let sterile atmosphere discourage you, however. Shops stock everything from Inuit art and locally made jewelry to luxurious beaver coats; some of Québec's finest designers have their creations in the **Diffusion Griff '3000** (p179) boutique. An exhibition hall was added upstairs in 1998 for displays on history and culture. Restaurants line the facade on rue St-Paul.

MUSÉE D'ARCHÉOLOGIE POINTE-À-CALLIÈRE Map p314

☎ 872-9150; www.pacmuseum.qc.ca; 350 Place Royale; adult/child/student/senior $12/4.50/6.50/8; ☽ 10am-6pm Mon-Fri, 11am-6pm Sat & Sun late Jun-early Sep, 10am-5pm Tue-Fri, 11am-5pm Sat & Sun rest of the year; Ⓜ Place-d'Armes

Built on the very spot where European settlers set up their first camp, the Pointe-à-Callière Museum of Archaeology & History provides a good overview of Montréal's beginnings. Visitors should start with *Montreal, Tales of a City*, a 20-minute multimedia show that illustrates the centuries with the aid of film, hologram characters and real drizzle.

For the most part the museum is underground. Head to the archeological crypt in the basement where you can explore the remains of the city's ancient sewage and river system and the foundations of its first buildings and first public square. Interactive exhibits include video monitors that allow visitors to ask questions of the hologramlike figures from the 17th and 18th centuries about their lives in the colony.

A whole floor depicts changing history exhibits, eg on the Canal de Lachine or Montréal's early merchants. An 18th-century market is re-created on Place Royale in summer.

The lookout at the top of the tower in the new building provides an excellent view of the Old Port, and can be visited free of charge.

MUSÉE DES SOEURS GRISES Map p314

☎ 842-9411; 138 rue St-Pierre; admission free; ☽ reservation only; Ⓜ Square-Victoria

Dedicated to Ste Marguerite d'Youville, founder of the community of the Sisters of Charity, better known as the Grey Nuns, this museum has a small but wonderfully presented set of exhibits. The sisters set out by canoe and founded a mission in what was to become Manitoba in western Canada in 1850. Folk legend has it that the nuns sold moonshine to the native Indians, getting them *gris* (grey) or tipsy. There are regularly scheduled tours of the museum in French and in English but you must call ahead for the schedule and availability.

MUSÉE MARC-AURÈLE FORTIN

Map p314

☎ 845-6108; 118 rue St-Pierre; adult/student/senior $5/3/4; ☽ 11am-5pm Tue-Sun; Ⓜ Square-Victoria

This museum has but a few viewing rooms dedicated to a sole Québec painter, Marc-Aurèle Fortin (1888–1970), whose depictions of lush trees and greenery transformed the art of landscapes. A self-taught genius, Fortin produced thousands of works. He painted until his death, even after he lost his both of his legs and later his eyesight to diabetes. His bold, colorful paintings are a sharp contrast to Fortin's tragic end.

PLACE D'ARMES

Map p314

This square is framed by some of the finest buildings in Old Montréal, including its oldest bank, first skyscraper and **Basilique Notre-Dame**. The square's name references the bloody battles that took place here, as religious settlers and First Nations tribes thrashed out control of what would become Montréal. At its center stands the **Monument Maisonneuve** dedicated to city founder Paul de Chomedey, sieur de Maisonneuve. The four bronze panels around the base of the monument depict key events in Montréal's history and quote from the great man himself: 'I am determined to go even if every tree on the island turns into an Iroquois.'

The red sandstone building on the east side of the square is the **New York Life Insurance Building** (Map p314), Montréal's first skyscraper (1888). It's said to be built with the blocks used for ballast on ships bringing goods to Montréal. The building is worth a close look for its lovely design flourishes like the bright clock faces that are illuminated at night.

Next door, the **Aldred Building** (Map p314) is made of limestone and was designed to emulate the Empire State Building. Completed in 1931, it has an opulent L-shaped, Art Deco lobby including a bronze of birds sitting on power lines, a shout-out to JE Aldred who ran a power and water company.

On the north side of the square, the **Bank of Montréal** was Canada's first permanent bank.

PLACE JACQUES-CARTIER
Map p314

The liveliest spot in Old Montréal, this gently inclined square hums with performance artists, street musicians and the animated chatter from terrace restaurants linings its borders. A public market was set up here after a château burned down in 1803. At its top end stands the **Colonne Nelson**, a monument erected to Admiral Nelson after his defeat of Napoleon's fleet at Trafalgar. The great likeness is now a fiberglass replica.

Nelson's presence is a thorn in the side of many French Quebecers, and there have been many attempts to have it removed (the last was by mayor Pierre Bourque in 1998). Francophones later installed a statue of an obscure French admiral, Jean Vauquelin, in the square **Place Vauquelin** just west of Hôtel de Ville on rue Notre-Dame.

PLACE ROYALE
Map p314

This little square in the west of Old Montréal marks the spot where the first fort, Ville-Marie, was erected. Defense was a key consideration due to lengthy fighting with the native Iroquois. In the 17th and 18th centuries this was a marketplace; it's now the paved forecourt of the **Old Customs House** (Vieille Douane; 1836; Map p314) and linked to the **Musée d'Archéologie Pointe-à-Callière** via an underground passage. The neoclassical building looks much the same today as when it was built, but now serves as the museum's gift shop.

RUE DE L'HÔPITAL & AROUND
Map p314

Named for a hospice set up by nuns in the 17th century, the rue de l'Hôpital and adjoining streets are full of architectural quirks and highlights. On the corner of rue St-François-Xavier, the **Canadian Pacific Telegraph Chambers** (Map p314) was the 19th-century equivalent of a national internet provider. It houses condominiums today but the wild-eyed keystone over the entrance remains. The **Lewis Building** (Map p314) was built as the head office of the Cunard Shipping Lines. One mischievous character on the facade is holding a bag full of loot; a more scholarly colleague is taking notes.

The **Sun Life Annex & Old Sun Life Building** (Map p314) is an ornate 1920s structure covered in beautiful granite with stately columns on the upper floors. In WWII the British crown jewels were moved here for safekeeping as well as the gold reserves of several European countries. The building is equipped with one of the Montréal's few carillons, which you can hear being played daily at noon.

A CAPITAL EXPERIMENT

Montréal would have a very different place in history but for a boozy rabble and a few newspaper articles. When the city became the capital of the United Provinces of Canada in 1844, the government moved into a two-story limestone building on the elongated square **Place d'Youville** (Map p314), which at the time was a public market. It was here that Canada's first prime minister, John A Macdonald, made his inaugural speech to a joint French-English parliament.

Montréal's tenure as capital came to an abrupt end in 1849. Egged on by inflammatory editorials in the *Gazette,* an anglophone mob set fire to the assembly and the building burned to a crisp. The crowd was protesting a law that would require the Crown to compensate French Canadians for damages inflicted by the British army in the rebellion of 1837. As a consequence Montréal lost its status as capital, and the seat of government shifted back and forth between Québec City and Toronto until 1858, when Queen Victoria declared Ottawa the new capital.

Nothing was saved from the Montréal flames except a legislative mace and a portrait of Queen Victoria; the latter now hangs in the federal parliament building in Ottawa. The location of the first Canadian parliament (the east end of the square) is today a parking lot.

Terrace featuring busy restaurants on Place Jacques-Cartier

The beer-brewing dynasty had its own bank, but the **Molson Bank Building** (Map p314) looks more like a royal residence; heads of founder William and his two sons grace the doorway.

The most glamorous of the lot is the **Royal Bank Building** (Map p314), the city's tallest building (22 stories) when it was built in 1928. Pass under the royal coat of arms into a banking hall that resembles a Florentine palace; the coffered ceilings are of Wedgwood and the walls display insignias of eight provinces, Montréal (St George's Cross) and Halifax (a yellow bird).

RUE ST-PAUL Map p314

This narrow cobblestone street, the oldest in Montréal, was once a dirt road packed tight by horses laden with goods bound for the Old Port. Today it's a shopping street with galleries, boutiques and restaurants, touristy in spots but undeniably picturesque and enjoyable to wander.

THREE COURTHOUSES

Map p314

Along the north side of rue Notre-Dame Est near Place Jacques-Cartier three courthouses stand bunched together. The most fetching is the neoclassical **Vieux Palais de Justice**, Montréal's old justice palace and oldest courthouse (1856) that's now an annex of the Hôtel de Ville. It's a popular backdrop for wedding photos. The **Édifice Ernest Cormier** from the 1920s was used for criminal trials before being turned into a conservatory and later a court of appeal. The ugliest of the lot is the oversized **Palais de Justice**, built in 1971 when sinister glass cubes were still in fashion.

VIEUX SÉMINAIRE DE ST-SULPICE

Map p314

116 rue Notre-Dame Ouest

The Catholic order of Sulpicians was given title to the entire island of Montréal in 1663. The order built the seminary in 1684 and the 3rd-floor apartments of the old seminary have been occupied ever since. The clock on the facade was a gift from French king Louis XIV in 1701; it is believed to be the oldest working clock in North America. Ancient oaks shade the rear garden laid out in 1715. The seminary and grounds are closed to the public.

The **Centaur Theatre** (p162) performs English-language plays in the old **Montréal Stock Exchange Building** (Map p314). Opened in 1903, the huge columns recall imperial Rome while the interior has sumptuous marble and wood paneling. The building backs onto the Secret Garden of the Sulpicians' seminary but forget about visiting – the Sulpicians are a secretive bunch.

RUE ST-JACQUES

Map p314

Known as the Wall Street of Canada into the 1930s, rue St-Jacques was lined with the head offices of insurance companies and banks that proclaimed Montréal's prosperity for the best part of a century. In those days it was known as St James St.

Some great edifices are veritable temples to capitalism. The **Guardian Insurance Building** (1902; Map p314) has helmeted women guarding the entrance while lions and mermaids watch over on the 2nd floor.

OLD PORT

The Old Port is a requisite stop during a visit to Old Montréal. Heaps of sites are set up along its four piers, and numerous tourist cruises sail in and out all day. In warm weather the **Promenade du Vieux-Port** is a favorite recreation spot for joggers and inline skaters, while cyclists can take in the view from the city bike path that runs parallel. There are plenty of benches and green space for those seeking a little relaxation or for phenomenal views of the **Loto-Québec International Fireworks Competition** (p22). In cold weather, skating at the outdoor rink, with the St Lawrence River shimmering nearby, is simply magical.

Rue de la Commune, a street still lined with many 18th-century buildings, faces the Vieux-Port and is the place to head for snack stands, restaurants or gear rental.

LABYRINTH Map p314

☎ 499-0099; www.labyrintheduhangar16.com; Quai de l'Horloge; adult/child $12/9.50; ⊙ 11am-9pm late Jun-late Aug, 11:30am-5:30pm late Aug-end Aug, Sat & Sun only end Aug-late Sep; Ⓜ Champ-de-Mars

Located in an old aircraft hangar, the winding corridors, obstacles and surprises of the Labyrinth are a kid's delight, in English or French. Themes change regularly. It takes about one hour to get through the maze; small children may be frightened.

QUAI ALEXANDRA & AROUND Map p314

This easternmost pier in the port is home to the Iberville Passenger Terminal, the dock for cruise ships that ply the St Lawrence River as far as the Magdalen Islands out in the Gulf of St Lawrence. Nearby the **Parc des Écluses** (Park of Locks) holds exhibitions of landscape architecture, shows and concerts. A bicycle path starts here and runs southeast along the pretty **Canal de Lachine** (p108).

The abandoned grain silo on the south side of the locks is the last big relic of Montréal's heyday as a grain port. **Silo No 5** is a concrete beast made up of 115 grain bins 17 floors high. In the 1920s ships bound for the Great Lakes or the Atlantic stopped here to fill up with grain but as the railways developed, ships bypassed Montréal for ports upstream. An eyesore for some, inspiration for others (like Le Corbusier, the Swiss architect), the silo was abandoned in 1994. It's too expensive to demolish. Several possible projects are being discussed to convert the silo into something that can actually be used. So far, turning it into some kind of cultural venue seems to generate the most excitement.

On the promenade just west of **Café des Éclusiers** (p159) you'll see a booth made out of four stone pillars. Venture inside to the **Silo Phone**, a set of speakers and microphones hooked up to the grain silo across the locks. Say something and the sound will be transmitted into four of the huge

---

SIGN WARS PART II

The red neon **Farine Five Roses** (Map pp308–9) sign has been flickering over Montréal since 1954 and is one of the city's most famous landmarks. Sadly, by the time you read this it may not be there anymore – and this time it has nothing to do with language wars or the Bill 101 sign law (p34).

Located about 100m southeast of the Parc des Écluses at the old locks, the sign sits on top of an old flour mill dating from 1946. A sign saying 'Farine Ogilvie Flour' was hoisted on top in 1948 before being changed in 1954 to the 'Farine Five Roses' sign Montrealers know and love today.

Though the Farine Five Roses company was bought out decades ago by ADM, the US-based agribusiness, the sign was judged too cool to tear down and has been there ever since, a kind of beacon for everyone all over the city whether from Little Burgundy, to Parc du Mont Royal to those coming down autoroute Bonaventure.

The merde hit the fan in 2006 when ADM was bought by Smuckers – who produces Robin Hood flour. The sign was turned off for two weeks and anonymous sources said the sign would soon be taken down for good. To say there was an uproar would be an understatement – as everyone from regular citizens to newspaper editorialists to the cyber community took up the cause. The brouhaha got the lights turned on again and fast by August 9, 2006. However, the company has made no promises about preserving this piece of the Montréal skyline, saying only it will keep the lights on for the foreseeable future while it decides the sign's fate. To keep track of the soap opera check out www .savefarinefiveroses.org.

grain chambers and bounced back at you. Its acoustic qualities fascinated a local architect, Thomas McIntosh, who raised a ton of cash for the project.

QUAI JACQUES-CARTIER & AROUND
Map p314

This pier is the anchor of the Old Port area, home to restaurants, an open-air stage and a handicraft center. The tourists' Jacques-Cartier Information Booth (☎ 496-7678; ⏰ 10am-7pm mid-May–late Jun & late Aug-early Sep, to 10pm late Jun-late Aug, 10am-5pm Mon-Fri, to 7pm Sat & Sun early-late Sep) can be found right in the center of things at the entrance. Every year the port stages a number of temporary exhibits, shows and events.

Montréal's Cirque du Soleil troupe of acrobats performs here every couple of years. Tours of the port area also depart from here, and a ferry goes to Parc Jean-Drapeau (opposite). The ferry can also stop at Parc de la Cité-du-Havre, where there's a restaurant and picnic tables.

Just east of Quai Jacques-Cartier is the Parc du Bassin-Bonsecours, a grassy expanse enclosed by a waterway and criss-crossed with footbridges. In summer cute paddleboats with a mock steamboat funnel can be rented by the half-hour for $4; in winter the ice skaters take over. Remote-control model sailboats can be rented as well at the Pavilion du Bassin Bonsecours (Map p314).

QUAI KING-EDWARD Map p314

This pier is home to the sparkling Centre des Sciences de Montréal (☎ 496-4724; www .centredessciencesdemontreal.com; adult $10-22, child $7-18, ⏰ 9am-4pm Mon-Fri, 10am-5pm Sat & Sun), a sleek glass-covered science center housing virtual and interactive games, technology exhibits and an 'immersion theater' that puts a video game on giant screens. There's a huge range of different admission prices depending on which combinations of films and/or exhibits you want to take in.

TOP FIVE PARKS IN MONTRÉAL

- Jardin Botanique (p97) – beautiful gardens and always some special event
- Parc LaFontaine (p100) – the perfect year-round park with performances at the bandstand in summer and ice-skating on the pond in winter
- Jardin des Floralies (p83) – little known bit of gorgeous-ity near the Montréal casino
- Parc du Mont Royal (p104) – climb up the mountain and watch the city unfold below
- Parc Jean-Drapeau (opposite) – trails, paths, gorgeous views of Montréal and plenty of unique sights along the way

Cycling through Plateau du Mont-Royal

The center includes an **IMAX cinema** (☎ 496-4629) showing vivid nature and science films.

RUE DE LA COMMUNE Map p314
Set back from the waterfront, 'The Common' is a showcase of the rejuvenation that has swept Old Montréal. Compare it with old photos and you'll see the warehouses and factory buildings haven't changed much on the outside, but the tenants are upmarket hotels, restaurants and converted condos. Though the street has lost its raw, industrial feel the original stone walls can still be viewed inside many buildings.

SAILORS' MEMORIAL CLOCK TOWER
Map p314

Quai de l'Horloge pier; ⏱ 10am-9pm mid-Jun–mid-Aug, 10am-7pm Mon-Thu, 10am-9pm Fri-Sun mid-May–mid-Jun & mid-Aug–early Sep, 10am-7pm Sat & Sun early-late Sep

At the east edge of the historic port stands the striking white Tour de l'Horloge. This notable clock commemorates all of the sailors and shipmen who died in the world wars. Normally the observation tower and historical exhibition are open to the public, but renovations were underway to correct a slight lean in the tower when we visited.

PARC JEAN-DRAPEAU

This is one of the most beautiful parks in the city, but relative to Parc du Mont-Royal and other outdoor areas, is little visited by locals. Even those who work on the island say their friends still ask them, 'What, you're going *where?*'

Fans of the park chalk this attitude up to a mental barrier on the part of locals because this bewitching green space is strewn over two islands, Île Ste-Hélène and Île Notre-Dame, both home to the Expo '67 World's Fair. Though the park is just a 20-minute bike ride from the Gay Village across Pont Jacques-Cartier, something about it feels very distant – which, of course, is absolutely part of its charm.

There's an infinite choice of recreational activities here during the summer along with a couple of terrific museums, but Parc Jean-Drapeau is also a lovely stop if all you're after is some peace, quiet and nature. Information kiosks open up on both islands during the summer and are good for detailed info on upcoming events.

Orientation
The park lies in the midst of the mighty St Lawrence about 1km east of the Old Port. If you're walking allow plenty of time to get around the islands, which are around 3km long and up to 750m wide. Jean-Drapeau is the sole métro stop but bus 167 runs along the east side of Île Ste-Hélène to Île Notre-Dame, stopping at the casino and beach.

ÎLE STE-HÉLÈNE
Walkways meander around the island, past gardens and among the old pavilions from the World's Fair. The western part of the island was transformed into an open-air stage for shows, concerts and even after-hours parties. A large metal sculpture, **L'Homme** (Humankind), was created by American artist Alexander Calder for Expo '67; to those who know the artist's mobiles, the style will be familiar. It's also here near the sculpture that the fantastic **Piknic Électronik** (admission $5; ⏱ 1-8pm late May–late Sep) takes place every Sunday. DJs spin techno and electronic music while you can dance or flop in the grass or amongst the trees. You can also get a combined ticket to the Biosphère and the Musée Stewart from either place (adult/child $15/9).

TOP FIVE SIGHTS IN PARC JEAN-DRAPEAU
- Biosphère (p82) – possibly the best interactive exhibits in town
- Casino de Montréal (p83) – spinning wheels got to go round
- Piknic Électronik (below) – where else can you picnic in a park and listen to the city's best DJs at the same time?
- Musée Stewart (p82) – keepers of Canada's stormy past
- Plage des Îles (p83) – sand, beer, what more can you say

BIOSPHÈRE Map p319

☎ 283-5000; adult/child/student & senior $9.50/5/7.50; ☽ 10am-6pm mid-Jun–early Sep, noon-5pm Mon, Wed-Fri rest of the year; Ⓜ Jean-Drapeau

Located in the striking spherical dome of the former American pavilion in the '67 World's Fair, the center has the most spectacular collection of hands-on displays in the entire city. The 'sphere's' raison d'être is to explain the Great Lakes–St Lawrence River ecosystem, which makes up 20% of the planet's water reserves.

Exhibits all involve real water (blow dryers line the wall!) and include work stations where you can experience what happens to the environment when you make a dam and even one station where you can walk on water (yes, *literally* walk on water). Though primarily geared to kids, it's hard not to be completely impressed no matter how old you are. Creative workshops for kids (eg boat-building from recycled materials) and various art and environment exhibitions are held in summer. The upstairs Visions Hall offers a great view of the river.

LA RONDE AMUSEMENT PARK
Map p319

☎ 397-2000; www.laronde.com; adult/child $36/24; ☽ 10am-8pm late May–mid-Jun, 10am-10:30pm mid-Jun–late Aug, irregular hours rest of the year; Ⓜ Jean-Drapeau, 🚌 169; Ⓟ $13.50

Québec's largest amusement park, La Ronde has a battery of rides including the 'Monstre' big dipper – the second largest in the world – a Ferris wheel and a gentle minirail that offers views of the river and city. The latest addition is the Vampire, a corkscrew roller coaster that races at speeds up to 80km/h. It's owned by Six Flags of the US. While amusement-park connoisseurs will no doubt have the times of their lives here, you hear a lot of grumbling from locals these days about the admission cost, especially from Montréal families who can't justify the prohibitively expensive prices. Concerts and shows like circuses and high-platform diving are held throughout the summer; the Loto-Québec International Fireworks Competition (p22) is a highlight on weekend evenings in June and July.

TRANSPORTATION TO PARC JEAN-DRAPEAU

Car Pont Jacques-Cartier leads to Île Ste-Hélène, while Pont de la Concorde leads to Île Notre-Dame.
Métro Jean-Drapeau stop
Bus 167 or 169
Bicycle Bike path from Old Montréal via Pont de la Concorde or Pont Jacques-Cartier
Parking At the Casino
Water Shuttle $4.50 single, pedestrians and bikes, 15-minute crossing, every hour, check schedule for seasonal changes.

MUSÉE STEWART Map p319

☎ 861-6701; www.stewart-museum.org; adult/child under 7/student $10/free/7; ☽ 10am-5pm late May-early Oct, 10am-5pm Wed-Mon early Oct-late May; Ⓜ Jean-Drapeau

Near La Ronde there is also an old fort where the British garrison was stationed in the 19th century. Inside the remaining stone ramparts is the Musée Stewart with artifacts and tools from Canada's past. Check out the enormous model of Old Montréal inside. There is a spotlight that sweeps over the buildings while old footage pops up on a video screen accompanied by narration, and the presentation is beautifully done. Demonstrations are also given outside by actors wearing period costume, and there's a military parade every day in summer. It is a 15-minute walk from métro Jean-Drapeau station; parking is free.

ÎLE NOTRE-DAME

This isle emerged in 10 months from the riverbed atop millions of tons of earth and rock excavated from the new métro created in 1967. The planners were creative with the use of water, carving out canals and pretty garden walkways amidst the parklands that stretch across the isle. The Formula One Grand Prix race is held every year in June here at the Circuit Gilles-Villeneuve (Map p319); the rest of the year it is popular with cyclists and inline skaters.

CASINO DE MONTRÉAL Map p319

☎ 392-2746; 1 ave du Casino; ⏰ 24hr;
Ⓜ Jean-Drapeau, 🚍 167

Québec's first (and biggest) casino looks like a cross between a spaceship and an airport terminal. Based in the former French pavilion from the World's Fair, the Montréal Casino opened in 1993 and was so popular (and earned so much money) that expansion occurred almost instantly. You can gather your winnings at 3000 slot machines and 120 gaming tables, but drinking isn't allowed on the floor (see p166).

Arched footbridges link the casino to the Jardin des Floralies (Map p319), a rose garden that is wonderful for a stroll.

CENTRE OPTION PLEIN AIR Map p319

☎ 872-0199; informations@optionpleinair.com; 1 Circuit Gilles-Villeneuve, Île Notre-Dame;
Ⓜ Jean-Drapeau, 🚍 167

Competitive rowers and kayakers, amongst other amateur athletes, train here at this former Olympic rowing basin. It's not open to the public except during special events, like when the famous dragon boat rowing races are held in late July. A youth hostel is also on site (p195).

DOWNTOWN

Eating p129; Shopping p181; Sleeping p195

Downtown Montréal is sharp, sleek and filled with energy. At the feet of its modern skyscrapers and condo developments lie heritage buildings and old-time mansions, top-notch museums and numerous green spaces. Businesspeople swing briefcases and talk on cell phones amongst thousands of backpack-toting students who flood the district each day for their classes at McGill or Concordia (see Downtown Tour, p116).

The city's major shopping district is also here: rue Crescent (also known as a popular drinking destination for anglophones), rue Ste-Catherine, rue Sherbrooke and the underground city. Explore the neighborhood with the local walking tour on p71.

HABITAT '67 Map p319

The artificial peninsula called Cité-du-Havre was created to protect the port from vicious currents and ice. Here, in 1967, architect Moshe Safdie designed a set of futuristic condominiums for the World's Fair when he was just 23 years old. The units are worth a fortune (around $750,000 for a 1250 sq ft two-cube apartment). A narrow spit of land connects Île Ste-Hélène with Old Montréal via the bridge Pont de la Concorde.

PLAGE DES ÎLES Map p319

☎ 872-6093; adult/child $7.50/4; ⏰ 10am-7pm, last admission 6:15pm Jun 24-Labour Day; 🚍 167

On warm summer days this artificial sandy beach can accommodate up to 5000 sunning and splashing souls. It's safe, clean and ideal for kids; picnic facilities and snack bars serving beer are also on-site. Volleyball competitions at the 2006 World Outgames were held here and there are still several professional-standard volleyball courts left over for anyone to use. The beach is closed on 'bad days,' but call to check if it's open – the authorities' idea of a bad day may not be the same as yours.

TRANSPORTATION TO DOWNTOWN

Métro The Green and Orange lines have over a dozen stops; Peel and McGill are central and convenient.
Bus 15 runs on rue Ste-Catherine & boul de Maisonneuve, 24 on rue Sherbrooke, 150 on boul René-Lévesque.
Parking Downtown is littered with paid parking lots, such as the one under the Eaton Centre.
Bicycle Only a few streets have separate cycle lanes.

Orientation

The chief shopping artery of rue Ste-Catherine bisects downtown, running roughly southwest to northeast (or as the locals say, east to west on an off-kilter compass). It passes Place des Arts, the performing arts complex and hub of the jazz festival, and runs parallel to boul de Maisonneuve and rue Sherbrooke. Some of the flashiest corporate buildings are on ave McGill College, which runs from Place Ville-Marie north into the McGill University campus with stunning views of Mont Royal.

At the foot of Mont Royal is a wealthy residential area still known by some as the Golden Square Mile. Rue Crescent and rue Bishop are the traditional anglophone centers of nightlife with an array of bars, clubs and restaurants. Rue Sherbrooke Ouest features upscale shops and turn-of-the-century residences with a decidedly English flavor.

BLACK WATCH HIGHLANDERS REGIMENTAL MUSEUM & ARCHIVES
Map pp310-11

☎ 496-1686; 2067 rue de Bleury; ◷ 1-8pm Tue, 1-4pm Thu & Fri; Ⓜ Place-des-Arts

The presence of the legendary Highlanders is usually reserved for holidays and official ceremonies, but military buffs can delve deeper at this small museum of military memorabilia that includes medals, insignia, munitions and small arms prior to 1969. The fanciful building – a faux Gothic castle, complete with turrets – also houses a national military archive and takes numerous requests for personnel documents. Few Montrealers know about this place because it never advertises.

CATHÉDRALE MARIE-REINE-DU-MONDE Map pp310-11

☎ 866-1661; 1045 rue de la Cathédrale; ◷ 7:30am-6pm; Ⓜ Bonaventure

The Cathedral of Mary Queen of the World is a smaller but still magnificent version of St Peter's Basilica in Rome. The architects scaled it down to one-quarter size, mindful of the structural risks of Montréal's severe winters. This landmark was built from 1870 to 1894 as a symbol of Catholic power in the heart of Protestant Montréal.

The 13 sculptures of saints over the entrance are sculpted in wood and covered with copper; at nighttime they're brilliantly illuminated. The neobaroque altar canopy, a replica of Bernini's masterpiece in St Peter's, is fashioned of gold leaf and copper with swirled roof supports. The overall impression, including the decoration of the vaults and their support, arguably rivals that of the famous Basilique Notre-Dame.

CENTRE CANADIEN D'ARCHITECTURE Map pp310-11

☎ 939-7026; www.cca.qc.ca; 1920 rue Baile; adult/child/student/senior $10/3/5/7; ◷ 10am-5pm Wed-Sun, 10am-9pm Thu; Ⓜ Guy-Concordia

The Canadian Centre of Architecture has a dual role: as a museum of the country's architectural heritage, and as a research center to promote future development.

TOP FIVE SIGHTS IN DOWNTOWN

- Cathédrale Marie-Reine-du-Monde (left) – scaled-down version of St Peter's in Rome
- Musée d'Art Contemporain (p89) – eclectic showcase of modern Canadian art
- Musée des Beaux-Arts (p92) – masterworks abound along with regular lectures and public activities
- Rue Ste-Catherine (p89) – for shopping and buzz galore
- Marché Atwater (p86) – quality produce and delis that draw people from all over town

This innovative building incorporates a modern museum with Shaughnessy House, the 1874 residence of a wealthy businessman and one of Montréal's few 19th-century homes open to the public. Highlights in this section include the conservatory, reception rooms and a wonderfully ornate sitting room with intricate woodwork and a massive stone fireplace. The busy, well-stocked bookstore has some wonderful coffee-table books on famous architects, styles and photography.

The exhibition galleries show prints, drawings, models and photos of remarkable buildings both local and international; sections are dedicated to urban planning and landscape design. Most visitors expecting an academic experience will be pleasantly surprised by the accessibility of the collection.

The CCA's sculpture garden is located on a grassy lot overlooking south Montréal, but separated from the main grounds by busy boul René-Lévesque. The dozen or so sculpture-models raised on pillars and beams are best viewed at night when they're illuminated. Here too you get an excellent look at the gray limestone annex of Shaughnessy House from the rear.

CHRIST CHURCH CATHEDRAL
Map pp310-11

☎ 843-6577; 635 rue Ste-Catherine Ouest; ◷ 7:30am-5:45pm; Ⓜ McGill

Modeled on a Salisbury, England, church, Montréal's first Anglican bishop had this cathedral built and it was completed in 1859. This church was the talk of the town in the late 1980s when it allowed a shopping center, the Promenades de la Cathédrale, to be built underneath it. Spectacular photos from 1987 show the house of worship resting on concrete stilts while construction went on underneath.

Some were scandalized, others thought the church had 'sold out.' However, the church maintains the extra revenue brought in by the development has added thousands of dollars to the church's coffers.

The interior is sober apart from the pretty stained-glass windows made by William Morris' studios in London. In the rear cloister garden stands a memorial statue to Raoul Wallenberg, the Swedish diplomat who saved 100,000 Jews from the concentration camps in WWII.

COMPLEXE DESJARDINS Map pp310-11
M Place-des-Arts
This shopping-and-office complex has three shopping levels, more than 150 stores and a central hall called La Grande Place that has 18m windows at either end of a huge, airy atrium. The space is often used for exhibitions and variety shows.

DRUMMOND MEDICAL BUILDING
Map pp310-11
1414 rue Drummond; M Peel
This university faculty building combines Art Deco with the Arts and Crafts style that was popular in the 1920s. Check the branches, pine cones and flowers on the facade, and the lacy artwork in the lobby.

> **MONTRÉAL ACCORDING TO TWAIN**
>
> 'This is the first time I was ever in a city where you couldn't throw a brick without breaking a church window.'
> *Mark Twain (1881)*

GARE WINDSOR Map pp310-11
☎ 287-8726; 1160 de la Gauchetière Ouest;
M Bonaventure
The massive Victorian building hugging the slope west of the Marriott Château Champlain is the old **Windsor Station**, opened in 1889 as the headquarters of the Canadian Pacific Railway. The Romanesque structure inspired a château style for train stations across the country; its architect, Bruce Price, would later build the remarkable Château Frontenac in Québec City. The station is no longer the terminus of the transcontinental railway but still serves commuter trains. Much of the building today houses offices and shops.

LES COURS MONT-ROYAL
Map pp310-11
1455 rue Peel; M Peel
This elegant shopping mall is a reincarnation of the Mount Royal Hotel (1922), at the time the largest hotel in the British Empire. The 1000-room hotel was converted into a snazzy mix of condos and fashion boutiques in 1988, with everything from the urban

Art classes at Musee d'Art Contemporain (p89), Place des Arts

THE UNDERGROUND CITY

Brilliant marketing that conjures up images of subterranean skyscrapers and roads has made this one of the first things visitors seek out when they travel to Montréal.

The underground city doesn't actually have any of these things. What it does have is a network of 2600 shops, 200 restaurants and 40-odd cinemas, theaters and exhibition halls, all hidden neatly beneath the surface of the congested city upstairs. For most travelers, it is a major let down, because no matter what tourism officials call it, it is basically just a kind of colossal network of interlocking shopping malls. Where it does get interesting, however, is for residents living in downtown Montréal, as it gives them a reprive from winter.

The sixty-odd distinct complexes that make up this network are linked by brightly lit, well ventilated corridors; fountains play to maintain humidity and the temperature hovers around 68°F (20°C). Add the métro and you've got a self-contained world, shielded from the subarctic temperatures. If you move to Montréal and pick the right apartment building, it could literally be the middle of winter and you would be able to go to work, do your grocery shopping, go see a movie and take in a performance at Place des Arts and never need more than a t-shirt.

The underground city was started, albeit inadvertently, when the Canadian National Railway laid a track through Montréal in 1918, splitting downtown in two and creating an ugly divide. Forty years later architect IM Pei was commissioned to build a skyscraper, Place Ville-Marie, to bridge the gap and link the Queen Elizabeth Hotel with CNR headquarters. Part of the new complex was underground, and in 1962 workers tunneled from the building to the hotel. The underground city was born. The métro was finished just in time for the Expo '67 World's Fair, and as 1% of the construction costs went into art, the entire network was conceived as a huge art gallery.

The underground city continues to evolve but with no master blueprint, making it easy to get lost. Plans are emerging to provide more artificial light and post more signposts to guide the perplexed. The easiest thing, however, is to seek out the info-points at main crossroads that will print you a plan of how to get to your destination. Other cities like Toronto have their own labyrinths but remember, they're piddling compared with Montréal's 29km of underground corridors.

wear of **Roots** (p184) to top-end garments of Club Monaco, Giorgio and Harry Rosen. Under the skylight you'll see six birdmen sculptures by Inuit artist David Pioukuni. These were shamans who transformed themselves into winged creatures and were powered by a wind god. The spectacular chandelier is from Monte Carlo's old casino.

MARCHÉ ATWATER Map pp310-11

☎ 937-7754; 138 ave Atwater; ☾ 8am-6pm Mon-Wed, 8am-8pm Thu & Fri, 8am-5pm Sat & Sun; Ⓜ Lionel-Groulx

This fantastic market is just off the Canal de Lachine and attracts a terrific range of people. Locals from the nearby condo developments come here to do their grocery shopping: stressed urbanites look for their organics and bikers and inline skaters stop for lunch or picnic items. There's produce from local farms, wine, fine cheeses and freshly butchered meats. The outdoor stalls operate March to October but the market's specialty shops inside operate year-round. The excellent **Premiére Moisson** (p136) is a popular café and bakery. It is swamped on weekends when approaching the counter for a pie or baguette feels like wading into the mosh pit at a punk concert. The high, golden brick building (1933) is framed by

a covered promenade and topped by a distinctive clock tower.

MONTRÉAL PLANETARIUM Map pp310-11

☎ 872-4530; www.planetarium.montreal.qc.ca; 1000 rue St-Jacques; adult/child/youth aged 5-17 $6.50/free/3.50; ☾ 12:30-5pm Mon, 9:30am-5pm Tue-Thu, 9:30am-4:30pm & 7-9:30pm Fri, 12:30am-4:30pm Sat & Sun, closed Mon Sep-Jun; Ⓜ Bonaventure

This 20m-high dome offers a window on the stars, space and the solar system via a celestial projector. The 50-minute shows run in shifts: mornings are geared toward kids and school groups, afternoons are for all ages and evenings are reserved for adult programs. Seasonal presentations run at Christmas and other times of the year.

MT STEPHEN CLUB Map pp310-11

☎ 849-7338; 1440 rue Drummond; Ⓜ Peel

The Mt Stephen Club, dating from 1880, was an exclusive businessmen's club named for the first president of the Canadian Pacific Railway. The 15 rooms of this Renaissance-style mansion have been completely renovated by a private foundation, and are rich with quality materials and skillful artistry, including a splendid mahogany staircase, marble mantelpieces and rather swanky furnishings. Still one of the swishest private clubs in town, the public can take it all in Sunday morning, when for $42 you'll get a tour of the digs followed by a 'musical' brunch. Reservations essential.

PALAIS DES CONGRÈS Map p314

☎ 871-8122; 201 ave Viger Ouest;
Ⓜ Place-d'Armes

Located on the new Place Jean-Paul-Riopelle in the heart of town, the facade of this convention centre resembles a pallet of popsicles with perky blue, orange, yellow and green panes; entering the hall is akin to strolling through a kaleidoscope. Day brings out the colors, night the transparency. More modern art lies within, including the Lipstick Forest that consists of 52 tree trunks daubed in electric pink.

The cutting-edge Palais adjoins the old convention center but also integrates several historic buildings: a 1908 fire station, the Art Deco Tramways building from 1928 and a Victorian-era office complex.

Immediately east of the Palais, the spanking new Esplanade is a slab of concrete that's been turned into a landscape garden. Stone pathways link 31 heaps of earth, each topped off with Montréal's official tree, the crab apple.

PLACE DU CANADA Map pp310-11

Ⓜ Bonaventure

This park immediately southeast of Square Dorchester is best known for its monument of John A Macdonald, Canada's first prime minister, who addressed the maiden session of parliament in Montréal. It's guarded by four bronze British lions and seven bronze figures holding shields of the seven Canadian provinces of the time. The two cannons around the base were captured in the Crimean War; if you look closely you'll see the dual-headed eagle of Czar Nicholas I. The statue was decapitated by vandals in 1992 and the head vanished for two years.

The overpass over boul René-Lévesque leads to the Marriott Château Champlain Hotel (p197), known as the 'cheese grater' for its windows shaped like half-moons.

PLACE JEAN-PAUL-RIOPELLE
Map pp310-11

cnr ave Viger Ouest & rue de Bleury; ☉ ring of fire every hour 6.30-10:30pm mid-May–mid-Oct;
Ⓜ Place-d'Armes

Inaugurated in 2003, the heart of the square is a fountain and sculpture by Jean-Paul Riopelle (1923–2002) called La Joute (The Joust). Formerly at the Olympic stadium, the statue was moved here to anchor the new square. Eleven species of tree typical to Montréal, including ash, oak and elm, are planted randomly over the rest of the square. In daytime this area is filled with nearby office workers having lunch, but summer nights are a big draw here as mists and a ring of fire erupts around the fountain, just as Riopelle had always wanted.

RUE BISHOP Map pp310-11

The stretch of rue Bishop north of rue Ste-Catherine has several university buildings of note. The Henry F Hall Building on the northwest corner of boul de Maisonneuve is the core of Montréal's English-language university Concordia. With no real campus to speak

---

RETURN OF THE MONTRÉAL MELON

In its heyday it was truly the Queen of Melons. Patrons in fancy restaurants of New York and Chicago would pay top dollar for a single juicy slice of the delicious green Montréal Melon; the 1938 handbook Vegetables of New York said that 'handled skillfully and intelligently, the melon produces the largest fruits of its type in American cultivation.' A single specimen might easily reach 20 pounds (9kg) and some have been twice that weight. Its unique spicy flavor earned it the nickname 'Nutmeg Melon.' And the market gardeners of western Montréal did a booming business in the fruit that resembles a flattened basketball.

After WWII the small plots vanished as Montréal expanded, and industrial farms had little interest in growing a melon with ultrasmooth rind. By the early 1950s the melon was gone – but not forever. In 1996 an enterprising Montréal journalist tracked down Montréal Melon seeds held in a US Department of Agriculture collection in Iowa. The first new crop was harvested in Montréal a year later in a new collective garden in Notre-Dame-de-Grâce, the heart of the old melon-growing district. To sample this blast from the past, visit markets such as Marché Atwater (opposite) or Marché Jean-Talon (p101) after the harvest every September.

of, the university acquires buildings around town as it expands. The **Bishop Court Apartments** (1904) are one-time luxury flats that bear some fantastic carvings and limestone decorations; the neo-Gothic building also has a manicured garden. Across rue Bishop, the **JW McConnell Building** (Map pp310–11) has screaming pink tiles and a terrific atrium where scattered extracts of literary works simulate an intellectual 'whirlwind.'

SEAGRAM HOUSE Map pp310-11
1430 rue Peel; M Peel
For almost seven decades this faux château served as headquarters for the world's largest distilling company – a child of the Prohibition era. Founder Samuel Bronfman ordered a design like a phony Tudor-Gothic castle and the result looks pretty funny today (note the scary imp over the entrance). When Seagram was sold to France's Vivendi in 2000 the building was donated to McGill University.

SQUARE DORCHESTER Map pp310-11
M Peel
This leafy expanse in the heart of downtown offers many visitors their first impression of Montréal – the main tourist office, **Centre Infotouriste** (p191), is located on the northwest side where many tour buses line up. Known until 1988 as Dominion Square, a reminder of Canada's founding in 1867, it was the site of a Catholic cemetery until 1870 and bodies still lie beneath the grass. Events of all kinds have taken place here over the years – fashion shows, political demonstrations and royal visits. In 1995 it was the site of a huge national rally for Canadian unity during the referendum on Québec sovereignty.

The square still exudes the might of the British Empire. The most striking statue in the square is of **Lord Strathcona** (Map pp310–11), a philanthropist who sponsored a Canadian regiment that fought in the Boer War (1899–1901). Other monuments in the park include likenesses of Queen Victoria, poet Robert Burns and Wilfrid Laurier, Canada's first francophone prime minister. Laurier faces a statue of John A Macdonald, the first anglophone prime minister, in **Place du Canada** (p87) across boul René-Lévesque.

Apart from home to the Centre Infotouriste, the **Dominion Square Building** on the north side of the square has a plush central hall and carved arches featuring dragons, gar-

goyles and demons on the east and west entrances. The frontage on rue Ste-Catherine is home to the **HMV** (p182) record store.

On the west side of the square stands the aristocratic rump of the old **Windsor Hotel** (below).

SQUARE VICTORIA Map pp310-11
M Square-Victoria
In the 19th century this was a Victorian garden in a swanky district of Second Empire homes and offices. Today Square Victoria is a triangle of manicured greenery and water jets in the midst of modern skyscrapers. The only vestige of the period is a statue of Queen Victoria (1872). The Art Nouveau entrance railing to the métro station was a gift from the city of Paris for Expo '67.

ST PATRICK'S BASILICA Map pp310-11
☎ 866-7379; 460 boul René-Lévesque Ouest; ☿ 9am-6pm; M Square-Victoria
Built for Montréal's booming Irish population in 1847, the interior of St Patrick's Basilica contains huge columns from single pine trunks, an ornate baptismal font and nectar-colored stained-glass windows. The pope raised its status to basilica in 1989, in recognition of its importance to English-speaking Catholics in Montréal. It's a sterling example of French-Gothic style and, as you might expect, is classified a national monument. The Irish-Canadian patriot D'Arcy McGee was buried here after his assassination in 1868; his pew (No 240) is marked with a small Canadian flag.

WINDSOR HOTEL Map pp310-11
☎ 393-3588; 1170 rue Peel; M Peel
The palatial Windsor was Canada's first grand hotel (1878) and played host to all manner of international guests and celebrities, including Mark Twain, Winston Churchill, King George VI, Queen Elizabeth and John F Kennedy, to name a few. The original Windsor had six restaurants and 382 sumptuous guest rooms, but a fire that devastated the hotel in 1957 left only the annex, the portion still standing today. The ballrooms are rented for receptions and filmsets – scenes from *The Jackal* with actor Bruce Willis were shot here. You can stroll down the magnificent main hall, Peacock Alley, and peek at the vast wooden dance-floors, chandeliers and high windows that recall turn-of-the-century splendor.

RUE STE-CATHERINE

A boutique-lover's delight and one of the 'happeningest' streets in town, rue Ste-Catherine is one endless orgy of shops, restaurants, bars and cafés on the hyperactive stretch between rue Crescent and rue St-Urbain. Shopping malls, department stores and multiplex cinemas are sprinkled along the way. Shoppers flood the streets on weekends, slowing pedestrian traffic to a mere shuffle in the afternoons.

CHURCH OF ST JAMES THE APOSTLE

Map pp310-11

☎ 849-7577; 1439 rue Ste-Catherine Ouest;
Ⓜ Guy-Concordia

Built in 1864 on a sports field for the British military, this Anglican church used to be called St Crickets in the Fields for the matches that unfolded here. The stained glass in the east transept, the Regimental Window, was donated in memory of the WWI fallen.

MUSÉE D'ART CONTEMPORAIN

Map pp310-11

☎ 847-6226; www.macm.org; 185 rue Ste-Catherine Ouest, Place des Arts; adult/student/senior $8/4/6, free 6-9pm Wed; ☙ 11am-6pm Tue & Thu-Sun, 11am-9pm Wed, English tours 1pm & 3pm Sat & Sun; Ⓜ Place-des-Arts

This showcase of modern Canadian and international art has eight galleries divided between past greats (since 1939) and exciting current developments. A weighty collection of 6000 permanent works includes Québec legends Jean-Paul Riopelle, Paul-Émile Borduas and Geneviève Cadieux,

Illuminated crowd sculpture (p91)

but also temporary exhibitions of the latest trends in current art from Canadian and international artists. Forms range from traditional to New Media, from painting, sculpture and prints to installation art, photography and video. The exhibition spaces are large and airy, ideal for regular modern and avant-garde performances held at the museum. The **sculpture garden** with Henry Moore's work *Upright Motive No 5* is worth a look.

English-language tours are at 6:30pm on Wednesday, and at 1pm and 3pm on Saturday and Sunday. The pleasant **restaurant** upstairs has a great dining terrace and the **gift shop** is full of tempting artistic stuff.

MUSÉE JUSTE POUR RIRE Map pp310-11

☎ 845-5105; www.hahaha.com; 2111 boul St-Laurent; adult/child $9/5; ☙ 9:30am-3:30pm Thu & Fri, 10am-5pm Sat & Sun; Ⓜ St-Laurent

The Just for Laughs Museum is the seat of the summer comedy festival of the same name. Apparently comedian George Burns was nearly killed by a brick of fake banknotes here, but otherwise guffaws are few and far between. This warehouse space runs the best 100 comedy clips from comics around the world, from Roberto Benigni to Steve Martin, in its International Humor Hall of Fame. A favorite with kids, the *Abracadabra* show reveals a fascinating glimpse of magic and magicians behind the scenes. The adjacent **Cabaret Theater** (☎ 845-2014) stages special events and shows.

PLACE DES ARTS Map pp310-11

☎ 285-4200 (box office); 175 rue Ste-Catherine Ouest; Ⓜ Place-des-Arts

Montréal's performing arts center is the kingpin of artistic and cultural events. Several renowned musical companies call the Place des Arts home, including the Montréal Symphony Orchestra and the McGill Chamber Orchestra; it's also the nexus of the **International Jazz Festival** (p22) and **Les Francofolies** (p23). Completed in 1963 but enlarged several times, the complex embraces an

THE MÉTRO MUSEUM OF ART

Primarily a mover of the masses, the Montréal métro was also conceived as an enormous art gallery, although not all stations have been decorated. Here are a few highlights from the central zone; many more await your discovery.

Berri-UQAM

A set of murals by artist Robert La Palme representing science, culture and recreation hangs above the main staircase leading to the yellow line. These works were moved here from the 'Man and His World' pavilion of Expo '67 at the request of Mayor Jean Drapeau, a buddy of La Palme.

Champ-de-Mars

The station kiosk boasts a set of antique stained-glass windows by Marcelle Ferron, an artist of the Refus Global movement. The abstract forms splash light down into the shallow platform, drenching passengers in color as their trains roll through.

Peel

Circles, circles everywhere: in bright single colors on advertising panels, in the marble of one entrance, above the main staircases, as tiles on the floor – even the bulkhead vents are circular. They're the work of Jean-Paul Mousseau of the québécois art movement Les Automatistes.

Place-des-Arts

The station's east wall has a back-lit stained glass mural entitled *Les Arts Lyriques,* by québécois artist and Oscar-winning filmmaker Frédéric Back. It depicts the evolution of Montréal's music from the first trumpet fanfare played on the island in 1535 to modern composers and conductors.

Further afield, there are plenty of interesting artistic quirks if you decide to ride along the blue line; check out the geometric stained glass by Claude Bettinger at métro **Côte-des-Neiges,** the colored brick designs by Gilbert Poissant at métro **Outremont,** or the elaborate hanging grills by Jean-Louis Beaulieu at métro **Snowdon.**

outdoor plaza with fountains and an ornamental pool and is attached to the **Complexe Desjardins** (p85) via an underground tunnel. The five halls include the 3000-seat **Salle Wilfrid-Pelletier** and the 1500-seat **Théâtre Maisonneuve**, and there's a small experimental space called the **Cinquième Salle.**

ST JAMES UNITED CHURCH

Map pp310-11
☎ 288-9245; 463 rue Ste-Catherine Ouest;
🕙 11am Sun; Ⓜ McGill
If you find yourself in front of its stunning facade, you'll have a hard time imagining that it was blocked from public view for 70 years. But it's true, a hideous three-storey

commercial building completely blocked this Methodist colossus from 1926 to 2005, when the only way to reach the church was through a dark lane underneath a gaudy neon sign. Thankfully, the commercial monstrosity was flattened and several years of restoration work have got the church camera-ready for the first time in decades.

Everyone from private enterprise to the Québec government has invested money into the project. The excellent acoustics at St James United are coveted for organ and choir concerts as well as performances of the **International Jazz Festival** (p22).

The church was originally opened in 1889.

RUE SHERBROOKE OUEST

Until the 1930s the downtown stretch of rue Sherbrooke Ouest was home to the **Golden Square Mile**, then one of the richest residential neighborhoods in Canada. You'll see a few glorious old homes along this drag, though most of them have been torn down to make way for skyscrapers. Those still standing serve mostly as private clubs, but there are good interpretation panels outside them explaining their history. The route is also home to worth-visiting churches, some first-rate museums and strings of energetic students en route to McGill.

ERSKINE & AMERICAN UNITED CHURCH Map pp310-11

3407 ave du Musée; M Guy-Concordia
One of Montréal's most attractive Romanesque churches features an extensive collection of beautiful Tiffany windows.

GRAND SÉMINAIRE DE MONTRÉAL
Map pp310-11

☎ 935-1169; 2065 rue Sherbrooke Ouest; admission by donation; ☺ tours 1pm & 3pm Tue-Sat Jun-Aug; M Guy-Concordia
The immense complex was built in 1860 to train priests for the Roman Catholic diocese. Shortly after construction the main instruction building, the Collège de Montréal, was requisitioned by the British army to house soldiers (who departed in 1870 after petitioning by the archdiocese). The seminary has a pretty Romanesque chapel, with hand-carved oak pews and walls covered with imported stone from Caen, France. Several shaded canals on the property are lovely for a stroll. Tours last about an hour and a half and the guides are excellent.

The Catholic Sulpicians built a farmhouse on this spot with four corner towers, but the farm was demolished when the Grand Seminary was built in the mid-19th century.

ILLUMINATED CROWD Map pp310-11
1981 ave McGill College; M McGill
Are you disturbed or compelled? That's more or less the conversation first-time visitors to Raymond Mason's 1986 statement on the human condition find themselves having. It's one of Montréal's most talked-about sculptures and arguably the most photographed piece of public art. The inscription reads in part: 'A crowd has gathered…the strong light casts shadows, and as light moves toward the back and diminishes, the mood degenerates; hooliganism, disorder and violence occur.' The group placed on four giant steps ranges from wide-eyed, upstanding citizens in the front to miscreants in the rear as the steps descend downwards. They're made of polyester resin with a vanilla-yellow coating that can appear sickly or radiant depending on the light.

LE CHÂTEAU Map pp310-11
1321 rue Sherbrooke Ouest; M Guy-Concordia
This fortresslike apartment complex was designed by the famed Montréal architects George Ross and Robert MacDonald. The style would do Errol Flynn proud: Scottish and French Renaissance with stone battlements, demons and pavilion roofs. In the early 20th century these were some of Montréal's most elegant apartments. You can walk into the romantic courtyard for a closer look at the walls; fossilized shells are visible in the granite blocks.

LOUIS-JOSEPH FORGET HOUSE
Map pp310-11

1195 rue Sherbrooke Ouest; M Peel
This Victorian mansion was built in the late 19th century for the first francophone chairman of the Montréal Stock Exchange. Forget was also a founding member of the Mont Royal Club and ran the Canadian Pacific Railway – much like George Stephen, an earlier CPR president who founded the Mt Stephen Club (p86).

MAISON ALCAN Map pp310-11
1188 rue Sherbrooke Ouest; M Peel
This mélange of four carefully restored 19th- and 20th-century buildings is not only an architectural wonder, but also the symbolic headquarters of the Alcan aluminum concern. It integrates the old Berkeley Hotel and four houses including the Atholstan House, a Québec historic monument. To the rear is an intriguing atrium with a pretty garden. Also on the property stands the Emmanuel Congregation Church (Map pp310–11), which belongs to the Salvation Army.

MASONIC MEMORIAL TEMPLE
Map pp310-11

☎ 933-6739; 2295 rue St-Marc; M Guy-Concordia
This Grand Lodge of Québec is one of the most imposing monuments on rue Sherbrooke, built in 1929 to honor the fallen in WWI. Huge classical columns frame the facade while two mysterious obelisks with dragons and globes guard the entrance. Free guided tours are offered on an irregular basis; check ahead for a worthwhile glimpse into the secretive world of Freemasonry.

MCGILL UNIVERSITY Map pp310-11
☎ 398-4455; www.mcgill.ca; 845 rue Sherbrooke Ouest; M McGill
Founded in 1828 by James McGill, a rich Scottish fur trader, McGill University is one of Canada's most prestigious learning

institutions with 15,000 students. The university's medical and engineering faculties have a fine reputation and many campus buildings are showcases of Victorian architecture. The entrance is located at the northern end of ave McGill College at the Roddick Gates, which house the university's clock and chimes. Two Romanesque buildings on the right house the physics, chemistry and architecture departments; further north stands the **Macdonald Engineering Building**, in English baroque style. At the top of the green stands the **Arts Building**, the oldest structure on campus (1839). The campus is rather nice for a stroll around at the foot of Mont Royal, and also incorporates the **Musée Redpath** (right).

MOUNT ROYAL CLUB Map pp310-11

☎ 933-6739; 1193 rue Sherbrooke Ouest; Ⓜ Peel
Founded as an exclusive men's society, the Mount Royal Club was formed in the 19th century as a one-up on the older **Beaver Club** (p132) across town. It's essentially a business-people's club today, and both men and women are welcome.

MUSÉE DES BEAUX-ARTS Map pp310-11

☎ 285-2000; www.mbam.qc.ca; 1380 rue Sherbrooke Ouest; permanent collection free, special exhibits adult/senior or student $15/7.50; ⏰ 11am-5pm Tue-Sun, to 9pm Wed; Ⓜ Peel
Montréal's Museum of Fine Arts, the oldest in the country and the city's largest, is housed in two buildings: the classical, marble-covered **Michal and Renata Hornstein Pavilion** at 1379 rue Sherbrooke Ouest, and the modern annex across the street, the **Jean-Noël Desmarais Pavilion**. The latter plays host to works by European and Canadian masters but also ancient artifacts from Egypt, Greece, Rome and the Far East, Islamic art and works from Africa and Oceania. The Old Masters collection has paintings from the Middle Ages stretching through the Renaissance and classical eras up to contemporary works. Exhibitions change but some great painters (such as Rembrandt, Picasso or Matisse) and sculptors (Henry Moore, Alberto Giacometti or Alexander Calder) are always on display. Researchers can consult 50,000 books and hundreds of periodicals on the visual arts. The building is an attraction in itself, a minimalist space with classical columns.

The classical pavilion is accessible via an underground tunnel and houses the

Musée des Arts Décoratifs (Map pp310–11), with works and handicrafts from some of the world's most influential designers. The eclectic collection includes glass vases, Victorian chests, home appliances and an Inuit gallery as well as sections on industrial and graphic design. After 5pm Wednesday entry for adults is half price. Regular English tours are given on various subjects. Call ahead for the schedule.

MUSÉE MCCORD Map pp310-11

☎ 398-7100; www.mccord-museum.qc.ca; 690 rue Sherbrooke Ouest; adult/child/student/senior $12/4/6/9; ⏰ 10am-6pm Tue-Fri, 10am-5pm Sat & Sun; Ⓜ McGill
With hardly an inch to spare in its cramped but welcoming galleries, the McCord Museum of Canadian History houses nearly a million artifacts and documents illustrating Canada's social, cultural and archaeological history from the 18th century to present day.

The eclectic collection has large sections on Canada's earliest European settlement and the history of Québec's indigenous people; other display highlights include embroidered gowns, toys, prints and First Nations' works. Sunday workshops (2pm) are geared toward children.

One notable highlight is the **Notman Photographic Archives**, regarded as one of the finest composite works of photojournalism in Canada. William Notman and his sons captured hundreds of thousands of images from 1850 to 1930. The museum ran a special exhibit comparing views of Montréal a century apart, and many hundreds of his other shots remain on display. Another exhibit focused on Montrealers of Scottish descent (such as James McGill, founder of McGill University) who steered the city's business, finance and industry in the 19th century.

The 2nd-floor gallery entitled 'Turning Point: Québec 1900' neatly encapsulates French-Canadian history in Québec. There's a gift shop with quality gifts and books, a documentation center and tearoom. Admission is free 10am to noon on the first Saturday of each month.

MUSÉE REDPATH Map pp310-11

☎ 398-4086; 859 rue Sherbrooke Ouest, McGill University; admission free; ⏰ 9am-5pm Mon-Thu, 1-5pm Sun; Ⓜ McGill
A Victorian spirit of discovery pervades this old natural history museum, though you

won't find anything more gruesome than stuffed animals from the Laurentians hinterland. The Redpath Museum houses a large variety of specimens including a life-sized dinosaur skeleton and seashells donated from around the world. A highlight is the 3rd-floor **Ethnology Gallery**, which traces the beginnings of mankind. It includes Egyptian mummies, shrunken heads, and artifacts from ancient Mediterranean, African and East Asian communities. There's also a section of minerals named after McGill scientists. In winter it's also open Friday.

PLACE VILLE-MARIE Map pp310-11
1 Place Ville-Marie; Ⓜ McGill
Known for its rotating rooftop beacon that illuminates downtown at night, the Place Ville-Marie tower marked the beginning of Montréal's **underground city** (p86) over four decades ago. Its cruciform shape was chosen to commemorate Maisonneuve's planting of a great cross on Mont Royal in 1642. The 42-story skyscraper is home to high-powered offices as well as a chic rooftop bar, **Club 737** (p159). The intriguing fountain in the forecourt is called Feminine Landscape (1972) by Toronto artist Gerald Gladstone.

REID WILSON HOUSE Map pp310-11
1187 rue Sherbrooke Ouest; Ⓜ Peel
This is one of Montréal's finest old mansions, built in 1902 with an old coach house out back and an attached conservatory, rare features amongst the remaining Golden Square Mile homes. Architecture buffs will have a good time here picking out the Gothic, Italian and Romanesque Revival elements.

CHINATOWN
Eating p133

Despite its diminutive size, Montréal's Chinatown percolates with energy that emanates from its nucleus at boul St-Laurent south of boul René-Lévesque and rue de la Gauchetière. These thoroughfares are packed with eateries, shops, knick-knack stalls and Taiwanese bubble-tea parlors. Over 36,000 Montrealers are of Chinese origin, and Chinatown is a popular pit stop both for them and residents of other backgrounds looking for unique shopping and low-priced produce.

The Chinese Catholic church **Église St-Esprit** (Map p314), near the corner of rue de la Gauchetière and rue Jeanne-Mance, serves the Chinese Catholic community with services in Mandarin and Cantonese. The two gold-leaf **ceremonial gates**, one on boul St-Laurent at boul René-Lévesque and the other at rue Viger, were gifts from the city of Shanghai.

MONTRÉAL AGAINST THE GRAIN

It's hard to imagine that there could still be a part of Montréal that hasn't been picked over with a fine-toothed comb and written about at length. But there are plenty of memorable experiences to be had all over town if you are looking for them.

Referred to as 'Parc-Ex' by locals, talk has been percolating for years that **Parc-Extension** is the next big thing and it's just a matter of time before it becomes, if not another Plateau, then at least heir apparent to the artsy mantel Mile End is sporting today. It hasn't actually happened yet, but there are still plenty of well-kept secrets in this neighborhood, from shops to eats, that locals from elsewhere in Montréal don't even know about. To see what's up, take the blue métro line to métro Parc. Parc-Ex is roughly bordered by Parc Jarry, rue Jean-Talon, boul de l'Acadie and boul Crémazie Ouest.

For all the Francophiles among you, the **Université de Montréal** is kind of like the French-speaking Harvard in Canada. Maybe because it's on the mountain far away from downtown and the rest of the student population is downtown at McGill, Concordia and Université du Québec à Montréal, but there are heaps of interesting things going on all the time on this campus that the student grapevine downtown never gets a hold of. There's wonderful DJs working at the campus radio station who've made its home here on 89.3FM one of best places in the city besides *Voir* for keeping track of up-and-coming francophone bands. Being the second biggest French-speaking university in the world, it attracts the best of the best in the French-speaking world and consistently stages wonderful colloquia and public talks by French academics and intellectuals.

Entrance gate to Chinatown

Orientation

The pedestrian mall along rue de la Gauchetière reveals the sights and smells of the district. The active section of the Chinatown district is only six blocks long and three blocks wide.

PLACE SUN-YAT-SEN Map p314

cnr rue de la Gauchetière & rue Clark

Dedicated to Sun Yat Sen, the ideological father of modern China, this small square was opened in 1988. The space was later refashioned by eight Shanghaiese craftsmen who used traditional methods and materials. The mural on the north and east walls is made of grey slate. There's a

TRANSPORTATION TO CHINATOWN

Car Drive and park on the street.
Métro Place-d'Armes.
Bus 55 runs along boul St-Laurent.

small concrete stage for performances and a pavilion from which souvenirs or knick knacks are sold. On any given day here you will find old timers sitting on stone stools together laughing and gossiping in Cantonese while a handful of Falun Gong demonstrators hand out their literature nearby.

QUARTIER LATIN & THE VILLAGE

Eating p134; Shopping p185; Sleeping p198

The Quartier Latin is one of Montréal's great artistic districts. Not only is it vibrant with terrific bars and restaurants, but thousands of students stream here every day to attend the Université du Québec à Montréal making the place pulse with energy around the clock.

After the Université du Montréal was founded in 1893 a number of cultural institutions followed, and the area blossomed as the French bourgeoisie settled into wealthy residences. The district fell out of fashion after the university relocated to a larger campus north of Parc du Mont Royal. Fortunes turned again when the Université du Québec was established in 1969, and the International Jazz Festival provided a further boost in the 1980s.

Gay-friendly doesn't even begin to describe the Village, hub of one of the world's most exuberant gay communities. During the day the streets bustle with workers from the big media firms nearby and people of all persuasions wander rue Ste-Catherine at all hours to take in the bistros, shops and nightlife. August is the most frenetic time as hundreds of thousands of international visitors gather to celebrate **Divers/Cité** (p23), the massive annual Gay Pride parade.

But though its main artery, rue Ste-Catherine, seethes with fun, and condo development is taking off on the side streets, this is not an area without its serious social problems; homelessness is prevalent, panhandlers are on most corners east of métro Berri-UQAM and used syringes are commonly discarded in alleys and residential parking lots.

Orientation

The Quartier Latin is a dwarf among Montréal neighborhoods, little over 1.5km square within the borders of rue Sanguinet, rue Sherbrooke Est, rue St-Hubert and boul René-Lévesque. The spine of the (Gay) Village is rue Ste-Catherine Est and its side streets between rue St-Hubert in the west and ave de Lorimier in the east.

BIBLIOTHÈQUE ET ARCHIVES NATIONALE DU QUÉBEC Map p315

☎ 873-1100, 800-363-9028; 475 boul de Maison-neuve Est; ◷ 10am-10pm Mon-Fri, to 5pm Sat & Sun; Ⓜ Berri-UQAM

Opened in 2005, this stunning building houses both the library and national archives of Québec and has been a success beyond planners' wildest dreams. Originally conceived as a place to receive between 5000 to 6000 people per day, the reality has been that 10,000 to 12,000 Montrealers flocking through its doors each day. The library itself is 33,000 sq meters, connected to the métro and underground city. Since 1968, everything published in Québec (books, brochures, sound recordings, posters) has been deposited here. It also buys historical documents and publications about Québec outside the province or internationally.

CHAPELLE NOTRE-DAME-DE-LOURDES Map p315

☎ 842-4704; 430 rue Ste-Catherine Est Ⓜ Berri-UQAM

Now hidden among the university buildings, this Romanesque gem was built by the Sulpicians in 1876 to cement their influence in Montréal. The chapel was designed by rue St-Denis resident, artist Napoléon Bourassa, whose imaginative frescoes dotted about the interior are regarded as his crowning glory.

TOP FIVE SIGHTS IN QUARTIER LATIN & THE VILLAGE

- Rue Ste-Catherine Est (p96) – alternative vibe with mainstream appeal
- Écomusée du Fier Monde (right) – putting a face on working-class heroes
- Prowling the side streets – every so often you still come across a 19th-century bungalow that's somehow escaped developers
- Église St-Pierre-Apôtre (right) – neoclassical gem with a gay-friendly flock
- Chapelle Notre-Dame-de-Lourdes (above) – story of Sulpician power and divine frescoes

---

TRANSPORTATION TO QUARTIER LATIN & THE VILLAGE

Car Drive and park on the street.
Métro Green Line Berri-UQAM to Papineau.
Bus 30 runs along rue St-Denis.

ÉCOMUSÉE DU FIER MONDE Map p315

☎ 528-8444; 2050 rue Amherst; adult/child $6/4; ◷ 11am-8pm Wed, 9:30am-5pm Thu & Fri, 10:30am-5pm Sat & Sun; Ⓜ Berri-UQAM

This magnificent ex-bathhouse explores the history of Centre-Sud, a former industrial district in Montréal until the 1950s and now part of the Village. The museum's permanent exhibition, *Triumphs and Tragedies of a Working-Class Society*, puts faces on the Industrial Revolution through a series of excellent photos and multimedia displays. The 1927 building is the former Bain Généreux, an Art Deco public bathhouse modeled on one in Paris. Frequent modern art exhibitions are also held here.

ÉGLISE ST-PIERRE-APÔTRE Map p315

☎ 524-3791; 1201 rue de la Visitation; Ⓜ Beaudry

The Church of St Peter the Apostle belonged to the monastery of the Oblate fathers who settled in Montréal in the mid-19th century. The neoclassical church in the Village has a number of fine decorations – flying buttresses, stained glass, statues in Italian marble – but nowadays the house of worship is more renowned for its gay-friendly Sunday services. It also houses the Chapel of Hope, the first chapel in the world consecrated to the memory of victims of AIDS.

MAISON FRÉCHETTE Map p315

306 rue Sherbrooke Est; Ⓜ Sherbrooke

Louis Fréchette, a 19th-century poet, journalist and member of parliament, lived in this striking Second Empire residence just off rue St-Denis. The French actress (and one-time courtesan) Sarah Bernhardt stayed here during her North American tours in the 1890s.

MONT ST-LOUIS Map p315
244 rue Sherbrooke Est; Ⓜ Sherbrooke
This charming greystone was converted to a Christian boys' school. The long, segmented facade is one of the best examples of French Second Empire style, with a mansard roof, arches and pavilions.

RUE STE-CATHERINE EST Map p315
Montréal's embrace of the gay community is tightest along the eastern end of rue Ste-Catherine, a one-time bed of vice and shabby tenements. This strip of restaurants and clubs has been made so presentable that middle-class families mingle with drag queens on the pavements, all hot on the trail of a good time. It's still in the delicious phase, long may it endure, where the alternative goes mainstream without losing its edge or identity.

Enlightened visitors will enjoy the campy, tongue-in-cheek shows at **Mado Cabaret** (p160).

TERRASSE ST-DENIS Map p315
Ⓜ Berri-UQAM
This little street off rue St-Denis was where Montréal's poets and writers met in the early 20th century. It is also nicknamed the 'hill of the Zouaves' for the houses built on the site of Sieur de Montigny, a Papal Zouave or guard.

UNIVERSITÉ DU QUÉBEC À MONTRÉAL Map p315
☎ 596-3000; 405 rue Ste-Catherine Est; Ⓜ Berri-UQAM
The modern, rather generic buildings of Montréal's French-language university are integrated into the cityscape and are linked to the underground city and the Berri-UQAM métro station. The most striking aspect here is the old Gothic steeple of the Église St-Jacques (Map p315), which has been integrated into the university's facade.

OLYMPIC PARK & AROUND
Eating p136

Nestled in the heart of the blue-collar Hochelaga-Maisonneuve district, the Olympic Park and Stadium area is probably the most popular destination for Montréal visitors after the Old Town. If you are planning to take in more than one of this area's sights, there are a number of combo tickets (on sale at the stadium) covering almost every constellation of attraction you can imagine.

Orientation
The Olympic Park is located 3km east of downtown in Parc Maisonneuve, also home to popular attractions like the Jardin Botanique, the Biodôme and the Insectarium. A free shuttle runs between the Biodôme and the Jardin Botanique.

The Château Dufresne stands on the edge of the residential district 150m west of the Olympic Stadium.

BIODÔME Map pp308-9
☎ 868-3000; www.biodome.qc.ca; 4777 ave Pierre-de-Coubertin; adult/child/senior & student $13/6.50/9.50; Ⓨ generally 9am-6pm mid-Jun –Aug, 9am-5pm Sep–mid-Jun; Ⓜ Viau
At this captivating kid-friendly exhibit you can amble through a rainforest, the Arctic Circle, rolling woodlands or along the raw Atlantic oceanfront – all without ever leaving the building. Be sure to dress in layers for the temperature swings.

The four ecosystems house many thousands of animal and plant species; follow the self-guided circuit and you will see

everything. Penguins frolic in the pools a few feet away from groups of goggle-eyed children; the tropical chamber is a cross-section of Amazonia with mischievous little monkeys teasing alligators in the murky waters below. The Gulf of St Lawrence has an underwater observatory where you can watch cod feeding alongside lobsters and sea urchins in the tidal pools. The appearance of the Laurentian Forest varies widely with the seasons, with special habitats for lynx, otters and around 350 bats.

The Biodôme is wildly popular so try to visit during the week, avoiding the middle of the day if possible. Plan two hours to do

THE BIG OWE

Built for the 1976 Olympic Games, Montréal's Olympic Stadium was plagued with difficulties right from the start. A strike by construction workers meant the inclined tower wasn't finished on time – in fact, you can almost ask which Olympics they had in mind as it took another 11 years to complete. The 'Big O' nickname for the huge oval stadium, was redubbed 'The Big Owe' by irate Montrealers.

The 65-ton stadium roof took another two years to complete but never worked properly. Made of Kevlar, the material used in bulletproof vests, the striking orange dome worked like a huge retractable umbrella that opened and closed by the tower cables. It was a sight to behold (if you were so lucky), but winds ripped the 'bulletproof' Kevlar and mechanical glitches led to its permanent closure. In 1998 the umbrella was folded up for good and replaced with a set model that doesn't open. The tower lost its hoist function but remains a great observation deck. The stadium too has required a litany of repairs. In one incident a concrete beam collapsed over horrified spectators during a football game, but no one was injured.

Provincial officials calculate that when the entire stadium is paid off in 2007 the total price tag will be $1.5 billion. It's a bittersweet ending to the saga as nobody in town is making much use of it these days. The city's baseball team the Montréal Expos moved to Washington DC and changed their name to the Capitals in 2005, leaving the stadium empty except for the odd rave or trade show.

it justice. You can bring a packed lunch for the picnic tables or dine in the cafeteria. The gift shop has an excellent choice of stuffed animals, educational games and native art. In summer there are educational day camps for kids.

CHÂTEAU DUFRESNE Map pp308-9

☎ 259-9201; www.chateaudufresne.qc.ca; 2929 ave Jeanne-d'Arc; adult/child/senior $7/3.50/6; ⏱ 10am-5pm Thu-Sun; Ⓜ Pie-IX

Brothers Oscar and Marius Dufresne made their fortunes in shoes and cement manufacturing in the early 20th century. They commissioned this beautiful beaux-arts mansion, along the lines of the Versailles Palace in France, in 1916 and moved in with their families – Oscar on one side and Marius on the other. The interiors are stunning – with tiled marble floors, coffered ceilings in Italian Renaissance style and stained-glass windows – and are open for the public to explore. Italian artist Guido Nincheri was in charge of interior decoration and painted many murals, including one of dainty nymphs in the Petit Salon. Marius' side of the building is furnished in a more masculine style, with a smoking room fitted to look like a Turkish lounge with hookah pipes. The furniture, art and other objects reflect the tastes of Montréal's bourgeoisie of the period, and the building has been declared a national monument.

The frequent temporary exhibits explore all aspects of early-20th-century culture from art to lifestyle.

JARDIN BOTANIQUE Map pp308-9

☎ 872-1400; www.ville.montreal.qc.ca/jardin; 4101 rue Sherbrooke Est; adult/youth aged 5-17/senior & student $10.50/5.50/8; ⏱ 9am-6pm mid-May–early Sep, to 9pm early Sep-Oct, to 5pm Tue-Sun rest of the year; Ⓜ Pie-IX

Montréal's Jardin Botanique is the third-largest in the world after London's Kew Gardens and Berlin's Botanischer Garten. Since its 1931 opening, the garden, some 75 hectares in size, has grown to include tens of thousands of species in 30 thematic gardens, and its wealth of flowering plants is carefully managed to bloom in stages. The rosebeds in particular are a sight in summer. Climate-controlled greenhouses house cacti, banana trees and 700 species of orchid. Bird-watchers should bring their binoculars.

A popular draw is the landscaped Japanese Garden with traditional pavilions, tearoom and art gallery; the bonsai 'forest' is the largest outside Asia. The twinning of Montréal with Shanghai gave impetus to plant a Chinese Garden. The ornamental penjing trees from Hong Kong are up to 100 years old. A Ming dynasty garden is the feature around Lac de Rêve (Dream Lake). In the northern part of the Jardin Botanique you'll find the Maison de l'Arbre (Tree House), a permanent exhibit on life in the 40-hectare arboretum. Displays include the yellow birch, part of Québec's official emblem. The First Nations Garden reveals the bonds between 11 Amerindian and Inuit nations and indigenous plants such as silver birches, maples, Labrador and even tea. The Orchidée Gift Shop in the main building has a wonderful selection including hand-made jewelry and crafts, stuffed animals and beautifully illustrated books.

In fall the Chinese garden dons its most exquisite garb for the popular **Magic of Lanterns** when hundreds of handmade silk lanterns sparkle at dusk (mid-September to early November). Montrealers are devoted to this event and it can feel like it's standing room only even though it's held in a huge garden.

Creepy crawlies get top billing at the bug-shaped **Insectarium**. Most of the 250,000 specimens are mounted but live displays include bees and tarantulas.

The ticket includes the gardens, green-houses and the Insectarium.

OLYMPIC STADIUM Map pp308-9

☎ 252-8687; www.rio.gouv.qc.ca; 4545 ave Pierre-de-Coubertin; tower adult/child/senior & student $14/7/10.50; ⏰ 9am-7pm mid-Jun–Labor Day, to 5pm rest of the year, closed for maintenance Jan–mid-Feb; Ⓜ Viau

The Stade Olympique seats 56,000 and re-mains an architectural marvel though these days it hosts mostly concerts and trade shows and only rarely hosts sports events.

The best thing to do is take the bilevel cable car up the **Montréal Tower** (Tour de Montréal, also called the Olympic Tower) that lords over the stadium. It's the world's tallest inclined structure (190m at a 45° angle), making it a whisper taller than the Washington Monument. The glassed-in ob-servation deck (with bar and rest area) isn't for the faint of heart but affords a bird's-eye view of the city. In the distance you'll see the pointy modern towers of the **Olympic Village**, where athletes stayed in 1976.

The **Centre Aquatique** (p173) is the Olympic swimming complex with six pools, diving towers and a 20m-deep scuba pool.

The **Tourist Hall** is a three-story informa-tion center with a ticket office, restaurant and souvenir shop, as well as the cable-car boarding station. There's regular English-language tours from 10am in spring and summer, and five tours a day starting at 11am in fall and winter.

PARC MAISONNEUVE Map pp308-9

4601 rue Sherbrooke Est; Ⓜ Viau

Once an 18-hole golf course, this vast green space next to the Jardin Botanique doesn't have much to look at but is pleasant for an extended walk or picnic. Golf can be played nearby at the nine-hole course adjoining the **Olympic Park** (p96).

PLATEAU DU MONT-ROYAL

Eating p137; Shopping p186; Sleeping p201

There's no other neighborhood in the city that captures Montrealers' imagination the way the Plateau does. Writers set their novels in it, Québec directors make it the backdrop for many of their films and most Montrealers would kill for a Plateau address. If you were to judge just by popular culture you'd be forgiven for thinking there was little else to Montréal beside it. Though you'll encounter streams of 'Plateau backlash' from locals, the fact is it's an extra-ordinary area to explore and you'll feel it as soon as you step within its boundaries.

There's a tremendous mix of people, several major streets each with their own special char-acter, restaurants and boutiques and the quintessential Plateau fingerprint, ornate wrought-iron balconies, pointy Victorian roofs and winding exterior staircases climbing up the front of multicolored residential dwellings.

Originally a working-class neighborhood, in the 1960s and '70s the Plateau became the place where writers, singers and all manner of artists lived. The district was made famous by play-wright Michel Tremblay who took an unvarnished look at some of its more colorful residents. Pockets of the district were famously poor. But over the past decade or so a quarter that used to be prone to barricading its buildings has become the most coveted neighborhood in town.

Orientation

The main drags are boul St-Laurent ('The Main'), rue St-Denis and ave du Mont-Royal, with an unbelievable wealth of sidewalk cafés, restaurants, clubs and boutiques. The streets of rue Prince-Arthur and ave Duluth are alive with bring-your-own-wine eateries. The district is bordered roughly by boul St-Joseph to the north and rue Sherbrooke Est to the south, ave du Parc to the west and ave de Lorimier to the east.

TOP FIVE SPOTS IN THE PLATEAU

- Ave du Mont-Royal (below) – hub of hipwear and dumpster chic
- Boul St-Laurent (below) – 'the Main' has been cruise central for over a century
- Parc LaFontaine (p100) – green lung with a sense of drama
- Rue St-Denis (p100) – cool boutiques and comfy cafés
- Carré St-Louis (right) – assess the Second Empire from an oasis of calm

ARMOURY OF THE MOUNT ROYAL FUSILIERS Map pp316-17

☎ 283-7444; 3721 ave Henri-Julien; Ⓜ Sherbrooke
The former munitions depot of this Canadian Black Watch regiment is a miniature château complete with steel turrets and battlements. Today it's an administrative center and a museum of old military gear, but you'll be hard-pressed to find it open.

AVE CHÂTEAUBRIAND Map pp316-17

This shady little lane is a classic story of Plateau renovation. Until the early 1990s this was one of the Plateau's poorer streets where residents painted murals on the facades to disguise the deterioration. The murals have long since gone and in their place have emerged colorful homes with trim little gardens and potted plants hanging under the windows.

AVE DU MONT-ROYAL Map pp316-17

Ⓜ Mont-Royal
Old-fashioned five-and-dime stores rub shoulders with a growing number of trendy restaurants and fashion boutiques on ave du Mont-Royal. The nightlife here has surged to the point that it rivals boul St-Laurent, with bars and nightclubs ranging from the sedate to uproarious. Intimate shops, secondhand stores and ultramodern boutiques offer the latest in urban chic.

BOUL ST-LAURENT Map pp316-17

Also known as 'the Main,' boul St-Laurent is such a figurative and literal part of Montréal it would take this whole book to do it justice. A dividing line between the city's east and west, the Main has always been a focus of action, a gathering place for people of many languages and backgrounds. In 1996

it was declared a national historic site, for its role as ground zero for so many Canadian immigrants and future Montrealers. The label 'the Main' or 'Rue Principale' has stuck in the local lingo since the 19th century. By 2007, St-Laurent will also be in the middle of phase two of its multimillion dollar face-lift which will see $25 million hit the streets to plant trees and widen sidewalks amongst a host of other improvements. Today it's a gateway into the Plateau and the epitome of Montréal urban chic – the city's most glamorous clubs, bars and restaurants are found at its southern end, above rue Sherbrooke.

If you have the time, consider devoting a whole day to exploring this street. Starting at the southernmost end and working your way up will lead you on a self-guided tour through some of the most vivid examples of Montréal's many sides, including the seedy, the überly slick and trendy and the artsy. If you time it right you'll end up in Little Italy in time for dinner. By the end of your boul St-Laurent jaunt, you'll be that much closer to feeling what really makes Montréal tick.

CARRÉ ST-LOUIS Map pp316-17

cnr rue St-Denis & rue Prince-Arthur; Ⓜ Sherbrooke
This lovely green space with a three-tiered fountain is flanked by beautiful rows of Second Empire homes. In the 19th century a reservoir here was filled, and a neighborhood emerged for well-to-do French families. Artists and poets gathered in the area back then, and creative types like filmmakers and fashion designers now occupy houses in the streets nearby. Students loll on the grass, taking in precious rays and street music; while others linger puffing on strange smokes.

Carré St-Louis feeds west into rue Prince-Arthur, a center of 1960s hippie culture that has refashioned itself as a popular restaurant-and-bar strip.

ÉGLISE ST-JEAN-BAPTISTE Map pp316-17

309 rue Rachel Est, off rue St-Denis; Ⓜ Mont-Royal
Dedicated to St John the Baptist, the patron saint of French-Canadians, this church was the hub of working-class Catholic families in the late 19th and early 20th centuries. Plateau residents weren't rich but they channeled large sums of money into the colorful interior, especially after two disastrous fires. The altar is white imported marble, the chancel canopy is in pink marble and there are two Casavant

organs. The acoustics are splendid and the church plays host to numerous classical concerts throughout the year.

INSTITUT DES SOURDES-MUETTES
Map pp316–17

☎ 284-2581; 3600 rue Berri; Ⓜ Sherbrooke

The little silver-plated cupola of the Deaf and Dumb Institute has reigned over the Plateau since 1900. An earlier building was built on clay, a problem typical to the area, and the soft ground gave way. The architects didn't take any chances the second time around and the newer version sits on 1700 stakes and a concrete slab two feet deep. The building still houses a private communications institute for the deaf along with other offices.

PALESTRE NATIONALE Map pp316–17
840 rue Cherrier; Ⓜ Sherbrooke

The neobaroque National Palace (1916) was formerly a sports center for local youth, drawing crowds to amateur athletic events in the 1980s. Note the horn-of-plenty motif above the portico. It now houses the university dance troupe **Agora de la Danse** (p165).

PARC DU PORTUGAL Map pp316–17
cnr boul St-Laurent & rue Marie-Anne

This quaint little park dedicated to Portuguese immigrants was spruced up in 2003, the 50th anniversary of the official founding of the Portuguese community in Montréal. At the rear of the park, next to the little summer pavilion, a plaque reads in translation: 'We arrived in this area seeking a new life and ample horizons.' The gates and fountain are covered with colorful glazed tiles.

PARC LAFONTAINE Map pp316–17
cnr rue Sherbrooke Est & ave du Parc LaFontaine;
Ⓜ Sherbrooke

This great leafy municipal park is the city's third largest after Parc du Mont Royal and Parc Maisonneuve. In the warmer months weary urbanites flock to leafy LaFontaine to enjoy the walking and bicycle paths, the attractive ponds and the general air of relaxation that pervades the park. The view down the steep banks from ave du Parc LaFontaine is stunning, especially if the fountains are in play. You can rent paddleboats in the summer and ice skate in winter. The open-air **Théâtre de Verdure** (p164) draws a relaxed crowd on summer evenings.

House in Carré Saint-Louis (p99)

PLACE ROY Map pp316–17
cnr rue Roy Est & rue St-André; Ⓜ Sherbrooke

Travelers in particular will identify with artist Michel Goulet's vision for this square. A giant stone map of the world sits in the centre, with water trickling alongside the continents, a symbol for getting out and exploring the world and what goes on in it. Goulet finished off the square by scattering several bronze chairs of all different types all over the pavement. Each one faces a different direction to express openness to new ideas. This is a wonderful place for pause in a quiet, sleepy corner of the Plateau.

RUE ST-DENIS Map pp316–17
The backbone of Montréal's francophone shopping district, rue St-Denis is lined with hat and garment shops, über-hip record stores and terrace cafés designed to keep people from getting any work done. It's a terrific place for browsing and seeing charming **old buildings** (p119). Summers here are spectacular when the street and every restaurant, café and bar on it positively groan with people.

TRANSPORTATION TO THE PLATEAU

Car You can drive and park on the street.
Métro Orange Line stations from Sherbrooke to Laurier.
Bus 55 runs along boul St-Laurent; 30 along rue St-Denis.

HIGH TIMES IN THE PLATEAU

The head of Québec's pro-cannabis party was all smiles as he cut a red, black and green ribbon opening Montréal's first marijuana café. 'It's time to stop the persecution,' Bloc Pot leader Hugo St-Onge said at the time.

The café, dubbed Chez Marijane, on rue Rachel Est did not sell pot but people can bring their own smokes. Police made several arrests of people found in possession, but smokers just continued given their extra-relaxed mood.

The then Liberal prime minister of Canada also began discussing the decriminalization of small amounts of marijuana: it would net a fine but no criminal record. However, an unrelated political scandal erupted and early elections were called and all things pot were put way on the backburner. The election brought Stephen Harper's Conservatives to power. Harper nixed the Liberal proposal for good, voiced his support for tougher sentences for pot producers and stopped government subventions for research into medical marijuana use.

So, so much for that. Pot is still very much illegal in Canada though the sweet smell has become a familiar odor on Montréal streets, and not just in the scuffed-chic areas of the Plateau.

LITTLE ITALY

Eating p141; Shopping p187

Italians are the third-largest ethnic group in Montréal after the French and British and many of them have been here just as long. Many families settled in the late 19th century and after WWII. Stroll through this neighborhood and you'll encounter a riot of dialects as businessmen lunch, seniors loll on balconies or in parks and Italian pop music flows from trattorias.

The zest and flavor of the old country find their way into this lively district where the espresso seems stiffer, the pasta sauce thicker and the chefs plumper. Italian football games seem to be broadcast straight onto boul St-Laurent, where the green-white-red flag is proudly displayed. Drink in the atmosphere on a stroll and don't miss the Marché Jean-Talon, always humming with activity.

Orientation

The main arteries are boul St-Laurent, with its row of restaurants, shops and cafés, and rue Dante. Tiny, manicured Parc Martel is the main square but it's dwarfed by Marché Jean-Talon, where almost everyone converges. The whole district is less than 1 sq km around and easily walkable.

TRANSPORTATION TO LITTLE ITALY

Car You can drive and park on the street.
Métro Jean-Talon or De Castelnau.
Bus 55 runs along boul St-Laurent.

ÉGLISE MADONNA DELLA DIFESA
Map p318

6800 ave Henri-Julien; Ⓜ **Jean-Talon**

Our Lady of Protection Church was built in 1919 according to the drawings of Florence-born Guido Nincheri (1885–1973), who spent the next two decades working on the decor of the Roman-Byzantine structure. The artist painted the church's remarkable **frescoes**, including one of Mussolini on horseback with a bevy of generals in the background. The work honored the formal recognition by Rome of the pope's sovereignty over Vatican City in 1929 and was unveiled a few years later as Hitler came to power. During WWII, Nincheri and others who had worked on the building were interned by the Canadian authorities. The fresco, still controversial, can be viewed above the high marble altar.

MARCHÉ JEAN-TALON Map p318

☎ 277-1588; 7075 ave Casgrain; ⏰ 7am-8pm Mon-Fri, 7am-6pm Sat & Sun; Ⓜ Jean-Talon

The pride of Little Italy, this huge covered market is Montréal's most diverse. Many chefs buy ingredients for their menus here or in the specialty food shops nearby. Three long covered aisles are packed with merchants selling fruit, vegetables and flowers as well as baked goods. The market is flanked by delis and café-restaurants with tiny patios. Even in winter the market is open under big tents.

Be sure to stop by the **Marché des Saveurs**, one of the few large stores in town devoted entirely to Québec specialties like wine and cider, fresh cheeses, smoked meats, preserves and a huge number of tasteful gifts.

MILE END

Eating p142; Shopping p187

Is Mile End the new Plateau? For good or for bad, things are shaping up that way. This area is just brimming with cool cafés, innovative shops, the best bagels in town and even better, a terrific community atmosphere that gentrification on the Plateau killed a long time ago. Mile End is a fascinating area where a large, established Hasidic community (that also overflows into neighboring Outremont) lives comfortably among Italians, Portuguese, Greeks, anglophones and francophones. There's not much in the way of formal sights but this is still a terrific place to spend an afternoon just walking around. The best way to tour this area is with one of Mordecai Richler's (p48) novels in your hand. *The Apprenticeship of Duddy Kravitz* (1959) or *The Street* (1969) are good places to start.

Orientation

Mile End is bordered roughly by boul St-Joseph to the south, ave Henri-Julien to the east, ave du Parc to the west and rue Bernard to the north. The main strips for bars, cafés and restaurants are ave Fairmount and ave St-Viateur (all running east–west) as well as ave du Parc (north–south).

ST MICHAEL'S & ST ANTHONY'S CHURCH Map p318

5580 rue St-Urbain; Ⓜ Rosemont

This Byzantine-style church positively dominates its corner of St-Urbain and St-Viateur. Its dome and soaring turret make it one of the more unique examples of church architecture in Montréal. Completed by 1915, it has since mainly served the Irish and Polish Catholic communities.

TRANSPORTATION TO MILE END

Car You can drive and park on the street.
Métro Laurier
Bus 55 runs along boul St-Laurent.

OUTREMONT

What Westmount is to rich anglophones, Outremont is to rich francophones. This area is thin on formal sights but is gifted with upscale dining and boutiques selling things like $200 ties or $400 bras. Heading north and northwest of rue Bernard, real-estate groupies will be rewarded with streets chock-full of fabulous old mansions and mammoth family homes along quiet, leafy green streets. There is a significant Hasidic community in Outremont though most of the synagogues and community centers are in neighboring Mile End.

Orientation

Outremont is bordered by Parc du Mont Royal to the west, ave du Parc to the east, boul St-Joseph to the south and ave Van Horne to the north. The two most interesting streets for travelers for boutiques, browsing and eating are ave Laurier Ouest and rue Bernard Ouest.

ÉGLISE ST-VIATEUR Map p318

cnr ave Laurier & ave Bloomfield; Ⓜ St Laurier, then bus 51

If you are already on ave Laurier for the shopping and food, poke your head into this church, opened in 1910. The interior is pure Gothic Revival with ornate paintings, stained glass, hand-crafted cabinets and sculptures by renowned Montréal artists; the impressive ceiling vaults depict the life of St Viateur. Funeral services for former prime minister Pierre Trudeau were held here in 2000.

TRANSPORTATION TO OUTREMONT

Car You can drive and park on the street.
Métro Outremont

PARC DU MONT-ROYAL AREA

Contrary to what people may try to tell you, this place is *not* an extinct volcano. Rather, Parc du Mont Royal is a hangover from when magma penetrated the earth's crust millions of years ago. A kind of ultrasuper erosion-proof rock was formed, so while time and the elements were wearing down the ground around it, the 232m-high hunk of rock, that locals affectionately refer to as 'the Mountain,' stood firm. Today, the leafy, masterfully planned Parc du Mont Royal affords terrific views of the city and teems with nature-lovers in all seasons. On the north side of the park lie two enormous cemeteries, Cimetière Notre-Dame-des-Neiges (Catholic) and the Cimetière Mont Royal (Protestant and nondenominational), and both have plenty of stories to tell.

Orientation

The Mont Royal area sits between downtown to the south and the Plateau to the east. It's contained within the oval marked by ave de Pins Ouest to the south, chemin de la Côte-des-Neiges to the west, chemin de la Côte-Ste-Catherine to the north and ave du Parc to the east.

BELVÉDÉRE CAMILLIEN-HOUDE

Map pp308-9

voie Camillien-Houde; Ⓜ Mont-Royal, 🚌 11

This is the most popular lookout on Mont Royal thanks to its accessibility and large parking lot. It's a magnet for couples once night falls, making it near impossible on summer nights to find a parking space.

You can walk to Belvédère Chalet about half an hour away. To get to this lookout take the stairs that lead from the parking lot. There's also a quick alternative: after the first set of stairs turn left and walk a few meters to an unofficial lookout point. The protruding boulder gives a fantastic panorama free of guard rails.

CHALET DU MONT-ROYAL Map pp310-11

stairs up from Redpath crescent; 🕙 seasonal

Constructed in 1932, this grand old white villa complete with bay windows contains canvases inside that depict scenes of Canadian history. Big bands strut their stuff on

the huge balcony in summer, reminiscent of the 1930s. Most people, however, flock here for the spectacular views of downtown from the Kondiaronk lookout nearby. It's about a 20-minute walk from the park entrance on ave de Pins.

CIMETIÈRE NOTRE-DAME-DES-NEIGES Map pp308-9

☎ 735-1361; 4601 ch de la Côte-des-Neiges; 🕙 8am-7pm Apr-Oct, 8am-5pm Nov-Mar; Ⓜ Côte-des-Neiges

More than one million people have found their final resting place here since this Catholic cemetery opened in 1854, replacing the old one at Dominion Square downtown. It has a fascinating bunch of mausoleums that emit solemn music including that of Marguerite Bourgeoys, a nun and teacher who was beatified in 1982 (see Chapelle Notre-Dame-de-Bonsecours, p74). The catalog of permanent guests includes 20 Montréal mayors, several ex-passengers of the *Titanic*

TOHU: THE WORLD'S ONLY GARBAGE-POWERED CIRCUS CITY

If you decide to take a jaunt to Montréal's circus mecca in its working class St-Michel district be prepared to be wowed. This innovative complex, named TOHU (which comes from the French expression *tohu-bohu*, for a hustle and bustle), includes an arena designed only with the circus arts in mind, the Cirque du Soleil's international headquarters and artists' residence and the National Circus School. Moreover, it was built on the sight of North America's second-largest waste dump and the whole complex is now powered completely by methane gas from the landfill garbage beneath it.

The 192 hectares started out as a limestone quarry before being turned into a landfill. By the end of the 1980s it was receiving about a million tons of waste a year. The whole kit and caboodle was taken over by the city in 1988 and one of Montréal's most exciting rehabilitation projects was in the works soon afterwards.

TOHU, rather than being imposed on the neighborhood, has made a real effort to be part of it. Priority is given to residents of St-Michel for jobs and TOHU has already won numerous environmental prizes.

and Calixa Lavallée, the composer of *O Canada*. The cemetery office (Map pp308–9; ⏱ 8:30am-4:30pm Mon-Fri, 9am-4pm Sat) has brochures for self-guided tours around the tombs but there's also a map posted at the entrance.

CIMETIÈRE MONT ROYAL Map pp308-9
☎ 279-7358; 1297 ch de la Forêt; ⏱ 10am-6pm; Ⓜ Édouard-Montpetit

Much smaller than Notre-Dame-des-Neiges, this cemetery was founded in 1852 for the last journey of non-Catholic Montrealers – Presbyterians, Anglicans, Unitarians, Baptists and nondenominationals. The most famous tomb is of Anna Leonowens, the inspiration for the heroine in the musical *The King and I*. The cemetery is laid out like a landscape garden and is perfect for the Goth-historically interested.

CROIX DU MONT-ROYAL Map pp310-11
About 1km northeast of the Chalet lookout stands the Mont Royal Cross, one of Montréal's most familiar landmarks. One-hundred-and-two feet tall and made of reinforced steel, the cross was erected in 1924 on the very spot where Maisonneuve planted a wooden cross as a tribute to the French king. The white illuminated cross is visible from anywhere downtown. Purple light signifies a pope's passing. In the past, it's been turned red in recognition of an AIDS march, and blue in recognition of St-Jean-Baptiste Day.

LAC DES CASTORS Map pp310-11
Created in a former marsh as part of a work-creation project, Beaver Lake is a center of activity year-round. You can rent paddleboats on the lake or, in winter, ice skates and sleds from the pavilion, and refreshments are sold in summer. The slopes above are served by a ski lift when it snows.

MAISON SMITH Map pp310-11
voie Camillien-Houde; ⏱ 9am-5pm Mon-Fri, 10am-6pm Sat & Sun; 🚌 11

Constructed in 1858 by a merchant who wanted to get away from the pollution and overpopulation of the rest of Montréal, this house was one of 16 private properties on the Mountain that were expropriated by the government in 1869 once the land was officially designated for a park. The building has gone though several incarnations including

---

TRANSPORTATION TO MONT ROYAL

Car You can drive most of the way and park your car in a paid lot.
Métro Mont-Royal and transfer to bus.
Bus 11 runs through the park and stops near the Belvédère Camillien-Houde.
Foot From downtown, you can walk via the staircase at the top of rue Peel, or from the George Étienne-Cartier monument, on ave du Parc, to the east.
Calèche Horse-drawn buggies (per hr $75).

art center and police station. These days it's been spiffed up with a small exhibition on the history of the park, a visitors centre and a café selling soups and sandwiches. There's also a gift shop selling bird-watching paraphernalia, maps of the park and souvenirs.

PARC DU MONT-ROYAL Map pp308-9
Montrealers are proud of their 'mountain,' so don't call it a hill as Oscar Wilde did when he visited the city in the 1880s. The charming, leafy expanse of Mont Royal Park is charged for just about any outdoors activity you can dream of. The wooded slopes and grassy meadows have stunning views that make it all the more popular for jogging, picnicking, horseback riding, bicycling and throwing frisbees. Winter brings skating, tobogganing and cross-country skiing. Binoculars are a good idea for the bird-feeders that have been set up along some walking trails.

The park was laid out by Frederick Law Olmsted, the architect of New York's Central Park. The idea came from bourgeois residents in the adjacent Golden Square Mile who fretted about vanishing greenery. Montrealers were horrified when the ice storm of 1998 destroyed thousands of trees but it remains the city's best and biggest park, spread over 100 hectares. Note that walking in the park after sunset isn't such a safe idea.

UNIVERSITÉ DE MONTRÉAL Map pp308-9
☎ 343-6111; 2900 boul Édouard-Montpetit; Ⓜ Université-de-Montréal

This is the second-largest French-language university in the world, after the Sorbonne in Paris. Located on the north side of Mont Royal, it's most recognizable building is an Art Deco tower and pale-yellow brick structure. The university was founded in 1920.

CÔTE-DES-NEIGES & NOTRE-DAME-DE-GRÂCE

The leafy, residential neighborhoods of Côte-des-Neiges and Notre-Dame-de-Grâce are perfect examples of the city's quiet, diverse residential areas.

Côte-des-Neiges (originally Notre-Dame-des-Neiges – Our Lady of the Snows) has always been home to a varied assortment of inhabitants. Even in the 19th century you'd find everyone from upper-class business folk to low-wage tannery workers. The breathtaking Oratoire St-Joseph and campus of the Université de Montréal are the main draws here.

Notre-Dame-de-Grâce (or simply NDG) is a bit of a sleepy district. However, ave Monkland's cafés and restaurants liven up the area, as do the students from Concordia University's Loyola campus and the home-team games held at Loyola's sports facilities. Frequent fires and rebuilding in NDG over the last century have left a hodge-podge of architectural styles. You'll hear a lot more English spoken on these streets than in other Montréal neighborhoods.

> ## TRANSPORTATION TO CÔTE-DES-NEIGES
>
> **Car** You can drive and park on the street.
> **Métro** Côte-des-Neiges

Orientation

Côte-des-Neiges lies off the western slope of Parc du Mont Royal, delineated by ave Devon to the south, ave de Vimy to the east, rue Jean-Talon Ouest to the north and ave Clanranald to the west.

Notre-Dame-de-Grâce lies to the southwest, marked by ave Connaught in the west, chemin de la Côte-St-Luc in the north, rue St-Jacques in the south and in a jagged line along ave Grey to the east.

AVE MONKLAND Map pp308-9

Over the past decade or so ave Monkland (or Monkland Ave) has been transformed, with coffee bars, restaurants and condominiums springing up like mushrooms after a warm rain. Called Monkland Village by anglo real-estate agents, it certainly has a village character as many people walk to the shops from their homes. Among the nightspots here is Ye Olde Orchard Pub (p145), a Celtic pub known for its waiters in kilts.

CONCORDIA UNIVERSITY, LOYOLA CAMPUS Map pp310-11

☎ 848-2424; 7141 rue Sherbrooke Ouest; Ⓜ Vendôme, then bus 105

Concordia's western campus started out as Loyola College, built by Jesuits on melon fields they had bought from the famous Décarie family. Its main building is an impressive Tudor-style structure built in 1913. Loyola Campus fused with downtown's Sir George Williams University in 1974 to form Concordia University. Today, the Loyola campus houses Concordia's journalism, communications and music departments.

HOLOCAUST MEMORIAL CENTRE

Map pp308-9

☎ 345-2605; www.mhmc.ca; 5151 ch de la Côte-Ste-Catherine; adult/student $8/5; Ⓨ 10am-5pm Mon, Tue & Thu, to 9pm Wed, to 3pm Fri, to 4pm Sun; Ⓜ Côte-Ste-Catherine

The Montréal Holocaust Memorial Centre provides a record of Jewish history and culture from pre-WWII Europe and holds seminars, exhibitions and other events. There's also a Jewish library open to the public. The museum is closed on Jewish holidays; call to confirm Friday hours between November and March.

ORATOIRE ST-JOSEPH Map pp308-9

☎ 733-8211; 3800 ch Queen-Mary; admission free; Ⓨ church & votive chapel 6:30am-9:30pm, museum 7am-5pm; Ⓜ Côte-des-Neiges

The gigantic oratory honors St Joseph, Canada's patron saint. The largest shrine ever built in honor of Jesus' father, this Renaissance-style building was completed in 1960 and commands wonderful views of the northern slope of Mont Royal. The oratory dome is visible from anywhere in this part of town.

TRANSPORTATION TO NOTRE-DAME-DE-GRÂCE

Car You can drive and park on the street.
Métro Vendôme
Bus 24 or 105

The oratory is also a tribute to the work of Brother André, the determined monk who first built a little chapel here in 1904. André was said to have healing powers and as word spread, a larger shrine was needed so the church began gathering funds to build one. Rows of discarded crutches and walking sticks in a votive chapel testify to this belief and the shrine is warmed by hundreds of candles. Brother André's heart is on view too. It was stolen by a zealot some years ago but later returned intact. Film buffs will know that scenes of *Jésus of Montréal* were shot along the Way of the Cross outside the oratory.

Religious pilgrims might climb the 300 wooden steps to the oratory on their knees, praying at every step; other visitors take the stone stairs or one of the free shuttle buses from the base parking lot.

There's a small museum dedicated to Brother André, who was beatified in 1982. Free guided tours are given in several languages at 10am and 2pm daily in summer. Sunday afternoons feature organ concerts at 2:30pm.

SAIDYE BRONFMAN CENTRE

Map pp308-9

☎ 739-2301; 5170 ch de la Côte-Ste-Catherine; ⌚ gallery 9am-9pm Mon-Thu, 9am-2pm Fri, 10am-5pm Sun; Ⓜ Côte-Ste-Catherine

There's a tremendous gallery in this performing arts center that focuses on art both by well-known and emerging talent in a variety of mediums and styles. Frequent talks and lectures are also given.

VIEWS OF MONTRÉAL

On the north side of downtown where rue Peel meets ave des Pins is a staircase that leads to **Parc du Mont Royal** (Map pp308-9). At the top of the stairs is the **Chalet lookout** (p103), which affords magnificent views of the city, the St Lawrence River and the rolling hills towards the Eastern Townships.

If your thirst for lookouts still holds, seek out the small park called Parc Summit just to the northwest of Parc du Mont Royal; if you're driving, take rue Guy from the downtown area to chemin de la Côte-des-Neiges and follow the signs for stunning views of the western residential districts.

Other good vantage points for panoramas are the **Montréal Tower** (p98) in Olympic Park, **Club 737** (p159) and **St Joseph's Oratory** (p105).

In **Old Montréal** (Map p314) the **Chapelle Notre-Dame-de-Bonsecours** (Sailors' Church; p74) and the clock tower on the **Quai de l'Horloge** (p81) afford unique views of Parc Jean-Drapeau and the Old Port.

The skyscrapers of downtown never looked better than from the northwest shore of **Île Ste-Hélène** (Map p319), especially at Alexander Calder's towering sculpture *L'Homme* (Map p319) near the ferry docks.

Old Port and Downtown

WESTMOUNT

Westmount's history as a bastion of rich anglos of good British stock is hard to shake. Though many francophones and people of other backgrounds have moved to the area, the name is still loaded, a hangover from the 1970s when if you said you lived in Westmount it meant you were part of the establishment, a red flag to the francophones of the era.

This little municipality, again its own little city after voting to demerge from greater Montréal, has always marched to its own drummer.

The district has a long and colorful history, starting in the 1670s as an outpost of the Catholic order of Sulpicians and growing into a village called Côte St-Antoine. After Canadian Confederation in 1867 the village grew rapidly and the influx of anglophone families led the name to be changed to Westmount in 1895. However, it was only after WWII that this anglo enclave assumed its poshness after some of the most moneyed families of the days, including the likes of the Birks and Bronfmans, decided to settle down in the neighborhood.

Though Westmount is not a place to come for formal sights, the extraordinary variety of 19th-century buildings, many in neo-Tudor or Georgian style, is superb.

Orientation

Westmount is roughly bordered by ave Atwater in the east, autoroute Ville-Marie in the south, ave Devon in the north and ave Claremont in the west. Most sights lie on or near rue Sherbrooke Ouest, the main artery.

TRANSPORTATION TO WESTMOUNT

Car You can drive and park on the street.
Métro Vendôme or Atwater and transfer to bus.
Bus 24 runs along rue Sherbrooke.

WESTMOUNT CITY HALL Map pp308-9
☎ 989-5200; 4333 Côte St-Antoine; ☻ 8:30am-4:30pm; Ⓜ Atwater
The faux medieval towers of Westmount City Hall come as a surprise after the skyscrapers of downtown. This Tudor gatehouse in rough-hewn stone looks like something from an English period drama. A lawn-bowling green as smooth as a billiard table lies to the rear.

WESTMOUNT PARK & LIBRARY
Map pp308-9
☎ 989-5300; 4575 rue Sherbrooke Ouest; ☻ 10am-9pm Mon-Fri, to 5pm Sat & Sun; Ⓜ Atwater
Once swamps then farmland, Westmount Park has developed into one of Montréal's prettiest parks, encompassing a series of pathways, streams and concealed nooks that recall the whimsical nature of English public gardens. The park is used extensively

WESTMOUNT ARCHITECTURE STROLL

Real estate groupies and architecture junkies will find Westmount fascinating and could easily spend a whole day strolling from one street to the next with a stop at one of the rue Sherbrooke Ouest bars, restaurants or cafés between ave Claremont and ave Lansdowne.

Though there is little left of the time when it was just a village made up of farms and a sprinkling of stately homes, several of Westmount's green spaces are actually the grounds of former estates that have been turned into parks.

For the most impressive mansions, you can start at **Westmount Park** and walk **north of rue Sherbrooke Ouest**. The closer you get to Parc du Mont Royal, the bigger and more imposing the houses get, and this is where many of the city's, and indeed the country's, movers and shakers reside, including former prime ministers.

South of rue Sherbrooke Ouest, between ave Greene and ave Lansdowne, there are some wonderful examples of houses from the late 1800s, though many of them have been converted or modified since then. You can often still pick out interesting carvings on the facades and elegant windows that were once such a fixture on residential homes in this area. **Ave Elm** has several two- and three-story residential houses dating from the late 1800s with characteristics like front doors raised far above ground level.

Some of the most impressive houses are along **boul Dorchester** east of ave Greene. There you'll find a clump of almost castlelike greystone residences dating from around 1890. Many of these homes still have their original doors, stained-glass windows and facades decorated with elaborate carvings.

in summer – by families pushing baby carriages, sunbathers around the pond, and kids playing on the swings. The park itself was originally named Westmount Jubilee Park in honor of Queen Victoria's diamond jubilee in 1897. At the western boundary the Westmount Public Library makes a weighty statement with its Romanesque brickwork, leaded glass and plaster details inside and out.

Two fine buildings are attached: the **Westmount Conservatory** (a Victorian greenhouse) and the **Victoria Jubilee Hall** fronted by a beautiful floral clock. Both can be visited during business hours.

WESTMOUNT SQUARE Map pp310-11
cnr ave Wood & boul de Maisonneuve Ouest; Ⓜ Atwater

Architect Ludwig Mies van der Rohe, a disciple of the Bauhaus movement, made a bold statement in 1966 with this black metal-and-glass office-apartment-shopping complex. Van der Rohe originally used marble for the plaza but it was eventually replaced by granite to weather the cold. It is linked to a section of the underground city, and its exclusive stores are frequented by rich Westmounters who are looking for a Hermes scarf or Gucci mini-handbag.

SOUTHWEST MONTRÉAL

This area encompasses many neighborhoods, including Petite-Bourgogne, St-Henri and Pointe-St-Charles. These mainly working-class districts have some worthwhile sights, even though the areas don't make it on many visitors' itineraries. The Canal de Lachine, which weaves through many of them, is lined by a cycling path, making a bike tour (p120) a great way to experience this area's highlights.

Orientation

This section takes in a flotilla of districts including Pointe St-Charles, Verdun and LaSalle – areas all becoming gentrified in Montréal's general sprawl. The rough borders are Old Montréal to the east, the St Lawrence River to the south and west, and the Canal de Lachine to the north.

CANAL DE LACHINE Map pp308-9
The Lachine Canal was built in 1825 as a means of bypassing the treacherous Lachine Rapids on the St Lawrence River. It was closed to shipping in 1970, but the area has been transformed into a 14km-long cycling and pedestrian pathway, with picnic areas and green spaces. Since the canal was reopened for navigation in 2002, flotillas of pleasure and sightseeing boats tootle along its calm waters (p71). The city of Montréal has plans for a marina along the canal near downtown, at the bottom of rue Peel. Condo construction is also springing up like mushrooms near the canal by Atwater Market.

Though the bike path is fantastic, be aware there's been an increase in Lance Armstrong wanna-bes treating the route like their own private training circuit instead of a recreational path that belongs to everybody.

FUR TRADE IN LACHINE NATIONAL HISTORIC SITE Map pp308-9
☎ 637-7433; 1255 boul St-Joseph, borough Lachine; adult/child/senior $4/2/3.50; ⏱ 9:30am-12:30pm & 1-5pm Apr-Oct, Wed-Sun only Oct-Nov; Ⓜ Angrignon

This old stone depot from 1803 is now an engaging little museum telling the story of the fur trade in Canada. The Hudson Bay Co made Lachine the hub of its fur-trading operations because the rapids made further navigation impossible, so business was conducted there. The warehouse contained goods imported from England or made

TRANSPORTATION TO SOUTHWEST MONTRÉAL
Car Drive west along rue Notre-Dame Ouest and park at Marché Atwater.
Métro Lionel-Groulx for the Marché Atwater; Angrignon.
Bus 195 to 12th Ave.
Bicycle From downtown, you can ride the Lachine Canal bicycle path.

THE WEDNESDAY NIGHT SALON

The Wednesday night 'salon' has been a Westmount institution since its inception in the 1980s. An eclectic group of 20 to 30 people gathers in a 19th-century Tudor home for lively exchanges on subjects ranging from astronomy to zoology, with the aid of video clips and internet references. As this is well-heeled Westmount there's a financial and economic angle to the chats.

Bigwigs are an important part of the tradition. Past guests included the managing director of the IMF, a former Québec premier, mayors of Montréal, officials from NAFTA and senior diplomats from around the world. Everything is off the record but weekly summaries are posted at www.wednesday-night.com. It's held every Wednesday without fail – the number of meetings has passed the 1100 mark. A guest moderator stands in when hosts David and Diana Nicholson go on vacation.

Not just anyone can attend, you understand – an introduction by an established 'regular' is the usual way in.

in Montréal awaiting trade. Visitors can view the furs and old trapper's gear, and costumed interpreters show how the bales and canoes were schlepped by the native *voyageurs,* or trappers. The presentation is held throughout the day and kids love it.

A little office display near the Fur Trade site relates the history of the Canal de Lachine, and guided tours are conducted along the canal on request.

This museum has a gorgeous little location, kissing Lac St-Louis, making it lovely to wander the side streets particularly behind the Collège Ste-Anne nunnery and the Hôtel de Ville, both along boul St-Joseph.

MAISON ST-GABRIEL Map pp308-9

☎ 935-8136; www.maisonsaint-gabriel.qc.ca; 2146 Place Dublin; adult/child/student $8/2/4; ⏰ 11am-6pm Tue-Sun late Jun-early Sep, 1-5pm mid-Apr–late Jun & early Sep-early Dec; Ⓜ Charlevoix

This magnificent farmhouse in Pointe St-Charles is one of the finest examples of traditional Québec architecture. The house was bought in 1668 by Marguerite Bourgeoys to house a religious order. Young women, called the *Filles du Roy,* who were sent from Paris to Montréal to find husbands also stayed here. The 17th-century roof of the two-story building is of particular interest for its intricate beam work, one of the few of its kind in North America. The museum has an excellent collection of artifacts going back to the 17th and 18th centuries, with unusual items including sinks made from black stone and a sophisticated water-disposal system. It all gives visitors a wonderful idea of how people *really* lived way back when. It also hosts fantastic temporary exhibits that are also beautifully executed and can cover anything from the history of French schools in North America to the art of making candy in the 1700s.

MOULIN FLEMING Map pp308-9

☎ 367-6439; 9675 boul LaSalle, borough LaSalle; admission free; ⏰ 1-5pm Sat & Sun May-Aug; Ⓜ Angrignon

This restored five-story windmill was built for a Scottish merchant in 1816, and a multimedia exhibit inside covers its two centuries of history. It's a nice diversion if you're out here visiting the other Lachine sites, and a great photo op.

MUSÉE DE LACHINE Map pp308-9

☎ 634-3471; www.lachine.ville.montreal.qc.ca; 110 ch LaSalle; admission free; ⏰ 11:30am-4:30pm Wed-Sun Apr-Dec; Ⓜ Angrignon

Practically right on the Lachine Canal, it's a great bike ride to this museum, also one of the oldest houses in the Montréal region (1669) with shooting holes inserted for defense. Back then Lachine was the last frontier for trappers heading west and the final stop for fur shipments. You can see and smell the old fur-storage building from the original trading days. Adjacent to the museum is a huge waterfront sculpture garden that you can visit anytime from dawn to dusk.

PARC DES RAPIDES Map pp308-9

☎ 367-6540; cnr boul LaSalle & 6e ave; Ⓜ De l'Église

This space on the St Lawrence is the spot to view the Lachine Rapids (and the jet boats that ride them). The park attracts hikers, anglers and cyclists who pedal the riverside trail, and it's a renowned bird sanctuary, with what's said to be Québec's largest heron colony. Information displays relate the history of the rapids and of the old hydroelectric plant on the grounds.

You can rent sailboats and light water craft like windsurfing boards nearby at the l'École de Voile de Lachine (p172).

OUTER DISTRICTS
KAHNAWAKE INDIAN RESERVE
Map pp306-7

The Kahnawake (gon-a-**wok**-ee) Indian Reserve is home to 6000 Mohawks. The best time to visit is the traditional powwow every year on the weekend closest to July 11, the anniversary of the Oka crisis. Over two days you can enjoy a variety of dances performed by indigenous people in traditional costume.

In the summer of 1990 the reserve was the site of a standoff between the Mohawks and the Québec and federal governments in a bitter territorial dispute. Local support of the Mohawks in Oka exploded into a symbolic stand against the mistreatment of First Nations people across the country, and the reverberations are still felt today.

The cultural center (☎ 450-638-0880; ⏱ 8:30am-noon & 1-4pm Mon-Fri) contains an extensive research library relating to the nations of the Iroquois Confederacy. Temporary exhibitions show off work by local Mohawk artists. The permanent display on the reserve and its history was taken down at the time of research, however it will likely be set up again by the time you read this. The St Francis Xavier Church (☎ 450-632-6031; ⏱ 9am-5pm Jun-Sep, 9am-5pm Mon-Fri rest of the year, Sunday mass year-round) was established as a Catholic mission for the natives and has a small museum with drawings and religious artifacts. Sunday Mass at 10:30am is in English but the choir sings in Mohawk.

The largest Iroquois art gallery in the country is in the Five Nations Village (☎ 450-632-1059; rte 138 east; ⏱ 9am-5pm) and you can also take an hour's guided tour (adult/child $10/5; English guides weekends only) of the reserve; kids in particular will enjoy seeing the deer and buffalo that wander the pastures. Traditional dance performances are staged for tour groups and independent travelers can call ahead for the schedule and are welcome to take part.

The reserve is located about 18km southwest of Montréal. By car take route 138 west and cross the St Lawrence River over the Mercier bridge; the reserve is below and to the right, on the riverbank. Then take Hwy 132 and turn off at Old Malone, the main road. You can also take the métro to the Angrignon station and have a taxi pick you up (about $11 one way).

COSMODÔME Map pp306-7
☎ 450-978-3600; www.cosmodome.org; 2150 autoroute des Laurentides; adult/child under 6/student/family $11.50/free/7.50/29.50; ⏱ 10am-5pm late Jun-early Sep, 10am-5pm Tue-Sun & holidays rest of year

You (or your kids) can experience the thrill of space flight in this interactive museum of space and new technologies a half-hour's drive north of Montréal. Exhibits focus on the solar system, satellite communications, teledetection and space travel, and there are mock-ups of rockets, the space shuttle *Endeavor* and planets. A multimedia show, *Reach for the Stars,* simulates space travel with special effects on a 360-degree screen. The center also runs space camps for one to five days for kids aged nine and up in a sort of mini-NASA training.

The center is a 25-minute drive north of downtown Montréal. It's a bit of a push by public transportation, but you can take the métro to Henri-Bourassa station and take bus 60 or 61 from Laval bus station outside (ask to be let out at the Cosmo dôme).

MORGAN ARBORETUM
Map pp306-7

☎ 398-7811; ch des Pins, Ste-Anne-de-Bellevue; adult/child $5/2; ⏱ 9am-4pm

This arboretum holds the country's largest grouping of native trees: fragrant junipers, cedars and yews but also exotic species like ginkgo, cork and yellowwood. There's a wonderful trail map and the area is perfect for a long hike in the woods, strolling through magnolia blossoms or having a family picnic. Spring and fall offer the best colors.

The grounds of the arboretum serve as an educational facility for McGill's MacDonald agricultural school. There's several species of wildlife and reptile as well as a stop for 170 species of wintering or migratory birds, making it a thrill for bird watchers.

In winter, this is a beautiful location for cross-country skiing.

Located about 15km west of Montréal on the western tip of the island, the arboretum can be reached most easily from autoroute 40. Take exit 41 and follow signs for chemin Ste-Marie; at the stop sign at the top of the hill, turn left onto chemin des Pins for the registration office.

MUSÉE FERROVIAIRE CANADIEN

Map pp306-7

☎ 450-632-2410; www.exporail.org; 110 rue St-Pierre (rte 209), St-Constant; adult/child/student/senior $12/6/7/9.50; ⏰ 10am-6pm mid-May–early Sep, 10am-5pm Wed-Sun early Sep-late Oct, 10am-5pm weekends & holidays only Nov-Apr

The Canadian Railway Museum contains more than 150 historic vehicles, ranging from locomotives, steam engines, Old Montréal street cars and passenger cars to snow plows. It's widely acknowledged as one of North America's most outstanding collections. Not particularly well known by Montrealers, this museum gets raves from those who make the trek, especially families, and many claim it's the best museum in the Montréal area.

The aerodynamic steam engine *Dominion of Canada* broke the world's speed record in 1939 by clocking over 200km/h. A special sight is Montréal's famous *Golden Chariot,* an open-air streetcar with tiers of ornate seats and gilt ironwork. Another good exhibit is the school car, a Canadian invention that served the railway towns of northern Ontario: two cars of each teaching train had a kitchen, living area and classroom with 15 desks.

There always seems to be something special going on here, whether it's the miniature railway or street car rides, weather permitting.

By car, take the Pont Champlain from Montréal to autoroute 15, then Hwy 132 at the Châteauguay cutoff to rte 209. It's a 20-minute drive.

PARC NATURE DU CAP ST-JACQUES

Map pp306-7

☎ 280-6871; 20099 boul Gouin Ouest, borough Pierrefonds; admission free; ⏰ 10am-7pm Jun-Aug, 10am-5pm May & Sep-Oct; Ⓟ $5

Arguably the most diverse of Montréal's nature parks, Cap St-Jacques has a huge beach, 27km of trails for hiking and skiing, a farm and even a summer camp. The maple and mixed deciduous forest in the interior is a great patch for a ramble, and in spring a horse-drawn carriage brings visitors to a sugar shack to watch the maple sap boil. On the north shore there's the Eco-Farm, a working farm with two barns and horses, pigs and chickens, as well as a large greenhouse for viewing. Picnic tables abound and a restaurant serves the farm's produce. The beach (adult/child $4.50/3) is a comfortably wide stretch of fine white sand, and the shallow water is wonderful for splashing with kids, but bear in mind it gets as popular as Cape Cod on summer weekends. You can also rent canoes, kayaks and pedalboats.

By car, take autoroute 40 west from Montréal to exit 49 (rue Ste-Marie Ouest), turn north on rue l'Anse-à-l'Orme and continue on to boul Gouin Ouest.

STE-ANNE-DE-BELLEVUE Map pp306-7
Situated on the western tip of Montréal island, this old-fashioned anglo town occupies a wonderful spot at the locks of the Ste-Anne-de-Bellevue Canal, also known as the Becker Dam (1877). The boardwalk is dotted with terrace restaurants and boutiques, and a green space along the canal is wonderful for a stroll.

For a meal with a view try the **Marco Restaurant** (☎ 457-3850; 82 rue Ste-Anne; ☺ lunch & dinner) serving pastas, veal scaloppini and steaks along with popular pizzas for $9 to $18.50. Grab a table overlooking the canal on the raised open-air terrace.

Drive the 20km from Montréal along autoroute 20 west, getting off at exit 39 (Ste-Anne-de-Bellevue) and drive 200m into town, where you can park on the edge of the canal and boardwalk.

ST LAWRENCE SEAWAY Map pp308-9
admission free; ☺ 9am-9:30pm Apr-Dec
This system of locks, canals and dams that opened in 1959 along the St Lawrence River enables oceangoing vessels to sail 3200km inland via the Great Lakes. Across Pont Victoria from the city is an observation tower over the first locks of the system, the St Lambert Locks, where ships are raised/lowered 5m.

From January to March, the locks are closed – they're frozen like the river itself until the spring thaw. The site can be reached by the bike trail on the south shore of the St Lawrence, about 300m southwest of Pont Jacques-Cartier.

Walking & Cycling Tours

Walking & Cycling Tours

OLD MONTRÉAL TOUR

Wigged colonists, top-hatted financiers and scheming spies are just some of the characters you'll run into in Old Montréal. It's a treasure-trove of period sets for visiting film crews and there's an historic building at every turn. You can recall what you've seen in the atmospheric cafés and restaurants of this very walkable district.

The starting point is the **Place d'Armes** (p76) the square where Paul de Chomedey, one of Montréal's early settlers, is believed to have met the Iroquois in battle. On the south side of the square stands the **Vieux Séminaire de St-Sulpice 1** (p78) that was constructed for the Catholic order named the Sulpicians. Just northeast of the Old Seminary is the magnificent **Basilique Notre-Dame 2** (p73), one of Montréal's most famous churches and tourist drawcards.

Still on the square, the **Aldred Building 3** (p76) was designed to emulate the Empire State Building, while the smaller **New York Life Insurance Building 4** (p76), with red Scottish sandstone and a clock tower, was Montréal's first skyscraper.

Rue St-Jacques was known as the Wall Street of Canada until the 1930s. The **Bank of Montréal 5** (p73) is the country's oldest bank, with a grand, colonnaded edifice modeled after the Pantheon in Rome. Heading along rue St-Jacques, note the helmeted women guarding the entrance, and the lions and greenish mermaids on the 2nd floor of the

WALK FACTS

Start/Finish Place d'Armes
Distance 2.5km
Transport Ⓜ Place-d'Armes

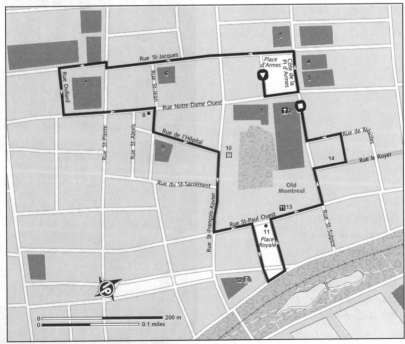

Guardian Insurance Building 6 (p78). The greatest temple of mercantilism around here is the **Royal Bank Building 7** (p78). Peek inside and gasp at a lobby that resembles a Florentine palace.

Our circuit now turns back toward the Old Port. The safes of the **Sun Life Annex & Old Sun Life Building 8** (p77) stored gold reserves of some European countries and the British crown jewels in WWII. On rue de l'Hôpital, dragons and mischievous gargoyles adorn the **Lewis Building 9** (p77) that was built as the head office of the Cunard Shipping Lines.

The magnificent **Montreal Stock Exchange Building 10** (p77) recalls imperial Rome with its stately columns and sumptuous marble interior. It's now home to the **Centaur Theatre** (p162).

Heading south down rue St-François-Xavier leads to rue St-Paul Ouest, where you then make a dogleg right to get to the **Old Customs House 11** (p77) on Place Royale, the square believed to be where the first settlers landed. The house is connected by a tunnel to the **Musée d'Archéologie Pointe-à-Callière 12** (p77), the museum of history and archeology.

Back on rue St-Paul Ouest, consider stopping off at congenial **Le Petit Moulinsart 13** (p127) for mussels or the magnificent cherry beer on draft. The lovely **Cours Le Royer 14** (p75) is a tranquil pedestrian mall with fountains and lush greenery. The passageway on the north side features a stained glass window of Jérôme Le Royer, one of the founders of Montréal.

Continue through the passage to rue de Brésoles and take a left back out onto rue St-Sulpice, where you'll make a right return to Basilique Notre-Dame.

ARTSY MONTRÉAL AMBLE

Art lovers are easily seduced by this city. Sculptures, galleries and art references are absolutely everywhere you look. This walk is a bit of a haul, but will be very much worth it. Start your day at the **Bibliothèque et Archives Nationales du Québec 1** (p95). Head into the main hall but don't go past security to where the books are. Keep moving left and you'll see a flight of stairs heading down into a sunken gallery. It's usually free here and has anything from installations to funky industrial sculpture.

Next, head out and straight ahead to **rue Ste-Catherine Est** and turn west. Here you'll be on the seedy part of the street between the 'party' section in the Village and the swank shopping section further west. There's always interesting graffiti and wall murals by urban artists in this part so keep your eyes peeled (hint: walk on the north side of the street for a better chance of picking one out and look over your shoulder occasionally too!)

When you reach Place des Arts you have a choice. For international and Canadian stars, there's the **Musée d'art Contemporain de Montréal 2** (p89) on your right, or for up and comers there are dozens of galleries for you to check out in the **Belgo building 3** (p182) across the street. Head south down rue Jeanne-Mance, turn right on ave Viger Ouest and you'll arrive at **Place Jean-Paul-Riopelle 4** (p87) named in memory of Canada's most famous contemporary artist. For decades, Riopelle dreamed of having the statue you see here surrounded by a ring of fire but couldn't find any takers. He never lived to see it finally realized here. Next head west on rue St-Antoine Ouest and then south on rue McGill. This is the perfect place to stop for lunch. **Restaurant Holder 5** (p128) is a classic French brasserie and has a terrific wine list. When you're done,

WALK FACTS

Start Bibliothèque et Archives Nationales du Québec
Finish Fonderie Darling
Distance 2.75km
Transport Ⓜ Berri-UQAM

continue down the street and you'll enter Griffintown, the historical center of Montréal's Irish community (p65). Turn west on rue William, nip immediately south on rue King, hang a right on rue Wellington and soon you'll come to the **Fonderie Darling 6** (☎ 392-1554; 745 rue Ottawa; $3, free Thu; ⏰ noon-8pm Wed & Fri-Sun, noon-10pm Thu) an old iron foundry now used as a modern art space. Don't go in yet however. Fonderie Darling owns several outdoor spaces around Griffintown (though not all of them are consistently in use). Look around on this block, up, down, high, low, back and forth and see if you can pick something up. If not, just duck inside for a peek at the spectacular installations and ask the staff. They are usually more than eager to help.

DOWNTOWN TOUR

Skyscrapers give downtown Montréal a distinctly North American feel, but the area is also dotted with historic buildings with plenty of stories to tell. Rue Ste-Catherine and rue Sherbrooke slice through the area in a blaze of trendy boutiques and department stores, and some are attractions in their own right.

Start at **Square Dorchester** (p88), the official center of town. The stern statue on the northeast side is of **Lord Strathcona 1**, a philanthropist who helped to sponsor Canada's efforts in the South African Boer War. Wander south a bit to check out the neglected rendition of **Sir Wilfrid Laurier 2** (1841–1919) one of Canada's most respected prime ministers. The square's historic buildings include the aristocratic rump of the **Windsor Hotel 3** (p88), opened in 1878 and inspired by New York's Waldorf Astoria. The **Dominion Square Building 4** (p88), home to the Centre Infotouriste office, has a plush central hall and carved arches.

WALK FACTS

Start Square Dorchester
Finish Musée des Beaux Arts or Winnie's Pub
Distance 3km
Transport Ⓜ Guy-Concordia

Cross over bustling rue Ste-Catherine Ouest and walk north up rue Metcalfe to the upscale shopping complex **Les Cours Mont Royal 5** (p183). The central atrium features bird sculptures with human heads and a chandelier from a Monte Carlo casino. Just west of the complex you will find the **Seagram House 6** (p88), a faux castle that once housed the distilleries company.

Now you hit the melee of Montréal's busiest shopping street, rue Ste-Catherine Ouest. In the space of a couple of blocks you can snap up New Age hits at **HMV 7** (p182), literary gems at **Chapters 8** (p181), fancy footwear at **Felix Brown 9** (p182) or a drop-dead chic gown at **Nadya Toto 10** (p183).

Up on rue Drummond you'll come to the **Emmanuel Congregation Church 11** (p91), which belongs to the Salvation Army but is located on the grounds of **Maison Alcan 12** (p91) the fancy restored headquarters of the aluminium company Alcan. To view its pretty atrium and rear garden, turn into the little passageway leading to rue Stanley.

Rue Sherbrooke Ouest was Montréal's most prestigious residential street in the early 20th century. The **Mont Royal Club 13** (p92) was founded as an exclusive men's society; the **Louis Joseph Forget House 14** (p91) is a Victorian mansion built for the first francophone chairman of the Montréal Stock Exchange. The adjacent **Reid Wilson House 15** (p93) remains one of Montréal's finest mansions.

The only grand hotel in Montréal to survive the beaux-arts era intact was the **Ritz-Carlton Hotel 16** (p197). Richard Burton and Elizabeth Taylor married each other here for the first time in 1964 and the afternoon tea here is legendary (reservations recommended).

At **Le Château 17** (p91), a fortresslike apartment complex, look closely for vestiges of shell fossils in the brick. Directly opposite, the fancy store with Art Deco motifs is **Holt Renfrew 18** (p182), the official supplier of furs to Queen Elizabeth. One of the area's most imposing churches is the **Erskine & American United Church 19** (p91) a solid neo-Romanesque structure built in the 1890s.

Now you can opt for art or ale. View the fine paintings in the **Musée des Beaux-Arts 20** (p92) or head down rue Crescent for lunch and a tall cool one at **Winnie's Pub 21** (p158).

Skyline view of downtown Montréal from Île Sainte Hélène across the St Lawrence River

QUARTIER LATIN TOUR

Much of the charm of the compact Latin Quarter lies not in official sights but in soaking up the laid-back atmosphere – allow yourself to linger, especially along the café-filled terraces of rue St-Denis.

A few buildings hark back to the area's French and religious roots of the early 19th century. The former boys' school of **Mont St-Louis 1** (p96) is a sober greystone with a mansard roof (now reinvented as an apartment complex), while the **Maison Fréchette 2** (p95) is the former home of Louis Fréchette, a well-known Québec poet of the day. French actor (and courtesan) Sarah Bernhardt stayed in his home during her North American tours in the 1880s and '90s.

Turn right onto rue St-Denis and plunge into the heart of the Quartier Latin. Many festivities are based here such as the popular Just for Laughs (p23) comedy festival. The little side street, **Terrasse St-Denis**, used to be a meeting place of Montréal's bohemian set at the turn of the 20th century. The tangle of alternative shops that lines rue St-Denis includes the quirky **La Capoterie 3** (p185), where you can purchase condoms for any occasion. Heading further south will take you to the former **Bibliothèque Nationale 4**, a branch of the Québec national library – which has now relocated to métro Berri-UQAM (see p95). The library (1914) was originally built for the Catholic order of Sulpicians and is a wonderful blend of beaux-arts and French-renaissance styles – you must step foot inside to admire the

WALK FACTS

Start Mont St-Louis
Finish Place Émelie-Gamelin
Distance 1.5km
Transport Ⓜ Berri-UQAM

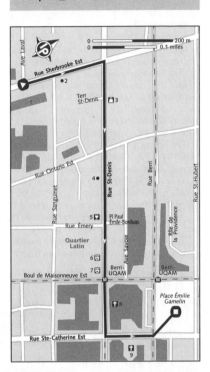

beautiful stained glass windows. Stop awhile for refreshments at brewpub **Les Trois Brasseurs 5** (p155), which opens its ceiling-high windows in summer.

One block south, an important venue for Just for Laughs is the **Théâtre St-Denis 6** (p164), the city's second-largest theater. Next door you can watch robot-activated movies at the **National Film Board 7** (p154), which occupies an ultramodern cinema and production complex.

The modern buildings of the **Université du Québec à Montréal** (p96), or UQAM, have been integrated into the cityscape and are linked to Montréal's underground city. The most striking thing here is the old facade of the **Église St-Jacques 8**, with its magnificent Gothic steeple.

Tucked away in the university premises on rue Ste-Catherine Est, you will find the **Chapelle Notre-Dame de Lourdes 9** (p95), which was commissioned by the Sulpicians in 1876 to secure their influence in this part of town. This Romanesque gem is filled with imaginative frescoes painted by artist Napoléon Bourassa and is regarded as his crowning glory.

From here you could continue your walk to **Place Émilie-Gamelin**, the site of spontaneous concerts, wacky metal sculptures and dozens of punks with their beleagured pets. Further west along rue Ste-Catherine Est is the Gay Village where further exploration of all sorts awaits.

PLATEAU TOUR

The Plateau du Mont-Royal area is best known for its hip bars, cafés and shops but its pretty residential streets, decked with brightly colored townhouses and the trademark Montréal swirling staircases are a treat to explore as well. This area perfectly epitomizes the Montréal success story. It draws an eclectic mix of grunge and chic – one moment it's as comfy as an old shoe, the next sizzling with edgy dynamics. It's also stacked with many points of historical interest.

The starting point for this walk is **Carré St-Louis** (p99) a pleasant, green, shady oasis with a splashing fountain that's a popular spot for lazing and people-watching. It's surrounded by beautiful old houses that were built for wealthy French people in the 19th century. Make sure to check out **the house on the west side of ave Laval 1** where Québec's most revered poet, Émile Nelligan once lived – there is an easy-to-miss-bronze plaque (see boxed text p74). Cut back through the square and head for rue St-Denis, and the immense buildings of the former **Institut des Sourdes-Muettes 2** (p100) – note the little silver cupola. Take a little detour west down ave des Pins Est to see the former **Armoury of the Mount Royal Fusiliers 3** (p99), a cute tin-soldier château with battlements and steel turrets. Continuing north along rue St-Denis, stay on the west side to see the pretty facades of the bars and shops to the east. Note the row of **terraced houses 4** with slate mansards and lantern roofs above the entrances on the northeast corner of ave Duluth Est.

Turn left into rue Rachel Est to see the winged angel on the **Sir George-Étienne-Cartier monument,** way down at the end of the street, site of the fabled **tam-tam concerts** (p149) at the leafy base of Mont Royal.

An interesting hub in the district is in the first few blocks west of rue St-Denis. On the northeast corner of ave Henri-Julien and rue Rachel Est stands the

WALK FACTS

Start Carré St-Louis
Finish Café Cherrier
Distance 3km
Transport Ⓜ Sherbrooke

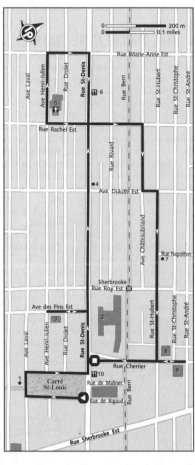

baroque **Église St-Jean Baptiste 5** (p99), with its entrance framed by double columns. Directly opposite stands Les Cours Rachel, which was once a boarding school but has now been earmarked for condos. The houses that stand on ave Henri-Julien are typical of this area's hodge-podge of styles.

Circle back onto rue St-Denis. If you're hungry by now, try **Rockaberry** (6; 4275 rue St-Denis) a place legendary for enormous pieces of pie, before continuing on. Zigzag to the southeast, onto ave Châteaubriand. A symbol of the poor through the 1970s, this cozy narrow street has been spruced up with blue, green and turquoise paint and potted plants hang outside the windows. Here too you'll spot another of this town's signature objects: the external staircase.

Closer to Parc LaFontaine, the neighborhood is visibly wealthier and the homes larger. At the corner of rue St-Hubert and rue Napoléon there's a magnificent **art deco apartment building 7** that's a pleasure to behold. Further along rue St-Hubert, the **École Cherrier (8**; 3655 rue St-Hubert) built in 1931 has the dominant vertical lines of the art deco style, while the nearby **Palestre Nationale 9** built in 1918, is Italian Renaissance – check the classical arch over the entrance. It's now one of Montréal's leading dance theaters, **Agora de la Danse** (p165).

From here you can hop back on the Sherbrooke métro or enjoy a drink on the wraparound terrace of pretty **Café Cherrier 10** (p138) opposite Carré St-Louis.

CANAL DE LACHINE TOUR

The prettiest cycle path in Montréal stretches along the Canal de Lachine and has easy access from downtown and the Old Port. Sunny days are terrific here; people flop on the grass to read and sunbathe, families lunch at picnic tables and the path is packed with cyclists and in-line skaters.

Bits of Montréal's suburban history and a busy outdoor market add to the variety of this tour – perfect for a summer afternoon.

Starting point is the **Canal Locks 1** at the southwestern end of the Old Port. This part of town has an industrial feel thanks to the abandoned **grain silo 2** (p79) just southeast of the locks and the enormous neon sign **Farine Five Roses 3** (see boxed text p79) which crowns a flour mill.

Pedaling southwest along rue de la Commune Ouest you'll pass under autoroute-10 and continue along the downtown side of the canal to where strips of greenery line both sides and the nicest part of the path begins. The path switches sides at the bridge at rue des Seigneurs, where you come to a **former silk mill 4** that ran its operations on hydraulic power from the canal. The red-brick factory has been reborn as lofts – one of many such conversions in prosperous Montréal.

Continue south on rue Shearer and turn right on rue Centre where soon you'll come to the massive, Romanesque **Église St-Charles 5** on your right which is worth a stop to see if there is a garage sale or something else going on. Next push your bike over to the French-style **Église St-Gabriel 6**, pedal on to rue Charlevoix and turn right and you'll come to **Taverne Magnan 7** (p146) on your left, a restaurant that stakes its reputation on excellent roast beef. (Best save this one for the return journey.) Continue on until

CYCLE FACTS

Start/Finish Canal Locks
Distance 7km
Transport Ⓜ Square-Victoria

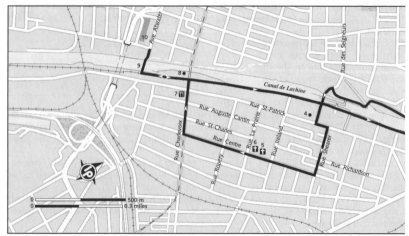

Cycling path in downtown Montréal

you are at the bike path again where you may want to lock up your wheels at the **electric-boat rental 8** (p70) and spend some time cruising on the canal. Afterwards, continue on the bike path and turn right at the **pedestrian bridge 9** to head to the **Marché Atwater 10** (p86), one of the city's absolute best markets. Apart from great produce, there are shops selling quality meats, cheeses and Québec's own maple-syrup whiskey.

If you're keen for more exploring, head west of the market. This is a hard-scrabble working-class area in transformation as condo development mushrooms and you may come across a new pub or trendy gallery when you least expect it.

To head back resume the route north along rue Centre to rue Shearer, where you take a left to rejoin the Canal de Lachine and the trail back to the Old Port.

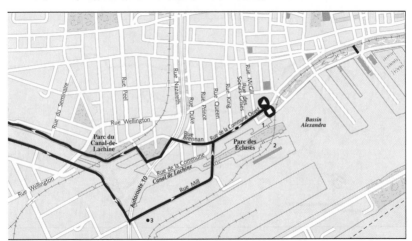

PARC DU MONT-ROYAL TOUR

Many of Montréal's neighborhoods hug the foot of this park making everyone in the city feel a bit like it's their own personal backyard. 'The Mountain,' as Parc du Mont-Royal is affectionately known by locals, is cherished for its winding trails, fresh air and terrific views. It also links the posh homes of the Golden Square Mile with those final destinations to the north, the big municipal cemeteries.

The starting point for this walk is on ave des Pins Ouest at the **staircase 1** into the park. It's a fairly brisk 10- to 15-minute climb that alternates between steps and inclined trail. You cross a large path and continue climbing to the signposted **Chalet Lookout 2** (p106). The lookout offers stunning views of the downtown area, best seen in the early evening when the skyscrapers begin to light up. Nearby the **Chalet du Mont-Royal 3** (p103) contains paintings of some key scenes from Canadian history, but most people turn up here for the truly magnificent view.

From the chalet, walk north along the trail named Chemin Olmsted about 500m to the **Cross of Mont Royal 4** (p104), the Montréal landmark that's illuminated at night. Bird feeders are hung along Chemin Olmstead from November to April making it ideal for bird watchers. Further along you can descend a set of stairs to reach the scenic lookout of **Belvédère Camillien-Houde 5** (p103), one of the most romantic views in the city.

Returning to Chemin Olmsted head south along the leafy paths towards **Maison Smith 6**, an historic building that's been rechristened as an art gallery; exhibitions are usually in the afternoons only. Another 500m further south, the manmade pond **Lac des Castors 7** (p104) is a haven of toy-boat captains in summer and ice-skaters in winter. Refreshments are available at the pavilion, and in warm weather the meadows around the pond are full of sunbathers.

> ## WALK FACTS
>
> **Start/Finish** ave des Pins Ouest, stairs into park
> **Distance** 6km
> **Transport** Ⓜ Peel, then bus 107

To the north you can venture across the wide road called Chemin Remembrance into Montréal's largest cemetery, the very Catholic **Cimetière Notre-Dame-des-Neiges 8** (p103) and its musical mausoleums. The entrance map reveals the plots of the famous departed. The smaller, mainly Protestant **Cimetière Mont-Royal 9** (p104) lies just to the north. Both are on rolling, leafy terrain and ooze Montréal history.

From Lac des Castors you wind your way back northeast to the Chalet lookout and the stairs down towards ave des Pins.

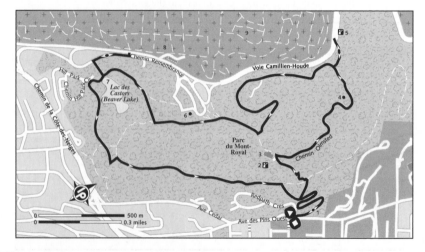

Eating

Eating

Montrealers are die-hard foodies. The city serves up more than 5000 restaurants and counting – that's more per capita than anywhere in North America, except for New York City. There's a mind-whirring assortment of ethnic, American and French cuisines, and it's all mixed together in such different variations that nearly every city block dishes out something exciting and new. Regardless of your budget, there are few places in the world where you can eat so well.

The dining scene took its big bow in March 2006, when *Gourmet* magazine devoted itself to Montréal. This, and the number of tourists still toting the magazine more than a year after its publication, helped solidify Montréal's standing as one of the continent's epicenters for gastronomic tourism.

Downtown and the Plateau are a diner's nirvana, linked by arteries boul St-Laurent and rue St-Denis. 'The Main,' as locals affectionately call boul St-Laurent, teems with trendy establishments but shades into the alternative as you move north. Still in the Plateau, rue Prince-Arthur Est and ave Duluth Est are popular for their good-time BYOW (bring your own wine) places, while in Mile End terrific new and original ethnic restaurants from Indonesian to Brazilian are always popping up.

Québec is also home to great microbrewers such as Boréale, St-Ambroise and Belle Guele; for a doomsday kick, try *Fin du Monde* (End of the World) with 9% alcohol.

Opening Hours & Meal Times

Standard opening hours for restaurants are 11am to 2:30pm (lunch) and 5:30pm to 11pm (dinner). Many places are closed Monday. Breakfast cafés open around 8am (9am on Sundays) and close by late afternoon. On weekends two dinner sittings are common at 5:30pm to 6pm and 8pm to 8:30pm. Places really tend to fill up from 8pm onwards in the francophone tradition.

How Much?

Eating out won't wallop your wallet in Montréal. Midrange places will, on average, charge $15 to $25 for a multicourse meal including a glass of wine. The top end runs upwards of $25; a culinary temple of some renown might charge $60 to $100 or more for a four-course gourmet dinner including wine. Count on $6 to $8 for a glass of drinkable red and $25 to $35 (and over) for a bottle from the house cellar.

PRICE GUIDE	
$$$	over $25 a meal
$$	$15–$25 a meal
$	under $15 a meal

At dinner look for the *table d'hôte,* a fixed-price meal including dessert or coffee that can be an incredible bargain starting around $15. Many restaurants have a policy of *apportez votre vin,* or bring your own wine. Pick up your tipple from an outlet of the government's alcohol retailer, Société des Alcools du Québec (SAQ), or a *dépanneur* (convenience store), from around $10.

Taxes amounting to 15% apply at all restaurants. Most don't include the taxes in their menu prices, but check the fine print.

Booking Tables

Reserve on weekends to avoid disappointment. During the week you needn't book a table unless the place is quite popular (or formal). Note that most budget eateries don't take reservations.

Tipping

A tip of 15% of the pretax bill is customary in restaurants. Some waiters may add a service charge for large parties; in these cases, no tip should be added unless the service was extraordinary. Leave the tip on the table or hand it directly to staff.

Groceries

The largest supermarket chains in Montréal are Provigo and Metro, always well-stocked and open long hours. In the Plateau, the section of boul St-Laurent between ave des Pins and ave Mont-Royal is renowned for its ethnic food shops. Little Italy has a multitude of small groceries and deli shops on boul St-Laurent, a few blocks south of rue Jean Talon.

There are four open-air food markets where farmers, butchers and cheese makers sell their produce directly. Most sites also have indoor sections that stay open all winter.

LE FAUBOURG

Map pp310-11   Food Court

1606 rue Ste-Catherine Ouest; 🕐 **10am-9pm daily;** Ⓜ **Guy-Concordia**

The best food court in the city is here on the third floor. Amongst the smorgasbord of international cuisines are German, Japanese and crepe stands. Keep your eye out for **Restaurant Bangkok** on the third floor for quality Thai food better than in many restaurants – line-ups of around 15 people at lunchtime are common. Also on the third floor try the fabulous Taiwanese stall in the northwest corner as well as **La Maison du Bédouin** for killer Moroccan mint tea served in beautiful silver pots. The Parisian-style multilevel mall-cum-

Sweets for sale at outdoor market Marché Jean-Talon

market also includes fruit vendors, a bakery, a bagel shop, a liquor store and is perfect for a meal or picnic goodies.

MARCHÉ ATWATER

Map pp310-11   Food Market

138 ave Atwater; 🕐 **8am-6pm Mon-Wed, to 8pm Thu, to 9pm Fri, 8am-5pm Sat & Sun;** Ⓜ **Lionel-Groulx**

Located right on the banks of the Canal Lachine, with scores of vendors outside and high-class delicatesans and specialty food shops inside, in the tiled, vaulted hall under the Art-Deco clock tower. Try the **Boucherie Claude & Henri** for beautiful racks of lamb, the bakery **Première Moisson** for baguettes or the astounding **Fromagerie du Marché Atwater**, whose hundreds of cheeses reach from runny triple crèmes to hard goudas.

MARCHÉ MAISONNEUVE

Map pp308-9   Food Market

☎ **937-7754; 4445 rue Ontario Est;** 🕐 **8am-6pm Mon-Wed, Thur, to 8pm Fri, to 5pm Sat & Sun;** Ⓜ **Pie-IX, then bus 139**

About 20 farm stalls, and inside, a dozen vendors of meat, cheese, fresh vegetables, tasty pastries and pastas in a beautiful beaux-arts building (1912–14) in Maisonneuve, girded by pretty gardens.

MARCHÉ JEAN-TALON

Map p318   Food Market

☎ **277-1588; 7075 rue Casgrain;** 🕐 **7am-8pm Mon-Fri, 7am-6pm Sat & Sun;** Ⓜ **Jean-Talon**

The city's largest market, right in the heart of Little Italy. There are several hundred market stalls on a huge square ringed by shops that stock all matter of produce year-round including fruits, vegetables, potted plants, herbs and (of course) maple syrup.

MARCHÉ ST-JACQUES

Map p315   Food Market

1125 rue Ontario Est; ☽ **8am-6pm;** Ⓜ **Beaudry**
Traditional food and vegetable stalls and shops still occupy their 1931 Art-Deco home, in the northern reach of the Village.

METRO Map p315   Supermarket

☎ **525-5090; 1955 rue Ste-Catherine Est;** ☽ **7:30-2am;** Ⓜ **Papineau**
Cavernous supermarket in the Village that's perfectly situated for picking up late-night snacks and party goods.

MILANO SUPERMARKET

Map p315   Supermarket

☎ **273-8558; 6862 boul St-Laurent;** ☽ **8am-6pm Mon-Fri, 8am-5pm Sat & Sun;** Ⓜ **De Castelnau**
This local institution has a mind-boggling selection of fresh pasta, antipasto and olive oil. The fun here is seeing the old timers do the rounds. Stop, watch, listen, buy what they buy. You'll be on your way to an authentic Italian meal before you know it.

PROVIGO Map pp310-11   Supermarket

☎ **932-3756; 1953 rue Ste-Catherine Ouest;** ☽ **8-2am;** Ⓜ **Guy-Concordia**
They're huge, well stocked and often have elaborate deli counters serving fried chicken and smoked-meat sandwiches. There's another outlet in the **Plateau** (Map pp316–17; ☎ 849-8028; 50 ave du Mont-Royal Ouest).

OLD MONTRÉAL

Vieux-Montréal used to be filled with mediocre food at tourist-oriented (ie expensive) prices. These days you'll find terrific eateries catering to all budgets, many with unforgettable ambience.

TITANIC Map p314   Café $

☎ **849-0894; 445 rue St-Pierre; mains $3.50-7.50;** ☽ **7am-4pm Mon-Fri;** Ⓜ **Square-Victoria**
The sandwiches are what has office workers scurrying to these cramped basement quarters from all over Old Montréal on their lunch breaks. The varieties are endless and can include pepper pâté, smoked mackerel or spicy Calabrese sausage.
Excellent salads, pastas, quiche and antipasto misto are popular takeouts that round out the mix.

CLUNY ARTBAR

Map p314   Mediterranean-Café $$

☎ **866-1213; 257 rue Prince; mains $5-12;** ☽ **8am-5pm Mon-Fri;** Ⓜ **Square-Victoria**
Hyper young chefs dole out ultra-stylish café fare in this renovated factory shared with the Fonderie Darling art space. Tables are made of recycled bowling lanes and consciously grimy beams and pipes hang from the high ceilings. The menu changes daily so try the lunch special, the hot or cold soups or the whopping antipasto plate with a glass of wine. The breakfast menu includes everything from croissants to *huevos rancheros* (a Mexican dish with fried eggs, tortillas and salsa).

BORIS BISTRO Map p314   Bistro $$

☎ **848-9575; 465 rue McGill; mains $5.95-27.95** ☽ **11:30am-midnight Mon-Fri, noon-midnight Sat, Sun;** Ⓜ **Square-Victoria**
You'll be elbowing your way through everyone from Armani-clad executives and disheveled artists to maple syrup-toting tourists in order to get a table at this popular bistro. Once settled, however, dishes range from artfully presented salads to the fantastic duck risotto with mushrooms. Whether you want to eat inside or underneath the high ceilings and exposed heat conductors or in the outdoor courtyard, it's a good idea to reserve ahead during the lunch rush.

CAFÉ ST-PAUL Map p314   Bistro $

☎ **844-7225; 143 rue St-Paul Ouest; mains $6.95-11.95;** ☽ **7am-7pm Mon-Fri, 8.30am-7pm Sat & Sun summer, 9-6pm Mon-Fri, 10-6pm Sat & Sun rest of year;** Ⓜ **Square-Victoria**
With so much hullabaloo in Old Montréal, this is the place visitors stop for a low-key rest from exploring the area or to start their days with breakfast while going over their brochures and guidebooks before heading out. It's got grey, exposed stone walls and understated bare, black and chrome colored tables and chairs. Burgers, salads and bacon and egg breakfasts.

SCOLA PASTA Map p314 — Italian $$

☎ 842-2232; 260 rue Notre-Dame Ouest; mains $8-14; ☷ 11:30am-10pm Mon-Fri, 5:30-10pm Sat; Ⓜ Place-d'Armes

A longtime favorite with office workers. Don't be intimidated by the pushy lunchtime crowds. Grab a tray, get in line, and prepare for mouth-watering daily specials served over the counter by some of the most gregarious cooks in town.

OLIVE + GOURMANDO

Map p314 — Deli/Bakery $

☎ 350-1083; 351 rue St-Paul Ouest; sandwiches from $8.50; ☷ 8am-6pm Tue-Sat; Ⓜ Square-Victoria

Named after the owners' two cats, this bakery/café is legendary in town for its sandwiches and baked goods and is as busy as a train station at rush hour when office workers from all over the Old Town flock here for lunch creating waits of up to 30 minutes for a table. Some of its most popular offerings include the fig bread ($5 available Tue, Wed, Sat), olive and rosemary loaves ($4, daily) and its sandwiches (try the trout variety which is slathered with herbed cream cheese, capers and spinach and sun-dried tomatoes).

USINE DE SPAGHETTI PARISIENNE

Map p314 — Italian-International $-$$

☎ 866-0963; 273 rue St-Paul Est; mains $8.95-16.95; ☷ 11am-11pm; Ⓜ Champ-de-Mars

The congenial stone and wood interiors with open hearth attract loads of tourists and families, but can you blame them? Its standard dishes like fettuccini with baby clams or filet mignon are great value and prices include all the bread and salad you can eat.

STASH CAFÉ Map p314 — Polish $-$$

☎ 845-6611; 200 rue St-Paul Ouest; mains $9.75-15.75; ☷ 11:30am-11pm; Ⓜ Place-d'Armes

Hearty Polish cuisine served up with good humor in a dining room with seats made of church pews and daringly low red lights illuminating the tables. An enthusiastic pianist hammers away in the corner and takes requests. Staff ranges from warm and gregarious to completely standoffish, but the food is consistent, with quality fare like *pirogi* (dumplings stuffed with meat or cheese, with

sour cream) and potato pancakes with apple sauce. The more ambitious should sample the Wild Boar *table d'hôte* ($29.95). Reservations are a good idea anytime of the year especially if you want a window table.

MARCHÉ DE LA VILLETTE

Map p314 — Deli $

☎ 807-8084; 324 rue St-Paul Ouest; sandwiches $7-12.99, mains $10-20; ☷ 9am-6pm Mon-Fri, 9am-5pm Sat & Sun; Ⓜ Square-Victoria

Here you'll find a convivial traditional deli serving made-to-order sandwiches with homemade pâté, cured ham, sausages, foie gras and an array of pungent cheeses. Also does meat and seafood mains to go, best followed by its flavorful ice cream or sherbet.

GANDHI Map p314 — Indian $$

☎ 845-5866; 230 rue St-Paul Ouest; $12.95-25.95; ☷ noon-2pm & 5:30-10:30pm Mon-Fri, 5:30-10:30pm Sat & Sun; Ⓜ Square-Victoria

Gandhi's has a core of loyal fans who come here for classics like Tandoori chicken as well as the extensive curry menu with adventurous fare like *malaya*, a curry of pineapple, lychees and cream. The starched white tablecloths and ochre walls are simple and understated letting the food take center-stage. Appetizers like pakoras or vegetable samosas are finely spiced, and faves such as tandoori duck, butter chicken and lamb korahi practically melt in your mouth. This place is a gem. Reservations are strongly recommended as it is often booked solid summer nights even on usual 'off-days' like Tuesday night. The *assiette* Gandhi ($20.50) of tandoori chicken, lamb and shrimp tikka and sheikh kebab will lead you to culinary joy.

LE PETIT MOULINSART

Map p314 — Belgian $$

☎ 843-7432; 139 rue St-Paul Ouest; mains $14.95-24; ☷ 11:30am-3pm & 5-11pm summer, Mon-Sat winter; Ⓜ Place-d'Armes

Fans of Tintin comic books will feel right at home here in a restaurant inspired by the Belgian hero and his sidekick Captain Haddock. There's a range of good dishes but it's the mussels (19 sorts!) accompanied by fries and mayonnaise that are the kicker. They've also got an extensive beer list that includes Kriek-Bellevue (a cherry beer) on tap with a head so creamy it could rival a Guinness. The dining room is tidy, done up in blue and white. The terrace out back, open in summer, makes for great eavesdropping. A fair share of politicos and their flaks quaff beers while going over papers in hushed tones. Shares space with Le Pharaon Lounge (p156).

LA GARGOTE Map p314 French $$

☎ 844-1428; 351 place d'Youville; table d'hôte lunch $16.50-19.50, dinner $18-23; ⏱ noon-2:30pm & 5:30-10pm, closed Sun low-season; Ⓜ Square-Victoria

An Old Montréal standard, this bistro pumps along seamlessly with quality bistro fare served in a cozy dining room with stone walls and beamed ceilings. There's nothing cutting edge or revolutionary about this eatery, but it works well on all levels whether you're sitting down with a digestive and the table d'hôte after skating at the Old Port or in summer, taking in the street life as you lunch on the terrace in place d'Youville across from the main building and watching the waiters dodge traffic as they ferry food to you from the kitchen.

RESTAURANT HOLDER

Map p314 Bistro $$

☎ 849-0333; 407 rue McGill; mains $18-27; ⏱ 11:30am-11pm Mon-Wed, 11:30am-midnight Thu, Fri, 5:30pm-midnight Sat, Sun; Ⓜ Square-Victoria

High ceilings, a terrific wine list and the best and most beautiful diners from the nearby multimedia offices. This French bistro buzzes with importance and fun during both lunch and dinner. Try the wonderful salad foie gras ($20), a meal in itself.

CHEZ L'ÉPICIER Map p314 French $$$

☎ 878-2232; 311 rue St-Paul Est; mains $24-36; ⏱ restaurant 11:30am-2pm & 5:30-10pm Mon-Fri, 5:30-10pm Sat & Sun, delicatessen 11:30am-10pm daily; Ⓜ Champ-de-Mars

This place, helmed by chef Laurent Godbout, has a permanent buzz around it. The menu changes regularly, but you'll find interesting, beautifully presented dishes that might include something like venison and red wine sauce. As for the desserts, there probably hasn't been one review in

---

TOP FIVE RESTOS IN OLD MONTRÉAL

- Chez l'Épicier (left) – fine delicacies for galloping gourmets
- Chez Queux (below) – an old-fashioned French pampering
- Boris Bistro (p126) – fantastic flavors and magnificent outdoor terrace
- La Gargote (left) – reliable French bistro fare and atmosphere
- Restaurant Holder (left) – perfect mix of bustle and snobbery

---

the entire history of this place that *hasn't* mentioned the chocolate club sandwich with pineapple fries ($7). The dining room is bright and cozy with large windows looking out onto the street. The six course tasting menu is $75. There's a gourmet delicatessen attached that is excellent for picnic food if you're off to the Old Port.

CHEZ QUEUX Map p314 French $$

☎ 886-5194; 158 rue St-Paul Est; mains $25-35; ⏱ 11:30am-3pm & 5-11pm; Ⓜ Champ-de-Mars

Housed in an historic warehouse from 1862, with stone walls, polished paneling and Third Empire furnishings this gem offers the epitome of old-fashioned French cuisine. Settle into a thronelike chair, order the delicious châteaubriand and prepare for a pampering. The little-known rear terrace overlooking the Old Port is a lovely dining spot in summer. The wine list of 300-plus varieties has been featured in *Wine Spectator*.

CUBE Map p314 International $$$

☎ 876-2823; 355 rue McGill; mains $29-42; ⏱ noon-2pm & 6-11pm; Ⓜ Square-Victoria; Ⓟ valet $15

Cube first offers a feast for the eyes with its simple designer decor (high ceilings, thick white drapes and herds of votive candles) and then for the taste buds with a menu that can include dishes like veal sweetbreads with parsnip and truffle purée or wild sweet bass with sweet peas. Textures and tastes contrast well in the mains, (succulent flaky fish and veggies al dente), as well as the desserts (chocolate crème with red pepper and raspberry sherbet or Québec strawberries with violet ice cream). Reservations essential.

PARC JEAN-DRAPEAU

Food at the park is synonymous with hot-dogs and ice-cream bars, but there are a couple of options if you want to kick it up a notch and linger over some good food.

RESTAURANT HÉLÈNE DE CHAMPLAIN

Map p319   French $$

☎ 395-2424; 200 Tour de l'Isle, Île Ste-Hélène; mains $14.50-24.50; ☽ 11:30am-2:30pm Mon-Fri, 5:30-10:30pm Wed, Thu, Sun, 5:30-11:30pm Fri & Sat; Ⓜ Jean-Drapeau; Ⓟ

Right by the Biosphère,with a relaxed, old-fashioned ambience, this is a wonderful place to take a relaxing break from exploring the park. Service is warm and friendly and there's a range of 'just-right' French dishes like scallop and shrimp brochette ($18.95) or duck confit ($18.50).

NUANCES Map p319   French $$

☎ 392-2746; 1 ave du Casino; mains $30-44; ☽ 5:30-11pm Sun-Thu, 5:30-11:30pm Fri & Sat; Ⓜ Jean-Drapeau, then bus 167; Ⓟ

Just past the roulette tables and slot machines inside the Casino de Montréal lies one of the town's classiest restaurants. One highlight is the roasted pigeon, succulent with crispy skin, served with gratinéed potatoes and a stew of giblets and chanterelles, all bathed in a delectable sauce of veal and chicken stock. The kitchen shines best when special events feature international guest chefs. Reservations and business attire are essential for both men and women.

DOWNTOWN

Downtown Montréal crackles with culinary energy well into the evening. With all this good food around, commuters are always looking for an excuse to linger.

BAGEL PLACE Map pp310-11   Bagels $

☎ 931-2827; 1616 rue Ste-Catherine Ouest, Le Faubourg; sandwiches $3-5; ☽ 7am-9pm Mon-Sat; Ⓜ Guy-Concordia

You can watch them haul the chewy bagels right out of the oven through the giant window on rue Ste-Catherine. There's a variety of toppings including smoked salmon, chicken salad, ham 'n' cheese and more and the cheese bagels are outstanding.

FRITES DORÉES

Map pp310-11   Burgers & Dogs $

☎ 866-0790; 1212 boul St-Laurent; sandwiches $3-7; ☽ 9am-4am; Ⓜ St-Laurent

If you can deal with the low-life area and derelict regulars muttering about alien invasions at the table next to you, this place does a classic toasté all dress hotdog (relish, mustard and onion, topped with chopped cabbage and on a toasted bun). A city institution, immortalized by renowned Canadian photographer Gabor Szilasi in one of his classic photos.

BEN'S Map pp310-11   Smoked Meat $

☎ 844-1000; 990 boul de Maisonneuve Ouest; mains $4.25-8; ☽ 7am-4am Sun-Thu, 7am-5am Fri & Sat; Ⓜ Peel

Hollywood stars used to have sandwiches flown in from this informal deli where time, if not the prices, stood still around 1950. This Montréal landmark has faded a bit in recent years but its smoked-meat sandwich – a two-inch-high pile of succulence, served with French mustard ($4.25) – remains a classic. The waiters are creaking old wisecrackers.

Diners enjoy alfresco atmosphere overlooking the popular rue St-Paul Est

Eating

DOWNTOWN

DUNN'S Map pp310-11 — Smoked Meat & Deli $
☎ 395-1927; 1249 rue Metcalfe; mains $5-15;
🕑 24 hr; Ⓜ McGill
One of Montréal's oldest smoked meat institutions with killer sandwiches slapped down on wax paper and served in baskets drowning with fries. The Reuben sandwich (smoked meat, sauerkraut and melted cheese, $11.45) is so filling it could knock you out. It's like a rush-hour train station in here at lunchtime.

MCLEAN'S PUB Map pp310-11 — Pub $
☎ 392-7770, 1210 rue Peel; mains $6-10;
🕑 11am-11:30pm Mon-Thu, 11am-3am Fri & Sat, noon-3am Sun; Ⓜ Peel
If you're after great pub fare you can't go wrong at McLean's. It does an excellent line in chicken wings, Reuben sandwiches and burgers with a mountain of crispy fries. Dark wood, dim lights and high ceilings make it easy to lose track of time at this Irish pub. The beer list features beers like Keith's and Euro-brews like Stella and Leffe. There's live music some evenings.

AMELIO'S Map pp310-11 — Italian $-$$
☎ 845-8396; 201 rue Milton; mains $6-20;
🕑 11:30am-9pm Mon-Fri, 4-9pm Sat & Sun;
Ⓜ Place-des-Arts
Smack in the middle of the McGill student ghetto, this joint has fed generations of students with generous portions of pizza and pasta and is an institution. A medium pizza (always crisp and heaped with toppings) is enough to stuff two people. And the pasta dishes come with sumptuous bread and crisp salads. Lineups outside the plain flat-top structure are common around 6pm.

REUBEN'S Map pp310-11 — Smoked Meat $
☎ 866-1029; 1116 rue Ste-Catherine Ouest; mains $8-15; 🕑 6:30am-midnight Mon-Wed, 6:30am-1:30am Thu & Fri, 8am-1:30am Sat, 8am-midnight Sun; Ⓜ Peel
Towering smoked-meat sandwiches served with big-cut fries are slammed down in booths and along the long counter that seems perennially crowded.

BUONA NOTTE Map pp310-11 — Italian $$
☎ 848-0644; 3518 boul St-Laurent; mains $8-22;
🕑 noon-3pm; Ⓜ St-Laurent, then bus 55
So slick, so hip it hurts. Wait staff are exclusively beautiful. The waitresses sway in such towering stilettos you'll hold your breath to see if they make it to the table carrying cocktail trays without keeling over. Despite all this, there's something *almost* democratic about the place. The staff exert a real effort to make you feel you're actually wanted even if you are a bit rough around the edges. With all the schmoozing going on, the food is irrelevant, but there's a range of dishes like pasta or steaks that all get decent reviews. Reservations a must on weekends.

MANGO BAY Map pp310-11 — Caribbean $
☎ 875-7082; 1202 rue Bishop; mains $11.95-14.95;
🕑 11:30am-10pm Sun-Thu, to midnight Fri & Sat;
Ⓜ Guy-Concordia
Situated in a converted Victorian house with pretty stained-glass windows, Mango Bay serves up authentic chicken jerk or stew, curried goat or island chicken fajitas with a terrific side order of plantain. Watch out for the incendiary hot sauces, and be sure to save room for a slice of the signature mango cheesecake or rum cake. There's

---

FIVE TOTALLY RANDOM LAPRISE EATING RECOMMENDATIONS

Toque! superchef Normand Laprise (p30) speaks of Montréal's other restaurants with as much enthusiasm as his own. Below are just five of his many top Montréal eating experiences.

- Au Pied de Cauchon (p140) - 'Martin (Picard, a former Toqué! chef) has done a great job here. It's modern, convivial, the portions are generous. They have *poutine* with foie gras and you have all kinds of Montrealers from students to lawyers.'
- Cocagne (☎ 286-0700; 3842 rue St-Denis; Ⓜ Sherbrooke) - 'is a French bistro with a wonderful price-quality relationship. A four-serving menu will only cost you something like $24 to $35.'
- Pullman Wine Bar (☎ 288-7779; 3424 ave du Parc, Ⓜ Place-des-Arts, then bus 80 or 129) - 'has a great atmosphere. We (Toqué! chefs) often go to have a drink here together after work.'
- Isakaya (opposite) – 'sushi in Montréal is not always such wonderful quality, not so fresh, but it's different here. I still see (Chef) Shige (Minagawa) out at the fish markets all the time making his own choices.'
- Schwartz's (p138) – 'of course.'

also a quick express lunch menu like a jerk chicken burger with fries and soda. There's live Jamaican music on Saturday evening.

SAFFRON Map pp310-11 Persian $$

☎ 937-7475; 1801 rue Ste-Catherine Ouest; mains $13-25; ⏰ 11:30am-10pm Mon-Thu, 11am-8pm Fri-Sun; Ⓜ Guy-Concordia

A vibrant mural of Persian ruins and bright blue sky dominates the dining room of this charming eatery, one of the newer Persian restaurants on the scene. The *ash reshteh*, a soup with pinto beans, veggies, garlic and mint ($4) is delicious and there's a range of meat and even vegetarian dishes. The most popular dinner choice is the hunters' platter for two ($34) with three types of brochettes, salad and rice. There's also a $6.95 lunch special and a take-out menu as well.

BOMBAY PALACE Map pp310-11 Indian $

☎ 932-7141; 2201 rue Ste-Catherine Ouest; dinner buffet $14; ⏰ 11:30am-3pm & 5:30-10pm Mon-Thu, 11:30am-11pm Fri & Sat, 5:30-10pm Sun; Ⓜ Atwater

One of the oldest Indian restaurants in town, now in new snazzy premises close to the Pepsi Forum. The midday buffet ($8.95 Monday to Thursday, $9.95 Friday to Sunday) is a good chance to try its excellent curries and tandoori specialties. Fans include Bill and Hillary Clinton – check out the foyer's photos.

ISAKAYA Map pp310-11 Japanese $$

☎ 845-8226; 3469 ave du Parc; mains $14-23; ⏰ 11.30am-3pm & 6-10pm Tue-Fri, noon-3pm & 6-11pm Sat, 6-10pm Sun; Ⓜ Place-des-Arts, then bus 80 or 129

One of the most authentic Japanese restaurants in town. The decor is fairly simple but the fish is frighteningly fresh – the owner, Shige Minagawa, is known for hand-picking his seafood and preparing it in classic Japanese fashion. Daily specials such as lobster sashimi, tuna belly or yellowtail are listed on the chalkboard by the kitchen. Reservations are essential.

LE CAVEAU Map pp310-11 French $$-$$$

☎ 843-3661; 2063 rue Victoria; mains $14-39; ⏰ 11:30am-11pm Mon-Fri, 4:30-11pm Sat & Sun; Ⓜ McGill

Nestled amid a forest of skyscrapers, this Victorian villa has been a Montréal institu-

TOP FIVE RESTOS DOWNTOWN

- Beaver Club (p132) – Canadian luxury edibles fit for a baron
- Les Chenêts (p132) – perfect bistro fare and the largest cognac collection in the world
- Queue de Cheval (p132) – carnivore's mecca with in-house pyrotechnics
- Toqué! (p132) – innovative fusion from a super-star chef
- Le Caveau (left) – solid French cooking in a Victorian atmosphere

tion since 1949. The fine *table d'hôte* ($12 to $15 at lunch, $16 to $20 at dinner) may include bourgeois French courses such as glazed snails, Provençal lamb or marinated salmon. The upper dining floors are most atmospheric, stuffed as they are with paintings and antiques. Reservations are recommended.

LE PARIS Map pp310-11 French $$

☎ 937-4898; 1812 rue Ste-Catherine Ouest; mains $15-29; ⏰ noon-3pm & 5:30-10:30pm Mon-Sat, 5:30-10:30pm Sun; Ⓜ Guy-Concordia

It's the quintessential neighborhood bistro and refreshingly, there's nothing slick or trendy about this place. The dated décor and core of loyal costumers gives it a casual, family, community feel. The menu is about no-frills French food – with classics like duck confit and *flétan menieur* (halibut dusted in flour and cooked in butter) alongside blood pudding and calf brains for the more adventurous. The place pulls loads of regulars so reserve ahead.

NEWTOWN

Map pp310-11 International $$-$$$

☎ 284-6555; 1476 rue Crescent; mains $16-39; ⏰ 11:30am-2:15pm Mon-Fri, 5:30-10:30pm Mon-Wed & Sun, 5:30-11pm Thu-Fri; Ⓜ Guy-Concordia

A showy design palace for the Grand Prix circuit, owned by star driver Jacques Villeneuve ('Newtown' refers to his surname). The grilled seafood and Grand Marnier crêpes are good but the main draw of this place is the clientèle – beautiful people souped up for a night out. There's a terrace on top with spectacular views of the city and the commotion on rue Crescent at night. Reservations are essential.

CAFÉ MÉLIÈS Map pp310-11 Media Café $$

☎ 847-9218; 3536 boul St-Laurent; mains $17-29; ⊗ 8am-11pm Mon-Wed & Sun, 8:30am-midnight Thu-Sat; Ⓜ St-Laurent, then bus 55

This chic, modern restaurant located in the Ex-Centris cinema and multimedia complex is tailor-made for Montréal's showbiz types. It's an excellent place to be seen over breakfast, lunch or afternoon coffee in front of the windows on the Main. The brunch is particularly upscale and popular. At night, moviegoers and politicians rub shoulders over plates of marinated salmon or roasted scallops.

RESTAURANT GLOBE

Map pp310-11 French-International $$-$$$

☎ 284-3823; 3455 boul St-Laurent; mains $18-30; ⊗ 6-11pm Sun-Wed, 6pm-midnight Thu-Sat; Ⓜ St-Laurent, then bus No 55

In such a pretentious part of town the Globe is a breath of fresh air. The menu is ingredient-driven: lowbrow items like dirty mashed potatoes alongside 'finer' dishes such as slow-cooked rabbit with crispy fried pancetta. The fine waiters excel in unobtrusive service, allowing patrons to focus on their meal (and the visiting movie stars). Reservations are essential.

QUEUE DE CHEVAL

Map pp310-11 Steakhouse $$$

☎ 390-0090; 1221 boul René-Lévesque Ouest; mains $28-41; ⊗ 11:30am-2:30pm Mon-Fri, 5:30-10:30pm Sun-Wed, 5:30-11:30pm Thu-Sat; Ⓜ Lucien-L'Allier

This mecca of expense-account carnivores serves up delectable prime beef that's dry-aged on the premises. Order from a dozen varieties of he-man-sized steaks that span filet mignon, T-bone and thick slabs of marbled tenderloin, and then watch as it's char-broiled in the pyrotechnics of the open kitchen. Service is impeccable, with attention paid to little details – chunky-handled steak knives for male clientèle, thin and sleek models for women. Reservations are a must.

TOQUÉ! Map pp310-11 French $$$

☎ 499-2084; 900 pl Jean-Paul-Riopelle; mains $29-35; ⊗ 5:30-10:30pm Tue-Sat; Ⓜ Place d'Armes; Ⓟ

No other place has generated so much excitement on the Montréal dining scene as Toqué!. It's hard to know what to write

about it that hasn't been trumpeted already 1000 times over. Chef Normand Laprise (see p30) gets rave reviews for his superfresh, innovative menus based on the products he gets from local farmers, and blending the ingredients into eclectic dishes. Even his desserts excite, created around fresh fruit with surprises like basil accents. The restaurant is a bright, wide-open space with high ceilings accented with playful splashes of color and a glass enclosed wine cave with suspended bottles front and center in the dining room.

LES CHENÊTS Map pp310-11 French $$-$$$

☎ 844-1842; 2075 rue Bishop; lunch $15-23, dinner *table d'hôte* $45-95; ⊗ 11:30am-2pm Mon-Fri, dinner 5:30pm-late daily; Ⓜ Guy-Concordia

Magnificent French food like duck *à l'orange,* is served here by chef and owner Michel Gillet in an intimate, magically ornate dinning room. Gillet is also owner of the world's largest cognac collection (830 different labels), immortalized in the *Guinness Book of Records*. If dinner prices seem a bit stiff, swing by for lunch. It's served in the bistro downstairs from the main dining room. On any given day, businessmen perch at the counter and chat up the smoky-voiced waitresses. The menu is written out on the chalkboard with classics like herring appetizers and mains like *steak frites* (steak and French fries). For dessert try the tremendous chocolate profiteroles.

BEAVER CLUB Map pp310-11 Canadian $$$

☎ 861-3511; 900 boul René-Lévesque Ouest, Fairmont Reine Elizabeth; *table d'hôte* $70-88; ⊗ lunch noon-2:30pm Tue-Fri, dinner 6-10:30pm Tue-Sat; Ⓜ Bonaventure; Ⓟ valet

The original Beaver Club was formed in 1785 by a group of Montréal fur barons, and to join you had to have wintered in the Northwest Territories. Membership is still elite – ask to see the pic of Bill Gates in trapper's furs – but anyone with the right currency can reserve in the impeccably serviced, old-fashioned dining room to enjoy a cross-section of Canadian luxury edibles. The $88-*menu découverte* is a multimenu focused on Québec produce like Gaspé lobster, Marieville foie gras and Île d'Orléans raspberries. Reservations are a must, especially at lunch. No jeans. Jacket and tie for men.

THREE AMIGOS Map pp310-11   Tex-Mex $

☎ 939-3329; 1657 rue Ste-Catherine Ouest; mains $8.95-14.95; ⏰ 11:30am-11:30pm Mon-Thu, 11:30am-1:30am Fri & Sat, noon-11:30pm Sun; Ⓜ Guy-Concordia

You know, sometimes it isn't all about the food. The chicken chimichangas ($11.95) here are lethally good, and the homemade salsa reeks to perfection with coriander, however the rest is fine but unremarkable Tex-Mex fare. Then why come? Because locals and students from the nearby universities and college pack this place to the gills, especially on weekends, turning it into a kind of loud, tacky and boisterous party.

CHINATOWN

Billowy steam and scrumptious odors waft out of kitchens and into the streets of Montréal's tiny but lively Chinatown. Cantonese, Szechuan and Vietnamese restaurants dominate boul St-Laurent and the pedestrian rue de la Gauchetière.

HOANG OANH Map p314   Vietnamese $

☎ 954-0053; 1071 boul St-Laurent; sandwiches $2.75; ⏰ 11am-3am; Ⓜ Place-d'Armes

The Vietnamese baguette sandwiches here are the very best in Chinatown. There's an endless choice of fillings but the grilled chicken or tofu varieties topped with mayonnaise, veggies and coriander are pretty unbeatable.

LA MAISON KAM FUNG

Map p314   Chinese $-$$

☎ 878-2888; 1111 rue St-Urbain; mains $3.50-12; ⏰ 7am-2:30pm & 5:30-9:30pm; Ⓜ Place-d'Armes

This is generally considered the best place in town for dim sum, and is especially popular for Saturday and Sunday brunch. Waiters circle the tables with carts of dim sum ($3.50 to $5.50 each) – you pick and choose from duck or chicken feet, spare ribs, mushrooms, cow's stomach or spicy shrimp. The entrance is hidden in the rear of a shopping passage up an escalator.

CALI Map p314   Vietnamese $

☎ 876-1064; 1011 boul St-Laurent; mains $5.95-9.95; ⏰ 10am-10pm; Ⓜ Place- d'Armes

A terrific hole-in-the-wall place, with friendly, good-humored wait staff no matter how busy things get. The deal with this place is to get you in and out as quick as possible, so don't be surprised if your order lands in front of you, piping hot, literally seconds after you order it. Even faster than McDonald's.

JARDIN DE JADE Map p314   Chinese $

☎ 866-3127; 67 rue de la Gauchetière Ouest; buffet $8.50-13.50; ⏰ 11am-10:30pm daily; Ⓜ Place-d'Armes

The chaotic, free-for-all Jardin de Jade buffet should be a must on your list if only to see it in action. Vegetarian, sushi, dumplings, fish, ribs, desserts, pizzas…The list just goes on. To see it in its full elbow-bumping glory, try

Eating

CHINATOWN

Slurping soup in Chinatown

weekdays when locals, business people and students battle it out over the stir-fry. One of the town's best deals. Prices vary depending on day and time.

PHÓ BANG NEW YORK

Map p314   Vietnamese $

☎ 954-2032; 970 boul St-Laurent; mains $8.95 & up; ☺ 10am-10pm; Ⓜ Place-d'Armes

Just a couple of doors down from Cali, the décor and service is geared more towards Westerners who want to have their tonkinese soups in swisher digs. The food here is still very good and regularly makes people's 'top' lists, but it lacks the kind of manic energy that makes the other Vietnamese places on this drag so atmospheric. Still a good place if you want to relax a bit over your meal.

QUARTIER LATIN

The terraced cafés and restaurants of the Latin Quarter are a great spot to watch the world go by, over coffee, croissants or even a bowl of borscht.

CAFÉ CROISSANT DE LUNE Z

Map p315   Café $

☎ 843-8146, 1765 rue St-Denis; ☺ 9am-9pm; Ⓜ Berri-UQAM

This is people-watching central anytime, for breakfast, lunch or dinner. A café au lait and one or two of the fresh sweet buns or croissants, served in the sun on the street-front terrace, will hold you over for hours. The burgers and sandwiches are great too.

LE COMMENSAL

Map p315   Vegetarian $-$$

☎ 845-2627; 1720 rue St-Denis; hot buffet $1.89 per 100g, dessert buffet $2 per 100g ☺ 11am-10:30pm Sun-Thu, 11am-11pm Fri & Sat; Ⓜ Berri-UQAM

This place still corners the market on quality self-serve vegetarian meals, salads and desserts, sold by the 100g. The usual suspects are all here (tofu, kale, bean sprouts etc) but they're all so well-seasoned and prepared that you'll forget it's health food. An average meal costs about $10 including a mineral water (but there's beer, too).

L'AMÈRE À BOIRE

Map p315   Brewpub $

☎ 282-7448; 2049 rue St-Denis; tapas $4.25, mains $6-8.50; ☺ 3pm-3am Mon-Fri, 2pm-3am Sat & Sun; Ⓜ Berri-UQAM

This bilevel brewpub with 25-ft ceilings, two outdoor terraces and a rustic brick interior is often filled with toe-tapping students enjoying the Spanish and jazz beats and unusually good pub food. Patrons slurp freshly brewed pints of the house German- or Czech-style lagers over tapas and burgers (downstairs), or borscht, pirogies and goat's cheese salad (upstairs).

LA PARYSE

Map p315   Diner $

☎ 842-2040; 302 rue Ontario Est; mains $8-10; ☺ 11am-11pm Mon-Fri, 2-10:30pm Sat & Sun; Ⓜ Berri-UQAM

Often credited with the thickest, juiciest burgers and best fries in town, this smart little retro diner offers an almost paralyzing variety of toppings and gorgeous thick milkshakes. This place is an integral part of

MAPLE SYRUP QUÉBEC STYLE

Sitting down for breakfast with Quebecers can be a shock sometimes. No sooner are the eggs, bacon and a side of baked beans put on the table, when, more often than not, they lunge for the maple syrup, pop the lid and then slather it over the whole kit-and-kaboodle without flinching. While in the rest of Canada, maple syrup is a treat for pancakes, in Québec it's practically a staple making regular appearances in desserts, on meat, on vegetables, in foie gras and in maple beer.

Many fans can discern the different grades of maple syrup and refuse to touch anything but their favorite. They can go on to discuss their texture, color and 'nose' as if they were discussing a great wine.

Québec produces about three-quarters of the world's syrup so it should hardly be surprising… they and it go back a long way. The French settlers began producing it regularly in the 1800s after being taught how to make it from maple tree sap by Canadian Aboriginals. Sap is usually extracted in spring after starch has been converted by enzymes into sugars over the winter. The sap starts to flow again once the weather warms up and the whole season is celebrated by Quebecers in *cabanes à sucre* (sugar shacks) out in the countryside all over the province. The experience involves a long, belly-busting multicourse meal made up of the kinds of foods French settlers ate way back in the day. It also gives people the chance to try the first saps of the season and do the taffy pull, where steaming maple syrup is poured into the snow and then scooped up on a popsicle stick once it's cooled. To check one out for yourself, go to www.cabaneasucre.org/

the neighborhood and when owner Madame Paryse recently celebrated 25 years in business, employees and customers alike sent her a flood of congratulatory emails.

THE VILLAGE

Great new eateries open (and close) frequently in the Village. But you'll always find an exciting mix of eating options, from Italian ristorantes to greasy spoons to Asian-fusion bistros. Most diners in this neighborhood concentrate on the kitchens around métro Beaudry, but consider getting off at Papineau instead (one stop east of Beaudry). Formerly a bit of a rundown area, stylish and flashy little restaurants are slowly popping up on this stretch of rue Ste-Catherine Est.

KILO Map p315   Café $
☎ 596-3933; 1495 rue Ste-Catherine; mains $5-11; ☽ 5-11pm Mon, 10:30am-11pm Tue-Thu, 10:30am-2am Fri, 1pm-2am Sat, 1-11pm Sun; Ⓜ Papineau
The house specialties are creamy cakes and tarts with a shot of Grand Marnier or some other liquid decadence, as well as hot sandwiches, snacks and salads. This favored Village meeting point is great for sussing out intentions before the evening gets going.

MI BURRITO Map p315   Mexican $$
☎ 525-8138, 1327 rue Ste-Catherine Est; mains $8.50 & up; ☽ noon-11pm daily; Ⓜ Beaudry
Opened in 2005 by a Mexican family with a passion for cuisine from the north of Mexico, this restaurant's décor is colorful but plain. The food here is simple (burritos, enchiladas, soups) and tasty, so unlike what you'll find elsewhere in the city, it's already amassed loyal champions. The margaritas are outstanding (real, and not made with syrup concentrate) and come in flavors like hibiscus or tamarind. And the spicy tortilla soup, with melted cheese is best described as addictive. Brunch dishes like *huevos rancheros* are spectacular and served Saturday and Sunday.

AU PETIT EXTRA Map p315   French $$
☎ 527-5552; 1690 rue Ontario Est; mains $15-21; ☽ 11:30am-2:30pm & 6-10pm Mon-Wed, 6-10:30pm Thu-Sat, 5:30-9:30pm Sun; Ⓜ Papineau
The party never ends at this little restaurant that resounds with the laughter of boisterous regulars and visiting film crews. Dishes written on the blackboards are simple – leg of

lamb, filet of mahi-mahi or stuffed hare – but flavors are full and distinct. Reservations are advised, but you can sip wine at the beautiful wooden bar if you have to wait.

LE SPIRITE LOUNGE Map p315   Vegan $$
☎ 522-5353; 1205 rue Ontario Est; mains $16; ☽ 6pm-midnight Tue-Sun; Ⓜ Beaudry
This eccentric restaurant with the squat-like exterior (Christmas lights and tinfoil) is an absolute gas. There's no printed menu but the main dish is always built around a hot crêpe with a legume-based filling, always organic and inventive. One little thing: you must finish each and every course, for if you don't you'll pay a small fine (donated to charity). Reservations are essential.

LE GRAIN DE SEL Map p315   Bistro $$
☎ 522-5105; 2375 rue Ste-Catherine Est; mains $17-25; ☽ noon-2:30pm Mon-Fri, 6-10:30pm Tue-Sat; Ⓜ Papineau, then bus 34
This tiny, friendly bistro just beyond the eastern edge of the Village exudes old-world ambience with a small bar and open kitchen. The menu has bistro favorites such as pheasant terrine, *bavette* (undercut steak), mussels cooked in beer and goat's cheese salad, but with Asian accents. The waiters will marry the right wines with your meal.

MOZZA Map p315   Italian $$
☎ 522-4116, 1208 rue Ste-Catherine Est; mains $20; ☽ 5-10pm Tue-Sun; Ⓜ Beaudry
One of the Village's best kept secrets, this little resto is tucked away in a pea-sized room near the métro and is easy to miss. (Look for the 'Mozza' sign they shine on to the pavement.) The menu includes salad, a starter like escargots in pastis and then a pasta meal of your creation. There's a choice of all kinds of noodle shapes and there are over a dozen sauces to choose from. The quality of food is consistently outstanding and the service expert. There are two dinner services a night and reservations are recommended. This is a bring-your-own-booze establishment.

BISTRO LE PORTO Map p315   Portuguese $$
☎ 527-7067 1635 rue Ste-Catherine Est; mains $20-30; ☽ 11am-10pm Mon-Fri, 5-10pm Sat & Sun; Ⓜ Beaudry
This is a charming and cozy bistro, with terrific Portuguese and Mediterranean food and a fantastic selection of ports of all

types, colors and vintages. The wait staff are friendly and knowledgeable and give great advice about what to pair with what. The menu changes regularly, but the fish *marmite* (a huge stew of seafood) is offered, it is well worth the price (usually topping $30).

AREA Map p315   International $$-$$$
☎ 890-6691; 1429 rue Amherst; mains $21-34; ⏰ 11:30am-2:30pm Tue-Fri, 6-11pm Tue-Sun; Ⓜ Beaudry

The most creative recent addition to the Village's culinary arsenal, Area has earned heaps of accolades since opening in 2000. This dining room is black and white with a menu divided into categories titled 'Fins,' 'Legs,' and the intriguing 'Why not?' section that includes numbers like green asparagus risotto with mushrooms, parme-

san, chives, shallots and 'milky juice' and grilled onion milk with parsley oil and jelly.

OLYMPIC PARK

This eastern district is called Hochelaga-Maisonneuve and was home to some of Montréal's most successful early industrialists. Few visitors make it out this far to eat so locals usually have the place to themselves.

CHEZ CLO

Map pp308-9   Québécois $
☎ 522-5348; 3199 rue Ontario Est; mains $5-7; ⏰ 6am-8pm, to 10pm in summer; Ⓜ Frontenac, then bus 125

Homey atmosphere and good-value Québécois breakfasts have made this corner diner

---

TOP FIVE BAKERIES IN MONTRÉAL

The bakeries in Montréal are bearers of light, crispy French tradition goodies, and like in France you'll see residents walking home with a baguette tucked under one arm. There are so many great bakeries scattered around town it's a wonder the supermarkets can still sell the mass-produced stuff.

- Au Pain Doré (Map pp316–17; ☎ 982-9520; 3611 boul St-Laurent; ⏰ 8am-7pm Mon-Wed, 8am-9:30pm Thu-Fri, 8am-6pm Sat & Sun; Ⓜ St-Laurent, then bus 55) – homemade and organic bread, Viennese pastries, sandwiches, panini, meats and cheese. There are 13 outlets around Montréal.
- Boulangerie M Pinchot (Map pp316–17; ☎ 4354 rue de Brébeuf; Ⓜ Mont-Royal, then bus 97) – locals swear by the croissants and baguettes.
- MBCo (Map pp310–11; 1447 rue Stanley; Ⓜ Peel) – with numerous locations around town, this place does particularly intriguing pastries and muffins with flavors that on any given day can run from chocolate-cranberry or orange-oatmeal
- Olive + Gourmando (Map p314; ☎ 350-1083; 351 rue St-Paul Ouest; sandwiches $8.50 and up; ⏰ 8am-6pm Tue-Sat; Ⓜ Square-Victoria) – famous for the fig loaves and olive and rosemary bread
- Première Moisson (Map pp310–11; ☎ 931-6540; Marché Atwater, 137 ave Atwater; Ⓜ Lionel-Groulx) – this legendary bakery (also with 13 branches) displays its 30-odd marvelous breads in wicker baskets, Parisian-style. Its cheery café inside the market is a great spot for a flaky croissant and a cup of dark-roast coffee.

Boulangerie M Pinchot (above), Plateau du Mont-Royal

an institution for the best part of two decades. Slide onto a breakfast stool and order eggs, bacon, baked beans and cretons (pork drippings) or return for Québec specialties such as *tourtière* (meat pie), poutine or *ragoût de boulettes,* all in view of the monumental Nativité de la Ste-Vierge church.

PLATEAU DU MONT-ROYAL

Moving north of rue Sherbrooke, rue St-Denis and boul St-Laurent are staked with some of the city's finest eateries. Rue Prince-Arthur Est is a narrow residential street that has been converted into a dining and entertainment enclave. The restaurant segment runs west from Carré St-Louis (just north of rue Sherbrooke) to a block west of boul St-Laurent. Many of the small, inexpensive and mostly ethnic restaurants here aren't licensed to serve alcohol, so BYOW.

Further north on boul St-Laurent, ave Duluth is a former red-light district that has been transformed into a restaurant center. And if you like Portuguese food, veer east when you reach rue Marie-Anne. This area is packed with tiny family-run Portuguese eateries, and you may just stumble upon a gem that even the locals don't know about.

COCO RICO Map pp316-17   Fast Chicken $
☎ 849-5554; 3907 boul St-Laurent; mains $3.50-7; ⏲ 10am-11pm Mon-Fri, 9am-11pm Sat & Sun; Ⓜ St-Laurent, then bus 55
People strolling the Main pop into this little Portuguese place all day for the plain, classic $3.50 chicken sandwich and a little Styrofoam cup of roasted potatoes so good you'll be writing home about them. With only one long counter and flimsy bar stools inside this place always looks empty, most people get their orders to go and eat them on the run.

LA BINERIE MONT ROYAL
Map pp316-17   Fast Québécois $
☎ 285-9078; 367 ave du Mont-Royal Est; mains $4-7; ⏲ 6am-8pm Mon-Fri, 7:30am-3:30pm Sat & Sun; Ⓜ Mont-Royal
Authentic québécois cuisine is served from this diner-like counter. It's full of typical Québécois dishes including *tourtière* pie, pork and beans or *pudding chômeur* (a bread pudding with brown sugar syrup) as well as universal comfort food like grilled cheese sandwiches ($3.50).

PATATI PATATA
Map pp316-17   Extra-Fast Québécois $
☎ 844-0216; 4177 boul St-Laurent; mains $4-7; ⏲ 8am-11pm Mon-Fri, 11am-11pm Sat & Sun; Ⓜ St-Laurent, then bus 55
This hole in the wall (literally, if more than 15 people are inside you'll probably have to wait) is known for its *poutine,* borscht and burgers. A Montréal classic.

ST-VIATEUR BAGEL & CIE
Map pp316-17   Bagels $
☎ 528-6361; 1127 ave du Mont-Royal Est; sandwiches $4-8; ⏲ 6am-midnight; Ⓜ Mont-Royal
A splendid café that serves its signature bagels, grilled or *nature,* with soup or salad. There are about a dozen sandwiches but most popular are the traditional smoked lox with cream cheese and roast beef with Swiss cheese, olive oil and tomato. There's also a breakfast bagel with eggs and ham.

CHEZ CORA Map pp316-17   Café $
☎ 525-9495; 1396 ave Mont-Royal Est; mains $4-13; ⏲ 6am-3pm Mon-Sat, 7am-3pm Sun; Ⓜ Mont-Royal
The beloved breakfast standard. You'll recognize this chain right away with its bright cheerful décor and menus. The menus are so creative and so varied you'll literally find anything you've ever wanted for breakfast and more. Try *Récolte 90,* that comes with egg, bacon, French toast with raisins and an avalanche of fruit ($8.95). There are several other branches around town including the one in the **The Village** (Map p315; ☎ 285-2672; 1017 rue Ste-Catherine Est).

MA-AM-M BOLDUC
Map pp316-17   Québécois $
☎ 527-3884; 4351 ave de Lorimier; mains $5-12; ⏲ 7am-9pm Mon-Fri, 8am-10pm Sat, 9am-10pm Sun; Ⓜ Papineau, then bus 10
This neighborhood eatery with piped-in punk and New Age music still serves mainstays of québécois cuisine: meatball stew, *tourtière,* and more *poutines* than you can shake a trotter at. Long departed, Mme Bolduc's friendly round face still graces the marquee above the terrace tables.

SCHWARTZ'S Map pp316-17 Smoked Meat $

☎ 842-4813; 3895 boul St-Laurent; mains $4.75-14.95; ⏲ 8am-12:30am Sun-Thu, 8am-1:30am Fri, 8am-2:30am Sat; M St-Laurent, then bus 55
Known far and wide, first port of call for ex-pats and new arrivals alike, this old-time Hebrew deli is widely considered to serve the best smoked meat in Montréal whether it's brisket, duck, chicken and turkey, all piled high on sourdough rye bread. The Romanian-style meat is cured on the premises and aged without chemicals. Waiters can be impatient with novices but it all just adds to the legend.

CAFÉ FRUITS FOLIE

Map pp316-17 Café $
☎ 840-9011; 3817 rue St-Denis; mains $5-14; ⏲ 7am-11pm; M St-Laurent, then bus 55
This agreeable café has a long list of crêpes, bagels, burgers and sandwiches, plus good vegetarian choices. The front terrace (one of many in this neighborhood) has a great view of the happenings on rue St-Denis, and people love to linger here over breakfast while watching the world go by.

CAFÉ SANTROPOL

Map pp316-17 Café $
☎ 842-3110; 3990 rue St-Urbain; mains $6-9; ⏲ 11:30am-midnight; M St-Laurent, then bus 55
This is an iconic Montréal eatery known for its towering and creative sandwiches, its colorful digs, and lush outdoor garden patio. Its creations range from the Sweet Root (carrots, raisins, coriander, nuts, mayo and fresh apple, $7.50) to Pepper Island with Ham (that comes with jalapeño pepper jelly, pesto and cream cheese spread, $8.25).

CAFÉ CHERRIER Map pp316-17 Café $-$$

☎ 843-4308; 3635 rue St-Denis; mains $7-18; ⏲ 7:30am-10pm; M Sherbrooke
Locals flock to the shady, wraparound terrace of this comfy café with the long zinc serving counter that wouldn't be out of place in Paris. This is an especially fun place after a performance at the nearby L'Agora de la Danse. A huge percentage of the audience usually swings by here for dinner or a drink setting the whole place abuzz. The breakfasts are popular here as is classic French bistro fare like steak frites.

TOP FIVE RESTOS PLATEAU

- Au Pied de Cochon (p140) – a symphony of French flavors and poutine foie gras
- Café Santropol (left) – utterly bizarre sandwiches at the goldfish pond
- Le Nil Bleu (p141) – Ethiopian food and spicy surprises
- Le Poisson Rouge (p141) – seafood specialist known for the freshest cuts
- L'Express (p140) – best Parisian bistro this side of the Atlantic

---

EURO DELI Map pp316-17 Italian $

☎ 843-7853; 3619 boul St-Laurent; mains $7; ⏲ 8am-midnight; M St-Laurent, then bus 55
One of the lower Main's gems – for people watching and its fresh pastas. Students and punks flop on the outside steps with pizza slices and drinks, inside regulars shoo away newcomers from 'their' tables. This sparse, bustling eatery is cafeteria-style and food changes daily – just go up and choose your pasta and sauce from the counter. If chocolate cake is on offer when you visit, pounce! It's phenomenal.

BRÛLERIE ST-DENIS

Map pp316-17 Café $
☎ 286-9158; 3967 rue St-Denis; coffees $2-4, sandwiches $6.50-8.50; ⏲ 8am-11pm Mon-Fri, 9am-midnight Sat & Sun; M Sherbrooke
This is coffee heaven: iced coffees, frappés, special blends like Café Dante (mocca espresso with whipped cream, cinnamon, chocolate and grated orange peel), made from beans fresh out of the big roaster. The front terrace is a great place to nurse a cup with a hot veggie sandwich or a slice of gooey gâteau.

L'AVENUE Map pp316-17 Bistro $-$$

☎ 523-8780; 922 ave du Mont-Royal Est; mains $7-25; ⏲ 7am-11pm Mon-Fri, 8am-11pm Sat, 8am-10pm Sun; M Mont-Royal
Socialites will line up outside at 40°F below for an overpriced breakfast, such is the pull of this hopelessly trendy restaurant. The chic set is always well represented, nibbling at a golden croissant or sculpted melon ball, fully aware of the other hipsters doing the same thing. The washrooms are so cool they're worth a visit.

TAMPOPO Map pp316-17 — Asian $

☎ 526-0001; 4449 rue de Mentana; mains $8-13;
🕑 11am-11pm; Ⓜ Mont-Royal

Plateau locals love this cozy place for its aromatic Vietnamese soups and filling noodle dishes with flank steak, grilled pork and rice vermicelli. Take a seat at one of three low tables with bamboo matting, or at the long wavy counter with a view of the open kitchen.

MAZURKA Map pp316-17 — Polish $

☎ 844-3539; 64 rue Prince-Arthur Est; mains $8-15; 🕑 11:30am-midnight; Ⓜ Sherbrooke

This Polish place has kept generations of students filled with cheap and hearty fare. The menu features *pirogi* and meat or cheese blintzes (filled pancake rolls), Polish sausage, potato latkes, or the restaurant's namesake, *mazurkas* (potato latkes filled with beef goulash). Make sure to wash it all down with one of Poland's most famous exports, Zubrowka, a vodka flavored with bison grass. The restaurant is a sprawling place, with nearly 200 seats over four levels and paintings from the Old Country on the walls.

RESTAURANT RAPIDO DU PLATEAU

Map pp316-17 — Fast Food $

☎ 284-2188; 4494 rue St-Denis; mains $7.95-10.95; 🕑 24 hr; Ⓜ Mont-Royal

If you're partying late on the Plateau you will probably end up here at least once. Is the food good? Impossible to say. By the time people end up here, that's kind of a moot point and they aren't really in the condition to recall what they ate anyway.

Whatever. Good or bad, most Montrealers have fond memories of watching the sun come up while tucking into a hamburger steak here at some point in their youth.

LA SALA ROSA Map pp316-17 — Spanish $

☎ 844-4227; 4848 boul St-Laurent; mains $10-16, tapas $5-8; 🕑 5-11pm Mon-Fri, brunch 10am-3pm & 5-11pm Sat & Sun; Ⓜ St-Laurent, then bus 55

Be prepared for anything at this little gem. The waiters may not speak anything other than Spanish, your orders may or may not come at the same time as your dinner companion's, or you may have an interminable wait, but the heaping portions of paella (which comes in five sorts including vegetarian) are masterful and will feed you for days afterwards. (People rarely make it out of here without a doggy bag the servings are so copious). Mains come with salad and dessert. A great tapas menu is also available. Try to make it here Thursday night when the flamenco show packs them in to the point that diners are practically sitting on top of each other.

BIÈRES & COMPAGNIE

Map pp316-17 — Mussels $$

☎ 844-0394; 4350 rue St-Denis; mussels $15-18, other mains $12-13; 🕑 11am-1am Mon-Tue, 11:30am-2am Wed-Sat, 11:30am-midnight Sun; Ⓜ Mont-Royal

Throbbing fusion pop and a grand ex-bank setting make this Belgian-style eatery a prime night spot. When you're not sipping on one of 100 varieties of beer, or slicing into savory wild boar or St-Ambroise beer sausage, check out the 30-odd types of mussels.

HOLY TREK TO THE BIG ORANGE BALL

Enough with Schwartz's and Toqué! already. When it comes to iconic Montréal eateries, give the giant orange ball on the Décarie Expressway a chance.

Orange Julep (☎ 738-7486; 7700 boul Décarie) was stuck up here in 1942 by Hermas Gibeau to sell his frothy orange-cream drink. It started out as a diner and still hasn't lost the retro vibe. Everyday dozens of cars screech into the parking lot and the drivers jump out for this classic orange drink, hotdog and fries, before hopping into their vehicles to tear off again.

In summer, people tend to linger. Pop music from the 1980s, like teen queen Tiffany, blares over the loudspeakers while people eat at the handful of picnic tables or spread the goods out on the hoods of their cars. In winter, people huddle inside their vehicles before tucking into what is arguably the best fast food in the city.

And in keeping with its drive-in roots, car maniacs hold weekly meetings here so they can admire each other's hot rods.

So, though plenty of expats worship at the cult of smoked meat or bagels when they roll into town, there's another core of ex-Montrealers for whom the Orange Julep trek is obligatory. It's their first port of call for a *toasté all dress* and a liter of the Julep under the stars. To get here take the Décarie Expressway to the exit Jean-Talon, but don't worry about the address too much. It's kind of hard to miss a three-storey high, 40-ft-in-diameter orange sphere plunked down in the middle of nowhere. You can also take the métro to Namur and walk.

PRODUITS DU TERROIR

If you hang around the Montréal food scene for any length of time, it won't be long before you start hearing about *produits du terroir* ('produce from the earth' loosely translated). While québécois cuisine has typically been heavy, using only a small number of ingredients, these days more and more young chefs and cooks are heading to the markets and the farms, and constructing menus around what they find. In foodie circles, it's also influencing menus and making minor celebrities out of small producers and farmers who weren't on anyone's radar even a few years ago. The mania for these types of local ingredients aren't just for star chefs however. More and more Montrealers are heading outside of town, to hit the farms to tote back jams, spreads, cheese and red pepper jellies from local producers than are raiding the shelves at their local Provigo. Though some people (see boxed text p30) are suspicious of its trendiness as everyone jumps on the band wagon, it seems like nobody will be hopping off anytime soon.

MISTO Map pp316-17 — Italian Bistro $$
☎ 526-5043; 929 ave du Mont-Royal; mains $12-20; ⏰ 11:30am-midnight; Ⓜ Mont-Royal
Misto was one of the first 'see-and-be-seen' restaurants to open on ave du Mont-Royal with a big rolling garage door facade. Readers give it consistent raves for everything from the food to the ambience. The bare brick walls, polished wood and opulent curved bar draw scads of urban professionals dressed to kill. The organic pastas, pizzas and dinner salads are as much about California cool as *la bella Italia*.

AU PIED DE COCHON
Map pp316-17 — French $$
☎ 281-1114; 536 ave Duluth Est; mains $12-30; ⏰ 5pm-midnight Tue-Sun; Ⓜ Sherbrooke
Chef Martin Picard takes normally heavy dishes and turns then into a symphony, like Alsacian *choucroute* (sauerkraut with meat and potatoes) or the trademark *ragoût de pattes de cochon* (tiny meatballs and vegetables topped with a crisp lid of breaded, deep-fried pig's feet). The logo is of a chef, frying pan in hand, riding a grinning pig. The *poutine* foie gras($8.50) still has critics buzzing.

L'EXPRESS Map pp316-17 — French Bistro $-$$
☎ 845-5333; 3927 rue St-Denis; mains $12.85-21.40, foie gras $27.20; ⏰ 8am-3am; Ⓜ Sherbrooke
L'Express has all the hallmarks of Parisian bistro – black-and-white checkered floor, Art Deco globe lights, papered tables, brown mirrored walls – but the food matches the presumption. Seafood dishes like grilled salmon with grey salt or almond-crusted pike are alarmingly fresh, and even standards such as *pot-au-feu* (poached chicken, ribs and marrow bone in clear broth with potatoes and cabbage) are consistently deli-

cious. The waiters can advise on the extensive wine list. Reservations are essential.

BYBLOS Map pp308-9 — Iranian $
☎ 523-9396; 1499 rue Laurier Est; meals $14-18, tapas $4.20-7.50; ⏰ 9am-11pm; Ⓜ Laurier
This Iranian café does such good food and is so comfortable and charming, people who come here tend to make a day of it. The big windows and tables invite lingering and though there are wonderful main courses, most people end up grazing on the Iranian tapas-like dishes all day and into the evening. The feta omelette is by far the most popular followed by the eggplant or chick pea purées. It's all served with pita bread perfect for dipping. The mint tea ($2.50 cup), is the perfect way to finish it all off.

OUZERI Map pp316-17 — Greek $$
☎ 845-1336; 4690 rue St-Denis; mains $15-24; ⏰ 11:30am-10:30pm Sun-Thu, 11:30am-11:30pm Fri & Sat; Ⓜ Mont-Royal
Recommended for its contemporary twist on traditional Greek food. Considering its oh-so-cool decor and multiple patrons dressed in black, dinner for two is a tremendous bargain for charcoal-grilled mint-flavored meat patties or moussaka, calamari or veal cutlets. There's an extensive wine list; batten down the hatches for Greek dancing on Friday.

VENTS DU SUD
Map pp316-17 — Basque-Catalonian $$
☎ 281-9913; 323 rue Roy Est; mains $16-23; ⏰ 5:30-10pm Tue-Sun; Ⓜ Sherbrooke
The cuisine is rustic terrines, conserves of duck, grilled meats and hearty sauces of garlic, peppers and tomatoes. It's one of the few places on the Montréal scene devoted to this kind of food. Service is warm and

welcoming and good at giving menu recommendations if you are not familiar with this type of cuisine. Its garage-sale chairs, salty regulars and moustached host give it the feel of a village eatery. Reserve ahead.

MAESTRO SVP Map pp316-17   Seafood $$-$$$
☎ 842-6447; 3615 boul St-Laurent; mains $17-55; ◷ 11am-10pm Mon-Wed, 11am-11pm Thu & Fri, 4pm-midnight Sat & Sun; Ⓜ St-Laurent, then bus 55

Hundreds of oyster shells are nailed to the wall in this seafood bistro with highbacked chairs and halogen spots. The calamari is a great appetizer and the oysters – a palette of 15 varieties – are served in a bewildering number of ways. Try the oyster shooter: a raw specimen in jalapeño vodka, cocktail sauce and horseradish, and you'll never have to prove your courage again.

LE NIL BLEU Map pp316-17   Ethiopian $$
☎ 285-4628; 3706 rue St-Denis; mains $18-27; ◷ 6pm-late; Ⓜ Sherbrooke

With water running down a kind of interior fountain, the relaxing ambience is the perfect accompaniment to the fantastic Ethiopian food. Order from a range of stews all served with a giant flatbread-like crepe – you then rip off pieces to pick up the food. This is a terrific unique dining experience.

LE POISSON ROUGE
Map pp316-17   Seafood $$$
☎ 522-4876; 1201 rue Rachel Est; mains $26; ◷ 5:30-11pm Tue-Sat; Ⓜ Mont-Royal

This seafood specialist with the cozy front terrace is renowned amongst market vendors for picking the best, freshest cuts. The pan-seared red tuna is juicy as can be with Cajun spices, but the ray braised in butter will also take your fancy. The four-course *table d'hôte* ($33) is tremendous value. There are two sittings on Friday and Saturday, at 6pm and 9pm. Bring your own wine.

JANO
Map pp316-17   Portuguese $$
☎ 849-0646; 3883 boul St-Laurent; mains $15; ◷ 11am-11pm; Ⓜ St-Laurent, then bus 55

If you're on this block of St-Laurent you'll see two lineups winding down the street, one will be for Schwartz's (p138) the other will be for this old-world Portuguese grill restaurant. Warm colors, small tables and a deafening buzz on Friday and Saturday nights mix with the smells of charcoal-grilled chicken, fish, meats and sausages. This is one restaurant where you can order anything on the menu without going wrong.

LITTLE ITALY
Come here for your Italian-food fix and you won't only get a memorable meal, but lots of street theater and old-world atmosphere to go with it. You have your choice of authentic family-style restaurants or one of the dozen or more cafés along boul St-Laurent, where the espresso is stiff and the cappuccinos so frothy the foam threatens to swallow up the cup. On summer evenings crowds fill the eateries and sidewalk cafés along the main drag, boul St-Laurent where the social buzz lasts into the wee hours.

Dining out in Little Italy

TOP FIVE POUTINE

For the traditional taste of Québec order a *poutine*, or fries smothered in cheese curds and gravy. Varieties include 'all dress' (sautéed mushrooms and bell pepper), 'richie boy' (ground beef), Italian (beef and spaghetti sauce), barbecue or even yer good ol' smoked meat. The idea is eat up quick 'cause the curds make the fries mushy in no time flat.

- Au Pied de Cochon (p140) – since they came out with their *poutine* foie gras no one can stop talking about it.
- Ma-am-m Bolduc (p137) – try *poutine* Italian style, with spaghetti sauce or red wine and garlic.
- Patati Patata (p137) – the house special is Patat-ine, with cheese curds served in an edible crispy potato basket.
- La Paryse (p134) – its burgers are so popular their poutine tends to fall under the radar, but it is wonderful!
- La Belle Province (Map p315; ☎ 845-0700; 1018 rue Ste-Catherine Est; ⊙ 24 hr; Ⓜ Beaudry) – Québec's most famous greasy spoon chain does a middling classic *poutine* but their Italian variety is the best in town.

CAFFÈ ITALIA Map p318   Café $

☎ 495-0059; 6840 boul St-Laurent; sandwiches $7.50, espresso $1.50; ⊙ 6am-11pm; Ⓜ Jean-Talon

Once this stretch of the Main was filled with gritty, dark old-world cafés where regulars would spend the day quaffing espresso and yelling at the Italian soccer team as they flitted across a rickety old TV. In recent years however cafés in this area have been getting Starbucked with slicker, more sexed up interior design and staff. Not this place. Caffè Italia is still rickety, rough around the edges and churning out the best espresso on the Main (if not the entire city) with staff that alternate between grumpy and terse to enthusiastically welcoming.

PIZZERIA NAPOLETANA

Map p318   Italian $

☎ 276-8226; 189 rue Dante; mains $9.50-15.50; ⊙ 11am-midnight Mon-Sat, noon-midnight Sun; Ⓜ De Castelnau

Homemade pasta sauces and thick-sauced pizzas (there's 31 sorts of each!) draw regulars here like flies. The dining room is simple with neat wood tables and chairs, and the friendly black-clad wait staff run between it and the kitchen. If you're visiting in the summer be prepared for big, loud crowds and lineups that stretch out the door.

LE PETIT ALEP

Map p318   Middle Eastern $$

☎ 270-9361; 191 rue Jean-Talon Est; mains $10-25; ⊙ bistro 11am-11pm Tue-Sat, restaurant 5-10pm Tue & Wed, 5-11pm Thu-Sat; Ⓜ De Castelnau

The complex flavors of Syrian-Armenian cuisine draw clientèle from all over Montréal. There's hummus, salads and *muhammara* (spread made of walnuts, garlic, bread crumbs, pomegranate syrup and cumin) and even the beef kebabs are an adventure, smothered in tahini, spices and nuts. You can either eat in the bright bistro (the front wall opens up onto the street during nice weather) or, in the evening, the slightly swish dining room next door.

IL MULINO Map p318   Italian $$

☎ 273-5776; 236 rue St-Zotique Est; mains $18-28; ⊙ 6-10pm Tue-Sat; Ⓜ Jean-Talon

Arguably the best Italian restaurant in town. This family-style restaurant is low-key and homey with old black and white photos on the walls. Lamb chops are the house specialty and the vegetarian starter plate with sautéed peppers and olives, stuffed eggplant and grilled mushrooms is still considered a classic.

MILE END

This neighborhood is a treasure trove of exotic flavors and gastronomic adventures. Strewn with low-key eateries and funky cafés, it also boasts that vedette of the city's culinary scene: the famous Montréal bagel shops. Some highlights follow but do your own exploring along ave Fairmount and ave St-Viateur, where you'll find everything from Senegalese to Mauritian cuisines.

WILENSKY'S LIGHT LUNCH

Map p318   Diner $

☎ 271-0247; 34 ave Fairmount Ouest; sandwiches $2.40-3.75; ⊙ 9am-4pm Mon-Fri; Ⓜ St-Laurent, then bus 55

It's like walking onto a 1950s movie set the moment you walk in the door at Wilensky's. Terminally grumpy staff make no effort to hide that cranking out your hand-pumped soda and Wilensky's special is likely the most disagreeable task they've had all day. Rickety wooden stools line the counter and photographs from the 1930s adorn the walls. This place was immortalized in Mordecai Richler's novel *The Apprenticeship of Duddy Kravitz* and the subsequent film but it is equally famous for its cheap sandwiches, burgers and hot dogs.

FAIRMOUNT BAGEL

Map p318   Bagels $

☎ 272-0667; 74 ave Fairmount Ouest; sandwiches $3.50-7; ⏱ 24 hr; Ⓜ Laurier

One of Montréal's famed bagel places, people flood in here around the clock to scoop them up hot the minute they come out of the oven. Bagels are one thing Montrealers don't get creative with. They stick to classic sesame or poppy seed varieties, though you can pick up anything from chocolate chip to sundried tomato bagels here too.

LA MAISON DU BAGEL

Map p318   Bagels $

☎ 276-8044; 263 ave St-Viateur Ouest; sandwiches $4-8; ⏱ 24 hr; Ⓜ Place-des-Arts, then bus 80

Also known as St-Viateur Bagel, this place has a reputation stretching across Canada and beyond for its perfectly crusty, chewy and slightly sweet creations – check out the newspaper articles from around the world.

CAFÉ L'ESPERANZA (CAFÉ LA PHARMACIE)

Map p318   Vegetarian $

☎ 948-3303; 5490 boul St-Laurent; mains $6.75; ⏱ 5pm-midnight Mon, 8.30am-2am Tue-Fri, 9am-2am Sat, 9am-midnight Sun; Ⓜ Rosemont

No mater how much the owner tries to change the name nobody seems able to stop calling this place Café L'Esperanza. The retro-kitschy décor complete with votive-candles burning on the tables is so on the ball with its references it's like traveling back in time. To anyone who grew up in Canada in the 1970s or '80s who may be reading this: Remember the white, unbreakable cups with tacky green flowers that our mothers all had? Well, that's what they serve the coffee in here! How cool is that? This place is vegetarian (and vegan wherever possible) with fantastic burritos, soups and sandwiches as well as baked goods like brownies with red peppers. Beer and cocktails are also served here. Café L'Esperanza has also become a real artists' hub and on any given day you might stumble across anything from a book launch to a spoken word recital to a bluegrass or electronic music performance.

BEAUTY'S

Map p318   Diner $

☎ 849-8883; 93 ave Mont-Royal Ouest; breakfast $10-15; ⏱ 7am-5pm Mon-Sat, 8am-5pm Sun; Ⓜ Mont-Royal

This sleek, retro '50s diner serves what many consider Montréal's best breakfast – all day long. Owner Hymie Sckolnick greets everyone with 'How are you, dahling.' Ask for 'The Special' – a toasted bagel with lox, cream cheese, tomato and onion. From the freshly squeezed juice to the piping hot eggs, sausages and pancakes, it'll be hard to go anyplace else once you've tried it. Lineups on Saturday and Sunday mornings can run up to 40 minutes long, even in winter.

MONTRÉAL'S SMOKED MEAT MUST

If you're in Montréal and the conversation turns to all things foodie, it won't be long before the subject of smoked meat comes up. Called pastrami in the rest of the world, Montréal has become as synonymous with the smoked meat sandwich as it is with bagels (see p145).

Smoked meat is made by smoking beef brisket with garlic, herbs and spices and then steaming it. It's generally agreed that the city can thank one Ben Kravitz, a Jew from Lithuania, for introducing the town to what would become one of Montréal's trademarks. Apparently Kravitz, who came to Canada in 1899, went on to found Ben's (p129) and got the inspiration for the recipe his grandparents used to make beef last longer without refrigeration.

There's terrific smoked meat all over the city but **Schwartz's** (p138) is the untopped king. Reuben Schwartz, a Romanian Jew, opened the-soon-to-be Montréal icon in 1928. It's been going gangbusters ever since. Schwartz's meat goes through a 14-day regime of curing and smoking before landing on your table after a final three-hour steam. There are usually long lineups outside, even in mid-winter weather but think of this as one of your integral Montréal experiences and if it's your first time, don't mess around, don't ask questions, just go with the medium fat.

SENZALA Map p318 — Brazilian $-$$

☎ 274-1464; 177 rue Bernard Ouest; dinner $10.50-16.75, breakfasts $6.95-14.95; ☉ 6pm-10pm Mon-Wed, 9am-late Thu-Sun; Ⓜ Place-des-Arts, then bus 80

Wonderful Brazillian meat and seafood dishes are served here. Try the *churrasquinho mixto* ($16.75) a medley of shrimp, chicken and beef brochettes marinated in garlic. The breakfasts here are also one-of-a-kind. The Tropicana ($9.95) has poached eggs gratinée in an avocado, with mango and tomato with cheese sauce and is served with plantain and fruit brochette. The restaurant is warm and causal with the dining room done up in bold colors and tended by terrifically friendly staff.

RESTAURANT BERLIN

Map p318 — German $$

☎ 270-3000; 101 ave Fairmount Ouest; mains $17-21; ☉ 4-11pm; Ⓜ Laurier

There really is nothing quite like hunkering down here on a frigid Montréal winter, stormy fall or spring day. Heaping portions of wholesome, piping hot Central and Eastern European fare is expertly served with a shot of schnapps after the entrée to prepare you for the main course. All the classics are here from pigs knuckles to potato dumplings, but the absolute best is the delicious but stomach punishing chef's platter ($21) which includes a sausage, roulade of beef, pork schnitzel, pork cordon bleu, potatoes and red cabbage.

MILOS Map p318 — Greek $$$

☎ 272-3522; 5357 ave du Parc; mains per pound $23-32; ☉ noon-3pm Mon-Fri, 5:30pm-midnight Mon-Sun; Ⓜ Place-des-Arts, then bus 80

Rock stars, socialites and business leaders flock to this fashionable restaurant with Mediterranean stucco, big urns filled with dried flowers and refrigerated counters of mouthwatering fish and fruits. Dinner for two (eg range of Greek appetizers, grilled seawolf, fried veggies with *tzatziki* and honey-laced milk yogurt) will run to $110 with wine. Reservations are essential.

MOISHE'S Map p318 — Steakhouse $$$

☎ 845-1696; 3961 boul St-Laurent; mains $24-38; ☉ 11:30am-2:30pm & 5:30-11pm Mon-Fri, 5-11pm Sat & Sun; Ⓜ St-Laurent, then bus 55

Feels a bit like a kind of social club, although guests from all backgrounds come to consume their legendary grilled meats and seafood. Its closely set tables amid hardwood paneling are perfect for eavesdropping. Skip the appetizers and launch straight into a gargantuan rib steak served with tasty fries or a Monte Carlo potato. Reservations are essential.

OUTREMONT

This is a tremendous area to seek out some upper-scale dining away from Downtown. You'll also find terrific bistros just by walking around.

LESTER'S Map p318 — Smoked Meat $

☎ 213-1313; www.lestersdeli.com; 1057 rue Bernard Ouest; mains $5-12; ☉ 9am-9pm Mon-Fri, 9am-8pm Sat; Ⓜ Outremont

Serving some of the city's best smoked meat for half a century, this deli is as much a part of Montréal lore as the three-hour lunch. With its Art Deco yet 1950s diner-style decor, the restaurant attracts a loyal following of locals looking for the perfect smoked meat sandwich (the dry-aged is formidable), but also smoked salmon or salads and awesome *karnatzel* (type of dried sausage) in fresh, medium or dry. You can also try to order through its website, though they do not deliver citywide.

LA MOULERIE Map p318 — Mussels $$

☎ 273-8132; 1249 rue Bernard Ouest; mains $15-20; ☉ 11:30am-11pm Mon-Fri, 10am-11pm Sat & Sun; Ⓜ Outremont

The mussels here seem bigger than elsewhere and the restaurant is renowned for its almost two-dozen sorts. Try the Greek mussels done up with umpteen ingredients including feta and ouzo ($19.95) or the Indian version with coriander and ginger ($18.45). Outremont locals usually crowd the simple dining room and the patio outside.

PARDON?

Menus in Montréal are increasingly bilingual but if you need help with *le français*, don't be shy to ask (the waiters are used to it). Important note: in French, an *entrée* is an appetizer, not a main course – that's *le plat principal*.

THE GREAT BAGEL DEBATE

The Montréal bagel has a long and venerable history. It all started in 1915 when Isadore and Fanny Shlafman, Jews from the Ukraine, opened a tiny bakery on rue Roy in the Plateau. They made the yeast bread rings according to a recipe they'd brought from the bakery where Shlafman's father worked. By 1919 they started the Montréal Bagel Bakery in a wooden shack just off boul St-Laurent, a few doors down from Schwartz's deli.

After WWII many holocaust survivors emigrated to Montréal and the bagel market boomed. Isadore Schlafman decided to build a bakery in the living room of his house at 74 ave Fairmount, where he opened **Fairmount Bagel** (p143) in 1950. Meanwhile Myer Lemkowicz, a Polish Jew who survived Auschwitz, went on to establish **La Maison du Bagel** (p143), also known as the St-Viateur Bakery, in 1957. A legendary rivalry was born and scores of other bagel bakeries sprang up in their wake.

Ask any Montrealer whose bagel is best and passions will flare. Year-in and year-out tireless critics tour the main bagel bakeries to chat, chew and cogitate. In recent years La Maison du Bagel has edged out Fairmount for the number-one slot. Lesser entries are dismissed with scorn – 'hockey puck' is a common assessment.

But locals do agree that Montréal's bagels are superior to their New York cousins. The Montréal bagel is lighter, sweeter and crustier, and chewy but not dense thanks to an enriched eggy dough that looks almost like batter. The dough hardly rises and the tender rings are formed by hand and boiled in a honey-and-water solution before baking (ideally in a wood-burning oven). Dry heat and woodsmoke produce bagels of a crusty, near-charred perfection.

But are they really tastier than New York's? When it comes down to it the standards are entirely different. Montrealers tout lightness while Big Apple natives may complain that their own bagels aren't dense enough. Nonetheless it's telling that your author met a Manhattan resident schlepping a dozen Montréal bagels back home just to compare.

CHEZ LÉVÊQUE Map p318   French $$

☎ 279-7355; 1030 ave Laurier Ouest; mains $18.50-23; ⏰ 8am-midnight Mon-Fri, 10:30am-midnight Sat & Sun; Ⓜ Place-des-Arts, then bus 80
This classic bistro attracts the beautiful people of Mile End and Outremont to chat about fashion, movies and business under irreverent religious art. Paris-born owner Pierre Lévêque presents a superb choice of traditional French cuisine with grilled meats (rack of lamb or caribou) and fresh seafood (red snapper, Atlantic salmon or bouillabaisse). Many of the fine wines are sold by the glass.

NÔTRE-DAME-DE-GRÂCE

This historically anglo area of Montréal is home to an increasing bevy of good restaurants west of the boul Décarie expressway along the main strips of rue Sherbrooke Ouest and ave Monkland.

YE OLDE ORCHARD PUB

Map pp308-9   Pub $

☎ 484-1569; 5563 ave Monkland; mains $8-16; ⏰ 12:30pm-2am Mon-Wed, 11:30am-3am Thu & Fri, noon-3am Sat, noon-2am Sun; Ⓜ Villa-Maria
Join hordes of chattering pubgoers for British Isles classics like bangers 'n' mash, fish and chips, Lancashire steak or Irish stout stew, all served to the strains of traditional Celtic music by kilt-clad waiters. As the night wears on, the empty Guinness glasses pile up below the pubroom TVs.

LA LOUISIANE Map pp308-9   Cajun $$

☎ 369-3073; 5850 rue Sherbrooke Ouest; mains $13.50-26; ⏰ 5:30-9:30pm Tue-Wed, 11:30am-3pm, 5:30-10pm Thu-Fri, 5:30-11pm Sat, 5:30-9:30pm Sun; Ⓜ Vendome, then bus 105
Montréal meets the Deep South in this casual NDG eatery, with amazing results. The menu bears the hearty, delicious flavors of jambalaya, shrimp Creole or chicken étouffé, all armed with mysterious peppers and spices. The diet-blowing Voodoo Pasta has spicy Cajun sausage and tomatoes in white wine and cream. While you're here, be sure to check out paintings of street scenes by N'awlins native James Michelopoulos.

WESTMOUNT

There are terrific cafés and bakeries along rue Sherbrooke Ouest and ave Greene is home to an interesting mix of eateries ranging from bistro to Japanese to diner.

TUTTI FRUTTI Map pp310-11   Diner $

☎ 934-0054; 4024A rue Ste-Catherine Ouest; mains $4.95-10.95; ⏰ 6am-3pm Mon-Sat, 7am-3pm Sun; Ⓜ Atwater
Plates are laden with gut-busting helpings at this bustling downtown breakfast place.

Don't expect much atmosphere from the no-frills dining room, the ambience here comes from the crowds that descend here, particularly on weekends. The *velours bleu*

BREAKFAST FAVORITES

Breakfast falls broadly into two camps: continental and the more voluminous Québécois variety. A continental breakfast will set you back a few bucks and typically consists of croissants or crusty bread and butter, jam and a mug of stiff coffee. For more variety (and bulk), the Québécois breakfast can include eggs, toast, bacon, sausage, potatoes, baked beans, fruit and coffee, on a sliding scale of about $3 to $8. If none of this appeals, you won't have to look far for bagels, pancakes or French toast.

- Beauty's (p143) – simply a Montréal legend that you have to come and experience for yourself
- Chez Cora (p137) – huge, gorgeously presented breakfasts, towering fruit salad structures, whimsical cartoony décor. Heaven!
- Tutti Frutti (p145) – copious breakfasts in a loud jovial atmosphere
- L'Express (**p140**) – a favorite with the Plateau crowd for the perfect flaky croissant, expert espresso and reading the morning paper
- Café Méliès (p132) – a favorite for a trendy, upscale breakfast

(two eggs, bacon and two blueberry pancakes served with potatoes, toast and coffee) is one of the most popular – you won't need to eat for the rest of the day it's so filling.

CHINE TOQUE Map pp310-11   Diner $$
☎ 989-5999; 4050 rue Ste-Catherine Ouest; mains $4.95-10.95; ☽ lunch 11:30-2:30pm Mon-Fri, dinner 5:30-11pm Fri & Sat, 5:30-10pm Sun-Thu; Ⓜ Atwater
Plates are laden with gut-busting helpings at this bustling downtown breakfast place. Don't expect much atmosphere from the no-frills dining room. It's calm, serious, and has just a few tasteful wall pictures and carvings. The food, on the other hand, is a joy. It's definitely toned down (nothing too fiery) but is perfectly prepared. Nothing is too heavy, fatty, or drowning in sauce. And the crispy beef is some of the best in the city. The dinner for two is endless, beautifully served and well worth the price (Menu 1 $41.99 or $53.99). Service is fantastic, discreet and knowledgeable without being pushy.

CHEZ NICK
Map pp310-11   Diner $
☎ 935-0946; 1377 ave Greene; mains $8-14; ☽ 7am-8pm Mon-Sat, 8am-6pm Sun; Ⓜ Atwater
This perfect little diner has been smack in the middle of swish Westmount since 1920. Despite the trendy stores and galleries that have mushroomed around it, it's stayed unabashedly dated and square. The Montréal diner staples are all here from burgers and fries, smoked meat and desserts so high and rich they threaten to topple over. But it's got something for everyone, including the foodie, fusion fanatics and you'll find health fare like brie and Granny Smith apple sandwiches with balsamic vinaigrette on black

Russian bread ($7.95) – wow. Lunchtime is rush time and lineups snake out the door.

SOUTHWEST MONTRÉAL

Watch this space: there are lofts and condos shooting up like crocuses in this old railway workers' district near downtown, so ambitious chefs are sure to follow.

GREEN SPOT
Map pp310-11   Diner $
☎ 932-2340; 3041 rue Notre-Dame Ouest; breakfast $3.50-6; ☽ 5am-midnight Mon-Thu, 24 hr Fri-Sun, closes midnight Sun; Ⓜ Lionel-Groulx
This diner near Atwater Market resembles a classic truck stop, with miniature jukeboxes at your booth and waiters who talk like they've heard it all. The fantastic breakfast specials, such as two eggs with sausage, fried potatoes, toast, baked beans and melon slices, run until 11am (later on weekends).

MAGNAN
Map pp308-9   Canadian $
☎ 935-9647; 2602 rue St-Patrick; mains $10-18; ☽ 6:30am-11pm Mon-Fri, 8am-11pm Sat & Sun; Ⓜ Charlevoix
Founded in the 1930s as a blue-collar diner, Taverne Magnan has long since raised meat and potatoes to an art form. Its reputation is fantastic roast beef – long-marinating, speckled with peppercorns and served in its own juice. This is the place to put back on the pounds after a day's cycling along the Canal de Lachine (near the front door).

Entertainment

Entertainment

Montréal parties with a vengeance, and the nightlife is legendary all over Canada. Those who have moved here from English Canada fondly recall the moment they first learned that midnight in Montréal is not when you start thinking about heading home and calling it a night, but when you go out in the first place. There's an endless choice of bars and clubs, and the exuberance is so contagious you'll forgive Montréal's flighty nature.

Music lovers are particularly well-served by the menu of classical to pop and New Age to world beats (see Music chapter p54). Jazz is never hotter or sweeter than at the International Jazz Festival. The performing arts enjoy theater and dance troupes of international renown; salsa dancing is so popular that Montréal calls itself the 'Latin capital of the north.' As a Hollywood film set Montréal has few equals, and its arthouse cinemas are showcases for up-and-coming directors (see p42).

To bone up on what's on, check the weekend editions of the *Montreal Gazette* as well as the French-language *La Presse*. Four free entertainment weeklies come out every Thursday: *Mirror* or *Hour* in English and *Voir* and *Ici* in French. All publications carry good reviews of cultural and arts events; pick up copies at bars and newsstands. Between the glossy covers of *ME* (Montréal Entertainment) you'll find all the details of the top clubs and DJs of the nanosecond.

Raves and loft parties rock this town like no other, and it's no secret that New England's best parties are held in Montréal. Check record stores and clubs for flyers, or do a basic Web search starting at www.nightmontreal.com.

Tickets & Reservations

For major pop and rock concerts, shows, festivals and sporting events, purchase tickets from the box office or call **Admission** (☎ 790-1245; www.admission.com) or **Ticketmaster** (☎ 790-1111; www.ticketmaster.ca). Admission has a dozen sales points around town including the **Centre Infotouriste** (☎ 873-2015 or 877-266-5687; 1001 rue Square-Dorchester) or the Place-des-Arts métro station. You can pay by credit card at all of these venues.

Info-Arts Bell (☎ 790-2787) is an information line for cultural events, plays and concerts.

The glass ceiling at Olympic Stadium (right)

Concert Halls & Arenas

BELL CENTRE
Map pp310-11

☎ 790-1245; 1260 rue de la Gauchetière; ☽ noon-6pm Mon-Fri, box office to 9pm on event days; Ⓜ Lucien-L'Allier or Bonaventure

When it's not hosting matches of the Montréal Canadiens hockey team, this 21,000-seat arena in downtown hosts all the big concerts. The likes of U2 and Céline Dion usually end up here when they're in town.

KOLA NOTE Map p318
☎ 274-9339; 5240 ave du Parc; ☽ box office noon-5pm Tue-Sat; Ⓜ Laurier

This cozy Mile End hall fits 450 people and hosts world music, rock, jazz and comedy acts.

OLYMPIC STADIUM Map pp308-9
☎ 252-8687; 4549 ave Pierre-de-Coubertin

Since the Montréal Expos baseball team moved to Washington DC it isn't getting the same workout it used to but it still occasionally hosts a variety of other events such as rock concerts, stunt car shows, trade fairs and the occasional Canadian Football League game.

PEPSI FORUM Map pp310-11
☎ 933-6786; 2313 rue Ste-Catherine Ouest; Ⓜ Atwater

This flashy entertainment arena is built on the site of the old Canadiens hockey rink. Cinemas with 22 screens, restaurants, a Jillian's pool and game emporium as well as the Comedy Nest (p162) rank among the biggest tenants. There are free shows staged in the central amphitheater.

TAM-TAM JAM

Hippie crowds gather every Sunday afternoon in summer for the legendary 'tam-tam' concerts at the edge of Parc du Mont-Royal (Map pp310-11). The action takes place at the Georges-Étienne-Cartier monument opposite Parc Jeanne-Mance, at ave du Parc and ave Duluth. The percussionists are tireless in their dedication, as some riffs go on for an hour or more, and other instruments join in on the odd occasion. Alternative handicrafts (eg Indian dream catchers, crystals and bead jewelry) are usually sold from suitcase displays.

PLACE DES ARTS
Map pp310-11

☎ 842-2112; rue Ste-Catherine Ouest; Ⓜ Place-des-Arts

Montréal's boxy but spacious municipal center for the performing arts (1992) has excellent acoustics. There are five theaters: the biggest, the 3000-seat Salle Wilfrid-Pelletier, hosts the city's symphony as well as ballet, opera and dance troupes. The eponymous square is the focal point of Montréal's International Jazz Festival.

POLLACK CONCERT HALL
Map pp310-11

☎ 398-4547; 555 rue Sherbrooke Ouest; Ⓜ McGill

McGill University's main music hall features concerts and recitals from its students and faculty, notably the McGill Chamber Orchestra. It's in the stately 19th-century building behind the statue of Queen Victoria.

SPECTRUM DE MONTRÉAL
Map pp310-11

☎ 790-1245; 318 rue Ste-Catherine; ☽ box office 10am-9pm Mon-Sat, 10am-5pm Sun ; Ⓜ Place-des-Arts

This converted cinema with great acoustics is a leading venue for rock and pop concerts as well as comedy acts. It serves as a main indoor venue for the International Jazz Festival in summer.

THÉÂTRE OUTREMONT
Map p318

☎ 495-9944; 1248 rue Bernard Ouest; ☽ box office noon-6pm Tue-Fri, noon-5pm Sat; Ⓜ Outremont

Built in 1929, this theater was both a repertory cinema and a major concert hall until it was shuttered in the late 1980s. The municipality of Outremont later brought it back to life and the theater was reopened in 2001. Now, everything from pop concerts and dance performances to Monday-evening film screenings take place here.

LIVE MUSIC

Montréal's independent music scene is legendary these days and there's a creative explosion in almost every club you go to. Everyone knows that little artsy band you're watching could one day be the next big thing.

Entertainment

LIVE MUSIC

JAZZ, BLUES & LATIN

BILY KUN Map pp316-17
☎ 845-5392; 354 ave du Mont-Royal Est; ⏰ 3pm-3am; Ⓜ Mont-Royal
One of the pioneers of 'tavern chic,' Bily Kun is a favorite local hangout that also draws party-goers across town for a chilled DJ-spun evening. First-time visitors usually gawk at the ostrich heads that overlook the bar but soon settle into the live music groove – jazz duos and trios (Tuesday to Friday and Sunday). Its cousin O Patro Vys (☎ 845-3855) is a performing-arts hall upstairs that features anything from electronic installations to Patagonian song and Haïku art.

BISTRO À JOJO Map p315
☎ 843-5015; 1627 rue St-Denis; ⏰ 11am-3pm; Ⓜ Berri-UQAM
This smoky venue in the Quartier Latin is the place for down 'n' dirty blues and rock groups nightly. If you are a fan and only have one night in Montréal this is the place to come. Sit close enough to see the band members' steam, or opt for a well-worn table at the rear that will take the edge off the decibels.

CLUB SODA Map pp310-11
☎ 286-1010; 1225 boul St-Laurent; adult/student $5/3; ⏰ 9pm-3am; Ⓜ St-Laurent
This venerable club hosts established acts such as Ranee Lee, a jazz singer in the Sarah Vaughan mold. New talent is embraced as well, with avant-garde groups, heavy metal and comedy acts performing in this hall with several hundred seats. Call for a recorded schedule.

CUBANO'S CLUB Map pp310-11
☎ 252-9749; 381 rue Ste-Catherine Ouest; ⏰ 10pm-3am; Ⓜ Place-des-Arts
This undisputed hub of Afro-Cuban and Latin jazz in Montréal gives dance classes during the day and sets standards of dexterity at night. Highlights here are the big Cuban orchestras and the mambo competitions during the International Jazz Festival.

HOUSE OF JAZZ Map pp310-11
☎ 842-8656; 2060 rue Aylmer; ⏰ 6pm-2am; Ⓜ McGill
Formerly known as Biddle's, a fixture on the Montréal jazz scene until owner-bassist Charlie Biddle passed away in 2003. The ambience is a tad touristy but fun with fin-de-siècle decor and musical instruments hanging from the ceiling. There's no cover charge, and you can eat ribs or chicken for about $15 per person including a drink. Prepare to wait if you haven't reserved.

JAZZ & BLUES
Map pp310-11
☎ 398-3319; www.mcgill.ca; 3840 rue McTavish; Ⓜ Peel
Located in the McGill University student union building, the Jazz & Blues club stages regular concerts by McGill's excellent student bands.

L'ESCOGRIFFE
Map pp316-17
☎ 842-7244; 4467a rue St-Denis; ⏰ 6pm-1am; Ⓜ Mont-Royal
This smoky, intimate Plateau club has quickly become one of Montréal's best jazz venues. It holds regular tributes to jazz legends like Charlie Parker or Herbie Hancock, and on Thursdays a jam session displays some of the greatest 'chops' on the Montréal scene, including some incredibly talented street musicians looking to break in. Blues and world music is woven into the agenda some nights.

LE VA-ET-VIENT
Map pp308-9
☎ 940-2330; 3706 rue Notre-Dame Ouest; ⏰ 11am-11pm; Ⓜ Lionel-Groulx
This smoky but popular venue straddles the boundaries between restaurant, music venue and exhibition space. Order one of its tasty microbrews and special bistro burgers and settle down to an evening of jazz, Irish folk or roadhouse funk.

LES BOBARDS Map pp316-17
☎ 987-1174; 4328 boul St-Laurent; ⏰ 3pm-3am; Ⓜ St-Laurent, then bus 55
This good-natured bar in the Portuguese area of the Plateau draws a hyper-fun 20s crowd for its sizzling Latin-American beats with French lyrics. It's pretty dead until around 10pm when it's standing room only. There are free peanuts and modern art exhibits. Expect a cover charge when bands are brought in.

QUAI DES BRUMES Map pp316-17
☎ 499-0467; 4481 rue St-Denis; ☼ 3pm-1am Mon-Thu, 3pm-3am Fri & Sat, 6pm-midnight Sun; Ⓜ Mont-Royal

A Parisian-style café with ornate framed mirrors, curlicued moldings and paneling that's been toasted brown by a million cigarettes. This fine venue for live jazz, rock and blues also has DJ-spun techno in the upstairs disco.

QUARTIER LATIN PUB Map p315
☎ 845-3301; 318 rue Ontario Est; ☼ 3pm-3am; Ⓜ Berri-UQAM

This cool bar with 1950s lounge-style decor has a small dance floor and a DJ playing New Wave on weekends, but Monday evenings you can catch rehearsals of the Vic Vogel Big Band for the price of a drink.

UPSTAIRS Map pp310-11
☎ 931-6808; 1254 rue Mackay; ☼ 6pm-2am, music from 9pm Mon-Sat; Ⓜ Guy-Concordia

This slick downtown bar hosts quality jazz and blues acts nightly, both local and touring talent. The walled terrace behind the bar is an enchanting place at sunset, and the dinner menu features some inventive salads and shark steak.

HIP-HOP, SOUL & WORLD MUSIC

JELLO BAR Map pp310-11
☎ 285-2621; 151 rue Ontario Est; ☼ 9pm-3am; Ⓜ St-Laurent

This perennial favorite is the quintessential lounge bar with garish-glitzy loveseats, lava lamps and a hot-to-trot clientele. Order one of 50-plus martinis and listen to the latest Marvin Gaye imitator at one of the extended jam sessions (weekends only).

LE DIVAN ORANGE
Map pp316-17
☎ 840-9090; 4234 boul St-Laurent; ☼ 11am-3am; Ⓜ St-Laurent, then bus 55

A new favorite on the main, this fantastic space was launched as a kind of restaurant-entertainment venue co-op. There's a terrific artistic vibe here. On any given night there may be a DJ, a world music performer or a record launch.

GAY & LESBIAN SPOTS

The majority of gay and lesbian entertainment is in the Village along rue Ste-Catherine Est, with a smattering of venues elsewhere in the city. For event listings, *Fugues* is a free monthly booklet for the gay and lesbian scene, in French but with easy-to-read club listings. Posters and flyers are also literally posted everywhere in these parts announcing new clubs, raves and gay friendly events.

MILE END Map p318
☎ 279-0200; 5322 boul St-Laurent; ☼ 5pm-3am Tue-Fri, 8pm-3am Sat; Ⓜ Laurier

Two levels of DJs can play up-level house without disturbing the laid-back 25s to 40s crowd drinking and chatting downstairs. The bar is affiliated with Montréal's Turbo Records and plays host to record launches throughout the year. Its identity shifts with the hour; dancefloors might form but it's not a club, and the top floor is more like a lounge.

POP & ROCK

BARFLY Map pp316-17
☎ 993-5154; 4026a boul St-Laurent; ☼ 3pm-3am Tue-Sat, 3pm-midnight Sun; Ⓜ Mont-Royal

This dubious cheap-beer dive appeals to chair-smashing patrons but also gritty local rock and blues bands of local renown. Wedge yourself in behind a raised cafétéria counter and take in the itinerant vibes, a bit like Tom Waits or Jack Kerouac in their first 15 minutes of fame. The Sunday afternoon blues jam is legendary.

CAFÉ CAMPUS Map pp316-17
☎ 844-1010; 57 rue Prince-Arthur Ouest; ☼ 3pm-2am; Ⓜ Sherbrooke

This eternally popular student club has great live acts, mostly French rock and live Québécois bands. In summer people wander in from the cafés and restaurants along rue Prince-Arthur for music and extra-cheap beer (happy hour is from 8:30pm to 10:30pm).

CAFÉ CHAOS Map p315
☎ 844-1301; 2031 rue St-Denis; ☼ 11:30-3am Mon-Fri, 2pm-3am Sat & Sun; Ⓜ Berri-UQAM

This down 'n' dirty basement bar is the place to catch the latest up-and-coming bands for a pittance in cover. Tuesdays there are two-for-one microbrews and turntable action with '80s glam rock, old pop classics and a pinch of punk. The bar is a workers' co-op that's definitely worth its weight in bong water. The downstairs **Bar les Conneries** (☎ 845-3889) runs a Wednesday oldies evening and hosts a variety of its own rock acts.

FOUFOUNES ELECTRIQUES
Map pp310-11

☎ 844-5539; 87 rue Ste-Catherine Est; ☉ 3pm-3am; Ⓜ St-Laurent

A one-time bastion of the alternafreak, the 'electric buttocks' has lost its edge but still stages some neat events (eg a DJ 'star-maker' night or indoor skateboard contest). On weekends the student-grunge crowd plays pool and quaffs brews till the dance floor starts to gel. The wall art is still vintage creepy-crawly.

LA SALA ROSSA Map pp316-17

☎ 284-0122; 4848 boul St-Laurent; Ⓜ Mont-Royal, then bus 55

This hall seats 250 people and its weathered digs show off the indie acts and rock bands that regularly take the stage (The Dears once played here). But with such an eclectic location – Spanish social club and restaurant (p139) – you can expect shows offering DJs, reggae, jazz or spoken word.

Electric guitar on bar at Bistro a JoJo (p150)

MAIN HALL Map p318

5390 boul St-Laurent; Ⓜ Mont-Royal

You'll find a mix of everything here from rock bands to world music. Check the local free entertainment guides around town to see what's coming up. You can usually buy tickets at the door (generally around \$10) when the doors open at around 9pm, but the entertainment guides will also mention which secondhand music shops or other venues you may be able to buy them from.

PASSEPORT Map pp316-17

☎ 842-6063; 4156 rue St-Denis; ☉ 10pm-3am Wed-Sat; Ⓜ Mont-Royal

A jewelry and clothing store by day, Passeport changes its spots after dark and becomes a small dance-music club spinning New Age and hip-hop. Québec's crème-de-la-crème shows up dressed to kill on weekends.

CHANSON & TRADITIONAL MUSIC

Québec folk music is integrated into the mainstream bar scene. The Irish and English pubs feature live folk music with acoustic guitar, red-hot Celtic fiddlers and rousing songs. Among the most popular venues are **Hurley's Irish Pub** (Map pp310–11; ☎ 861-4111; 1225 rue Crescent), **McKibbin's** (Map pp310–11; ☎ 288-1580; 1426 rue Bishop) and **Ye Olde Orchard Pub** (Map pp310–11; ☎ 484-1569; 5563 ave Monkland).

LES DEUX PIERROTS Map p314

☎ 861-1686; 104 rue St Paul Est; ☉ 6pm-1am Thu-Sat; Ⓜ Champ-de-Mars

This club has been serenading an adoring public for over three decades. Québec singers encourage you to join in sing-alongs of heart-on-your-sleeve chansons in thick dialect. The lyrics waft out over the rear terrace in summer.

CABARET MUSIC HALL Map pp310-11

☎ 845-2014; 2111 boul St-Laurent; Ⓜ St-Laurent

You'll never see québécois chanson the same way again. Right at the Musée Just for Rire (p89) this venue fits 800 people and hosts everything from DJs to comedy shows, but it's the massively popular **Soirées C'est Extra** nights that most Montréalers know

TOP FIVE LIVE MUSIC

- Les Bobards (p150) – hot Latin-American beats
- Café Campus (p151) – student mecca with great French acts
- L'Escogriffe (p150) – smoky showcase of top jazz talent
- Les Deux Pierrots (opposite) – heart-on-your-sleeve chansons in Québec dialect
- Boîte à Marius (below) – kick-ass off-the-beaten-track chanson

and love it for. Taking place every second Saturday, DJs remix popular québécois folk hits and have people dancing and singing their hearts out until the wee hours.

BOÎTE À MARIUS Map pp308-9

☎ 274-9090; 5585 ave Papineau; M Rosemont, then bus 197

A wickedly cool, off-the-beaten track location for classic chanson. Les Deux Pierrots (see above) is so centrally located, this one falls off people's radars (even for Montrealers) but the place is killer.

COFFEEHOUSES & SPOKEN WORD

The spoken word scene is becoming more and more popular in Montréal each year. Some of the most exciting and interesting stuff is being done on university campuses. Check out the bulletin boards or flyers at McGill or Concordia University where new and underground performances are regularly announced. Bars such as **Barfly** (p151) also hold spoken-word events.

INVISIBLE CITIES

☎ 847-9583; 1st Sat every month, other dates possible

This support group for local writers and publishers holds poetry and literature readings at venues around town. Contact organizer Christina Manolescu for a schedule of upcoming events.

YELLOW DOOR Map pp310-11

☎ 398-6243; 3625 rue Aylmer; Sep-Jun, closed Jul & Aug; M McGill

This earthy coffeehouse is Canada's oldest, having given refuge to US draft dodgers in the '60s. The program is English-language folk and blues acts, poetry and literature readings, but the schedule is erratic; call for upcoming events. There's no alcohol license and smoking is taboo.

CAFÉ LA PHARMACIE/L'ESPERANZA

Map p318

☎ 948-3303; 5490 St-Laurent; 5pm-midnight Mon, 8.30am-2am Tue-Fri, 9am-2am Sat, 9am-midnight Sun; M Rosemont

This fantastic café (p143) regularly opens its space for performances and events. On any given night you could stumble across a book launch, a spoken word performance, a bluegrass band or an electronic music performance. Check their board for upcoming events.

CINEMAS

Montréal hasn't escaped the trend toward multiplex cinemas; but they aren't necessarily as bad as they sound, many of them also regularly include foreign or independent films. More interesting are the several independent movie houses and repertory theaters. The website www.cinema-montreal.com is excellent with reviews and details of discount admissions. The repertory houses offer double bills and midnight movies on weekends. These cinemas are generally cheaper than the chains showing first-run films but a small membership fee may be charged.

AMC FORUM Map pp310-11

rue Ste-Catherine Ouest, cnr ave Atwater; M Atwater

This may seem like just another multi-theater monster cinema, but it's worth keeping an eye on these 22 screens. They are likely to have the most recent Bollywood smash or subtitled-québécois film hit somewhere amongst all the Hollywood blockbusters.

CINÉMA IMAX DU CENTRE DES SCIENCES DE MONTRÉAL Map p314

☎ 496-4629; adult/child $11/9; Quai King-Edward; M Place-d'Armes

Brings a range of specially-produced adventure, nature or historical films on oversized screens. Watch the Cirque du Soleil, dinosaurs or marine life come tumbling into your lap with the aid of 3D glasses and translation headsets.

FILM CITY MONTRÉAL

With its European ambience and big-city energy Montréal is a movie-maker's dream. Since the 1970s the city has hosted hundreds of productions, helped by the favorable exchange rate that makes it a bargain for US filmmakers. Hollywood celebrities like Robert de Niro, Cate Blanchett and Julia Roberts can be spotted dining in the sleek restaurants along boul St-Laurent or sipping a cognac at the scenic Old Port. The stars feel so comfortable mixing in public because Montrealers don't make a fuss about them.

The diversity of the urban landscape hands the producers a great variety of scenery choices. Especially popular are Old Montréal, the Plateau and the McGill University campus where you'll run across 'film-in-progress' signs throughout the year. In George Clooney's *Confessions of a Dangerous Mind* (2002) the cobblestone streets of Old Montréal stood in for East Berlin and Helsinki.

The city's largest and traditionally most turbulent cinematic event is the **Montréal World Film Festival** (p23), attracting fans from around the globe to view 400-plus films from six continents. Controversy is virtually guaranteed: in 2003 the festival lost its international accreditation as a competitive film festival, its schedule conflicted with events in Toronto and Venice, and some prize money was nearly a year late due to persistent financial woes. A saving grace is the cornucopia of films by first-time directors from the far corners of the earth, which keeps the festival fresh and unpredictable. For every high-profile picture like the American Gus van Sant's *Elephant* there are dozens more from places with scarcely any film industry like Afghanistan, the Philippines and Slovenia.

CINÉMATHÈQUE QUÉBÉCOISE
Map p315

☎ 842-9763; 335 boul de Maisonneuve Est; admission $4; ⏰ 1-9pm Tue-Sun; Ⓜ Berri-UQAM
A university-flavored venue noted for its French and Québécois avant-garde films. In the lobby there's a permanent exhibition on the history of filmmaking as well as a TV and new-media section.

EX-CENTRIS CINEMA
Map pp310-11

☎ 847-2206; 3536 boul St-Laurent; Ⓜ St-Laurent
A showcase for independent films from around the world founded by the creator of Softimage, a Montréal special-effects company. It's sleek and geared to provide pure movie enjoyment (pop corn and soft drinks are banned because they distract from the movie-watching experience, for example). Besides several cinemas, this place is full of high-tech film gadgetry you have to see to believe, starting with the box-office cashier whose disembodied head speaks to you through electronic port holes when you buy your tickets.

LE NOUVEAU CINÉMA DU PARC
Map p315

☎ 281-1900; 3575 ave du Parc; tickets $10; Ⓜ Place-des-Arts, then bus 80
Montréal's only English-language repertory cinema is getting a second chance! Financial problems forced the original owner to close down this much-loved theater and the city's movie-lovers were heart-broken. However, local businessman Roland Smith recently snapped up the space and re-opened the theater, determined to make a go of the institution this time around.

NATIONAL FILM BOARD
Map p315

☎ 283-9000; www.nfb.ca; 1564 rue St-Denis; ⏰ noon-9pm Tue-Sun; Ⓜ Berri-UQAM
This cutting-edge cinema in the Quartier Latin is worth a visit for serious cinephiles. There are regular screenings from the archive of 6000 films, documentaries and animated shorts, but the real attraction is its Cinérobothèque – make your choice, and a robot housed in a huge, glass-roofed archive plucks your selection from the stacks. Then relax and settle back into individual, stereo-equipped chair units to watch your personal monitor. There is also a huge Canadian-video collection available.

PARAMOUNT & IMAX CINEMAS
Map pp310-11

☎ 842-5828; 977 rue Ste-Catherine Ouest; Ⓜ Peel
An entertainment monstrosity with crowds darting through junk-food kiosks amidst a riot of flashing lights and booming sounds to get to the IMAX theatre and screens showing Hollywood blockbusters in this multilevel cinema.

FILM FESTIVALS

Montréal has so many film festivals (22 at last count) it's hard to keep track. In addition to Fanstasia, the Montréal World Film Festival and Festival du Nouveau Cinéma listed in the City Calendar section of this book, check out the festivals below.

CINEMANIA

www.cinemaniafilmfestival.com
Cinemania features films from French-speaking countries, all subtitled in English for non-native speakers.

FESTIVAL INTERNATIONAL DU FILM SUR L'ART

www.artfifa.com
A festival devoted to films and documentaries about art from all over the world.

DRINKING

The Plateau Mont-Royal has some of the best drinking spots in town – cruise boul St-Laurent, rue St-Denis and ave du Mont-Royal and you'll find a mix of trendy bars with plenty of splash, and creaky old pubs with a pool table, a few stools and more of a neighborhood feel. Concordia University,

---

McGill University and Dawson College are all just a few minutes from rue Crescent, making this strip of bars particularly popular with Anglophone Montrealers.

The Old Town's bars still have a reputation for being a bit of a drag as they can get overrun with visitors during the summer, but don't write them off altogether – employees from the new media and communications firms opening nearby are making the drinking crowds more and more diverse each year.

BREWPUBS

BIÈRES & COMPAGNIE Map pp316-17

☎ 844-4394; 4350 rue St-Denis; ☯ 3pm-1am; Ⓜ Mont-Royal or Sherbrooke
This relaxed pub has a great choice of European and local microbrews alongside excellent pub grub and mussels (see also p139).

BRUTOPIA Map pp310-11

☎ 323-9277; 1219 rue Crescent; ☯ 3:30pm-3am Sun-Fri, noon-3am Sat; Ⓜ Guy-Concordia
This fantastic brewpub has eight varieties of suds on tap including honey beer, nut brown and the more challenging raspberry blonde. The bare brick walls and wood paneling are conducive to chats among this relaxed student crowd. Live blues bands play some evenings; pints are $2.50 until 8pm and all night Monday. Really picks up after the night classes from nearby Concordia get out.

DIEU DU CIEL Map p318

☎ 490-9555; 29 ave Laurier Ouest; ☯ 4pm-2am; Ⓜ Laurier
There's no better bar then this in Montréal. Packed every night this bar drips atmosphere, is totally unpretentious and serves a phenomenal rotating menu of microbrew beers, running from classic ales to stouts that taste like chocolate or espresso, to a beer so smoky it's like sucking ash. (If you should find yourself staggering towards St-Laurent afterwards, that building on the corner is a former city hall, transformed into the coolest fire station in town.)

LES TROIS BRASSEURS Map p315

☎ 845-1660; 1660 rue St-Denis; ☯ 11am-1am, to 3am in summer; Ⓜ Berri-UQAM
This chain of European beer-brewers has set up a great locale in the Quartier Latin.

Québec's top artisanal beers

- McAuslan Brewing – keep an eye out for its apricot wheat ale and especially its St-Ambroise oatmeal stout
- Boréale – has everything from black beer to blond, but the red variety is by far the prefered.
- Unibroue – *Fin du Monde* (The End of the World) is a triple-fermented monster with 9% alcohol that more than lives up to its name and *La Maudite* (The Damned) is a rich spicy beer that clocks in a close second at 8%.
- L'Alchimiste – this Joliette-based brewer (about 60km northeast of Montréal) turns out a stable of different brews but its Bock de Joliette, an amber beer, is the star of the bunch.
- Lion D'Or – this Lennoxville brewer (p263) is one of the best in the province and does an outstanding, *very* bitter, bitter beer. For some reason, finding the label in Montréal these days is a bit like searching for a needle in a haystack (you know it's there somewhere but...) so if you come across this mark scoop it up fast!

Four homegrown brews are always on tap and the menu has a number of great bistro-style bites. Summer's the best time because the sliding garage doors let in the cool night air.

LOUNGES

GO-GO LOUNGE Map pp316-17
☎ 286-0882; 3682 boul St-Laurent; Ⓜ Sherbrooke
The retro-kitsch decor here looks like it was copied from an Austin Powers movie: '60s psychedelics, flower-power motifs, glistening vinyl and teardrop chairs. Regulars give this place raves for the cocktails and raspberries for the music rut that has the same music playing night after night. Look for bizarre weekend antics like women in schoolgirl costumes paddling passersby on the butt for fun.

LE PHARAON LOUNGE Map p314
☎ 843-4779; 139 rue St-Paul; Ⓨ 11:30am-3pm; Ⓜ Place-d'Armes
The Tintin theme of its neighboring restaurant spills over into this small, laid-back casual lounge. Like the nearby office workers that frequent it, you won't come here for gimmicks, pickups or trendiness, but rather for a place to hang out with friends when all you really want is a drink while you chat or unwind at the end of the day. Walls are brick and have a couple of pharaoh posters on the wall but don't try to push the connection too hard. It often hosts jazz acts and tickets are usually $10 to $15.

LUBA LOUNGE Map pp310-11
☎ 514-2109; 2109 rue Bleury; Ⓨ 9pm-3am; Ⓜ Place-des-Arts
Montréal is a mecca for lounge lizards and Luba has got the scene down pat. An unhurried crowd of 20- and 30-somethings settle into 'seating zones' with plush velvety sofas, easy chairs and soft lighting to sip on a microbrew while New Age, hip-hop and electronic music plays every night from 11pm. On Monday night there's a jam session of amateurs playing whatever.

SOFA Map pp316-17
☎ 285-1011; 451 rue Rachel Est; Ⓨ 3pm-3am; Ⓜ Mont-Royal
This cigar-and-port lounge with the comfy lounge gear is often standing room only on

the weekends when 20- and 30-somethings crowd in for live R&B, funk and soul bands. Hot snacks like nachos and designer burgers are served.

TYPHOON LOUNGE
Map pp308-9
☎ 482-4448; 5752 ave Monkland; Ⓨ 6pm-2am; Ⓜ Vendôme, then bus 105
Young yuppies, anglo and francophone, slip in to this Côte-des-Neiges watering hole for a beer and chicken legs on the way home or camp out for jazz, blues and world beats. It's hard to shake the office-worker ambience but on summer nights it's a good pitstop while cruising ave Monkland.

PUBS & BARS

Montréalers do much of their socializing over drinks, and the variety of the watering holes is astounding. Don't be put off by the sometimes scruffy appearances. Pubs here live or die by the kind of clientele they attract, not so much by the décor.

BAROUF Map pp316-17
☎ 844-0119; 4171 rue St-Denis; Ⓨ 3pm-1am; Ⓜ Mont-Royal
This French watering hole is the perfect spot to stop for a drink or three while cruising the Plateau. Brews can be ordered in giant plastic towers with a tap at the bottom. More conventional vessels are available for the 25 draft beers including extra-potent brands from Belgium.

BLIZZARTS Map pp316-17
☎ 843-4860; 3956a boul St-Laurent; Ⓨ 8pm-3am; Ⓜ St-Laurent, then bus 55
Virtually unmarked from the street, this cool discreet bar/club usually has teams of local club DJs who serve up jazz, funk, hip-hop, roots and dub to a small but sophisticated crowd.

EDGAR HYPERTAVERNE Map pp316-17
☎ 521-4661; 1562 ave du Mont-Royal Est; Ⓨ 3pm-3am; Ⓜ Mont-Royal
Once a trashy dive, Edgar's appeals to the well-educated, cognac-sipping crowd of the Plateau. When they're not air-kissing groupies, the DJs serve up a discriminating mix of acid jazz and New Age music. The wine list is copious.

PARTY CAPITAL OF CANADA

By: PhilipS

With 'dépanneurs' that sell wine and beer till 11pm, bars that serve drinks till 3am and 18 the legal drinking age you've got everything you need for a good time. The European feel of the city, tons of bars and clubs make for a good night out any day.

(blu,list) v. to recommend
a travel experience.
www.lonelyplanet.com/bluelist **BLUELIST.**

ELSE'S Map pp316-17

☎ 286-6689; 156 rue Roy Est; ⊙ 10am-3am; Ⓜ Sherbrooke

A warm and welcoming neighborhood bar where, as the saying goes, everyone knows your name. Settle into one of the worn chairs for an order of nachos, a tasty microbrew and a big portion of chat in front of the ceiling-high windows. Late-night jazz is a joy on weekends.

HURLEY'S IRISH PUB

Map pp310-11

☎ 861-4111; 1125 rue Crescent; ⊙ noon-3am; Ⓜ Guy-Concordia

This incredibly cozy place features live rock and fiddling Celtic folk on the rear stage and beer-soaked football and soccer matches on big-screen TVs. Standard pub grub is also served – fish 'n' chips, meat pies and burgers.

LE MAGELLAN BAR Map p315

☎ 845-0909; 330 rue Ontario Est; ⊙ 3pm-1am; Ⓜ Berri-UQAM

Once past the mock lighthouse out front you can enjoy a pleasant evening of eclectic offerings, from jazz to chansons. The interior is sprinkled with maritime doodads and the front terrace is great for people-watching.

LE ST-SULPICE Map p315

☎ 844-9458; 1680 rue St-Denis; ⊙ 11am-3am (dancing from 10pm); Ⓜ Berri-UQAM

This student evergreen is spread over four levels in an old Victorian stone house – a café, several terraces, disco and a sprawling back garden for drinks 'n' chats. The music changes with the DJ's mood, from hip-hop and ambient to mainstream rock and jazz.

LE SWIMMING

Map pp316-17

☎ 282-7665; 3643 boul St-Laurent; ⊙ 4pm-3am, live music Thu-Sun; Ⓜ St-Laurent

This quirky bar started life as a pool lounge ('Swimming,' get it?) but added a stage venue that plays indie rock, pop, hip-hop and jazz. Pot your balls or savor a cocktail on the cool terrace overlooking the Main (boul St-Laurent).

LE VIEUX DUBLIN PUB & RESTAURANT Map pp310-11

☎ 861-4448; 1219a rue University; ⊙ 11:30am-3pm & 5pm-3am; Ⓜ McGill

The city's oldest Irish pub has the expected great selection of brews (about $6 per pint) and live Celtic or pop music nightly. Curries rub shoulders with burgers on the menu.

LES FOLIES Map pp316-17

☎ 528-4343; 70 ave du Mont-Royal Est; ⊙ 11am-midnight; Ⓜ Mont-Royal

A cross between a bar, café and club, the oh-so-chic Folies has a DJ every night spinning trendy music and, much more importantly, the only sidewalk terrace on ave du Mont-Royal. Too-thin models and creative types breeze in for a quick 'Zen' sandwich or a 'Buddha' salad with mineral water before evaporating into the night.

MAD HATTER Map pp310-11

☎ 987-9988; 1220 rue Crescent; ⊙ 3pm-1am; Ⓜ Guy-Concordia

This bar in a nondescript area of de Maisonneuve kept generations of students from the nearby Concordia and McGill Universities happy. It has recently picked up and moved to the ultra-trendy rue Crescent nearby. The regulars used to the old location seem a little disoriented here but bizarrely the new spot is working. It has a comfy bar and a DJ-driven house with R&B and hip-hop on different nights of the week.

MCKIBBIN'S Map pp310-11

☎ 288-1580; 1426 rue Bishop; ⊙ 10am-3am Wed-Sat; Ⓜ Guy-Concordia

With its garage-sale furniture, McKibbin's cultivates a familiar, down-at-the-heels pub atmosphere. Its live entertainment varies from Celtic, pop and punk music to drinking contests. The office crowd pops in at lunch for burgers, chicken wings and salads.

PEEL PUB Map pp310-11
☎ 844-6769; 1107 rue Ste-Catherine Ouest; ☾ 8am-3am; Ⓜ Peel
This barn of a pub is a student institution for its cheap pitchers of beer and greasy-spoon menu. During televised sporting events fans hurl vocal abuse at the 30 big-screen TVs and it gets so crowded it's hard to move.

PUB STE-ÉLISABETH Map pp310-11
☎ 286-4302; 1412 rue Ste-Élisabeth; ☾ 4pm-3am Mon-Fri, 6pm-3am Sat & Sun; Ⓜ Berri-UQAM
Tucked off a side street, this awesome little pub is positively revered by Montrealers for its vine-covered courtyard and drink menu that includes beers galore, whiskeys and ports. It's got a mind-whirring repertoire of beers on tap, including imports and rare-to-find elsewhere microbrewery fare like Boréal Noir and Cidre Mystique.

SALOON Map p315
☎ 522-1333; 1333 rue Ste-Catherine Est; ☾ 11:30am-11pm Mon-Fri, 10am-midnight Sat & Sun; Ⓜ Beaudry
This bar-bistro with the Big Ben clock face earned a spot in Village hearts for its chilled atmosphere, cocktails and 'five-continents' menu including some good vegetarian options. This is a stylish pre-club pit stop.

SIR WINSTON CHURCHILL PUB
Map pp310-11
☎ 288-3414; 1459 rue Crescent; ☾ 11:30-3am; Ⓜ Guy-Concordia
Winnie's cavernous, split-level pub draws an older anglo crowd with its multiple bars, pool tables and pulsating music. The late great author Mordecai Richler used to knock back cold ones in the bar upstairs. Meals are served all day and drinks are half-price from 5pm to 8pm.

THURSDAY'S Map pp310-11
☎ 288-5656; 1449 rue Crescent; ☾ 11:30am-3pm & 6:30pm-2am; Ⓜ Guy-Concordia
Right next door to Winnie's, this lively singles place attracts hordes of fun-loving tourists and Montrealers looking for an easy place to paint the town red. Smoked bagels with cream cheese are the specialty on a menu

that spans gourmet bites. The mammoth bars and two-level dance floor appeal to the after-work crowd as well as night owls.

TOUR DE VILLE BAR Map p314
☎ 879-1370; 777 rue University; ☾ 6pm-midnight; Ⓜ Bonaventure
This padded upscale bar at the top of the Delta Hotel tower affords a splendid view of downtown Montréal. Cocktails are particularly costly but nursing one is fun, as is sizing up the office crowd from the nearby financial district.

CLUBBING

In Montréal, you have a great choice of venues from stylish monster clubs to smaller more laid-back party places. Following the Gallic tradition, things don't get going until after 11pm, and on Fridays and Saturdays expect the reveling to spill over into the after-hours clubs once the 3am closing time rolls around.

At some of the trendier places, especially the part of boul St-Laurent south of ave des Pins Est, expect line ups and a selection process that can run from subtle to not so subtle. If you are downtown around rue Crescent, rue de la Montagne and rue Bishop you'll hear more English

Sky Pub, a resto-bar in The Village (p160)

than French, while on rue St-Denis the reverse is true. Boul St-Laurent draws a pretty even mix of French and English speakers.

BELMONT Map pp316-17
☎ 845-8443; 4483 boul St-Laurent; ☽ 8pm-3am Thu-Sun; Ⓜ St-Laurent
A big draw on weekends for yuppie francophones in jeans and leather jackets who dig the laser light shows and the DJ trancemeisters. Some don't get past the pool table, cheap beer and big-screen sports in the front bar.

BOURBON COMPLEX Map p315
☎ 268-4679; 1574 rue Ste-Catherine Est; ☽ 3pm-3am; Ⓜ Beaudry
This gay entertainment complex looks like a wedding cake and is big enough to get lost in. There's La Track, a popular disco-bar with a leather boutique, and the Mississippi Club for dancing, live cabaret and drag shows.

CAFÉ DES ÉCLUSIERS Map p314
cnr rue McGill & rue de la Commune; ☽ 11am-11:30pm daily May-Sep; Ⓜ Square-Victoria
This club-café is right on the water at the Old Port with great views of the locks, the cruise ships and the hulking old grain silo across the water. Fantastic atmosphere, especially Friday and Saturday nights. Happy hour is from 5pm to 7pm.

CASA DEL POPOLO Map pp316-17
☎ 284-3804; 4873 boul St-Laurent; Ⓜ St-Laurent, then bus 55
One of Montréal's very best live venues, this place amazes with its diversity. As a café it's known for its vegetarian platters; as a funky bar for its talented DJs and great New Age and world mixes; and as an exhibition space for showing arthouse films and spoken word performances. It's associated with the tapas bar La Sala Rosa (p139) and concert venue La Sala Rossa (p152) across the street.

CLUB 737 Map pp310-11
☎ 397-0737; 1 pl Ville-Marie; ☽ 5-7pm Wed, 5-10pm Thu, 5pm-3am Fri & Sat; Ⓜ McGill
Try pre-dinner drinks with the glam set on the 43rd floor – the romantic skyline never disappoints. A Latin American dance contest is held Monday evening, but whatever the day there's always some serious cruising going on among the office crowd of 30-somethings.

CLUB ONE Map pp310-11
☎ 398-9875; 1186 rue Crescent; ☽ 4pm-3am; Ⓜ Lucien-L'Allier
This big stage venue with table service and a bar serves up an eclectic mix of music, from pop and jazz to New Wave lounge. A product of its recent renovation is a nifty tap dispenser for Jägermeister to settle trendy stomachs.

ELECTRIC AVENUE
Map pp310-11
☎ 285-8885; 1469 rue Crescent; ☽ 10pm-3am Thu-Sat; Ⓜ Guy-Concordia
Duran Duran, INXS, Depeche Mode…the spirit of '80s video pop lives on in this basement club in party-down rue Crescent. A few mirrors and lamps on satin-covered walls make up the decor, but no matter; from around 11pm on weekends you'll find the dance floor is packed with nostalgic 30-somethings. It also draws quite a few single women so guys listen up.

EXIT Map pp310-11
☎ 285-2223; 3553 boul St-Laurent (entrance on St-Dominique); ☽ 10pm-3am Fri & Sat; Ⓜ St-Laurent
Exit is one of those clubs where what's exciting is the people who fill it and not the space itself. This house and R&B mainstay doesn't look like much on the inside with its sparce interior, but when the star DJs show up this place is packed – it's one of the best nightclubs around.

LAÏKA Map pp316-17
☎ 842-8088; 4040 boul St-Laurent; ☽ 9am-3am; Ⓜ Sherbrooke
Get lost in the minimalist space of this intimate lounge bar where several DJs spin New Wave, house, techno and dub. It also serves a great continental breakfast (brunch on weekends)

LE DRUGSTORE Map p315
☎ 524-1960; 1366 rue Ste-Catherine Est; ☽ 8am-3am; Ⓜ Beaudry
This cavernous eight-story complex is modeled after a drugstore on New York's Times Square. It has big-city neon props, nine

theme bars, boutiques, a large delicatessen and a dance club in the basement. For bad hair days there's even a hairdresser. Lesbians and gays have staked out their terrain on different floors.

LE LOFT
Map pp310-11

☎ 281-8058; 1405 boul St-Laurent; ⌚ 9pm-3am Tue-Sat; Ⓜ St-Laurent

A spiffed-up crowd of 18 to 25s turn up for the mainstream rock and alternative on two dance floors, rough-edged murals and a great rooftop terrace. The wide metal staircase and ventilation ducts give the place a warehouse feel; the usual gear is jeans and T-shirts, now that the in-black crowd has sought more pretentious pastures.

LION D'OR Map p315

☎ 526-6849; 1676 rue Ontario Est; ⌚ varies; Ⓜ Papineau

This classy 1930s-style club draws beautiful people and visiting film-production crews. Patrons spin on the spacious wooden dance floor to killer party bands playing sophisticated rock and retro-pop. It's often used for private events so check the listings.

MADO CABARET
Map p315

☎ 525-7566; 1115 rue Ste-Catherine Est; ⌚ 11:30am-late; Ⓜ Beaudry

The drag shows usually start around 11:30pm and are legendary. The standup comedy features biting satire, with performers in eye-popping costumes. Mado is a flamboyant celebrity who writes a column in *Fugues*, the gay entertainment mag. The Tuesday night show is *the* event in the Village.

METROPOLIS
Map pp310-11

☎ 844-3500; 59 rue Ste-Catherine Est; Ⓜ St-Laurent

Housed in a former Art-Deco cinema that started off as a skating rink, this mega venue (capacity 2300) features live bands and DJs over three floors and has killer laser shows. Buy tickets at the box office around the corner at 1413 rue St-Dominique.

PARKING NIGHTCLUB
Map p315

☎ 282-1199; 1296 rue Amherst; ⌚ 3pm-3am; Ⓜ Berri-UQAM

With the right wardrobe you can celebrate Halloween every night at Parking, a very cruisy, steamy, and for the time being, utterly sexy gay nightclub. Located in an old garage repair shop, the club is decorated with car parts and tools. The **Cruising Bar** upstairs opens nightly, the disco Wednesday to Saturday with theme nights. The **Le Parking** bar and the fetishist **Donjon** club are eventful arms of the same complex. Since the only lesbian bar Magnolia closed down (lesbians in Montréal don't seem to be big clubbers, it's been years since a lesbian-oriented club stuck for any amount of time) there's been talk of a lesbian-Thursday night at one of the rooms here.

SAT Map pp310-11

☎ 844-2033; 1195 boul St-Laurent; ⌚ 3pm-3am; Ⓜ Berri-UQAM

The clock runs backwards over the bar at the Societé des Arts Technologiques, a cutting-edge warehouse space that promotes partying as much as digital art. DJs and performance artists push the envelope with banks of multimedia installations, but the wooden picnic tables and plastic beer cups recall its university links.

SKY PUB & CLUB Map p315

☎ 529-6969; 1474 rue Ste-Catherine Est; ⌚ 3pm-3am; Ⓜ Beaudry

This is one of those popular Village complexes designed to suck you in for an entire Saturday night of partying. If you're a gorgeous guy or looking for one, start the

---

TOP FIVE CLUBS

- Casa del Popolo (p159) – artsy venue with a split personality
- La Sala Rossa (p152) – anything from punk to world music
- Parking Nightclub (above) – gay meat market with Halloween flair
- Unity II (opposite) – newly renovated and full of attitude and flair
- Les Bobards (p150) – feels like you're at a giant house party

evening in the 1st-floor pick-up pub (low lighting for intimate chat) before heading up to the dance floors (disco and energized house/hip-hop). The roof terrace is a perfect place to catch the **Loto Québec International Fireworks Competition** (p22) in summer.

STUD BAR Map p315
☎ 598-8243; rue Ste-Catherine Est; ⏱ 6pm-3am; Ⓜ Papineau

This Village meat market has poor visibility, lots of guys with no hair, and persistent hopes for the night ahead.

TOKYO BAR
Map pp310-11

☎ 842-6838; 3709 boul St-Laurent; ⏱ 10pm-3am; Ⓜ Sherbrooke

Draws a dead chic crowd in their late 20s and early 30s for its water-filled backlit bar and sunken circular sofas that dwarf their occupants. Infectious pop, rock and New Age wafts over its impeccably wrapped patrons on two dance floors. The rooftop bar gets going around midnight.

UNITY II Map p315
☎ 523-2777; 1171 rue Ste-Catherine Est; ⏱ 10pm-3am Thu-Sun; Ⓜ Beaudry

This old Village favorite tragically burnt down just before the 2006 World Out-games – a tragedy given the windfall businesses on the strip were expecting from the thousands of people that would be partying in the streets each night. But the owners attacked this project with a vengeance and miraculously managed to open just in time. It's now got the attention of everyone not just for the shirtless techno-ravers and muscle queens but for its tenacity and work ethic in pulling off the impossible and anchoring its part of the Village despite the odds. The kitsch Bamboo bar is good for an incense-filled pop break while the Chill-Out Room appeals for its pool tables and leather benches for watching. The lovely rooftop terrace is a quiet getaway on summer evenings.

AFTER-HOURS CLUBS

After-hours clubs pick up the slack once the bars close at 3am. They don't serve alcohol but you can dance and listen to DJs until it's almost lunch time.

ARIA Map p315
☎ 987-6712; 1280 rue St-Denis; ⏱ 1:30am-10am; Ⓜ Berri-UQAM

This old Latin Quarter movie theater is now a refuge for sleepless party-goers, boasting three very individual floors and some of the ablest DJs in the industry including Christian Pronovost, Fred Everything and Yaz. The crowd is mixed straight, gay, and fashion victim, and exhibitions are held in the same very chilled space.

STEREO Map p315
☎ 286-0325; 858 rue Ste-Catherine Est; ⏱ 2am-11am Fri & Sat; Ⓜ Berri-UQAM

Montréal's house music giant, the sound system here is so amazing regulars gush about out-of-body-experiences. Stereo attracts everyone – gay, straight, students, drag queens – in short, anyone looking to lose sleep in style. You can warm up at the adjacent **Stereobar** from 10pm to 3am.

BALLROOM & WESTERN DANCE CLUBS

CLUB BOLO Map p314
☎ 849-4777; www.clubbolo.com; 960 rue Amherst; ⏱ 7:30-10pm Tue, 7:30pm-2am Thu-Sun; Ⓜ Beaudry

This is a gay country-and-western line dancing bar that is a one-of-a-kind in the Village. Line dancers should aim for Tuesday night; beginners show up for Friday classes at 7:30pm skilled kickers have Saturday nights to themselves.

DOREMI Map pp308-9
☎ 274-5456; 505 rue Belanger Est; ⏱ 6pm-midnight Thu-Sun; Ⓜ Beaubien

If you want to keep your fox trot fresh and your polkas perky, this all-round dance club in north Montréal has excellent music for ballroom dancing. The crowd is 30s and 40s, dedicated amateurs, a refreshing change from some of the presumptions downtown.

LE BALLATOU Map pp316-17
☎ 845-5447; 4372 boul St-Laurent; ⏱ 9pm-2am Tue-Sun; Ⓜ Mont-Royal

This dark, smoky Afro-Caribbean nightclub draws a multiethnic crowd and dancers of awesome sophistication. Shows are presented on weeknights for a varied cover; on weekends the cover (around $7) includes one drink. Check out the happy dancers in the photo gallery out front.

LATIN DANCE CLUBS

CACTUS Map pp316-17
☎ 849-0349; 4461 rue St-Denis; ☾ 10pm-3am Thu-Sat; Ⓜ Mont-Royal

Two floors of infatuation with things Latin, the Cactus is always packed with dancers ready to strut their stuff. Salsas and meringues are performed with astonishing ease by patrons poured into sexy outfits. Regulars are more than happy to show you the moves if your timing is off after a few *cervezas*.

L'ACADÉMIE DE TANGO ARGENTIN
Map pp316-17
☎ 840-9246; www.academietangoargentin.com; 4445 boul St-Laurent; ☾ varies; Ⓜ Mont-Royal

Tango dancing has enjoyed a surge of popularity in Montréal and the Academy is an excellent place to learn all the moves. Ascend through the beat-up door to the 3500 sq ft studio where owner Santiago teaches this sensual dance in private and intensive workshops as well as private parties. Prices and schedules vary by course, but you can reckon on $20 per hour.

LE SALONI DAOMÉ Map pp316-17
☎ 843-1755; 141 ave du Mont-Royal; ☾ 8:30pm-2am Thu-Sat; Ⓜ Mont-Royal

Latin dancing doesn't get much steamier than this, in a small Plateau club above an imported African goods shop. Enter via the unpretentious stairs and give yourself over to the small dance floor where the living room lamps and music make everyone look sexy. The stuffed chairs are usually occupied by enthralled couples.

SALSATHÈQUE Map pp310-11
☎ 875-0016; 1220 rue Peel; ☾ 9pm-3am Wed-Sun; Ⓜ Peel

This bright, busy, dressy place presents large live Latin bands pumping out tropical rhythms. During the breaks slurp a margarita in one of the movie-theater seats and watch the 25s to 50s crowd gyrate into exhaustion. Practice your one-liners and prepare to meet people Latin-style. Salsa, meringue and bachata lessons are given Sunday nights.

THEATER

From Shakespeare to Shepard and Carey to Carrey, there's drama and laughter on a Montréal stage every night.

CENTAUR THEATRE Map p314
☎ 288-3161; 453 rue St-François-Xavier; Ⓜ Place-d'Armes

Montréal's chief English-language theater presents everything from Shakespearean classics to works by experimental Canadian playwrights. It occupies Montréal's former stock exchange (1903), a striking building with classical columns. The season runs from October to June but other groups perform during the summer.

COMEDY NEST Map pp310-11
☎ 932-6378; Pepsi Forum, 2313 rue Ste-Catherine Ouest, 4th fl; shows ☾ 9pm Wed-Sun, also 11:15pm Fri & Sat; Ⓜ Atwater

Features Canadian comics like Jim Carrey as well as talent from all over North America. There's a dash of cabaret with singers, dancers, musicians, and female impersonators. Tickets for dinner and show are available.

COMEDYWORKS Map pp310-11
☎ 398-9661; 1238 rue Bishop; ☾ 9pm daily, 11:15pm Fri & Sat; Ⓜ Guy-Concordia

This upstairs venue presents standup comics nightly, usually in English. Events include open-mike nights, improvisation and headline acts on weekends. Audience participation and heckling is encouraged, and acts tend to be racier than at Comedy Nest.

I MUSICI DE MONTREAL
☎ 982-6038

Under the leadership of Moscow-born violin-cellist Yuri Turovsky this 15-member chamber ensemble has won many awards for its baroque and contemporary performances. Over the past 20 years I Musici, which has its home stage at the Place des Arts (p149), has recorded 43 CDs and toured in Europe and the USA.

L'OPERA DE MONTRÉAL Map pp310-11
☎ 985-2258; Place des Arts; box office ☾ 9am-5pm Mon-Fri; Ⓜ Place-des-Arts

Holds lavish stage productions that feature big names from Québec and around the world. The specialty is classics such as *Mefistofeles*, *Aïda* and *Carmen;* translations (French or English) are run on a video screen above the stage. Tickets cost around $40 to $100 during the week and slightly more on Saturday.

MCGILL CHAMBER ORCHESTRA
☎ 487-5190
Founded in 1939, this fine chamber ensemble is one of Canada's oldest. Concerts series are held at **McGill's Pollack Concert Hall** (p149) and other venues around the city. Its annual performance of the *Messiah* is extremely popular.

MONUMENT NATIONAL THEATRE
Map pp310-11
☎ 871-2224; 1182 boul St-Laurent; Ⓜ St-Laurent
Shows here run the gamut from Oscar Wilde to Sam Shepard with everything from acting, directing and technical production performed by graduating students of the National Theatre School. There are two halls, one with 800 seats, the other with 150 seats. The smaller theater stages about three original works a year by student playwrights. Tickets are on sale a month before opening and productions are in either English or French.

ORCHESTRE MÉTROPOLITAIN DE GRAND MONTRÉAL
☎ 598-0870; Place des Arts
This hip 58-member orchestra is made up of young professional musicians from all

over Quebec led by conductor Yannick Nézet-Séguin. The orchestra's mission is to democratize classical music so besides the swish Place des Arts, you may see it playing Mahler or Hayden in churches or colleges in even the city's poorest neighborhoods for reduced admission. A free 30-minute concert talk is given by one of its musicians one hour before each performance.

ORCHESTRE SYMPHONIQUE DE MONTRÉAL
☎ 842-9951; Place des Arts
Begun in 1934 as an amateur outfit for music-lovers, the Montréal Symphony Orchestra has grown into an international powerhouse that plays to packed audiences at Carnegie Hall. Its Christmas performance of *The Nutcracker* is legendary. Conductor Kent Nagano, a Californian with a leonine mane and stellar credentials, took over as music director in 2006. Until then the OSM was performing under the baton of guest conductors. Check for free concerts at the **Basilique Notre-Dame** (p73), **Olympic Park** (p98) and in municipal parks in the Montréal area.

SAIDYE BRONFMAN CENTRE
Map pp308-9
☎ 739-2301; 5170 Chemin de la Côte-Ste-Catherine; Ⓜ Côte-Ste-Catherine
Montréal's Jewish theater stages dramatic performances in English, Yiddish and Hebrew during the summer. The center also hosts a variety of other events throughout

Casino de Montréal (p166), Île Notre-Dame

the year, including dance and musical recitals, puppet shows and readings.

STATION C
Map p315

☎ 523-1450; 1450 rue Ste-Catherine Est; Ⓜ Beaudry

Alternative plays, circus and art exhibitions are held in this Village post-industrial space with living-room furniture. Some events have a gay flavor (this being the Village after all) but the artistic objective is much broader. It's worth a visit if only for the nonsensical whizz-bang machines by Florent Veilleux, a permanent exhibit.

THÉÂTRE DE QUAT' SOUS
Map pp316-17

☎ 845-7277; 100 ave des Pins Est; Ⓜ Sherbrooke

Housed in a former synagogue, this cosy theater is a launch pad for the careers of young singers, directors and playwrights. The forté is intellectual and experimental drama.

THÉÂTRE DE VERDURE
Map pp316-17

☎ 872-2644; Parc La Fontaine; ⏲ Jun-Aug; Ⓜ Sherbrooke

This open-air theater hosts musical, dance and drama events in the summer months, and something of a folks festival atmosphere prevails. Movies are also shown at a big pondside screen, and everyone shows up with blankets and ice chests.

THÉÂTRE DU NOUVEAU MONDE
Map pp310-11

☎ 866-8668; 84 rue Ste-Catherine Ouest; Ⓜ St-Laurent

The New World Theater specializes in classic dramas like Shakespeare's *Hamlet* or Molière's *Les Précieuses Ridicules*. The French-language venue is a 1912 movie house and theater renovated in 1996, now with snappy technical gear. There are matinee and evening performances.

THÉÂTRE DU RIDEAU VERT
Map pp316-17

☎ 844-1793; 4664 rue St-Denis; Ⓜ Laurier

This quality French-language venue has an elegant stage that's well suited to classic plays. Its lineup includes both repertory

and contemporary works with a preference for timeless works. The stage designs, costumes and lighting have earned accolades.

THÉÂTRE ST-DENIS
Map p315

☎ 849-4211; 1594 rue St-Denis; box office ⏲ noon-9pm; Ⓜ Berri-UQAM

This Montréal landmark and historic movie house hosts touring Broadway productions, rock concerts and musical comedies. Its two halls (930 and 2200 seats) are equipped with the latest sound and lighting gizmos and figure prominently in the Just for Laughs festival.

USINE C
Map p315

☎ 521-4198; 1345 ave Lalonde, off rue Panet; Ⓜ Beaudry

This former jam factory in the Village is home to the Emmy-award-winning Carbon 14 drama and dance troupe that performs here regularly. Its two flexible halls (450 and 150 seats) can be rejigged to accommodate circuses or raves. To bump into its talented performers head for the cosy basement café next to the changing rooms. Dinner-and-show tickets are available.

THEATER FESTIVALS
FESTIVAL DE THÉÂTRE DES AMÉRIQUES

⏲ 842-0704; www.ftq.qc.ca

Around 160 shows from countries throughout the western hemisphere are featured at this festival from late May to early June.

FESTIVAL JUSTE POUR RIRE (JUST FOR LAUGHS)

☎ 845-2322; www.hahaha.com

This festival draws big names like Jerry Seinfeld or Drew Carey plus Canadian comics (in both French and English) in late July.

MONTRÉAL FRINGE FESTIVAL

☎ 849-3378; www.montrealfringe.ca

This famous festival features avant-garde dancing, music and plays in intimate venues around town during the second half of June.

DANCE & PERFORMING ARTS

Montréal has a vibrant scene for jazz dance, traditional dance and ballet. It's home to internationally renowned troupes like Les Grands Ballets Canadiens and several avant-garde companies such as LaLaLa Human Steps (☎ 277-9090) or Margie Gillis (☎ 845-3115). Innovative companies such as O Vertigo Danse (☎ 251-9177) and Tangente (☎ 525-5584) have expanded the idiom and offered fresh direction.

AGORA DE LA DANSE
Map pp316-17

☎ 525-1500; www.agoradanse.com; 840 rue Cherrier; adult/child $23/16; Ⓜ Sherbrooke
Based in the striking old Palestre National building in the Plateau, this university dance troupe with a growing reputation focuses on modern and experimental forms. Two studios are open for instruction to the public; its student and independent dance companies stage regular performances.

CIRQUE DU SOLEIL
Map pp308-9

☎ 722-2234; www.cirquedusoleil.com; 8400 2nd ave
Over the past two decades the Cirque du Soleil (literally 'Circus of the Sun') has pushed back the boundaries of traditional circus with its astounding acts of dexterity and ethereal costumes. From its humble beginnings this one-time troupe of stilt-walkers has grown into an international phenomenon that thrills millions of spectators the world over.

Every few summers the circus erects its familiar striped tent for shows at the Old Port, but a new 'big top' called the Cité des Arts has been built for the premieres of its elaborate shows (see the boxed text on p46).

LES BALLETS JAZZ DE MONTRÉAL
☎ 982-6771; www.balletsdemontreal.com
This Montréal modern-dance troupe has achieved international acclaim since its birth in the 1970s. Artistic director Louis Robitaille showcases the talents of his classically trained dancers in experimental forms while encouraging up-and-coming choreographers as well. The dance troupe's performances are full of sensual grace and physical fireworks. When they are not out on an international tour they play at their home stage in Place des Arts (p149) and venues like the Théâtre de Verdure (opposite) in Parc LaFontaine, where they often kick off the fall arts season.

LES GRANDS BALLETS CANADIENS
☎ 849-8681; www.grandsballets.qc.ca; 4816 rue Rivard
You can be assured of a treat with tickets to Québec's leading ballet troupe. Aside from playing four shows annually in Montréal, the 34 dancers play a major role on the world stage, when they embark on two major tours every year. Its classical and modern programs are regarded as innovative while still remaining accessible to general audiences. There are dance classes for children that are also organized.

BILLIARDS

The pool lounge is alive and well in Montréal. Bars and pubs listed earlier might also have a table or three.

ISTORI
Map pp310-11

☎ 396-2299; 486 rue Ste-Catherine; ☽ 11am-midnight Mon-Wed, 11am-3am Thu-Sat; Ⓜ McGill
Unwind at two bars or 20 pool tables at this loft-style pool hall on the 2nd floor, a world away from rue Ste-Catherine below. Beers are tasty and potent (Hoegaarden, Leffe, Stella Artois) and you can obliterate an order of nachos or tacos before your next full clearance. Pool is free on Mondays and Tuesdays from 4:30pm to midnight.

SHARX
Map pp310-11

☎ 934-3105; 1606 rue Ste-Catherine Ouest; ☽ 11am-3am; Ⓜ Guy-Concordia
This underground cavern has no less than 36 pool and billiard tables, rows of TV screens beaming sports and a post-apocalyptic feel. The cool bowling alley is bathed in fluorescent light with glowing balls and pins.

CASINOS

CASINO DE MONTRÉAL

Map p319

☎ 392-2746; Île Notre-Dame; ☯ 24 hr; Ⓜ Jean-Drapeau, then bus 167

One of the 10 largest casinos in the world, occupying the former French pavilion from the Expo '67. Methods of separating yourself from your hard-earned cash include roulette, baccarat, blackjack and a few thousand slot machines. There is no alcohol served in the gambling halls. The dress code is not very strict but turning up in shorts and beachwear is a definite no-no.

The upstairs gallery offers a stupendous view of downtown and the attached restaurant, Nuances (p129), is one of the city's finest eateries. Glitzy Las Vegas-style shows are staged here too. A free bus service takes patrons to and from Square Dorchester (p88).

Activities ■

Activities

Montréal is known for its urban flash and cutting edge culture, but if you want a break from the museums, bars and bistros, there are all sorts of activities in town.

Sporting events draw huge numbers of Montrealers and visitors whether they are participants or spectators. To channel your inner athlete, the **Tour de l'Île** (p22) is definitely one of the most fun events and has a good mix of hardcore bike enthusiasts and casual riders. Some streets are shut off for the cyclists and there's a palpable energy in the city that even nonriders enjoy.

On the spectator side, the **Grand Prix du Canada** Formula One race (see p175) is unbeatable for the excitement. The roars from Parc Jean-Drapeau are heard all over town and many downtown streets are made pedestrian to accommodate the thousands of late-night partyers. The rest of the year, sports fans can take in hockey, soccer and the hugely popular Canadian Football League.

You certainly don't need to wait for organized events however. Montrealers get out and get moving no matter what the season. There are over 600km of bike paths in town and two of the most beautiful and pleasant stretches are along the **Canal de Lachine** (p108) and around **Île Notre-Dame** (p82). In winter, green spaces become cross-country ski trails and ponds and lakes at places like the Old Port or Parc La Fontaine become outdoor skating rinks.

After all the physical activity, there are also plenty of places around town where you can relax, whether it's in a downtown yoga studio or a popular spa.

OUTDOOR ACTIVITIES

Like elsewhere in Canada, the choice of outdoor activities in Montréal is terrific no matter in which season you visit. There are some lovely areas of the city for simple pastimes like jogging or walking, but plenty of options await those wanting to experience something a little more daring, like white-water rafting on the Lachine Rapids.

CYCLING & IN-LINE SKATING

Montréal teems with cycling and skating paths. One very fine route leads 13km southwest from the edge of Old Montréal along the **Canal de Lachine** (p108) with a lot of history en route. Picnic tables are scattered along the canalside park, a grand place to relax with a packed lunch.

The smooth **Circuit Gilles Villeneuve** (Map p319) is the coolest track in town for in-line skating and cycling. It's open and free to all except in mid-June, when it hosts the Grand Prix du Canada's Formula One race.

In the river northeast of downtown at **Parc des Îles de Boucherville** (Map pp306–7), there are 22km of trails around a string of island parks connected by bridges. A ferry departs from Quai Jacques-Cartier in the Old Port hourly in the summer.

Gear Rental

ÇA ROULE MONTRÉAL
Map p314
☎ 866-0633; 24 rue de la Commune Est; bicycle per hr/day $9/24, in-line skates $8/25; ☎ 9am-8pm Apr-Oct; Ⓜ Place-d'Armes
This place has a wide selection of bicycles, spare parts and a good repair shop. It provides cycling maps and locks on request.

LE GRAND CYCLE
Map pp316-17
☎ 525-1414; 901 rue Cherrier Est; bicycle per 4 hr/day $20/30; ☎ 9am-6pm; Ⓜ Sherbrooke
This is too cool a bike place with a kind of dinner counter set up at the side of the shop where people end up drinking coffee and noshing on vegan brownies. A good place to come to ask about new bike routes and the like.

LOCAL VOICES: FACES OF MONTRÉAL

Chantal Petitclerc, Paralympian

Montrealer Chantal Petitclerc was always a force to contend with in wheelchair racing, but her performance at the 2004 Olympic and Paralympic Games in Athens sent her career into the stratosphere. Canada's best performing athlete of the entire games, Petitclerc smashed three world records, set an Olympic record in the 800m where wheelchair racing is an exhibition sport, and brought home five gold medals, one for each race she entered. In addition to countless sports awards, she was named Canadian of the Year by *Maclean's* magazine and Nation Builder of the Year by the *Globe and Mail*. She is now Canada's most famous amateur athlete.

Born December 15, 1969 in Saint-Marc-des-Carrières, Québec, she's lived in Montréal since 1994. Despite a successful public-speaking career and promising future in broadcasting, Petitclerc is a long way from retirement and already has her sights on the 2008 Olympic and Paralympic Games in Beijing.

What's your typical Montréal day?
I'm up early and training by 7:30am at the Formula One Racing Circuit. I finish around 5pm. In the evening, I'll either cook at home or go out to a movie or the theater.

Where do you take your friends who've never been to Montréal before?
Mostly I take them for really long walks, for coffees, to restaurants and to go shopping – Montréal is really good for all of that. I live in the Latin Quarter so I am within wheeling or walking distance of everything. I'll take visitors out for really long walks to Chinatown, the Old Port, then come back, go up boul St-Laurent for the nice restaurants, maybe go all the way to Mile End district – the coffee places are really neat there – then come back on rue St-Denis. That would be a big, big day but that's the first thing I like to do. After that it depends where they're from. If I've got friends from Europe, usually they like to see the nature and big lakes outside of town. If I have friends from the U.S.A., Old Montréal is really nice for them.

Where's your favorite place for an upscale meal?
The classic is Toqué! (p132). Very expensive but when I come back from a very important sporting event and have been training hard for so many months, Toqué! is my once-a-year treat.

What's your favorite greasy spoon?
La Paryse (p134). I think it's got the best burgers and fries. Fortunately for me, being in a wheelchair, it's got two steps up so it's not easy for me to get in. That's good – if not for the stairs I'd be there everyday.

Favorite Montréal musician?
Jean Leclerc (ex Jean Leloup p55). He's always been my favorite – he's one of the very best singers to come from Québec.

Favorite night out?
In Montréal I'm usually training so I don't go out much, but **Soirées C'est Extra** (p152) is really special – a DJ plays classic French songs from the '60s, '70s and '80s all night. Everybody knows all the lyrics, and people go there because they just love French music – they're all singing and dancing. It's a really unique experience.

Favorite Québec film?
Léolo is one of my very favorites. *La Grande Séduction*. Also Denys Arcand's two films, *Les Invasions Barbares* and *Le Déclin de l'Empire Américain*.

What you miss most about Montréal when you're away?
The people. Whenever I come back I'm always happy just to be on the streets in Montréal. There are all kinds of styles, different languages. It's multicultural – everyone is doing and eating different things. The city is open-minded about everything. It feels good just being around that.

VÉLO AVENTURE Map p314

☎ 847-0666; www.veloaventure.com; Conveyor Pier, Old Port; bicycle per hr/day $7.50/25, in-line skates $9/30; 🕙 9am-9pm Apr-Oct; Ⓜ Place- d'Armes

The most convenient rental service for cyclists and rollerbladers on the waterfront. Also offers guided tours, skating lessons and repairs.

WALKING & JOGGING

Montréal has terrific places for jogging. Dedicated pavement pounders favor Parc du Mont Royal (p103) which is laced with walking and jogging trails. Parc La Fontaine (p100) and Île Ste-Hélène in Parc Jean-Drapeau (p81) offer less challenging terrain. You can also jog the trails of the Canal de Lachine (p108).

THE RUNNING ROOM Map pp308-9

☎ 483-4495; www.runningroom.com; 4873 rue Sherbrooke Ouest; 🕙 9:30am-9pm Mon-Fri, 9:30am-6pm Sat, 8:30am-5:30pm Sun; Ⓜ Vendôme

This terrific Canadian chain store is devoted completely to running; clothing, gadgets, everything. It holds all kinds of clinics touching on everything from walking to marathon training. If you are just looking for some company, it has free group runs Wednesday at 6:30pm and Sunday at 8:30am. (Just show up at the store.) The hours are the same all across Canada in every single store. The theory being, wherever you may be, you will know when and where to hook up with fellow joggers, even if you are new in town. There's also terrific downloadable running route maps on their website for all the cities they have stores in. There's another store in Outremont (☎ 274-5888; 1159 ave Bernard).

ICE SKATING

ATRIUM LE 1000 Map pp310-11

☎ 395-0555; www.le1000.com; 1000 rue de la Gauchetière Ouest; adult/child $5.50/3.50; skate rental $5; Ⓜ Bonaventure; Ⓟ

Enjoy year-round indoor ice skating at this excellent glass-domed rink. On Saturday kids and their families have a special session from 10:30am to 11:30am and a DJ hosts a 'dance and skate' from 7pm to 10pm. Call for operating hours as the schedule changes frequently.

LAC DES CASTORS Map pp310-11

☎ 872-6559; Parc du Mont-Royal; admission free, skate rental $6; 🕙 9am-6pm weather permitting; 🚍 11; Ⓟ

Nestled in the woods near the large parking lot and pavilion, the 'Beaver Lake' makes wonderful ice skating in the bucolic surrounds of Mont Royal.

PARC DU BASSIN BONSECOURS
Map p314

☎ 496-7678; Old Port; adult & youth $3, family $10, child under 6 free, skate rental $6; 🕙 11am-6pm weather permitting; Ⓜ Champ-de-Mars, bus 14; Ⓟ

This is one of Montréal's most popular outdoor skating rinks, located on the shore

Ice skating at Atrium Le 1000 (above)

of the St Lawrence River next to the Bonse-cours Pavilion. At Christmas time there's a big nativity scene.

SKIING & SNOWBOARDING

Though Montrealers often flock to the nearby mountains to ski and snowboard, several areas within the city limits have cross-country trails. Parc du Mont-Royal (p103) is criss-crossed with ski paths and has a couple of slopes; it's best to go during the week as the crowds wear the snow thin on weekends. Parc La Fontaine (p100), Île Ste-Hélène (p81) and the trails along the Canal de Lachine (p108) are easy for beginners. The Parc Nature du Cap-St-Jacques (p111) to the west of Montréal is one of the prettiest options, with 46km of trails about a half-hour's drive northwest of downtown. By public transport, take the métro to the Henri-Bourassa stop and bus No 69 west to the park.

Gear Rental/Purchase
ALTITUDE SPORTS PLEIN AIR
Map pp316-17

☎ 847-1515; 4140 rue St-Deñis; ⌚ 10am-6pm Mon-Wed, 10am-9pm Thu-Fri, 10am-5pm Sat, noon-5pm Sun; Ⓜ Mont-Royal

This well-stocked Montréal sports boutique has various outdoor and ski gear available for hire.

DIZ Map pp308-9

☎ 486-9123; 48 ave Westminster, Montréal West; ⌚ noon-6pm Mon-Wed, noon-9pm Thu-Fri, noon-5pm Sat & Sun; 🚌 Décarie Expressway to Westminster Exit

If you are not a snowboarder it's kind of hard to figure out what the fuss is about just by looking around, but fans of the sport say if you're in Montréal and need a board or any kind of accessory under the sun, then this place is it. A good smattering of skateboards rounds out the offerings but it's clearly their sideline.

LAC DES CASTORS PAVILION
Map pp310-11

☎ 872-6559; Parc du Mont Royal; ⌚ 10am-6pm Wed-Sun in winter; 🚌 11; Ⓟ

This place rents out ski equipment, snow-shoes and toboggans right on the slopes of 'The Mountain'.

JET-BOATING & RAFTING
SAUTE MOUTONS
Map p314

☎ 284-9607; www.jetboatingmontreal.com; Old Port; jet boat & raft adult/teen/child $60/50/40, speed boat adult/teen/child $25/20/18; ⌚ 10am-6pm May-Oct; Ⓜ Champs-de-Mars; Ⓟ

Thrill-seekers will get their money's worth on these fast, wet and bouncy boat tours to the Lachine Rapids. The aluminum jet boats take you through foaming white waters, from Quai de l'Horloge, on hour-long tours. There are also speedboats that take half-hour jaunts around the Parc des Îles from the Jacques Cartier pier. You can combine the two activities by jet-boating up the rapids and rafting down them (teens and adults only). Reservations are a must.

TENNIS
JARRY PARK TENNIS CENTRE
Map pp308-9

☎ 273-1245; 285 rue Faillon Ouest; per hr $35; ⌚ 9am-9pm; Ⓜ de Castelnau, bus 55; Ⓟ

Montréal has hundreds of free public tennis courts in Parc La Fontaine, Parc Jeanne-Mance and other municipal parks. The City Parks & Recreation Department (☎ 872-1111) can locate the ones nearest you.

This modern complex near Little Italy is home to indoor and outdoor courts that host the Tennis Masters Canada. Racket rental is available.

CANOEING & KAYAKING
PARC DE LA RIVIÈRE-DES-MILLES-ÎLES
Map pp306-7

☎ 450-622-1020; www.parc-mille-iles.qc.ca; 345 boul Ste-Rose; ⌚ 9am-6pm mid-May–Sep; Ⓜ Henri-Bourassa, bus 72; Ⓟ

This is one of the most beautiful spots for canoeing and kayaking. This park on the Riv-ière des Mille-Îles near Laval has 10 islands where you can disembark on self-guided water tours, and about 10km of the river (including calm inner channels) are open for paddling. Canoe rentals cost $8/28 per hour/day, two-person kayaks cost $13/46, and rowboats will set you back $10/35. You can even rent 20-seat *rabaskaw* – canoes like those used by fur trappers.

SAILING & WINDSURFING
L'ÉCOLE DE VOILE DE LACHINE
Map pp308–9

☎ 634-4326; www.ecoledevoiledelachine.com; 2105 boul St-Joseph, Lachine; boat rental per hr $15-30; ⏰ 10am-6pm Mon-Thu, 9am-8pm Sat & Sun May-Sep; Ⓜ de l'Église, bus 58

The Lachine Sailing School organizes regattas on the St Lawrence River, gives free boat tours in late June and early July and rents light craft (windsurf boards, small sailboats and catamarans). Qualified instructors give windsurfing and sailing courses in summer.

GOLF

The Montréal region has some impressive courses but most are outside the city proper, such as in the resort areas of the Laurentians. **Tourisme Québec** (☎ 873-2015; www.bonjourquebec.com) has a complete listing.

GOLF DORVAL Map pp306–7

☎ 631-6624; www.golfdorval.com; 2000 rue Reverchen; Mon-Thu $25-36, Fri-Sun $28-39; ⏰ dawn-dusk May-Oct; Dorval train station, 🚌 204; Ⓟ

This semi-private club near Pierre Trudeau Airport has two fairly challenging 18-hole courses, a lighted driving range and two putting greens. It's a 20-minute drive northwest of downtown; take Autoroute 20 Ouest to exit 53, boul des Sources Nord.

LE VILLAGE GOLF
Map pp308–9

☎ 872-4653; 4235 rue Viau; 9 holes $20; ⏰ 6:30am-7pm; Ⓜ Viau, bus 132; Ⓟ

Hone your drives and putts at this straightforward municipal course just east of Olympic Stadium.

SKATEBOARDING
UNDERWORLD
Map p315

☎ 284-6473; 289 rue Ste-Catherine Est; ⏰ 10am-6pm Mon-Wed, 10am-10pm Thu & Fri, 11am-5pm Sun; Ⓜ Berri-UQAM

Skateboarding is popular in Montréal and devotees come out with a vengeance after winter. Place Émile-Gamelin is right nearby

and is the first place kids head after swinging by here.

SPEED KARTING & PAINTBALL
CIRCUIT 500/ACTION COMMANDO PAINTBALL
Map pp306–7

☎ 254-4245; www.circuit500.com; 5592 rue Hochelaga Est; admission $18-25; ⏰ karting 24 hr, paintball noon-midnight Mon, Fri & Sat, noon-10pm Sun; Ⓜ L'Assomption, bus 85; Ⓟ

Do you want to be the next Schumacher or Villeneuve? Sharpen your skills in 10-minute races on North America's largest indoor karting track. The racers blaze around the circuit at speeds of up to 75km/h. Uniforms and safety helmets will be provided but it's up to you to bring the guts.

You can also let off steam in a round of paintball on four terrains strewn with obstacles, bunkers, pyramids and catacombs. The games pit security agents against thieves in a dozen splattering scenarios. A one-hour package includes mask, paintgun and 100 paintballs.

HEALTH, FITNESS & PERSONAL CARE

If you are a fitness freak you will have a field day in town where great facilities range from gyms to yoga studios. Swimmers in particular should be thrilled with choices that range from welcoming neighborhood pools to Parc Jean-Drapeau's World Aquatic Championship facilities on Île Ste-Hélène or the artificial beach found on Île Notre-Dame. The city's wide variety of trendy hair salons and unique spas will also provide you with no shortage of places to go if you want to look or feel your best.

SWIMMING
CÉGEP DU VIEUX MONTRÉAL
Map p315

☎ 982-3457; 255 rue Ontario Est; admission free; ⏰ 5:30pm-9:15pm Tue-Fri, 9am-4:30pm Sat; Ⓜ Berri-UQAM

This junior college has a large indoor pool with diving boards that's open to all. It's wonderful for serious training or just paddling around.

CENTRE AQUATIQUE
Map pp308-9

☎ 252-4622; www.rio-gouv.qc.ca; 4141 ave Pierre-de-Courbertin; adult/child $4/2.90; ☺ 9:15am-10pm Mon-Fri, 1-4pm Sat & Sun; Ⓜ Viau; Ⓟ
The competition pools at the Olympic Stadium are great for laps – they're among the fastest in the world thanks to a system that reduces water movement. The six indoor pools include a wading pool for tots, a water slide and a diving basin.

COMPLEXE AQUATIQUE DE L'ÎLE STE-HÉLÈNE Map p319

☎ 872-6120; l'Île Ste-Hélène, Parc Jean-Drapeau; adult/senior/6-13 yr/under 6 yr $5/4/2.50/free; ☺ 10am-8pm daily Jun 17-Aug 27; 11am-4pm Sat, Sun & holidays May 13-Jun 11 & Sep 2-17; Ⓜ Jean-Drapeau
The city's first outdoor pool complex was opened here in 1953. It was completely demolished and rebuilt when Montréal got the 2005 World Aquatic Championships. The state-of-the-art facilities are now open to the public. The diving pool (complete with underwater viewing windows) and competition pool are mainly reserved for hosting competitions or for training competitive swimmers and athletic teams. But the championship's magnificent 55m by 44m warm-up pool is open for recreational swimming. There's also a bay-like portion of the pool with a shallow, gently sloping bottom that's great for kids and families.

NATATORIUM Map pp308-9

☎ 765-7230; 6500 boul LaSalle, Verdun; admission free; ☺ 11am-8pm, late Jun-late Aug; Ⓜ de l'Église, bus 58; Ⓟ
Québec's first outdoor pool (1920) harks back to the era when bathing wasn't just about recreation. It occupies a beautiful spot on the shores of the St Lawrence River, reachable via a pretty bicycle trail through greenery.

PISCINE SCHUBERT Map pp316-17

☎ 872-2587; 3950 boul St-Laurent; admission free; ☺ 2-9:30pm Tue-Fri, 11am-4:30pm Sat; Ⓜ St-Laurent, bus 55
This former bathhouse in the Plateau is chock-a-block with pretty Art Deco details. There are special sessions throughout the day so call ahead to check the schedule.

PLAGE DES ÎLES
Map p319

☎ 872-6093; adult/child $7.50/3.75; ☺ 10am-7pm, last admission 6:15pm Jun 24-Labour Day; Ⓜ Jean-Drapeau, then bus 167
On warm summer days this artificial sandy beach can accommodate up to 5000 sunning and splashing souls. It's safe, clean and ideal for kids, and picnic facilities and snack bars serving beer are also on-site. Volleyball at the 2006 World Outgames was held here and there are still several professional-standard volleyball courts left over for anyone to use. The beach is closed on 'bad days,' but call to check if it's open – their idea of a bad day may not be the same as yours.

GYMS & HEALTH CLUBS
NAUTILUS PLUS
Map pp310-11

☎ 843-5993; 1231 rue Ste-Catherine Ouest; nonmembers per session $11; Ⓜ Peel
This high-tech fitness center offers a barrage of weight-lifting, cycling and climbing machines. Various courses like aerobics, spinning and targeted muscle training are available. There are 18 branches around town including a slick one in the Village (Map p315; ☎ 905-9999; 1231 rue St-André; métro Beaudry).

YOGA & PILATES
ASHTANGA YOGA STUDIO
Map pp310-11

☎ 875-9642; www.ashtangamontreal.com; 372 rue Ste-Catherine Ouest, Suite 118; beginner's class $10; Ⓜ Place-des-Arts
Ashtanga, also known as 'power' yoga, is an intense, aerobic form of the exercise. This professional center has big, bright studios, very friendly staff and offers 30-plus classes for all age groups and skill levels.

MORETTI STUDIO Map pp310-11

☎ 285-4884; www.pilates-montreal.com; 1115 rue Sherbrooke Ouest; group session $15; Ⓜ Peel
This is a relaxed pilates studio providing a practical, down-to-earth approach to getting and staying in shape. Its small group sessions are tailored to suit personal needs, with an emphasis on abdominal work, joints and spinal articulation.

MARTIAL ARTS

CULTURAL MARTIAL ARTS ACADEMY
Map pp310-11

☎ 281-9928; www.montrealmartialarts.com; 1121 rue Ste-Catherine Ouest; ☺ Sun-Fri; Ⓜ Peel
This large, well-equipped center offers an awesome choice of on-demand courses in martial arts like Jiu Jitsu, Muay Thai, Kuntao Silat and Jeet Kune Do (Bruce Lee's art) by fully qualified instructors. There's Western-style boxing too.

MASSAGE, BEAUTY & DAY SPAS

BLÜ SALON SPA URBAIN Map p314

☎ 866-2222; 120 rue McGill; ☺ 9am-7pm Mon, 9am-8pm Tue & Wed, 9am-9pm Thu & Fri, 9am-3pm Sat; Ⓜ Square-Victoria
A few hours at Blü will leave you feeling like a new (wo)man, relaxed and irresistible. This spa enjoys one of the best reputations in town. It's chic yet snob-free and combines all the professional services for hairstyling, facial and body treatments, manicures and foot care, waxing and massage therapy. There's a cool café to aid re-entry into the outside world.

COUPE BIZZARRE
Map pp316-17

☎ 843-3433; 3770 boul St-Laurent; ☺ 10am-8pm Mon-Fri, noon-8pm Sat, noon-7pm Sun; Ⓜ St-Laurent, then bus 55
One of Montréal's funkiest hairdressers. Apart from wash-cut-blown you can order sculpted, vicious, voluptuous or whatever suits your mood.

OVARIUM
Map p318

☎ 271-7515; 877-356-8837; 400 rue Beaubien Est; ☺ 9am-9pm; Ⓜ Beaubien
The excellent staff and Ovarium tanks have developed a loyal following for this terrific day spa. For total relaxation take the massage ($62) followed by one hour in one of Ovarium's flotation tanks ($47). The egg shaped tubs are filled with water and 2000 cups of Epson salts making you gravity free. You can leave the lid open or close it as much as you feel comfortable with.

TATTOOS AND PIERCING

Many of the city's tattoo and piercing places are in the 'seedier' or more alternative parts of town like boul St-Laurent or rue Ste-Catherine Est. But funnily enough **Adrenaline** (Map pp310–11 ☎ 938-8884; www.adrenalinetattoos.com; 1541 rue Sherbrooke Ouest; h11am-8pm Mon-Wed, 11am-9pm Thu-Sat, 11am-7pm Sun; Ⓜ Guy-Concordia) chose to set up right next to toney Westmount in the shadow of a university and a hospital (Is it the upper middle-class Westmounters that are keeping this place afloat?). It's now considered one of the best in town and claims to have a better sterilization process than most hospitals. Jeff Weit is considered one of the best artists in town. Choose from thousands of tattoo images on file or bring in your own drawing or photograph.

TERRA SPA
Map pp316-17

☎ 288-0152; 3821 boul St-Laurent; ☺ 10am-8pm Tue-Fri, 10am-6pm Sat; Ⓜ St-Laurent, then bus 55
Terra Spa's hardwood floors, bubbling Zen fountain and comforting incense make you feel more like you're visiting a friend who happens to have healing hands. Treatments have interesting perks such as an optional oxygen mask while receiving your body wrap. It also offers pilates training to improve your posture through the strength of back and abdominal exercises.

TONIC Map pp316-17

☎ 499-9494; 3616 boul St-Laurent; ☺ 9am-5pm Mon, 9am-8pm Tue & Wed, 10am-9pm Thu & Fri; Ⓜ St-Laurent, then bus 55
This spa/salon doesn't have the slickest digs but it does have one of the best reputations based largely on the stylists' personalities.

WATCHING SPORT

From the revving race cars of the Formula One to the city's legendary hockey team the Canadiens, Montréal has an endless list of both professional and amateur teams to keep sports fans happy.

Tickets for many sporting events can be purchased from **Admission** (☎ 790-1245; www.admission.com). It has dozens of sale outlets in Montréal including **Centre Infotouriste** (p191) on Square Dorchester and the **Place des Arts** (p89) concert halls. Montréal lost their professional baseball team, the

Montréal Expos, in 2005 but there is still plenty to keep sports fans happy all over town. And don't forget amateur sport! The McGill Redmen (www.football.mcgill.ca) or the Concordia Stingers (www.stingers.ca) are sometimes more fun to watch along with thousands of university student fans than going to a professional game.

HOCKEY

BELL CENTRE
Map pp310-11

☎ 790-1245; www.centrebell.ca; 1260 rue de la Gauchetière Ouest; tickets $25-182; ☸ Oct-Apr, playoffs until Jun; Ⓜ Lucien-L'Allier or Bonaventure
The Canadiens of the National Hockey League have won the Stanley Cup 24 times. Although the team has struggled in recent years Montrealers have a soft spot for the 'Habs' and matches sell out routinely. Scalpers hang around the entrance on game days, and you might snag a half-price ticket after the puck drops. Bring your binoculars for the rafter seats.

MCCONNELL WINTER STADIUM
Map pp310-11

☎ 398-7000; 3883 rue University; adult/child $5/2.50; ☸ Oct-Mar
The perfect place to experience a classic rivalry when the McGill Redmen face off against the Toronto Varsity Blues. It's a pleasure to warm the comfy seats in this indoor college stadium.

AUTO RACING

CHAMP CAR SERIES Map p256
www.champcarworldseries.com; Mont-Tremblant, Secteur St-Jovite; ☸ July 1, 2007
Champ Car lost its place on the Montréal's 2007 race calendar in favor of NASCAR, but you can still see the race if you make your way to Circuit Mont-Tremblant (www.lecircuit.com) 140km north of Montréal.

FORMULA ONE GRAND PRIX Map p319
☎ 350-0000; www.grandprix.ca; Parc Jean-Drapeau's Île Notre-Dame; 3-day grandstand tickets $195-495, 1-day general admission tickets $25-75; ☸ June; Ⓜ Jean-Drapeau
This is North America's biggest Formula One event and Montréal goes bonkers when the world's flashiest drivers, crews and entourages hit the city in early-to-mid June for the three-day event. The race takes place on Park Jean Drapeau's Circuit Gilles-Villeneuve but the festivities continue to spill over into the city core until late.

NASCAR: BUSCH SERIES EVENT
Map p319

www.nascar.com; Jean-Drapeau's Île Notre-Dame; ☸ Aug 4; Ⓜ Jean-Drapeau
NASCAR has added a 2007 Montréal race to its events calendar, which will take place on the legendary Circuit Gilles-Villeneuve. If all goes well, it may become a permanent Montréal event. There will be a Grand-Am series race held on August 3, 2007.

Olympic Park tower at Centre Aquatique (p173)

FOOTBALL & SOCCER
MOLSON STADIUM
Map pp310-11

☎ 871-2255; www.montrealalouettes.com; 475 ave des Pins Ouest; tickets $17.50-80; ⏱ Jun-Nov; Ⓜ McGill; Ⓟ

The Montréal Alouettes, a once-defunct football team of the Canadian Football League, is the unlikely star of the city's sports scene. The Alouettes (French for 'larks') folded several times before going on to win the league's Grey Cup trophy in 2002. Rules are a bit different from American football: the field is bigger and there are only three downs. The **Alouettes Box Office** (Map pp310–11; ☎ 254-2400; 646 rue Ste-Catherine Ouest; open 9am to 5pm Monday to Friday) sells advance tickets. Despite its address, the entrance is off rue University. Look for the big red sign.

MONTRÉAL IMPACT Map pp308-9

☎ 328-3668; www.montrealimpact.com; 1000 ave Emile-Journault, Claude-Robillard Sports Complex; tickets $5-20; ⏱ Apr-Sep; Ⓜ Crémazie; Ⓟ

This team regularly pulls in15,000 people per game.

HORSE RACING
HIPPODROME DE MONTRÉAL
Map pp308-9

☎ 739-2741; www.hdem.com; 7440 boul Décarie; ⏱ 7:25pm Wed, Fri & Sat, 1pm Sun; Ⓜ Namur; Ⓟ

Horse racing has been a feature of Québec life since the 18th century and the harness races of the Hippodrome enjoy world renown. Major events include the Coupe de l'Avenir and Coupe des Éleveurs every autumn, with a total purse of over $2 million. A free shuttle runs on race days from the Namur metro stop.

Shopping

Shopping

Rivaling eating and partying, shopping is swarmingly popular in Montréal. There's something for virtually everyone and prices are reasonable by North American standards, so why not let loose?

With a mix of American and European influences, the offerings, even in the commercial megastores, tend to be more varied and original than those you'd find in the rest of Canada. Montréal also has a great choice of vintage clothing, CDs and records, and retro/antique furnishings. The plethora of well-stocked bookshops is yet another treat. Fashion (p32) and designer clothing deserve special mention: Montréal's designers are trendsetters and their styles have an irrepressible Gallic flair. Bargain hunters won't pay dearly at wholesalers or factory outlets such as those in the Chabanel area.

Traditional Canadian gifts and goods are a specialty: Inuit and First Nations crafts, country furniture, outdoor and winter clothing and anything related to maple syrup. Most of Canada's fur companies are based in Montréal so pelts are in abundance here (as well as nonanimal furs). Museum shops at **Musée McCord** (p92) or the **Jardin Botanique** (p97) sell beautiful wooden toys, handmade jewelry and colorful quilts and garments.

Shopping Areas

Montréal's shopping districts are such a pleasure to browse that even the tightest wallets will be tempted. Rue Ste-Catherine, the main shopping strip, has recovered its old glitz and is now abuzz with trendy clothing stores, consumer-goods retailers and several famous department stores. Behind (and below) the facade lie shopping complexes like the **Centre Eaton** (p181) or **Les Cours Mont-Royal** (p183), impressive architecture with links to the underground city. Swanky boutiques, galleries and jewelry can be found on rue Sherbrooke and at the top end of rue Crescent.

For more intimate shopping you definitely need to explore the **Plateau** (p186). The pocket-sized shops here tend to be cheaper than downtown and their small-output labels are exclusive. Boul St-Laurent and ave Mont-Royal are famous for hip clothing boutiques and record stores, with stock that varies wildly. Rue St-Denis has some alternative shops in the Quartier Latin but turns trendier as you move into the Plateau.

In **Old Montréal** (opposite), the main street rue St-Paul is stacked with commercial art galleries, pricey designer boutiques and snazzy interior furnishers.

Dozens of antique shops jostle for business on **Antique Alley** (p181), the stretch of rue Notre-Dame Ouest in the southwest part of downtown between ave Atwater and rue Guy. Several antique places are also dotted along rue Amherst in the **Village** (p185).

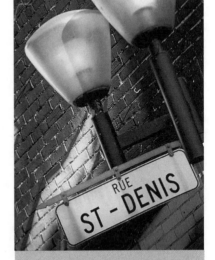

TOP FIVE SHOPPING STRIPS

- Ave du Mont-Royal (p99) – for gritty, off-the-rack style, and surprising specialty stores
- Boul St-Laurent (p99) – funky new designer boutiques mixed in with second-hand fashion
- Rue Notre-Dame Ouest (opposite) – treasure trove of galleries and antiques
- Rue Sherbrooke Ouest (p90) – for furs, stogies and expense accounts
- Rue St-Denis (p100) – classy European-style boutiques galore

Bookshops large and small are scattered among the downtown skyscrapers. Boul St-Laurent has some good independent booksellers.

The **Chabanel district** (p188) in north Montréal is the central wholesale outlet for the city's textiles industry, generally open Saturday mornings only.

Opening Hours

Most stores open Monday to Wednesday 9:30am or 10am to 6pm; clothing boutiques usually open their doors at 11am. Thursday and Friday are late opening days for retailers, usually until 9pm; Saturday hours are 10am to 5pm. Opening hours on Sunday afternoon (noon to 4pm or 5pm) are fast becoming standard along rue Ste-Catherine and boul St-Laurent as well as in the large malls. Some convenience stores such as the chain Couche Tard stay open 24 hours.

> ### TAXES AND REFUNDS
> Federal goods and services tax (called TPS in Québec, or GST in the rest of Canada) applies on just about every transaction except groceries. Québec also charges sales tax (TVQ) of 6% to 12% on top of that. Keep your receipts because foreign visitors can apply for a partial refund – see p181 for details.

Be aware that in summer you may find extended weekday hours at many stores. Where opening hours are listed with a store, it indicates that they vary from the usual opening times. Where incomplete or no opening hours appear with a review, assume that the hours as stated here apply.

OLD MONTRÉAL

The cobblestoned rue St-Paul is *the* shopping artery of Old Montréal. It has clusters of commercial art galleries and gift shops selling Canadian souvenirs such as maple-syrup chocolates and Inuit handicrafts. The **Marché Bonsecours** (Map p314) is a shopping gallery in a pretty old market building, offering expensive tourist goods as well as some quality Québec designer garments.

CENTRE DE COMMERCE MONDIAL

Map p314   Shopping Mall

☎ 849-1999; Suite 2100, cnr rue St-Jacques & rue McGill; Ⓜ Square-Victoria

The World Trade Centre is hidden completely behind the old facade of the ruelle des Fortifications. A lane marks the former location of the northern wall of the Old Town. Inside is a sweeping concourse with luxurious Italian fountains, an elegant carved stairway and a section of the Berlin Wall; above lie multiple layers of chic boutiques and stores.

DIFFUSION GRIFF '3000

Map p314   Boutique Fashion & Furs

☎ 398-0761; Marché Bonsecours, 350 rue St-Paul Est; Ⓜ Champ-de-Mars

French fashion diva Anne de Shalla studied fashion in Paris and came to Montréal in the 1970s. She now selects from up to 30 Québec designers every year for her exclusive shop collection – stretchy leathers, semi-sheer dresses, blouses and wraparound casuals, not to mention just about every fur in the animal kingdom.

FOURRURES DUBARRY

Map p314   Fashion & Fur

☎ 844-7483; 206 rue St-Paul Ouest; Ⓜ Place-d'Armes

This place carries oodles of off-the-rack fur jackets, hats, fur-trim capes and coats, plus a selection of sheepskin coats and leather jackets. There are no middlemen, which keeps prices low and you can trade in your old garment towards your purchase.

GALERIE 2000 Map p314   Art Gallery

☎ 844-1812; 45 rue St-Paul Ouest; ◷ 10am-9pm

Always fresh and entertaining, this eclectic gallery has large, flashy, tasteful displays from classic landscapes to neo-Cubist portraits, with the occasional well-charted flight into the alternative.

GALERIE LE CHARIOT

Map p314   Art & Craft

☎ 875-4994; 446 pl Jacques-Cartier; Ⓜ Champ-de-Mars

This arts emporium claims to have the largest Inuit collection in Canada. Choose from First Nations art carved mainly from soapstone, as well as walrus tusks, fur hats, mountain goat rugs and fleecy moccasins. It satisfies a variety of tastes and budgets.

GALERIE ORANGE Map p314   Art Gallery

☎ 396-6670; 81 rue St-Paul Est; Ⓜ Place-d'Armes
Fantastic, bright new addition to Old Montréal's gallery scene, representing established and up-and-coming contemporary artists like Francine Simonin and Elmyna Bouchard and a terrific collection of works on paper.

GALERIE PANGÉE Map p314   Art Gallery

☎ 845-3368; 40 rue St-Paul Ouest; ⏱ 10am-7pm;
Ⓜ Champ-des-Mars
Formerly known as Galerie Parchemine, a kind of framing cooperative, the owner recently decided to shut down that side of the business, chuck out all the framing equipment and reopen under the name Galerie Pangée. It's a wonderful, bright space devoted to showing off contemporary art.

GALERIE ST-DIZIER Map p314   Art Gallery

☎ 845-8411; 20 rue St-Paul Ouest; Ⓜ Champ-de-Mars
This spacious Old Town gallery has always been at the forefront of the contemporary avant-garde scene in Montréal. Works are split between local and heavyweight artists known abroad, including Besner, Missakian, Tetro, and Walker. Its forté is naïve and modernist art and sculpture.

KAMKYL Map p314   Men's Fashion

☎ 281-8221; 439 rue St-Pierre; Ⓜ Champ-de-Mars
Kamkyl has a fine Italian-made collection of men's suits with understated lines that beam self-confidence. Son of a German master tailor, designer Douglas Mandel (formerly of Hugo Boss and DKNY) also snagged a design award for this stylish post-industrial atelier of parquet, light and space.

LIBRISSIME Map p314   Books

☎ 841-0123; 62 rue St-Paul Ouest Ⓜ Place-d'Arms
It bills itself as more than just a bookstore, and it's right, there really is no other place like this in the city. Gorgeous books here are imported from all over the world including Italy and India and white gloves are laid on the displays for you to put on before touching the tomes, including giant sized books that cost upwards of $1000.

LA GUILDE GRAPHIQUE
Map p314   Art Gallery

☎ 844-3438; 9 rue St-Paul Ouest;
Ⓜ Champ-de-Mars
This place exhibits works of more than 200 contemporary artists in a variety of media and techniques. Most works are sketches, woodcuts, etchings and lithographs on paper, and you can visit the artists working in the upstairs studio.

SIMON'S CAMERA
Map p314   Photography

☎ 861-5401; 11 rue St-Antoine Ouest; Ⓜ Place-d'Armes
A real shopping icon in the Old Town, Simon's has one of the city's best selections of photography equipment. On any given day, a lineup may include old-timers bringing in their radio-sized hulks as well as young kids with credit card sized digital cameras. New and used digital cameras, darkroom gear, video and sound equipment go at competitive prices, with trade-ins possible. It also does a sideline in rental equipment.

CLOTHING SIZES
Measurements approximate only, try before you buy

Women's Clothing

Aus/UK	8	10	12	14	16	18
Europe	36	38	40	42	44	46
Japan	5	7	9	11	13	15
USA	6	8	10	12	14	16

Women's Shoes

Aus/USA	5	6	7	8	9	10
Europe	35	36	37	38	39	40
France only	35	36	38	39	40	42
Japan	22	23	24	25	26	27
UK	3½	4½	5½	6½	7½	8½

Men's Clothing

Aus	92	96	100	104	108	112
Europe	46	48	50	52	54	56
Japan	S		M	M		L
UK/USA	35	36	37	38	39	40

Men's Shirts (Collar Sizes)

Aus/Japan	38	39	40	41	42	43
Europe	38	39	40	41	42	43
UK/USA	15	15½	16	16½	17	17½

Men's Shoes

Aus/UK	7	8	9	10	11	12
Europe	41	42	43	44½	46	47
Japan	26	27	27½	28	29	30
USA	7½	8½	9½	10½	11½	12½

DOWNTOWN

Rue Ste-Catherine is the place to hit for all the glittery, big name items, flagship department stores and boutiques extravagant in both space and price. It's a window-shopper's paradise whether you're buying or not.

An excellent range of shops selling collectibles and memorabilia can be found on Antique Alley, the section of rue Notre-Dame Ouest between rue Guy and the Marché Atwater.

1.000.000 COMIX

Map pp310-11   Comics
☎ 989-9587; 1418 rue Pierce; ☺ 9:30am-11pm Mon-Fri, 9am-6pm Sat, 9am-5pm Sun; Ⓜ Guy-Concordia

This living archive could document the history of the comic book. *Marvel* and *DC* of course but also left-field titles like *Crumb* and *Tom of Finland*. It also does a sideline in toys, T-shirts and cards.

BIRKS JEWELLERS

Map pp310-11   Jewelry
☎ 397-2511; 1240 Square Phillips; Ⓜ McGill
For more than a century this upscale vendor of baubles and bangles has been Montréal's answer to Tiffany's of New York. Henry Birks opened his first store in 1879 and expanded throughout Canada. By 1936 the store won the right to supply the British royal family, and the warrant from the Prince of Wales is prominently displayed inside the main door (although it expired in 1950). After the business went bankrupt an Italian group took over and completely refurbished the weighty Romanesque-Renaissance building in 2001. Just the coffered ceiling in Wedgewood blue warrants a visit to the sales floor.

BOUTIQUE EVA B

Map pp310-11   Vintage Clothing
☎ 849-8246; 2013 boul St-Laurent; ☺ 10am-7pm or later Mon-Sat, noon-5pm Sun; Ⓜ St-Laurent
In a space reminiscent of a theater's back stage, this boutique is a riot of recycled women's clothing, retro gear and new streetwear. It's the kind of place where 1950s bowling shoes are proudly arranged beneath a flock of floaty feather boas and yet it all seems very normal. The store doesn't have regular closing hours and stays open into the night as long as there are still customers.

CENTRE EATON

Map pp310-11   Shopping Mall
☎ 288-3708; 705 rue Ste-Catherine Ouest; Ⓜ McGill

This five-story retailing palace on the main shopping drag is home to 175-plus stores and restaurants, and six movie screens. The tax-refund service **Global Refund Canada** is on the 4th floor. The **Promenade de la Cathédrale** is an underground passage of the complex that runs beneath the Cathédrale Christ Church.

CHAPTERS BOOKSTORE

Map pp310-11   Books & Music
☎ 849-8825; 1171 rue Ste-Catherine Ouest; ☺ 9am-10pm; Ⓜ Peel
Peruse three huge floors of English- and French-language books and a fantastic choice of travel-related items in the sunken floor at the back. There's a coffee bar and internet café on the 2nd floor ($2 per 20 minutes).

CHEAP THRILLS

Map pp310-11   Books & Music
☎ 844-8988; 2044 rue Metcalfe; Ⓜ Peel
Montréal's oldest used CD and cassette shop is so full you could hardly swing a cat. The selection covers everything from electronica, noise and indie-rock to jazz, blues and R&B, including hard-to-find imports. Upstairs you can snap up new recordings usually several dollars below prices elsewhere, and there's a decent collection of paperbacks.

COMPLEXE DESJARDINS

Map pp310-11   Shopping Mall
150 rue Ste-Catherine Ouest; Ⓜ Place-des-Arts
This 1970s multifunctional complex links three office towers, a shopping mall and a big public plaza with atrium, trees and tinkling waterfalls in what's still Montréal's largest commercial building. The food court in the basement is usually buzzing with shoppers exhausted by the selection from 110 stores.

COMPUSMART
Map pp310-11   Computers
☎ 398-0782; 1195 pl Phillips; Ⓜ McGill
Probably the best all-round retailer of computer software and hardware in Montréal – Future Shop will even refer you here iif it doesn't have the right item. Prices are competitive though higher than across the border in the US, but if you need it, you need it.

FELIX BROWN Map pp310-11   Shoes & Suits

☎ 287-5523; 1233 rue Ste-Catherine Ouest; Ⓜ Peel
Black pumps with 10cm heels, overly ego-stroking staff and suits that mean business are the hallmarks of a shopping-trip to this place. All items are imported from Italy and styles are sharp as a tack.

FUTURE SHOP Map pp310-11   Electronics

☎ 393-2600; 470 rue Ste-Catherine Ouest;
Ⓨ 9am-9pm Mon-Fri, 10am-9pm Sat, noon-9pm
Sun; Ⓜ Place-des-Arts
Canada's one-stop-shop for music systems, computers and software, printers, cell phones, video cameras and entertainment gadgets. Watch out for the weekly flyers with awesome sales. Your specialist computer needs, however, are more than likely better served at Compusmart.

GALERIES D'ART CONTEMPORAIN
DU BELGO Map pp310-11   Art Gallery

372 rue Ste-Catherine Ouest; Ⓜ Place-d'Armes
Over a decade ago the Belgo building was a run-down haven for struggling artists. It quickly earned a reputation as one of Montréal's most important exhibition spaces with galleries, dance and photography studios. Designers, art dealers and architects now make up three-quarters of the tenancy. Take the elevator up to the 5th floor and conduct an art walking tour down to street level.

HARRICANA Map pp310-11   Fashion & Fur

☎ 287-6517; 3000 rue St-Antoine Ouest;
Ⓜ Lionel-Groulx
Milan-trained fashion designer Mariouche uses top-grade materials to create fur and woven garments of unparalled style and beauty; soft, comfortable and for the most part affordable. Her creations are regular features in the fashion magazines. This airy corner boutique occupies an old bank and uses its safe as a changing room.

HMV Map pp310-11   Music & DVD

☎ 875-0765; 1020 rue Ste-Catherine Ouest; Ⓜ Peel
This cavernous, multilevel store is like a department store for music with fantastic sections of everything you could ever want from classical, world music, techno and francophone to pop and jazz. You can listen to CDs before buying or lounge on the ground-floor sofas and watch the latest DVD.

Shopping at Centre Eaton (p181)

HOLT RENFREW

Map pp310-11   Department Store
☎ 842-5111; 1300 rue Sherbrooke Ouest; Ⓜ Peel
This Montréal institution is a godsend for label-conscious, cashed-up professionals of both genders. Styles of this former furrier are subdued, yet the simplest designs ooze exclusivity. January and August are the big sales months, with treasures for half-price or less.

HUDSON BAY CO

Map pp310-11   Department Store
☎ 281-4422; 585 rue Ste-Catherine Ouest; Ⓜ McGill
La Baie, as it's called in French, found fame three centuries ago for its striped wool blankets used to measure fur skins – and the stripes still adorn the main entrance. Pass the legions of perfumery stands on the ground floor and take the escalators to the clothing boutiques on the 2nd floor, or make a strategic move for the cut-price garments on the 8th floor. It's an excellent stop for crystal, china and all things Canadian including Inuit handicrafts.

INDIGO Map pp310-11   Books & Music

☎ 281-5549; 1500 ave McGill, Place Montréal
Trust; Ⓜ Peel
This sister store of Chapters is a three-floor emporium with comfy reading chairs that keep you browsing for hours. It has a great selection of Canadian and Montréal literature, a good CD section and Starbucks coffee bar. A wonderful travel and map section is on the 2nd floor at the back.

LA CASA DEL HABANO

Map pp310-11   Cigars

☎ 849-0037; 1434 rue Sherbrooke Ouest;
Ⓜ Guy-Concordia

This well-stocked stogie temple has 50
brands of Cuban cigar. Be aware that bringing these across the border to the USA is
illegal although some travelers separate the
bands when packing. Cigaraphernalia sold
here includes cutters, humidors, lighters
and books. The lounge and espresso bar
attracts young important puffers.

LE BARON Map pp310-11   Outdoors

☎ 381-4231; 932 rue Notre-Dame Ouest;
Ⓜ Square-Victoria

For survival, sporting and leisure gear this
is the top address in town in a spanking
new warehouse location. Backpack buyers
should set aside a few hours just to look.

LES COURS MONT-ROYAL

Map pp310-11   Shopping Mall

cnr rue Peel & boul de Maisonneuve Ouest; Ⓜ Peel
This capitalist emporium was once the jewel
in the crown of the Mount Royal Hotel,
then the largest hotel in the British Empire.
It's terrific for wandering around – the
skylit atrium, designer ponds and winding staircases are the height of sumptuous
elegance. The airborne sculptures of birds
with human heads are a special touch.

LES ANTIQUITÉS GRAND CENTRAL

Map pp310-11   Antiques

☎ 935-1467; 2448 rue Notre-Dame Ouest;
🕑 9am-6pm Mon-Sat; Ⓜ Lionel- Groulx
The most elegant store on Antique Row is
a pleasure to visit for its English and Continental furniture, lighting and decorative
objects from the 18th and 19th centuries.
Get buzzed in to see the Louis IV chairs,
full dining-room suites and chandeliers in
Dutch cathedral or French Empire style,
with price tags in the thousands.

LIBRAIRIE ASTRO

Map pp310-11   Books & Comics

☎ 932-1139; www.astrolib.com; 1844 rue Ste-Catherine Ouest; 🕑 noon-7pm Mon-Wed, noon-8pm Thu &
Fri, noon-6pm Sat, noon-5pm Sun; Ⓜ Guy-Concordia
Rollicking wit and helpful service are as ubiquitous as the collectible comics, books, cards
and CDs stocked at this little family-run shop.

They know their customers by name and will
email you if they come across something you
might like. A downtown institution – check
out the owners' blogs on the website.

LILI-LES-BAINS

Map pp310-11   Boutique Fashion & Swimwear

☎ 937-9197; 1336 rue Notre-Dame Ouest; 🚌 150
Montréal's larger-than-life swimsuit maker
started out making cruise-ship gear. Her
philosophy is: every woman should have the
dress of her dreams – size makes no difference. Cuts can reveal or conceal. Lili uses
gorgeous fabrics flown in from Europe and
has clients from all over the world. A made-
to-order swimsuit costs from $200.

LUCIE FAVREAU ANTIQUES

Map pp310-11   Collectibles

☎ 989-5117; 1904 rue Notre-Dame Ouest;
🕑 closed Sun; Ⓜ Georges-Vanier
This colorful museum-like store on Antique
Alley is chock-a-block with giggle-inducing
housewares, advertising plaques, toys and
sports memorabilia like signed baseballs,
among other collectibles.

MAISON DE LA PRESSE
INTERNATIONALE Map pp310-11   Newsagent

☎ 861-6767; 1166 rue Ste-Catherine Ouest;
🕑 7:30am-11pm Mon-Wed, 7:30am-midnight Thu-
Fri, 8am-midnight Sat, 8am-11pm Sun; Ⓜ Peel
This is a slick international newspaper chain
with papers from a couple of dozen countries, row upon row of magazines on every
imaginable subject and best-selling novels.

METROPOLITAN NEWS AGENCY

Map pp310-11   Newsagent

☎ 866-9227; 1109 rue Cypress; Ⓜ Peel
Missing your January 19, 1984 copy of the
Winnipeg Free Press? Chances are, you'll be
able to find a yellowed copy here amongst
over 5000 newspapers and magazines from
across the globe. It just gets weirder and
weirder the longer you poke around. If you
can't find it here it probably doesn't exist.

NADYA TOTO Map pp310-11 Boutique Fashion

☎ 350-9090; 2057 rue de la Montagne; 🕑 10am-
6pm Mon-Wed, 11am-9pm Thu & Fri, 11am-5pm
Sat, noon-5pm Sun; Ⓜ Peel
Defined by a unique recipe of spandex and
wool in asymmetric cuts, Nadya's garments

183

offer a wonderful mixture of flexibility, comfort and warmth. Not to mention that just about every woman looks great in these gems that cost only about $150 each.

ODYSSEY BOOKS

Map pp310-11   Books & Music

☎ 844-4843; 1439 rue Stanley; ⏲ 10am-8pm Mon-Wed, 10am-8:30pm Thu, 10am-9pm Fri, 11am-6pm Sat, noon-6pm Sun; Ⓜ Peel
Odyssey has soft- and hardcover books as well as a good classical and jazz CD selection. Strong in mystery, literature, jazz, philosophy, history, art and cookbooks, and recent arrivals have a special section so you can check out the latest gems.

OGILVY Map pp310-11   Department Store

☎ 842-7711; 1307 rue Ste-Catherine Ouest; Ⓜ Peel
Once a Victorian-era department store, Ogilvy has transformed itself into a collection of high-profile boutiques without losing its heritage. When it was remodeled in the late 1920s the owner had a concert hall built on the 5th floor called 'The Tudor' – this remarkable paneled room is still open for viewing. Here too is a collection of historic photos of visitors, from Queen Elizabeth to Martin Luther King. Since 1927 a bagpiper winds his way through the building every day at noon. Ogilvy's front window displays mechanical toys that are a Montréal fixture at Christmas.

PARASUCO JEANS

Map pp310-11   Designer Jeans

☎ 284-2288; 1414 rue Crescent; Ⓜ Guy-Concordia
Newly renovated and reopened, this store shines with self confidence and shows its sexy denim designs to terrific impact. What was a rough-and-ready garment for gold-miners has clearly got out of hand. Parasuco caught some thieves on security camera saying 'take only the Parasucos' and it became the basis of a successful ad campaign.

PARISIAN LAUNDRY Map pp310-11

☎ 989-1056; www.parisianlaundry.com; 3550 rue St-Antoine Ouest; ⏲ noon-5pm Tue-Sat; Ⓜ Lionel-Groulx
A former industrial laundry turned monster gallery, this 15,000 sq ft space is worth a trip for the building itself even if you are not a fan of the large-format contemporary art that it shows off so well. There's wood floors, exposed beams and hanging vents. Natural

light floods through enormous 19th-century-era windows into two floors of exhibition rooms. Recent exhibitions include print artist Francine Simonin and international star Jean-Paul Riopelle. It also holds occasional artists' talks or lectures. Admission is usually free.

PLACE MONTRÉAL TRUST

Map pp310-11   Shopping Mall

1500 ave McGill College; Ⓜ Peel
One of downtown's most successful malls, with enough rays from the skylights to keep shoppers on their day-clock. Major retailers here include Athletes World Superstore, Indigo books, Mexx, Winners and Zara. It has a tremendous water fountain with a spout 30m high, and during the holidays a Christmas tree illuminates the same five-story space. The mobility-impaired can also borrow wheelchairs from the concierge.

PLACE VILLE-MARIE

Map pp310-11   Shopping Mall

☎ 861-9393; cnr ave McGill College & rue Cathcart; Ⓜ Bonaventure
Begun in the late 1950s, Montréal's first shopping complex marked the start of the underground city, was Montréal's most important skyscraper for years and set the standards for similar complexes around the city. The square consists of several towers in cruciform that recalls the religious origins of the city – Montréal was first called Ville-Marie. It now hosts around 80 boutiques, restaurants and service stores.

ROOTS Map pp310-11   Streetwear

☎ 845-7995; 1035 rue Ste-Catherine Ouest; Ⓜ Peel
Its reputation is now soooo big worldwide that customers may forget Canada's own Roots started off as a humble shoemaker in the '70s. Now its range includes Roots for kids, Roots athletics, leather and home accessories. Tastes are easily accessible and geared to teens and 20-somethings, fashionable and at times even innovative.

SCANDALE Map pp310-11   Boutique

☎ 842-4707; 3639 boul St-Laurent; Ⓜ St-Laurent, then bus 55
The magnificent Marie-Josée Gagnon has been running this boutique since 1977, bringing in exotic Parisian imports and more recently showing off the creations of Georges Lévesque, one of Québec's most exciting designers.

SEXE CITÉ Map pp310-11 — Sex & Fetish
☎ 937-3678; 1821 rue Ste-Catherine Ouest;
🕓 10am-midnight daily; Ⓜ Guy-Concordia

Spicy, sexy gear is all over this place, one of the most popular sex boutiques in town. It also stocks the gamut of sex toys, games and joke items. It's all so upfront that any inhibitions are checked at the door.

SIMONS Map pp310-11 — Streetwear
☎ 282-1840; 977 rue Ste-Catherine Ouest; Ⓜ Peel

This Québec City chain is a phenomenon that everyone, no matter their age or style seems a fan of. The selection runs the gamut from $15 T-shirts to $5000 designer coats. Simons is known for stocking fashionable, trendy creations from its own designers that aren't available anywhere else.

URBAN OUTFITTERS
Map pp310-11 — Streetwear
☎ 874-0063; 1246 rue Ste-Catherine Ouest; Ⓜ Peel

An impossibly trendy garment store for the teens and 20-somethings. Music thumps from morning to night throughout the warehouse-style building and the front mini-boutique is full of amusements like Homer Simpson bookmarks, vampire teeth or solar-powered toothbrushes.

QUARTIER LATIN & THE VILLAGE

This is more of a bar and restaurant area, but there are some interesting stores tucked in the midst of it all.

ARCHAMBAULT Map p315 — Books & Music
☎ 849-6201; 500 rue Ste-Catherine Est;
Ⓜ Berri-UQAM

Behind the Art Deco portals you'll find Montréal's oldest and largest book and record shop. Spread over four floors, this emporium boasts a great selection of CDs and books, apart from assorted musical supplies such as pianos and sheet music. Some recordings sold here are hard to find outside Québec.

LA CAPOTERIE Map p315 — Sex & Fetish
☎ 845-0027; 2061 rue St-Denis; Ⓜ Berri-UQAM

If you're wondering what to wear for that special occasion, then trot on down to the Capoterie for late-night fashion advice. Its exhaustive array of condoms comes in all giggly shapes, colors and sizes.

LE CHÂTEAU Map p315 — Streetwear
☎ 279-6391; 6729 rue St-Hubert; Ⓜ Berri-UQAM

This trendy concept store is where to go for one-season fashion and cheap designer knockoffs. Very popular for buying cheap, trendy club wear. There's also a shop in the Centre Eaton (☎ 288-3708).

PRIAPE Map p315 — Sex & Fetish
☎ 521-8451; 1311 rue Ste-Catherine Est;
Ⓜ Beaudry

Montréal's biggest gay sex store has made a career out of parodying itself in great style. It's been on the scene for a quarter of a century so it's plugged into the mainstream erotic wares (videos and DVDs, mags and books) but has recently branched out into high-quality clothing with a titillating edge – shrink-wrapped jeans but also a vast choice of black leather gear in the basement studio.

RENAUD BRAY Map p315 — Books & Music
☎ 876-9119; 1376 rue Ste-Catherine Est; 🕓 9am-midnight; Ⓜ Beaudry

One of 14 branches in greater Montréal, this bright 'n' cheery bookstore specializes in French titles but has a decent choice of English bestsellers, travel and literature titles. A good portion of the store is dedicated to CDs in both languages, with a vibrant choice of local rock and pop.

TABAGIE PAT & ROBERT
Map p315 — Cigars
☎ 522-8534; 1474 rue Ontario Est; Ⓜ Beaudry

Pat & Robert has a marvelous selection of the aromatic leaf – canned, rolled, displayed in plastic dispenser bins, with whatever accessory to make those rising coils a heavenly trip.

UNDERWORLD Map p315 — Streetwear
☎ 284-6473; 289 rue Ste-Catherine Est;
🕓 10am-6pm Mon-Wed, 10am-10pm Thu & Fri, 11am-5pm Sun

Underworld is a 1st-class punk refuge and supply house on an appropriately grungy stretch of rue Ste-Catherine. They've got jeans, a big CD and record store in the basement and a killer selection of skates and snowboards.

ZÉPHYR Map p315   Retro Art & Furniture

☎ 529-9199; 2112 rue Amherst; ☽ noon-6pm
Mon-Fri, noon-5pm Sat & Sun; Ⓜ Berri-UQAM,
then bus 61

Breathtakingly cramped, this bright little
emporium on the fringe of the Village is
dedicated to showing art from Montréal
artists. The proprietor, Daniel Roberge, will
also rent his stock of prized faux Victorian
mirrors, beanbags and cube chairs for
movie shoots.

PLATEAU DU MONT-ROYAL

This is one of the most exciting places to
troll for one-of-a-kind boutiques, used
clothes and books and the kind of quirky
stores that you remember as much for the
experience as for what you bought. The
main arteries are boul St-Laurent and ave
du Mont-Royal and are a delight for their
offbeat and ethnic goods. There's a brilliant
collection of small, independent record
shops, each quirkier than the last, along
stretches of boul St-Laurent, ave du Mont-
Royal and rue St-Denis. Wherever you go,
make sure to nose around the back streets.
Often there are interesting things there that
even the locals don't know about.

CRUELLA Map pp316-17   Gothic & Fetish

☎ 844-0167; 257 ave du Mont-Royal Est; Ⓜ Mont-
Royal

With a coffin centerpiece and one of the
biggest arrays of Gothic and fetish clothing
in Montréal, Cruella is undoubtedly the
biggest apparition in the Plateau grave-
digger's scene. Slip into a chain-link
miniskirt, dominatrix leggings or a Victorian
shroud to give your party that something
extra, or pick up vampire fangs and bond-
age icons for your pale-faced friends.

FRIPERIE ST-LAURENT

Map pp316-17   Vintage Fashion

☎ 842-3893; 3976 boul St-Laurent; Ⓜ St-Laurent,
then bus 55

A *friperie* is a used clothing store and there
are several in this area. This one however
gets the highest marks from hard-core
secondhand hounds for the general selection, condition of the clothes and the best
chances of funky 'eureka!' finds.

KANUK Map pp316-17   Winter Fashion

☎ 527-4494; 485 rue Rachel Est; Ⓜ Mont Royal

When people in Québec say 'Kanuk' they
mean the winter coats that last a lifetime,
and although they're available throughout
the province, this store has the best selection. Most jackets stay toasty in temperatures dipping to -30ºC, so in winter they're
perfect for roaming downtown Montréal
or slipping away to the chalet. It also carries raincoats, swimsuits, backpacks and
hiking gear.

LIBRAIRIE MICHEL FORTIN

Map pp316-17   Bookstore

☎ 849-5719; 3714 rue St-Denis; Ⓜ Sherbrooke

A mecca for every foreign-language student and linguist freak in town, you can
find books, cassettes or novels on just
about every language in the world from
Thai to Basque to Georgian.

REVENGE

Map pp316-17   Boutique Fashion

☎ 843-4379; 3852 rue St-Denis; Ⓜ Sherbrooke

This renowned showcase store for Québécois designers displays subtle designs for
professional women who want to balance
chic with audacious. The men's ready-to-
wear garments have a less challenging task,
stressing confidence and masculinity in
direct, commanding lines.

SCHRETER Map pp316-17   Men's Fashion

☎ 845-4231; 4358 boul St-Laurent; Ⓜ Mont-Royal

This rambling cut-rate Jewish-run store has
been going for 75 years thanks to its inexpensive brand-name clothing in all sizes.
It hasn't changed much since its opening
in 1928 except for the plate-glass display
installed during a recent expansion. Parents
remember how *their* parents brought them
here to stock up on the equivalent of Nike,
Reebok and Adidas at great savings. You
seriously have to wonder how the place
stays in business.

TWIST ENCORE Map pp316-17   Vintage Fashion

☎ 842-1308; 3972 boul St-Laurent; Ⓜ Sherbrooke

Close to Mojo and Friperie St-Laurent, this
is another favorite *friperie* because of its
small but extremely well-chosen selection.
Famous 1940s ties and Gothic-flavored
blouses proudly adorn window displays
that are always fresh and very colorful.

Places like this pooh-pooh the upstarts shops from Toronto that may not have the same instinctive feel for the street.

U&I Map pp316-17 · Boutique Fashion

☎ 844-8788; 3650 boul St-Laurent; Ⓜ Sherbrooke

Eric Toledanone, owner of one of Montréal's chicest designer boutiques U&I, put local designers in the spotlight from day one – YSO, Morales, Denis Gagnon – with an international sprinkling of offerings from Paris and other fashion meccas. The boutique itself has won a design award; and a film loop in the front window has people unselfconsciously dressing and undressing, constantly stopping foot traffic on boul St-Laurent.

LITTLE ITALY & MILE END

Mile End is a fascinating up and coming shopping area. Best of all, many of the stores are very community minded, running talks and supporting artists by showing their work in the stores. Little Italy is terrific for grocery shopping and cooking items.

AU PAPIER JAPONNAIS

Map p318 · Origami

☎ 276-6863; 24 ave Fairmount Ouest; Ⓜ Laurier

You'd never have guessed how many guises Japanese paper can come in until you visit this gorgeous little shop. The lamps and kites make great gifts and you can fold them for easy transport. This store has also become a bit of an arts and crafts hub and offers dozens of workshops and seminars a year, on things like bookbinding or how to make lampshades.

BODYBAG BY JUDE Map p318 · Boutique

☎ 274-5242; 17 rue Bernard Ouest; Ⓜ Laurier

The brainchild of Montréal designer Judith Desjardins, her Bodybag label is reasonably priced (around $100 per piece) and full of interesting shapes, volumes and fabrics like microfleece. The wonderful staff are big cheerleaders for the clothes without being pushy.

GENERAL 54 Map p318 · Streetwear

☎ 270-9333; 54 ave St-Viateur Ouest; Ⓜ Laurier

The hats! The bags! The community consciousness! Mile End artists have created almost everything stocked at this great little boutique. Goods here are sold on consignment with creators getting the lion's share of the proceeds from the store. You'll find stuff here you won't find anywhere else including funky T-Shirts and some of the coolest leather handbags ever.

LE MARCHÉ DES SAVEURS

Map p318 · Québébecois products

☎ 271-3811; 280 pl du Marché du Nord; ☻ 9am-6pm; Ⓜ Jean-Talon

Everything here is Québécois, from the food to the handmade soaps to one of the best collections of artisanal local beer in the city. The store was established so local producers could get wider exposure for their regional products, and it's a joy just to browse.

LOCAL 23

Map p318 · Second-hand

☎ 270-9333; 23 rue Bernard Ouest; Ⓜ Laurier

This tart little *friperie* stocks recycled clothing and heaps of interesting vintage finds. Even if you are not a secondhand clothing freak, this is an interesting place to stop by. There's nothing junky about it and pieces have been carefully chosen and arranged. Watching regulars attack the racks and turn up killer ensembles is part of the fun.

QUINCAILLERIE DANTE

Map p318 · Cooking/Hardware

☎ 271-2057; 6851 rue St-Dominique; Ⓜ De Castelnau

This quirky little Italian-owned hardware and cooking supply store is a household name in Montréal, selling everything from 1st-class pots and pans to espresso makers, fishing rods and hunting gear. Owner Elena Vitelle shows how real pasta is made on Saturday at 2pm.

OUTREMONT

Rue Laurier is Outremont's main shopping drag and is filled with ultra-pricy, slick boutiques. Most people won't be able to afford much on this stretch but it is a fun place to window shop. Rue Bernard is another interesting place to stroll, with its small sprinkling of specialty boutiques.

JET-SETTER Map p318   Travel Goods

☎ 271-5058, 800-271-5058; http://jet-setter.ca; 66 ave Laurier Ouest; M Laurier

An orgy of state-of-the-art luggage and every travel gadget known to man, it's got luggage alarms, pocket-sized T-Shirts, 'dry-in-an-instant' underwear and towels, mini-irons and hairdryers. This list goes on and on. There is also an on-line catalogue to browse so you can still order these hard-to-find thing-a-ma-bobs if you're not in Montréal.

UN AMOUR DES THÉS Map p318   Tea Shop

☎ 279-2999; 1224 ave Bernard Ouest; M Rosemont

Over 160 types of loose tea sit in canisters behind the counter of this charming shop. It stocks leaf varieties and flavors you've likely not only never heard of, but never imagined (red-berries and maple syrup, tea with chocolate oils, cream of Earl Grey). Regular tea tastings and ceremonies are also held.

WESTMOUNT

Ave Greene has interesting bookstores and galleries while Westmount's stretch or rue Ste-Catherine Ouest has high-fashion boutiques frequented by moneyed Westmounters and includes children's boutiques where the clothes cost more than most adult's elsewhere in town.

GALERIE DE BELLEFEUILLE

Map pp310-11   Art Gallery

☎ 933-4406; 1367 ave Greene; M Atwater

Even Montréalers may not know this gallery is one of the top private agents of Canadian art abroad, representing the likes of Nicola Hicks, Stephen Conroy or Jim Dine. Sculpture, paintings and limited edition prints are given excellent space in this grand ex-bank with its winding staircase. The manager, Anthony Collins, is a gold mine of knowledge on the local arts scene.

OINK OINK Map pp310-11   Toys & Children's Wear

☎ 939-2634; 1343 ave Greene; M Atwater

Westmount parents flock to this place for the latest and greatest of everything from toy gadgets to fashionable clothing for children. You'll find that pink mini-ghetto blaster, Barbie wig set or Sunday picnic garb in this adorable little shop.

WESTMOUNT SQUARE

Map pp310-11   Shopping Mall

Cnr rue Ste-Catherine Ouest & ave Wood; M Atwater

Designed by Bauhaus architect Ludwig Mies Van der Rohe, this modern complex with office towers, terrace and shopping concourse was opened in 1967. It has a variety of boutiques, gift shops and art galleries, as well as a good selection of liqueurs and wines from the local SAQ outlet. The Marché Westmount Square is a pretty food court and market with an English flavor.

OUTER DISTRICTS
CHABANEL WAREHOUSES

Map pp308-9   Garments & Textiles

900 boul St-Laurent; ☻ 9am-1pm Sat; M Crémazie

Bargain-sniffers from far and wide flock to the Chabanel, an eight-block expanse of old factory buildings in northern Montréal west of boul St-Laurent. Inside are hundreds of 'suites' or warehouse storage rooms stuffed with locally made and imported items. From Buffalo jeans to Monte Calvo coats to Indian skirts, the choice is so huge it's almost paralyzing. Just start on a top floor (the buildings have up to nine floors) and work your way down. Bring cash and be prepared to bargain. Prices are good even if you don't bargain – we know someone who bought a lacy tailor-made wedding dress for $50! The shops open their doors on Saturday morning only, when something of a funfair atmosphere prevails. A few buildings are open normal hours during the week.

Sleeping

Sleeping

Montréal's accommodation scene is blessed with a tremendous variety of rooms and styles. Though rates aren't particularly cheap, they are very reasonable by international standards – or even compared to Canadian cities like Toronto or Vancouver. French- and Victorian-style inns and independent hotels cater to a variety of budgets. The many B&Bs, in particular, offer heaps of character – the precious commodity that can make all the difference – and their owners are often invaluable sources of travel advice. There are many comfortable but bland chain hotels in town, however you should not write them off all together: in peak seasons or around key events, the B&Bs and guest houses are booked solid in Montréal. Especially if you've trundled off the bus, out of your car or off your airplane in summer without a reservation, this kind of hotel may be home to the only available bed in town.

Planning in advance is key to finding accommodation during big events. The Grand Prix (mid-June) and the Montréal Jazz Festival (late June to early July) are ultrapeak periods, and conventions can crimp availability in late summer. In the off-season (October to April), rates can be 20% to 30% lower, except over Christmas and New Year.

Accommodation Styles

Small, European-style hotels are a Montréal specialty. Located downtown and in the Quartier Latin, they occupy Victorian-era homes that are plain and functional or comfy and charming. Prices are graded by facilities (eg with sink, toilet and/or full bathroom), but note that not all places have air-con, and for some, air-con can mean a simple air fan though the standard is improving.

PRICE GUIDE	
$$$	over $160 a night
$$	$60–$160 a night
$	under $60 a night

B&Bs are a wonderful alternative. Many of them are set in attractive, 19th-century stone houses close to the Plateau's bar-and-restaurant strips of boul St-Laurent and rue St-Denis, or near rue Ste-Catherine Est in the Village.

Almost every establishment serves some kind of continental breakfast, and quantities can be lavish – croissants or rolls, jam, cheese, several cereals and a selection of coffee. More upscale hotels also offer hot English breakfasts with eggs, bacon and sausage.

The luxury hotels have a surprising number of rooms that fall into the midrange category, even if you book at the last minute and especially in low season. Keep an eye out for cut-rate weekend and internet specials, or special package deals from your travel agent. Prices

BIDDING FOR BEDS

Everyone knows Montréal accommodations can be a little pricey but whether they're looking for a cut-rate deal on a boutique hotel or a stay at an independent inn, deal hunters are turning to online bidding services to nab the best travel steals – www.priceline.com and www.hotwire.com are by far the most popular.

It works like this: hotels sign up with the service and put their lowest acceptable prices in the system. Then you come along. Enter your preferred budget and how many stars you want your accommodation to have. The search engine will match your request with what's available, then if you accept, click away and the money is whooshed off your credit card. No refunds. No changes. The name of your hotel will be emailed to you.

The bidding wars have become as much a game as a travel service and devotees can spend hours discussing tricks for getting the best prices and decoding what the hotel may be. The most popular (and least convoluted strategy) is to book as close to the last minute as you can as hotels are willing to accept lower prices if they hear time ticking away on an empty room. While Priceline is by far the most popular, some people favor Hotwire, because it occasionally gives out enough details for you to actually guess where you might be staying. Check out www.biddingfortravel.com to learn even more from people who post their winning bids for all to see.

at B&Bs and hotels sky-rocket in the summer especially around festival season when small and midsized hotels are often booked weeks in advance.

Montréal has an abundance of good budget accommodation. Apart from the usual dorm beds, hostels may offer single and double rooms at hotel standards. In addition, the universities throw open their residence halls to nonstudents in summer and prices are competitive.

Check-in & Check-out Times

Most hotels in Montréal operate on a similar kind of time frame: check-in is around 3pm, check-out some time between 11am and noon. A minority of hotels have a later check-in time of around 6pm so clarify when making your reservation.

Reservations

The following services will make bookings for free. You may need to guarantee with a credit card, bearing in mind that a fee may be charged if you cancel a couple days before you are due to arrive.

Most B&Bs are listed by agencies. If you're staying a while ask about a weekly rate, and check if the breakfast is cooked or continental. All places listed in this chapter have a private bathroom unless otherwise stated.

CENTRE INFOTOURISTE Map pp310-11

☎ 873-2015, 877-266-5687; www.tourisme
-montreal.org; Square Dorchester
For all types of accommodation in Montréal.

DOWNTOWN B&B NETWORK

Map pp316-17
☎ 289-9749, 800-267-5180; www.bbmontreal
.qc.ca; 3458 ave Laval
Owners Bob and Mariko Finkelstein have over 50 private homes on their books, mostly downtown and in the Quartier Latin, all checked for quality and hospitality beyond minimum requirements. Hosts range from students to lawyers; places range from mansions with fireplaces in the bedrooms, to Victorian homes and apartments filled with antiques. Reasonable rates from $55/65 for a single/double, to $95/150 with bathroom.

HOSPITALITÉ CANADA

☎ 287-9049, 800-665-1528; www.hospitality
-canada.com
This company handles reservations throughout Québec and Canada, including gay and gay-friendly accommodations. It also has the best overview of what's available where and when.

MONTRÉAL OASIS Map pp310-11

☎ 935-2312; www.bbcanada.com; 3000 ch de
Breslay
Montréal Oasis represents five B&Bs in pleasant old houses in Old Montréal and downtown. Prices range from $65 to $105; triples are also available. Most places welcome children.

RELAIS MONTRÉAL HOSPITALITÉ

Map pp316-17
☎ 287-9635; http://martha-pearson.com;
3977 ave Laval
Provides referrals to small inns, furnished apartments and European-style B&Bs downtown, near Old Montréal.

Long-Term Rentals

Most long-term options will require you to guarantee your stay by check or money order, with a cancellation period of two days or more. The universities offer good deals from May to August, though you should not expect much more than dormitory amenities.

STUDIOS DU QUARTIER LATIN

Map p315   Studio Apartments $$
☎ 845-6335; www.studiosquartierlatin.com;
1273 rue St-André; apt per day/week from $65/315,
per month $550-800; Ⓜ Beaudry
For a taste of life in the 'real' Montréal, away from the hotel circuit, seek out these cosy efficiency apartments in the Quartier Latin, the Village and the Plateau areas. All studios have fully equipped kitchenette, TV, private telephone and bed linen. Bathrooms are private or shared – ask for details.

TOP 10 MONTRÉAL SLEEPS

- Auberge du Vieux-Port (p194) – bare-brick chic, country charm and great views
- Hôtel Le Jardin d'Antoine (p199) – romantic hideaway in the Quartier Latin
- Maison Pierre du Calvet (p194) – landmark inn harking back to Ben Franklin
- A2K (p196) – charming little rooms with Indian influences and a discount on the Maharaja Buffet next door.
- Hôtel Champs-de-Mars (opposite) – an elegant Old Montréal option away from the crowds
- Hôtel Nelligan (p194) – if only to be surrounded by the poetry
- Auberge Bonaparte (opposite) – a perennial readers' favorite
- Auberge de la Fontaine (p202) – parkside gem with Provençal flavor
- Anne ma Soeur Anne (p202) – smartly equipped studios
- All Suite VIP Loft (p199) – newly renovated rooms in a sizzling part of town

LA TOUR CENTRE VILLE

Map pp310-11   Hotel Residence $$

☎ 866-8861; www.hotelcentreville.com; 400 blvd René-Lévesque Ouest; studios $119, ste $129-170; Ⓜ Square-Victoria

This is a conventioneer's favorite. Roomy full-service apartments, midrange hotel grade, in a 169-room tower in the middle of downtown. Studios also available. All quarters have a separate kitchen – not exactly Martha Stewart, but perfectly OK. Slip away to the indoor swimming pool, sauna or gym with a city panorama. They're normally rented on a weekly basis but exceptions can be made.

MARRIOTT RESIDENCE INN

Map pp310-11   Hotel Residence $$$

☎ 935-9224; www.residencemontreal.com; 2170 ave Lincoln; ste from $189; Ⓜ Atwater

Marriott swooped down on an aging apartment tower and created a snappy business option: spacious one- and two-bedroom suites with fully equipped kitchen and balconies with great views of Mont Royal (ask for the north side). Bits of worn chipboard are still around but you can't argue with the amenities – new pool and sauna, free high-speed internet and a designer restaurant.

TRYLON APARTMENTS

Map pp310-11   Apartments $$$

☎ 843-3971; www.trylon.qc.ca; 3463 rue Ste-Famille; apt per month $1350-1800; Ⓜ Place-des-Arts

This modern high-rise is a plush alternative to top-end hotels at a fraction of the price. Microwaves, crockery and linen are a cut above and guests can enjoy the indoor swimming pool, sauna and exercise room.

OLD MONTRÉAL

Old Montréal has the most atmospheric and most expensive digs in town. Over the last decade, many of the area's old buildings have been converted into impeccable boutique hotels with unique ambience and careful, confident service. The proliferation of such distinctive hotels has also inflated the area's B&B and inn rates, but don't let that put you off right away – considering the overall experience, value in this area is generally terrific.

ALTERNATIVE BACKPACKERS

Map p314   Hostel $

☎ 282-8069; www.auberge-alternative.qc.ca; 358 rue St-Pierre; dm $18-20; Ⓜ Square-Victoria

This laid-back hostel near the Old Port is like a muesli bar in designer wrapping. It has 48 beds in pastel and orange dorms, over two nicely kept floors in a converted commercial space, with one private double room for $55. Organic breakfast costs $3.50, and you can use the cooking facilities.

MAISON BRUNET

Map p314   B&B $$

☎ 845-6351; www.maisonbrunet.ca; 1035 rue St-Hubert; d with/without bathroom $76/66; ste $120; Ⓜ Berri-UQAM

Not far from the Quartier Latin and the Village, this charming little guesthouse has a splash of old-fashioned decor with touches of sugary rococo. Rooms are spacious with polished-wood floors, colorful linens and air-con, and the congenial owner is full of local tips. Breakfast (included) is served in the garden next to a cute little fountain and has received enthusiastic reviews from readers.

LES PASSANTS DU SANS SOUCY B&B

Map p314   B&B $$

☎ 842-2634; www.lesanssoucy.com; 171 rue St-Paul Ouest; d $125-175, ste $145-215; Ⓜ Place-d'Armes

Built in 1723, this B&B feels more like a fancy country inn, set back from the road at the rear of a quiet courtyard in the heart of Old Montréal. Its comfy rooms are furnished with tasteful antiques, the breakfast room is a treat (with a stained-glass skylight above the dining table) and the foyer doubles as an art gallery. Be sure to reserve well ahead.

UQAM RESIDENCES

Map p314   University Apartments $

☎ 987-6669; www.residences-uqam.qc.ca; 303 boul René-Lévesque; studios $63-121; Ⓜ Berri-UQAM

This place offers beautiful, modern studio apartments with kitchenette in a great location not far from the club district along boul St-Laurent. Readers have given them rave reviews, but like McGill, it's only open to nonstudents during the summer.

AUBERGE BONAPARTE INN &

RESTAURANT Map p314   Boutique Hotel $$$

☎ 844-1448; www.bonaparte.com; 447 rue St-François-Xavier; r $145-355, ste $325; Ⓜ Place-d'Armes; Ⓟ

Readers just can't seem to get enough of this place. Wrought-iron beds and Louis Philippe furnishings lend a suitably Napoleonic touch to this historic 30-room inn, a former judge's residence ('Berthelot 1886' is engraved in stone over the entrance). Rooms are decorated in a warm European style; those at the rear overlook a pretty garden with views of the Basilique Notre-Dame. Breakfast (included) is served in the fine **Bonaparte Restaurant**, which has been done up in Napoleonic Imperial style.

HÔTEL CHAMP-DE-MARS

Map p314   Hotel $$

☎ 844-0767, 888-997-0767; www.hotelchampdemars.com; 756 rue Berri; r $155-210, ste $310; Ⓜ Berri-UQAM

Because it's tucked off the main Old Montréal stomping grounds, this place tends to get overlooked. And while it's not as slick or trendy as the boutique hotels closer to town, its small, intimate rooms are done up in a lovely timeless style. There's a complementary breakfast served each day in the little attached restaurant.

INTERCONTINENTAL MONTRÉAL

Map p314   Luxury Hotel $$$

☎ 987-9900, 877-424-2449; www.ichotelsgroup.com; 360 rue St-Antoine Ouest; d $155-260, ste from $315; Ⓜ Square-Victoria; Ⓟ

This Interconti has a unique location between a new high-rise and a restored annex of the 19th-century Nordheimer building. Guests enjoy links to the Centre de Commerce Mondial shopping mall. Photography and paintings by local artists adorn all 357 rooms; the turret suites in particular really ooze character, with superb views to Mont Royal. The large complex includes a piano bar and gourmet restaurant as well as extensive conference facilities.

AUBERGE BONSECOURS

Map p314   Inn $$$

☎ 396-2662; www.aubergebonsecours.com; 353 rue St-Paul Est; d $160-175; Ⓜ Champ-de-Mars; Ⓟ

The unusual ambience of the renovated stables lends this secluded hotel particular appeal. All seven rooms have bare brick walls, designer halogens and floral linen piled high, but each room is cut differently. The front-facing room with the pinewood

Auberge Bonaparte Inn, Old Montréal

floors and sloping ceiling is especially popular, and all quarters are quiet thanks to its location on an inner courtyard.

AUBERGE DU VIEUX-PORT

Map p314 Boutique Hotel $$$

☎ 876-0081, 888-660-7678; www.aubergedu vieuxport.com; 97 rue de la Commune Est; d $165-199; Ⓜ Champ-de-Mars; Ⓟ

Combine cultivated bare-brick chic with the wrought-iron bedsteads of a country inn and, voilà, you've got a boutique hotel unlike any other in Old Montréal. The 27 portside rooms occupy an 1882 warehouse with views of the Old Port. The buffed floors and original wooden beams help lay on the romance.

HÔTEL NELLIGAN

Map p314 Boutique Hotel $$$

☎ 788-2040, 877-788-2040; www.hotelnelligan .com; 106 rue St-Paul Ouest; d $190-295, ste $295-2000; Ⓜ Place-d'Armes; Ⓟ

Housed in two restored buildings and named in honor of Québec's most famous and tragic poet Émile Nelligan (see boxed text p74) this is one of the Old Town's most tremendous boutique hotels. Warm wood, bare brick and a lobby filled with plush armchairs and a fireplace. We don't know what kind of draft machine they've got, but the Boréal Rousse the bartender pulls here is the best in town. Verses, a plush bar and restaurant, is next door. The decor is gorgeous and the food good but the service has been disappointing on occasions, especially given the prices. Hopefully that's been addressed of late.

HÔTEL PLACE-D'ARMES

Map p314 Boutique Hotel $$$

☎ 842-1887, 888-450-1887; www.hotelplace darmes.com; 701 Côte de la Place-d'Armes; r/ste from $225/$325; Ⓜ Place-d'Armes; Ⓟ

Charcoal-tile floors, white-marble countertops and a flickering hearth set the warm tone at this ex-headquarters of a Scottish life insurance company. Room decor is nearly identical but everything's first-class – antique moldings, brick or stone walls, black granite and white marble in the bathrooms, and a CD player/entertainment system in every room. Even small quarters feel spacious thanks to the views of Mont Royal or the Basilique Notre-Dame. There's a fitness

center, restaurant and bar, but the crowning touch is the splendid rooftop terrace.

HÔTEL ST-PAUL

Map p314 Boutique Hotel $$$

☎ 380-2222, 866-380-2202; www.hotelstpaul .com; 355 rue McGill; d $229-299, ste from $329; Ⓜ Square-Victoria; Ⓟ

The lobby greets you with a fireplace made out of translucent alabaster, a siren's call to linger in this swanky beaux-arts structure. The 120 rooms and 24 suites exhort the four elements but cool sophistication has the upper hand, with marble bathtubs, dark-wood furnishings and airy open-plan suites with a touch of Japanese elegance. Amenities galore, from high-speed internet to fax machines in rooms. The attached Cube (p128) restaurant is a draw in its own right.

HÔTEL GAULT

Map p314 Boutique Hotel $$$

☎ 904-1616, 866-904-1616; www.hotelgault .com; 449 rue Ste-Hélène; d $235-589; Ⓜ Square-Victoria; Ⓟ

The Gault's 30 loft-style rooms are a study in modern design – a Flou bed, Artemide lamps, ergonomic chairs. All quarters have king- or queen-size bed, workstation and a flat-screen TV – and the bathrooms have toasty floor heating. The top-flight rooftop suites with terraces are gorgeous. There's a small exercise room and more amazing design items in the lobby, but no restaurant. Web bookings can mean great deals (from around $200).

MAISON PIERRE DU CALVET

Map p314 Historic Inn $$$

☎ 282-1725, 866-544-1725; www.pierreducalvet .ca; 405 rue Bonsecours; d $265-295; Ⓜ Champ-de-Mars; Ⓟ

The heritage hotel experience par excellence! This historic landmark in Old Montréal was built right into the city defense walls in 1725, and staying here is like stepping back in time: massive stone fireplaces with original carvings, gilded picture frames, four-poster beds surrounded by carefully preserved antiques. Benjamin Franklin stayed here in 1775 while trying to garner support for the American Revolution. The salon, library and dining rooms all drip the moneyed elegance of the period. Breakfast is taken on a secluded courtyard amid pretty flowering plants.

HÔTEL LE ST-JAMES

Map p314   Boutique Hotel $$$

☎ 841-3111, 866-841-3111; www.hotellestjames
.com; rue St-Jacques; r $400-475, ste $575-5000;
Ⓜ Square-Victoria; Ⓟ

Three years' renovation went into this careful mosaic of contrasting styles, and against all odds, everything fits: the Greek columns with oriental wall blossoms, the Italian Renaissance moldings with the English antique chairs. An interior designer's fantasy, this former merchant bank has candle-lit basement spa and art treasures from five continents. The Rolling Stones booked out the entire hotel – 25 rooms and 28 suites – Mick quipped that it was a shame they couldn't just take the place along. The Terrace Apartment is a snippet at $5000 per night.

PARC JEAN-DRAPEAU

The youth hostel on Île Notre-Dame is the only accommodation in Parc Jean-Drapeau and is likely the park's best kept secret.

AUBERGE DE JEUNESSE-CENTRE
OPTION PLEIN AIR Map p319   Hostel $

☎ 872-0199; 1 Circuit Gilles-Villeneuve, Île Notre-Dame; dm $20-25; Ⓜ Jean-Drapeau, bus 167

If you want to take in all the summer activities and outdoor concerts at Parc Jean-Drapeau but don't want to slog back and forth over the bridge everyday you couldn't ask for a better location than this. The only downside is the lack of facilities in the park. Though the hostel has a small cafeteria on site where you can buy a continental breakfast or snacks, there are no restaurants, grocery stores or other amenities on the islands. Rooms here are clean but very plain and stark and may appeal more to younger travelers. Women's showers are private, but men's are communal. The park hosts many summer sports competitions and out-of-town teams book here so reservations are essential.

DOWNTOWN

The city center is the bastion of the business hotel and the large upper-end chain. There are some interesting independent hotels as well as budget establishments scattered throughout the area. Most of the B&Bs are around the residential areas around McGill.

HI AUBERGE DE MONTRÉAL

Map pp310-11   Hostel $

☎ 843-3317, 866-843-3317; www.hostelling
montreal.com; 1030 rue Mackay; dm/r $26/65;
Ⓜ Lucien-L'Allier

This large, central and well-organized HI hostel has shared rooms (all with air-con) from four to 10 beds, but is edging upmarket with an increasing number of private rooms. Its energetic staff are always organizing something – trips to the Laurentians, a local sugar shack or walking tours of town. This is one of those hostels that is always buzzing no matter what time of year (or day) that you drop by. Reservations are strongly recommended in summer.

MCGILL UNIVERSITY RESIDENCE
HALLS Map pp310-11   University Dorms $

☎ 398-8299; www.mcgill.ca/residences; 3935 rue University; s student/nonstudent $40/45; Ⓜ McGill

These three 1960s residence halls are located at the top of a steep hill right by Mont Royal. It's practically a town of its own: 600 dorm rooms with shared kitchen but no air-con. Guests can visit the university cafeteria, pool, gym and tennis courts. Weekly rates are good – but it's only available mid-May to mid-August. The only complaints visitors make about this place is the steep walk back and forth from the rooms to town.

B&B REVOLUTION

Map pp310-11   B&B $-$$

☎ 842-0938; www.bbrevolution.com; 2091 rue St-Urbain; r $50-160; Ⓜ Place-des-Arts

This fine little place offers splendid rates and neighborhood ambience – like from a friend who's just renovated a Montréal loft. All its rooms have TVs, air-con, bare brick and access to kitchen and laundry. Staff are extremely personable and there's no curfew. A single/double with shared bathroom costs only $50/60.

HÔTEL DU NOUVEAU FORUM

Map pp310-11   Independent Hotel $$

☎ 989-0300, 888-989-0300; www.nouveau-forum
.com; 1320 rue St-Antoine Ouest; s/d $60/65;
Ⓜ Lucien-L'Allier

Behind the old stone facade lie cheery, newly renovated rooms, all with air-con and disabled access, but no telephones. Ideally placed for a Canadiens hockey match as it's right next to the Bell Centre.

HÔTEL CASA BELLA

Map pp310-11   Independent Hotel $-$$
☎ 849-2777, 888-453-2777; www.hotelcasabella
.com; 264 rue Sherbrooke Ouest; s/d without bathroom $50/65, with bathroom $80/85; Ⓜ Place-des-Arts; Ⓟ

This intimate greystone at the north end of the Quartier Latin charms with its comfy, mismatched furniture, carved wooden Victorian staircase and accommodating staff. It also now has wi-fi in each room. The free continental breakfast includes home-baked croissants made by the staff, who are happy to help plan your day – just ask.

HÔTEL L'ABRI DU VOYAGEUR

Map pp310-11   Independent Hotel $$
☎ 849-2922, 866-302-2922; www.abri-voyageur.ca;
9 rue Ste-Catherine Ouest; s/d $59/69; Ⓜ St-Laurent

It's on a grimy, seedy slice of rue Ste-Catherine but if you're not put off by that or the nearby sex clubs, you'll be nothing but comfortable once you're buzzed inside the security doors of this immaculately kept hotel. Rooms have original pinewood floors, exposed brick, a sink and air-con. Bathrooms are all shared. The front desk staff are wonderfully friendly and a gold mine of visitor information.

Y DES FEMMES Map pp310-11   YWCA Hotel $
☎ 866-9942; www.ydesfemmesmtl.org; 1355 boul René-Lévesque Ouest; s/d without bathroom $60/75, with bathroom $75/86; Ⓜ Lucien-L'Allier

Freshly renovated in 2003, the YWCA's hotel welcomes both sexes to rooms that are comfy and modern – a welcome step up from its predecessor's institutional rooms. Each floor has a kitchen with fridge and microwave, and being a 'Y', there's a fitness center and heated indoor pool.

MANOIR AMBROSE

Map pp310-11   Independent Hotel $$
☎ 288-6922, 888-688-6922; www.manoirambrose
.com; 3422 rue Stanley; s/d without bathroom from $70/85, s/d with private bathroom from $80/95; Ⓜ Peel

This hotel consists of two merged Victorian homes in a quiet residential area. Its 22

smoke-free rooms offer a wealth of quirky charms and some of the best bathroom amenities in town. The nicely renovated superior (single occupancy from $95, double occupancy from $110) has a striking split-level ceiling and private bathroom while even the shared bathroom in the corridor has a luxury corner bathtub. Continental breakfast is included.

HÔTEL A2K

Map pp310-11   Independent Hotel $$
☎ 932-9300, 877-563-9300; www.a2khotel.com;
1475 boul René-Lévesque Ouest; r $90;
Ⓜ Guy-Concordia

One of a kind! Recently opened by the charmingly friendly owner of Restaurant Maharaja next door (one of the best in town!), rooms here are small, simple but with lovely touches like Indian gold and red accents on the bed. The staff makes you feel like they are welcoming you into their homes. Breakfast is included and if you are a guest, you get 25% off the Indian buffet.

CASTEL DUROCHER

Map pp310-11   B&B $$
☎ 282-1697; www.casteldurocher.com/francais
.html; 3488 rue Durocher; r 3 days from $119, ste from $179; Ⓜ McGill; Ⓟ

This establishment occupies a tall, turreted stone house a couple of blocks east of McGill University. The two standard rooms are anything but standard – the Penguin room has a king-sized bed in a Victorian tower, with access to a kitchen and a private living and dining room. Both suites have a private bathroom and terrace. Breakfast includes fresh croissants, cheese and pastries from the nearby Belgian bakery, and chocolates are made in-house. Room rates will vary depending on how many days you stay.

ARMOR MANOIR SHERBROOKE

Map pp310-11   Independent Hotel $$
☎ 845-0915; www.armormanoir.com; 157 rue Sherbrooke Est; s&d $99-139; Ⓜ Sherbrooke

This conversion of two fine Victorian houses is replete with atmosphere. Its 30 rooms range from standard (a bit snug but cheerful) to the deluxe faux-French style, with bedstead grilles, ceiling stucco and Jacuzzis. A continental breakfast is included.

MARRIOTT CHÂTEAU CHAMPLAIN

Map pp310-11   Luxury Hotel $$$

☎ 878-9000, 800-721-7033; www.marriott.com;
1 Place du Canada; d $145-260; Ⓜ Bonaventure; Ⓟ
Known as the 'cheese grater' for its half-
moon windows, this bold skyscraper has
large luxury rooms and amenities like an
indoor pool, health club and sauna. Ask for
quarters facing Square Dorchester for an
absolutely stunning view over downtown
to Mont Royal. Las Vegas-style revues are a
regular feature.

MARITIME PLAZA

Map pp310-11   Hotel $$

☎ 932-1411, 800-363-6255; www.hotel
maritime.com, 1155 rue Guy; r from $150; Ⓜ Guy-
Concordia
This is a big commercial hotel near Concordia university that gets terrific reviews
from both business travelers and vaca-
tioners. The lobby is usually a bit of a zoo
with a mix of families and conventioneers
clamoring for the desk's attention, but
once you get checked in the rooms are
quiet and comfortable. Room rates here
are always in flux and change drastically
based on occupancy and time of year.
There is also an on-site swimming pool
and bar with pool table.

SOFITEL

Map pp310-11   Luxury Hotel $$$

☎ 285-9000; www.sofitel.com; 1155 rue
Sherbrooke Ouest; r $170-460; Ⓜ Peel; Ⓟ
The western part of Montréal, between
Concordia and McGill universities is
packed with nice but bland chain hotels. If
you want to stay in the area but are look-
ing for accommodation with a little more
style, Sofitel is the place. Part of the French
luxury chain, this hotel opened downtown
in 2002 and was a breath of fresh air with
its stylish, modern rooms and European
feel. Staff hit the right note of sophistica-
tion without too much snobbery and the
rooms are immaculate – usually done up
in cool black and whites or white and
wood tones with a piece of interesting
artwork hanging on the walls. The down-
stairs Renoir restaurant is close to perfec-
tion with wonderful brunch and dinners,
fantastic staff and every detail considered
including shawls for the women if the air-
conditioning gets too cold.

HÔTEL DU FORT Map pp310-11   Hotel $$

☎ 938-8333, 800-565-3333; www.hoteldufort
.com; 1390 rue du Fort; r $145-175, ste $199-245;
Ⓜ Guy-Concordia; Ⓟ
This hotel is in a terrific location, near
Concordia University and the downtown
core. A post office and internet café are
right across the street and there are dozens
of terrific bars, restaurants and shopping
centers nearby. The decor is done in sober
vanilla and brown shades that you'll be
unlikely to remember the moment you've
left these clean, comfortable rooms. But
that's not necessarily a bad thing – from
service to amenities, there are no surprises
at this hotel which has a reputation for
good steady quality. High speed internet is
available in rooms for $10.95 a day.

RITZ-CARLTON Map pp310-11   Luxury Hotel $$$

☎ 842-4212, 800-241-3333; www.ritzcarlton
.com/hotels/montreal; 1228 rue Sherbrooke Ouest;
r/ste from $175-265; Ⓜ Peel; Ⓟ
This has been *the* place in Montréal for the
ultimate splurge ever since Liz Taylor and
Richard Burton got married here (once). The
marble-floored bathrooms are wired for TV
and radio sound, and rooms are stuffed with
antique writing desks and shelves of leather-
bound classics – just a small taste of what's
available in the Royal Suite ($5000). The
old-world character of the place is maybe as
good as the amenities. Its afternoon high tea
is about as authentic as you can get (down
to the crustless cucumber sandwiches and
clotted cream) and reservations are recommended. In warm weather, it's served by
white-uniformed waiters, in front of the
alfresco fountain and duck pond.

LOEW'S HOTEL VOGUE

Map pp310-11   Luxury Hotel $$$

☎ 285-5555, 866-563-9792; www.loewshotels
.com/hotels/montreal/; 1425 rue de la Montagne;
d from $189; Ⓜ Peel; Ⓟ
This upmarket hotel has managed to blend
French-empire style with modern perks
and conveniences – some travelers really
love the TVs attached to the baths and the
caviar-stocked minibar. The rooms them-
selves are comfy but short on individuality,
although the air-kissy designer bar is abso-
lutely gorgeous. Hollywood stars and their
crews stay here but good family packages
are on offer too.

HILTON MONTRÉAL BONAVENTURE

Map pp310-11   Luxury Hotel $$$

☎ 878-2332, 800-445-8667; www.hiltonmontreal
.com; 900 rue de La Gauchetière Ouest; d $195, ste
from $250; Ⓜ Bonaventure; Ⓟ

Your standard business Hilton with deluxe
amenities, but the best part is arguably
the panoramic view of downtown. All
rooms have on-command video movies,
mahogany furniture, marbled bathrooms
and large working areas. The absolute
highlight is the 2.5-acre rooftop garden
with a duck pond and heated pool. Ask
about the famous UFO sighting here a few
years back.

HÔTEL LE GERMAIN

Map pp310-11   Boutique Hotel $$$

☎ 849-2050, 877-333-2050; www.hotelgermain
.com; 2050 rue Mansfield; d $210-475; Ⓜ Peel; Ⓟ

This ultrachic hotel boasts loft-like luxury
rooms for a hip business crowd that treasures intimacy. Dark woods contrast nicely
with the blanched walls, glass and mirrors,
and the fine range of creature comforts
including 27-inch TVs, cotton bathrobes
and an exercise room. The sumptuous
bathrooms gleam with chrome and crafted-
porcelain fittings.

FAIRMONT LE REINE ELIZABETH

Map pp310-11   Luxury Hotel $$$

☎ 861-3511; www.fairmont.com; 900 boul
René-Lévesque Ouest; d/ste from $219/$350;
Ⓜ Bonaventure; Ⓟ

This is the grande dame of Montréal
business hotels with over 1000 tastefully
renovated rooms and suites. Its celebrity
guest list is longer than a stretch limousine,
including Queen Elizabeth, the Dalai Lama
and several presidents and prime minis-
ters. The most famous was arguably John
Lennon, who wrote the song *Give Peace a
Chance* here during his 1969 bed-in; you
can stay in the same suite, which contains
memorabilia such as the framed seven-inch
single.

QUARTIER LATIN

In this nightlife hub known for new bars
opening nearly weekly, luckily there are a
few decent places to stay within staggering
distance.

HÔTEL ST-DENIS

Map p315   Independent Hotel $$

☎ 849-4526, 800-363-3364; www.hotel-st-denis
.com; 1254 rue St-Denis; d $69-119, ste $110-140;
Ⓜ Berri-UQAM

These standard albeit fairly spacious hotel
rooms are pepped up with Ikea-style furniture, comfy beds and, in the case of the
suites, by a whirlpool tiled right into the
living area. Pluses are the cozy attached
restaurant, and being located near the
Quartier Latin pubs and clubs. Rooms are
quite OK for the price and have air-con.

CHEZ TAJ B&B (LA MAISON JAUNE)

Map p315   B&B $$

☎ 524-8851; www.maisonjaune.com; 2033 rue
St-Hubert; s/d $60/80; Ⓜ Berri-UQAM

Known until recently as La Maison Jaune, this
B&B has hard wood floors, high ceilinged
rooms in beautiful bright shades of blue, red,
yellow and green; the ambience here is just
charming. Breakfast typically includes choco-
late croissants, French toast and banana-
cranberry bread, served in a salon with
chandeliers and stucco moldings. Ask for the
quietest room with balcony overlooking the
garden. There are no private bathrooms.

HÔTEL LORD BERRI

Map p315   Independent Hotel $$

☎ 845-9236, 888-363-0363; www.lordberri.com;
1199 rue Berri; d $89-$129; Ⓜ Berri-UQAM; Ⓟ

This modern high-rise is a heartbeat away
from the nightlife of rue St-Denis. Furnishings are tasteful and contemporary in its 148
rooms with big comfy beds, air-con, in-room
movies and an in-house restaurant *Il Cavaliere*.

MONTRÉAL ESPACE CONFORT

Map p315   Independent Hotel $$

☎ 849-0505; www.montrealespaceconfort.com;
2050 rue St-Denis; r $89; Ⓜ Berri-UQAM

Back in the 1990s this stretch used to be
the stomping ground for the transient and
the confused, and this address was a noto-
rious flop house. Things have changed all
along this street since then and this new
hotel is one of the most charming exam-
ples. Though one guest described his room
as 'comfortable but nothing special,' he
didn't do the place justice. It's simple and
modern with plain furnishing but it abso-
lutely sparkles with newness. Gay friendly.

HÔTEL LE ROBERVAL

Map p315   Independent Hotel $$

☎ 286-5215, 877-552-2992; www.leroberval
.com; 505 boul René-Lévesque Ouest; d $99-129,
ste $119-149; Ⓜ Berri-UQAM; Ⓟ

On the southern edge of the Quartier
Latin, perky Roberval has nicely appointed
doubles with good business amenities –
including air-con, telephone with voicemail,
a work desk and a high-speed internet out-
let. Regular suites and family suites have a
kitchenette. The hotel's boxy exterior belies
the charms that lie within.

HÔTEL LE JARDIN D'ANTOINE

Map p315   B&B $$

☎ 843-4506, 800-361-4506; www.hotel-jardin
-antoine.qc.ca; 2024 rue St-Denis; d $105-145, ste
$150-181; Ⓜ Berri-UQAM

Romantic Victorian decor is the chief selling point at this cute hotel, handily located
in the thick of the Latin Quarter action. All
rooms are newly renovated with wrought-
iron bedsteads, some with flowery wallpaper
and others bare brick. The peacock-back
chairs make the breakfast salon feel like a Parisian café. Wi-fi now available in every room.

HÔTEL DE PARIS

Map p315   Independent Hotel $$

☎ 522-6861, 800-567-7217; www.hotel-montreal
.com; 901 rue Sherbrooke Est; r high season $69-
169, low season $59-139; Ⓜ Sherbrooke

A turreted Victorian mansion with a wide
range of upgraded rooms and suites with
kitchens. Most rooms have private bath-
room and air-con – ask for the fine front
rooms with balconies overlooking rue
Sherbooke. There is a fine little café on the
premises and the location is excellent. The
main drawback is the noise emanating
from the cramped hostel downstairs. Apart-
ments in a renovated stone building across
the street are rented by the week.

ALL SUITE VIP LOFT

Map p315   Independent Hotel $$

☎ 448-4848, 866-563-8847; www.cosytel
.com/viploft; 329 rue Ontario Est; r $89-149;
Ⓜ Berri-UQAM

Newly renovated, the rooms here have hard
wood floors and are oozing with character.
Little flourishes personalize each room
whether it's with an interesting floor mat

or unique color combination. Located on
the less trafficked rue Ontario, this hotel is
just seconds away from the action on rue
St-Denis. A terrific bar and two wonderful
restaurants are across the street.

THE VILLAGE

Delightful, superb-quality B&Bs dominate
the accommodation choices in this part of
town. The Village is also so central and well
served by métro lines that it's one of the best
locations in the city to base yourself. All the
options listed here are gay-friendly – open
but not limited to gay and lesbian guests.

LE GÎTE DU PARC LAFONTAINE

Map p315   Hostel $

☎ 522-3910, 1877-350-4483; www.hostel
montreal.com; 1250 rue Sherbrooke Est; dm $25,
d $55-70; Ⓜ Sherbrooke

This converted Victorian house has an
atmosphere more like that of a guesthouse
or inn than a hostel. It's located just a 10-
minute walk from the main bus station and
close to bar-filled rue St-Denis. Continental
breakfast (included in the price) is served
on the terrace and guests can use the
kitchen, TV room and laundry. There's also
bike rental for exploring the city.

LE CHASSEUR B&B Map p315   B&B $-$$

☎ 521-2238, 800-451-2238; www.lechasseur.com;
1567 rue Saint-André; r low season $34-74, high
season $44-99; Ⓜ Berri-UQAM

Right across from the métro station, this
place is run by a charming accountant M
Lachasseur. The rooms here are simple but
immaculately kept up and you'll be well
situated to take in the Village, Downtown,
the Plateau or Old Montréal.

TOP FIVE GAY STAYS

- Alexandre Logan (p200) – splendid 19th-century ambience
- Turquoise B&B (p200) – so you know what it feels like to live in a glossy magazine spread
- Montréal Espace Confort (opposite) – simple, sparkling and welcome-to-all digs
- Revolution B&B (p195) – gorgeous antiques in a 1830s setting
- Ruta Bagage B&B (p200) – what other place in town has a designated place for sunbathing?

TURQUOISE B&B Map p315 B&B $$
☎ 523-9943, 877-707-1576; www.turquoisebb
.com; 1576 rue Alexandre-de-Sève; s $60-80,
d $70-90; Ⓜ Beaudry
The decor in this plush two-story greystone
looks like something out of *Better Homes &
Gardens*. Each bedroom has a queen size
bed and is individually appointed with
Victorian ceiling moldings, shiny wood
floors and carved faux gables (yes, indoors).
Breakfast is served in the large backyard
next to the fish pond. Bathrooms shared.

HÔTEL LE BRETON
Map p315 Independent Hotel $
☎ 524-7273; www.lebreton.ca; 1609 rue St-
Hubert; s/d $45/85; Ⓜ Berri-UQAM, bus 30
This small family-run hotel is just a five-
minute walk from the action in either the
Quartier Latin or Village. Ask for a fully
renovated room with air-con and you'll get
a great deal – frilly bed linen in large and
well-kept (if not luxurious) quarters.

RUTA BAGAGE B&B Map p315 B&B $$
☎ 598-1586; www.rutabagage.qc.ca; 1345 rue
Ste-Rose; s/d $70/85; Ⓜ Beaudry
Tucked away in a quiet side street near
bustling rue Ste-Catherine Est, this old
Victorian house is one of the worst-kept
secrets in the Village. There are only four
rooms, impeccably decorated – you'll love
the 'Russian room' with dark-wood furnishings and swirling carved bedstead. There
are two outdoor terraces, one designated
for breakfast and the other for sunbathing.

ALCAZAR Map p315 B&B $$
☎ 223-2622, 866-589-8964; www.alcazarmontreal
.com; 1589 rue Alexandre-de-Sève; r without bathroom $85-95, r with bathroom $95-115; Ⓜ Beaudry
A former clergy's residence, this greystone
Victorian home is furnished with beautiful
crafted mahogany, antique stained glass
and contemporary art. Everything is wonderfully kept and inviting – the fluffy linen,
the modern kitchen and dining salon and
there's a little swimming pool for summer
evenings. Only one room has a private
bathroom. Bryan is the charming host and
chats easily in English, French and Spanish.

LA CLAIRE FONTAINE Map p315 B&B $$
☎ 528-9862; www.laclairefontaine.com;
1652 rue La Fontaine; r $65-95; Ⓜ Papineau
This place is minutes away from the village
nightlife, but tucked away in a quiet corner
of the village with its own lush spacious
patio garden so you get the best of both
worlds. Rooms are on the old-fashioned
side but still cheery and bright.

ALEXANDRE LOGAN Map p315 B&B $$
☎ 598-0555, 866-895-0555; www.alexandrelogan
.com; 1631 rue Alexandre-de-Sève; r $90-155;
Ⓜ Beaudry
Your friendly hosts Luc and Alain have an
eye for details like original plaster moldings, ornate woodwork and Art Deco glass
patterns in this splendidly renovated home
from 1870. The hard wood floors and
big windows make the rooms bright and
cheerful. The breakfast room couldn't be
more welcoming and the living room is set
up with a games table and a computer for
internet access. The outdoor terrace is great
for lounging under the tiki torches. Prices
here vary widely depending on the time of
week and year.

LA CONCIERGERIE Map p315 Guesthouse $$
☎ 289-9297; www.purpleroofs.com/la
conciergerie-qc.html; 1019 rue St-Hubert;
r $98-200; Ⓜ Berri-UQAM
This 17-room Victorian house from 1885 has
invested a lot in the guests' wellbeing and
it shows. Modern furnishings of solid-grain
wood, subtle touches of lighting and high-
class bathroom fixtures create comfort the
second you open the door. There's a private
sunroof, indoor Jacuzzi and gym and all

rooms have bathrooms. A generous continental breakfast is included. No children.

HÔTEL GOUVERNEUR

Map p315   Hotel $$-$$$

☎ 842-4881, 888-910-111; www.gouverneur.com; 1415 rue St-Hubert; d $139-199; Ⓜ Berri-UQAM

There are lovely B&Bs in the Village, but if you need something in the same location where you can be more independent and come and go as you please, this business hotel is a good option and is attached to the métro and the Village's Place Dupuis. There's usually a lot of action going on here and this is where press conferences are frequently staged. Rooms are done up in rich reddish woods and have a bit of character about them against the generic nature of the rest of the hotel. Rates will depend on season and occupancy.

PLATEAU DU MONT-ROYAL

Staying in the most fashionable district of Montréal means being close to some of the best eateries and nightlife in town. Like the Village, the Plateau is packed with B&Bs; hotels are few and far between.

AUBERGE DE JEUNESSE MAEVA

Map pp316-17   Hostel $

☎ 523-0840; www.aubergedejeunessemaeva montreal.com; 4755 rue St-Hubert; dm $22, r $45-50; Ⓜ Laurier

As close to the perfect hostel as you can get. Not only is it family run, but it's in a quiet residential neighborhood making it easy to forget you are in a new city and not just visiting some long-lost cousins. Highly recommended.

TOP FIVE MONTRÉAL B&BS

- Alexandre Logan (opposite) – old-world charm and two of the most welcoming hosts in town
- Au Piano Blanc (right) – homey haven with colors of the sun
- Couette et Café Cherrier (p202) – pretty greystone stacked with perks
- Les Passants du Sans Soucy B&B (p193) – arty surroundings and careful attention to detail
- Le Rayon Vert (p202) – country comforts and a stylish terrace

---

PIERRE ET DOMINIQUE B&B

Map pp316-17   B&B $-$$

☎ 286-0307; www.bbcanada.com; 271 Carré St-Louis; d $50-100; Ⓜ Sherbrooke

One of several inviting B&Bs snuggled in the rows of stone Victorian houses overlooking Carré St-Louis. The light, airy bedrooms are decked out in Swedish-style furniture and have a sink, but no bathroom. Pierre serves a different organic breakfast every day, along with a heart-stopping espresso.

MINI HOTEL B&B DES PINS

Map pp316-17   Independent Hotel $

☎ 849-6059, 888-806-8086; www.minihotel despins.com; 109 ave des Pins Est; s $55-80, d $60-99; Ⓜ St-Laurent, then bus 55

Convenient to the main boul St-Laurent, this affable little budget hotel offers a range of simple but clean rooms with views of the residential Plateau. The beds have down comforters and all rooms have pine floors and ceiling fans (no air-con). The more expensive rooms have a private bathroom. Continental breakfast is included.

AU PIANO BLANC Map pp316-17   B&B $$

☎ 845-0315; www.aupianoblanc.com; 4440 rue Berri; r $60-125; Ⓜ Mont-Royal

The 'colors of the sun', as owner Céline puts it, radiate from this delightful B&B a stone's throw from Mont-Royal métro station. It's certainly homey, with cheerful yellow and white decor, garden views and French country furniture. The three rooms are distinctively themed; the 'Royale Suite' has a touch of *Arabian Nights* with lacy curtains between bed and the bathroom (with freestanding French tub). Readers have consistently given this place good reviews.

À LA BONNE HEURE B&B

Map pp316-17   B&B $$

☎ 529-0179; www.alabonneheure.ca; 4425 rue St-Hubert; s/d/tr without bathroom from $65/80/95, with bathroom from $95/105/120; Ⓜ Mont-Royal

This is a typical turn-of-the-century Montréal terrace home with five bright, spacious rooms that exude an old-fashioned charm. Breakfast is quite an event in the grand dining room with high ceiling, French doors and cornice molding. The location, just one block from the Mont-Royal métro station, can't be beaten.

AIRPORT SHUT-EYE

If you need to catch an early-morning flight, this hotel in the vicinity of Pierre Elliott Trudeau International Airport is a practical option, albeit a bit short on atmosphere. **Best Western Hotel International** (Map pp308–9, ☎ 631-4811, 800-361-2254; www.best western.com; 13000 Côte Côte-de-Liesse; d from $99; AMT train Gare Dorval, bus 201) is a pleasant midrange chain hotel 1.5km from the airport. It has standard hotel amenities including a decent restaurant and interior corridors, a plus in winter. If you're flying in and out of town, you can park your car here free for three weeks, with one night's stay, and a shuttle is provided to the airport.

ANNE MA SOEUR ANNE

Map pp316-17   Studio Apartments $$

☎ 281-3187; www.annemasoeuranne.com; 4119 rue St-Denis; s $70-180, d $80-210, ste $155-230; M Mont-Royal

A real treat, these smart, fully equipped studios fill a valuable niche in the Plateau. They're suitable for short or longer stays, each unit having a 'microkitchen' with a microwave and stove, work space and Ikea-style furnishings built into the walls. Four of the 17 studios have private terraces, some overlooking the shady backyard. Business interests are looked after with a high-speed internet link and telephone with answering service. Croissants are delivered to your door as breakfast.

SHÉZELLES Map pp316-17   B&B $$

☎ 849-8694; www.bbcanada.com/2469.html; 4272 rue Berri; s $65-140, d $80-160; M Mont-Royal

A bastion of warmth and hospitality with its paneled walls, large fireplace and some utterly luxurious rooms. The studio apartment ($170 for two) is superb, occupying the entire ground floor with king-sized beds and a spacious bathroom with a whirlpool. There are smaller but welcoming doubles, as well as a 'love nest' behind a Japanese sliding door (the bed is directly under a skylight).

LE RAYON VERT Map pp316-17   B&B $$

☎ 524-6774; www.lerayonvert.ca; 4373 rue St-Hubert; s $72.50-77.50, d $85-90; M Mont-Royal

This centennial greystone has three comfortable, individual rooms not far from the alternative bustle of ave du Mont-Royal.

The yellow room has a queen-sized bed and Victorian furnishings, the rustic room is simple, and the garden room has two single beds (or one king, depending) a sink and a view of the garden. The breakfast room recalls a French country inn, but the clincher is the wonderful rear terrace – in summer it's as green as the tropics.

COUETTE ET CAFÉ CHERRIER

Map pp316-17   B&B $$

☎ 982-6848, 888-440-6848; www3.sympatico .ca/couette; 522 rue Cherrier; s $70-90, d $85-105; M Sherbrooke

This pretty greystone with lantern gables is stacked with perks: a living room with a fireplace; a separate guest floor with private access; and English-language newspapers in the morning. The rooms are immaculate and come with a variety of beds (double, queen, king) and personal touches, like dressing gowns. An open staircase leads to the 3rd floor where the congenial hosts Steve and Stephan serve their legendary breakfasts.

AUBERGE DE LA FONTAINE

Map pp316-17   Inn/B&B $$

☎ 597-0166, 800-597-0597; www.aubergede lafontaine.com; 1301 rue Rachel Est; d/ste from $120/159; M Mont-Royal

A gem of an inn on the edge of Parc La Fontaine. Provençal hues, bare brick, cheerful art and furnishings and staff a cut above the norm set the tone. Prices include a generous continental breakfast and guests can raid the fridge for snacks until midnight. The hotel is also well outfitted with tourist information. Room rates will vary widely depending on occupancy and your dates.

HÔTEL DE L'INSTITUT

Map pp316-17   Hotel $$

☎ 282-5120, Québec only 800-361-5111, ext 5120; www.ithq.qc.ca; 3535 rue St-Denis; r $120-295; M Sherbrooke

Run as a training center for the Québec tourism and hotel board, this lovely little hotel occupies what must be one of the ugliest buildings in town. The rooms, however, are spacious and comfortable, decked out in pretty oranges and greens, and the large suites have a salon and massive oak furniture. The only drawback is the smallish bathrooms.

Québec City ∎

Québec City

INTRODUCING QUÉBEC CITY

Québec City is the crown jewel of French Canada and if you're coming for the first time, look out – there's simply no other place like it in North America.

It's pure Old World Europe right smack in North America, the heart and soul of francophone culture in the New World, and it's got a boisterous and down-to-earth population proud to show it all off.

In short, it's hard not to be completely wowed by the place.

Perched atop a cliff that swoops down to the St Lawrence River, Québec City is the only walled city on the continent north of Mexico.

These fortifications now protect an entire old town that's become a kind of living museum. Narrow cobbled streets are lined with 17th- and 18th-century houses and almost every step will bring you to another historical plaque marking the battles between the French and British Empires for this symbolic piece of land, or a statue representing the French colonists' subsequent struggle for survival in English-speaking North America.

Plenty of first-time visitors just spend their time walking around the city with their jaws dropped open, muttering 'I can't believe this is in North America.'

Québec City's one-of-a kind history and cultural significance has even got the attention of Unesco. And since 1985 the entire old town has been placed on the UN's prestigious world heritage list.

Any time of year is good for a visit. Summer draws the mother load of tourists. The crowds create fascinating street life and a buzz wherever you go. And in turn, the city really pulls out the red carpet for visitors: everyone from musicians to acrobats to actors in period costume take to the streets. There's also terrific festivals and oodles of special museum exhibitions and tours. Fall and spring bring beautiful colors, dramatically reduced prices and thinner crowds. And in the winter, Caribou, an alcoholic drink enjoyed by the early settlers, is sold everywhere to keep people warmed up. Even in the darkest and coldest months of January and February, Quebecers have found a way to have fun: throwing the annual Winter Carnival, arguably the biggest, most colorful and most successful winter festival around.

The city has gone to great lengths to make the city as traveler-friendly as possible. Explanation panels are everywhere both inside and outside the walls pointing out historical events and things of interest to travelers – many of the plaques on historical buildings are translated into English. Even most of the street signs have explanations underneath, telling you who the street was named after and why.

Most visitors never venture outside the Old Town, but there is plenty to explore outside the walls as well.

The St-Jean-Baptiste neighborhood has wonderful shopping, cafés and bars as does the nouveau St Roch (New St Roch), another downtown neighborhood that's become one of the most striking and exciting examples of urban renewal in the province's recent history.

You will also be visiting Québec City at one of the most interesting times in its development. The entire region is gearing up for 2008, when it will celebrate Québec City's 400th birthday. Year-round festivities are planned and everything from museums to infrastructure is getting a spruce up in anticipation of the event.

Though Québec City was once considered little more than a day or weekend trip from Montréal, more and more visitors seem to be bypassing Montréal altogether and spending their entire vacation here and the surrounding regions.

Nine million tourists come to Québec City each year and it's regularly voted one of the top 10 tourist locations by everyone from Condé Nast to *National Geographic Traveler Magazine*.

About 622,000 people live in the Québec City municipality and around 95% of them have French ancestry. The English minority is miniscule here, but everyone associated with the tourism industry, including staff at hotels, restaurants, shops or tourist sites speaks English. Québec City is the capital of the province of Québec, which means once you leave those Old Town walls and head for its compact downtown you'll be rubbing shoulders with the province's elite: the rich, the powerful, the lobbyists, the wheelers, dealers and decision makers.

Québec City is also an important port and is developing its high-tech sector. In conjunction with Laval University, 'new-economy' high-tech enterprises are developing, particularly in such specialized fields as photonics, geomatics, biotechnology, nutraceuticals and software.

CITY LIFE
QUÉBEC CITY TODAY

Québec City these days is all about the birthday, and the big 4-0-0 in 2008 looks like it's shaping up to be a hell of a party. The preparations are everywhere you look; the celebrations dominate the news media and everywhere you go there is some kind of renovation, excavation or rejuvenation going on.

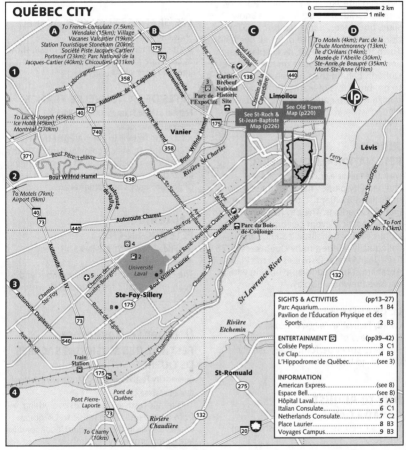

QUÉBEC CITY

SIGHTS & ACTIVITIES	(pp13–27)
Parc Aquarium	1 B4
Pavilion de l'Education Physique et des Sports	2 B3

ENTERTAINMENT	(pp39–42)
Colisée Pepsi	3 C1
Le Clap	4 B3
L'Hippodrome de Québec	(see 3)

INFORMATION	
American Express	(see 8)
Espace Bell	(see 8)
Hôpital Laval	5 A3
Italian Consulate	6 C1
Netherlands Consulate	7 C2
Place Laurier	8 B3
Voyages Campus	9 B3

France is kicking in money to redo the Parc de l'Amérique Française, Ottawa is kicking in $110 million and the province of Québec handing over another $40 million. Though there has been some scandal because the head of the organizing committee has been changed a whopping four times in just the last two years, it hasn't put a damper on the fun.

The same year, Québec City will also be hosting the summit of the world's francophone countries and the world Eucharistic conference.

Even citizens are getting into the action with prominent Québec City locals like Peter Simons (of Simons Department Store fame, see p247) spending $4 million to buy the Tourny fountain (presently in Bordeaux), renovate it and set it up smack in front of the Québec City parliament buildings in honor of the occasion.

CITY CALENDAR

January to February

WINTER CARNIVAL

www.carnaval.qc.ca

This famous annual event, unique to Québec City, bills itself as the biggest winter carnival in the world. Held sometime between late January and mid-February, there's parades, ice sculptures, a snow slide, boat races, dances, music and lots of drinking. Activities take place all over Old Town (many at the Parc de l'Esplanade) and include a giant slide on the Terrasse Dufferin behind the Château. If you want to go, bring lots of warm clothes and organize the trip early, as accommodations fill up fast.

June

FÊTE NATIONALE DU QUÉBEC

www.fetenationale.qc.ca/

Québec City parties hard on June 24, honoring John the Baptist, the patron saint of French Canadians. The day has evolved into a quasi-political event celebrating Québec culture and nationalistic leanings and is colloquially referred to by Quebecers as 'La Saint-Jean.' Major festivities on the Plains of Abraham start around 8pm ending with a massive fireworks display.

LE GRAND RIRE

Comedy Festival; www.grandrire.com
Eleven days of comedy, from stand-up shows to street performances, usually kick off mid- to late June.

July to August

CANADA DAY

Yes, it's celebrated even here, smack on July 1.

FESTIVAL D'ÉTÉ

Summer Festival; www.infofestival.com
Early July attracts musicians from all over Québec, Canada and even the world. The delightfully eclectic mix features everyone from Québec *vedettes* Garou and Éric Lapointe to German heavy-metal band the Scorpions. The 11-day festival is a fabulous place to see plenty of concerts by the province's stars.

LES GRANDS FEUX LOTO-QUÉBEC

www.lesgrandsfeux.com
It's a spectacular fireworks and music show at La Chute Montmorency, held between late July and mid-August.

FÊTES DE LA NOUVELLE-FRANCE

Festival of New France; ☎ 418-694-5560; www.nouvellefrance.qc.ca
A fab little festival in early August that commemorates Québec's colonial period. There's historical re-enactments and people running around in period costumes along with a slew of performances and other events.

September

FÊTE ARC-EN-CIEL

Gay Pride Festival; ☎ 418-809-3383; www.fetearcenciel.qc.ca
The celebrations early in September end in an enthusiastic rally through downtown Québec City.

October to November

FESTIVAL DES MUSIQUES SACRÉES DE QUÉBEC

Québec City Festival of Sacred Music; www.festivalmusiquesacree.ca
This terrific festival showcases everything from gospel and Celtic music to Gregorian chants and Inuit throat singing. Look for it in late October or early November.

CULTURE

Québec City has a reputation for being square and conservative (that is, at least from the Montréal perspective) and locals often refer to Québec City as a 'village' with equal parts affection and derision. Though it has all the big-city trappings, the core, downtown population numbers just 167,000.

Québec City is also known in Montréal and the rest of Canada as being a notoriously challenging place for people born outside of Québec City to establish themselves in the long term.

With a near homogenous French-Catholic background, community ties go back, way, way back. In fact, professional and future business networks are pretty much established by the time the city's citizens leave high school, if not primary school. Even French-speaking Quebecers from elsewhere in the province who come to Québec City to work or do business say these networks are extremely difficult to penetrate both professionally and socially.

However, the average visitor certainly doesn't need to concern themselves with this. About the first thing you hear from any traveler to Québec City is how great the locals are. Once they know you are from elsewhere (ie not an anglophone Quebecer) they will bend over backward to speak in English and help you out in any way they can.

Identity

Québec City locals are very proud but there's a time in pretty much all of their lives, usually after high school or university, when they decide whether they are going to 'try' Montréal or stay put. As the 'everything' capital of French Canada, from arts to business, science, technology and media, Montréal's pull is hard to resist. However, that means that those creative, dynamic people who chose to stay in Québec City are there because they really love the city and want to be there. So you'll find the way they identify with the city is very strong.

Lifestyle

Québec City has the best of both worlds. It has the feel of a small town but all the conveniences of the small city that it is. In 2001 the Canadian magazine *Today's Parent* ranked it the 'Best Canadian City for Families.' And it's easy to see why with its low crime rate, plenty of green spaces and a real sense of community.

BONHOMME CARNAVAL

You don't even need to be around for the winter festivities to know about Bonhomme. He's now as much a symbol of Québec as the Château Frontenac.

The official mascot of the Winter Carnival and the unofficial mascot of the provincial capital, Bonhomme was created with the founding of the carnival in 1954, along with a fantastical back story.

He lives in a land of ice and snow called Knulandis, whose residents are called Knuks; Grrrounches form a minority in the population. In the Knulandis tales, there is a town chief, ritualistic dances, and natural elements like the wind, moon and sun that all play a formative role in the destiny of their land. The clear references to First Nations' beliefs and customs cleverly link Québec's past and present.

This friendly snowman dresses in a red québécois *tuque* (winter hat) and an arrowed, colorful belt like those his *coureurs des bois* ancestors wore, purportedly to 'support the kidneys' and prevent the cold from seeping into the cracks between the *coureurs* pants and jackets.

He makes appearances at many of the festival's activities. A month before festivities begin, he unofficially sneaks into town, throws a big party, then reappears only at the solemn, official opening of the Carnival, in which Québec City's mayor hands him the keys to the city.

According to his official description, Bonhomme loves to dance and be merry, expresses his feelings through gestures, loves everyone equally and without prejudice, and represents the joy and the hardy spirit with which the Québécois handle their winters.

Université Laval is one of the most renowned universities in the province and 26,000 students attend each year.

The average cost of renting an apartment these days is $540, heaven to Montrealers who find themselves staring rents of $800 plus in the face.

The civil service in Québec City generates some 40,000 jobs and while unemployment overall in Québec rates about 8.4%, in Québec City it's only 5.9%.

And the employment outlook continues to be optimistic.

The only downside is what some consider the transformation of the Old Town. As recently as the early '90s, even students were able to afford to live there, and the place still had somewhat of a community feel. However, rents have pushed out almost all but the very moneyed and fewer and fewer locals can actually afford to live in the area. It's also pushed out the day-to-day businesses like grocery stores that gave the neighborhood a sense of community. While the Old Town is still breathtaking it's hard not to be a little wistful about the change.

Food

French food is king in Québec City. The lack of a significant immigrant population means that there is not the kind of massive ethnic smorgasbord that you'll find in Montréal, though the quality of restaurants here is outstanding. While for years Québec City locals were known to drive to Montréal for fine dining, these days Montrealers are making their way to Québec City to dine in the more than half dozen fine restaurants like **Laurie Raphaël** (p238) or **Le Panache** (p237).

Then there's Caribou, something you won't find in Montréal. It's an alcoholic beverage that resembles a very powerful and sweet red wine, kind of like a port and sherry mixed together, which is very warming. It's sold on streets around Québec City during Winter Carnival.

Fashion

Some of Canada's most famous and iconic clothing stores were founded in Québec City. Simons is a province-wide department store chain, known for stocking fashions by its own designers that aren't available in the other major stores. It's particularly known for its Twik clothing line for woman.

On the high-fashion front, Holt Renfrew, now the flagship of high fashion all across Canada, got its start in Québec City as a modest hat shop, established by an Irishman named William Samuel Henderson. However, it was only when the store started stocking furs that it drew national and then international attention. The store still proudly boasts that it received 'the prestigious honor of five generations of royal warrants under Queen Victoria's reign and was appointed Furrier-in-Ordinary to her Majesty.'

Unlike Montréal, Québec City isn't known as a hotbed of fashion. With so many locals being government workers, the dark navy or grey suit reigns supreme among both men and women, leaving little room for spicy fashion or experimentation.

THE QUÉBEC JUMPING WHAT?

The big sports news in Québec City isn't the imminent arrival of a CFL franchise or even the highs and lows of the Remparts. No, it's about the green guy dribbling a basketball on the logo of the new Québec City American Basketball franchise. When the man behind bringing the franchise to Québec City, businessman Réal Bourassa, said the new team name would be either the Québec Jumping Frogs or Kebekwa (how Québécois is pronounced in English), the uproar was heard across the country and all the way to France. 'Frog' has long been a derogatory name the English have used for French-speaking people and is considered very racist. That a professional sports team was considering it as part of their name scandalized the province. Bourassa told people they should just relax. 'We are in 2006 and we have to be able to laugh at ourselves,' Bourassa told the Canadian Press newswire service. However polls suggest locals didn't find it so funny — over 65% favored Kebekwa. You can keep track of the team, now known as the 'Kebs' for short, at www.quebecbasket.com.

When the most recent fashion scandal did hit, it was iconoclastic Québec City Mayor Andrée Boucher (see Government & Politics, p210) of all people who set it off. Mayor Boucher was on a business trip to Paris when she was snapped wearing a bright lime-green sundress with red lace-up ballet flats. Quebecers were scandalized and the picture made its way across English Canada where she was pilloried as well.

In fine form as always, Mayor Boucher said it was a $3000 Yves St-Laurent dress and that the picture just didn't do it justice. Still, the story had legs for weeks and we'll go out on a limb here to give Mayor Boucher a standing ovation for taking a risk and for being the only person to get 'Québec City' and 'fashion' together in every single major national newspaper in recent memory.

Sport

Until 1995 the Québec Nordiques hockey team were the sports sensation in town and the city alternately laughed with their every success and cried at their every defeat. When rumors began to seriously circulate that the team would be moved, protests were launched and gallons of ink spilled but they left town anyway. Pretty much any Quebecer you talk to will admit the loss of the city's National Hockey League team was the saddest day in sport. But there was also province-wide outrage, as the move put an end to one of the most infamous sports rivalries – between the Nordiques and the Montréal Canadiens. It was especially wrenching as pretty much every hockey fan felt the Nordique's time had come and that they were on their way to Stanley Cup glory. And win they did. Exactly a year after they moved, the ex-Nordiques, now Colorado Avalanche, took home the 1996 trophy.

These days fans content themselves with supporting the Québec Remparts, who play in the Québec Major Junior Hockey League. They play regularly at the **Colisée Pepsi** (p241). You can keep track of the team on their website (www.remparts.qc.ca/eng).

There are rumblings that Québec City may be getting a Canadian Football Team (CFL) franchise, but so far there doesn't seem to be much interest in spending the kind of money needed to build a stadium for them.

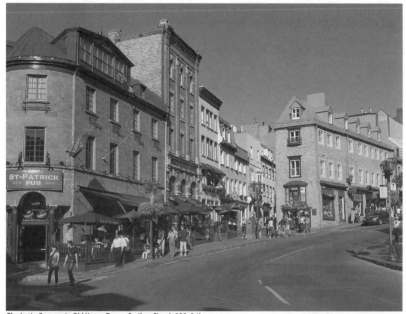

The Latin Quarter in Old Upper Town, Québec City (p222-24)

Québec City **CULTURE**

Media

Weekly newspaper the *Quebec Telegraph Chronicle* (www.qctonline.com) is Québec City's only English-language publication. It claims to be the oldest newspaper in North America, having published continuously since 1764. Though it does have some interesting editorials and columns, it is actually more of a community newspaper and has only limited distribution. The city's two daily newspapers are the French-language *Le Soleil* (www.cyberpresse .ca/apps/pbcs.dll/section?Category=CPSOLEIL) which has the best coverage of the city, and the tabloid, *Le Journal de Québec* (www.lejournaldequebec.com).

Voir Québec (www.voir.ca/une.aspx?zone=2) is the city's free entertainment weekly with pages of listings each Thursday for what's going on around town. Though it shares some of the same editorial content with its Montréal incarnation, the listings are all focused on the Québec City scene.

Language

Though many young people will be comfortable chatting to you in English, it is far less commonly spoken here than in Montréal. English is learned from primary school and locals grow up listening to anglophone music, but given the tiny English community in Québec City, if you venture outside the walls you may find many locals who are not used to speaking or listening to the language.

Within the walls, where almost all locals are somehow engaged with the tourist industry, you will have no problem finding English speakers.

If you speak some French and are coming from Montréal, you may find the accent here thicker and more challenging to understand. Montrealers and Quebec City locals can easily recognize each other at parties just by their accents.

ECONOMY & COSTS

Québec City has gone through an exciting about-turn over the last decade. Poor urban planning through to the 1980s led to an exodus to the suburbs, leaving the downtown core depopulated and prone to crime in some areas. The huge mega-malls being built in the suburbs were also a capital drain on the downtown businesses. The area started to turn around in the 1990s, with the rejuvenation of St-Roch and diversification of the economy. Laval University moved some of its departments downtown as well, bringing an influx of young students into the neighborhood.

Other urban projects included a fountain and landscaping in front of the train station as well as projects around the parliament buildings and the Dufferin-Montmorency expressway.

Québec City also reached out to the high-tech industries and now there are research centers in everything from lasers and optics to health and biotechnology. The government established the National Center of New Technology (CNNTQ) in St-Roch and now there are over 20 IT firms that bring over 800 workers into the neighborhood each day.

The 'rebranding' of Québec seems to be working. In a recent poll of North American and European cities, Québec City ranked number two for its software, plastics and metal manufacturing.

So like modern Montréal, Québec City has a new sheen on it with both the pluses and minuses that that brings: locals are struggling with their property taxes which are sky-rocketing just as they have in Montréal.

GOVERNMENT & POLITICS

Québec City has a great tradition of colorful, rabble-rousing mayors. Jean-Paul L'Allier, mayor from 1989 to 2005, had a reputation as a bit of an egoist but he did wonders for the city by taking the initiative to diversify the economy and clean up the St-Roch neighborhood. Present mayor Andrée Boucher is arguably the most colorful in Canada. She was the mayor of Ste-Foy before it became part of Québec City during the province-wide mergers, then was elected mayor of Québec City in the best punk-rock tradition – Boucher pummeled her competition, which included a slick campaign by former provincial Justice Minister Marc Bellemare, with a grassroots campaign. She participated in public debates but did not do any advertising and limited her campaign spending to just $5000.

ENVIRONMENT

There are wonderful parks and green spaces here, including Parc du Bois-de-Coulonge, Jardin Jeanne-d'Arc and of course, Battlefields Park. The city says about 45% of greater Québec City is wooded territory. Recycling programs are high on the city's environmental to-do list. Presently, only 26% of household waste is recycled, something the city is hoping to boost to 60% by 2008. Québec City recently spent $7 million on 110,700 recycling carts.

ARTS & ARCHITECTURE

MUSIC

Québec City has plenty to offer music lovers. For classical music fans there's the **L'Orchestre Symphonique de Québec** (☎ 418-643-8486; www.osq.org), a respected 100-year-old symphony orchestra. Its season runs from September to May and they perform at **Le Grand Théâtre de Québec** (p244). There's also the terrific **Opéra de Québec** (☎ 418-529-0688; www.operadequebec.qc.ca), which performs at the same place. Its season runs from October to May.

Some of the province's biggest rock stars started out here. Jean Leloup of rock and pop fame was born here and Loco Locass are a hip-hop group that formed in the city. But the scene here is so small, both bands and singers end up relocating to Montréal at some point in their careers to be where the music industry is concentrated and to be closer to the thriving club scene.

If you're interested in original music, there's still enough here to keep you busy. Heavy metal and goth are extremely popular (for advice on that area just ask the kids who hang out in the graveyard at Église St-Matthew off rue St-Jean). For more off-the-wall stuff check out the electronic music of Millimetrik (www.millimetrik.com) and for New-York-Dolls-/ Hanoi Rocks-ish dance music keep an eye out for Uberko (www.uberko.com).

There's a brash and independent spirit amongst the eclectic mix of active bands here so ask around at record stores about what's new and check out the weekly listings in *Voir Québec* every Thursday.

LITERATURE

There are many wonderful Québec City writers but few are translated. For a great sense of the city that still applies today, read one of the horror/fantasy stories by American writer HP Lovecraft. Lovecraft was obsessed with cities in which the past and present exist on top of each other, and Québec City was one of his favorite locations.

VISUAL ARTS

Many of Canada's top artists have been inspired by the beauty of Québec City and its surrounding scenery.

Jean-Paul Lemieux (1904–90) is one of Canada's most accomplished painters. Born in Québec City, he studied at L'Ecole des Beaux-Arts de Montréal and later in Paris. He is famous for his iconic paintings of Québec's vacant and endless landscapes and Quebecers' relation to it. Many of his paintings are influenced by the simple lines of folk art. There's a whole hall devoted to his art at the **Musée National des Beaux-Arts du Québec** (p221) and it is definitely worth a visit.

Alfred Pellan (1906–88) was another famous artist who studied at the local École des Beaux-Arts before moving to Paris. He later became famous for his portraits, still life, figures and landscapes, before turning to surrealism in the 1940s.

Other artists born elsewhere have moved to Québec City after being bewitched by its countryside.

Cornelius Krieghoff (1815–72) was born in Amsterdam but was acclaimed for chronicling the customs and clothes of Quebecers in his paintings and is known especially for the portraits he did of the Wendats (p233) who lived around Québec City.

Francesco Iacurto was born in Montréal but moved to Québec City in 1938 and his acclaimed works are dominated by the town's streetscapes, landscapes and portrayals of Île d'Orléans (p232).

ARCHITECTURE

You'll find a fascinating architectural mix here ranging from old buildings from the 18th century, to newer and more daring buildings springing up in the outer districts. The soaring cathedrals and basilicas encompassing everything from Gothic to neo-classic elements will likely be the highlights for many architecture buffs. These awesome religious structures are generally of such colossal size, they positively dwarf everything around them, whether it's the Église St-Jean-Baptiste (p225) casting shadows over the residential St-Jean-Baptiste neighborhood or the Église St-Roch (p228) that completely overpowers even the flashiest and ritziest boutiques of the St-Roch district.

Québec's Old Town is the place to head for a taste of what residential dwellings were like in New France. One feature you'll notice is the tiny doors on many of the buildings. While some people say their small size is because people were shorter in the 17th and 18th century, another explanation is that these doors were actually delivery ports, small only because they were meant for cargo deliveries and not for humans at all. For some of the city's most interesting modern buildings, the up-and-coming St-Roch neighborhood is likely the most interesting. Even run-of-the mill buildings like parking garages have been given a makeover and are worth a look. Check out the Stationnement Odéon (rue de la Chapelle) that got an overhaul in 2002.

CINEMA

The Québec film industry is firmly based in Montréal both from the production and creative angles.

The well-preserved state of the Old Town makes it extremely popular with foreign productions as it can easily stand in for medieval Europe. However, there is no production studio in Québec nor are there many Québec City–set stories being made today, strange for a capital and the second-biggest city in the province.

Robert Lepage's Ex Machina, a multidisciplinary performing arts company, is still based here. Though Lepage had hoped to turn a giant tunnel under the city into a movie production studio, negotiations are stalled for the moment. Lepage is one of the only contemporary filmmakers who regularly sets his films in the city.

Film Reviews

All names listed here refer to the director of the film. Below are some films in which Québec City gets centre stage.

Les Plouffe by Gilles Carle (1981) – based on a novel by Roger Lemelin, this film depicts a family's struggles in depression-era Québec City. If you want to understand the turbulent changes going on in the province at that time, it's hard to find a better film than this.

Les Yeux Rouges ('The Red Eyes' or 'Accidental Truths') by Yves Simoneau (1982) – a Québec City–set thriller with two cops on the trail of a deranged strangler.

Ma Vie en Cinémascope (My Life in Cinemascope) by Denise Filiatrault (2004) – singer Alys Robi was Québec's first international superstar (Never heard of her? Alys' *Tico-Tico* was as well known in the 1940s as Céline' s *My Heart Goes On* is 50 years later). Robi reached a level of fame that most Canadians could never dream of, let alone a French-speaking girl from conservative, isolated Québec City. The brilliant (as always) Pascale Bussières plays the adult Alys as she realizes her wildest dreams before mental illness sees her shut up in a mental institution for years where she receives electroshock treatments and a lobotomy.

I Confess by Alfred Hitchcock (1953) – a film-noirish suspense thriller, Québec City has never looked better than when Hitchcock is caressing its atmospheric Old World edges with his lens. It's based on a French play about a priest who hears a murderer's confession that his covenant with God won't let him break, even when he finds himself accused of the murder instead. Hitchcock was so taken with Québec City he based the entire story here and made the characters Canadian (see the boxed text on the Château Frontenac, p253).

Le Confessionnal (The Confessional) by Robert Lepage (1995) – an homage to the above Hitchcock film, Lepage's character starts off the film saying the days that had the most impact on his life were the re-election of Maurice Duplessis as premier of Québec, the arrival of TV, and Hitchcock arriving in Québec City. It only gets better from there. Sometimes retracing Hitchcock's steps, Lepage builds a beautiful portrait of Québec City through a man's quest to uncover a family secret that coincided with Hitchcock's arrival in town.

La Neuvaine (The Novena) by Bernard Émond (2005) – OK...so it's not *exactly* in Québec City, but if you're in this section, you may very well be nipping off to **Ste-Anne-de-Beaupré** (p233) whose shrine has a starring role in this film. It brings together a young man who comes to the cathedral to pray for his grandmother's life and a guilt-ridden Montréal doctor who arrives to put an end to her own. It's all too easy to ridicule Ste-Anne-de-Beaupré's religious rock-concert vibe, but as the director Bernard Émond said so well of this film 'I don't want to mock the crutches and exvotos...you don't mock hope.'

THEATER

Canada's French-language TV and film industries are firmly based in Montréal, but when it comes to theater, Québec City is still holding its own. Pretty much every actor who graduates from the local drama conservatory here asks themselves whether it's the big city and bright lights of Montréal that they seek, or if they'll stick around in the capital's tight-knit theater community.

Actors in Québec City can't always completely support themselves just through performing so usually combine it with a related job like teaching or drama coaching.

There's a lot that's attractive about staying. An actor here with a creative or original idea can write a script and have it produced, something that would take years, if it happened at all, in Montréal.

One of the most infamous examples was the brilliant one-woman-show *Gros et Détail* by Québec City actor Anne-Marie Olivier about the different people who live in the

WHY QUÉBEC CITY?

By: dhelenhall – Jan 22, 2006

The View from the Château Frontenac

While seated on a bench in front of the Château Frontenac, the sunshine formed imaginary diamonds on the tips of the waves on the St Lawrence, as it wound north towards the Laurentian Mountains. My breathing ceased for a brief moment.

Conversing with the Québécois

I learned very quickly to start a conversation with 'Bonjour' then look slightly puzzled when the response is in rapid québécois French, even if I understand a little. Seeing my look they will say 'Oh, English!' and speak English from then on!

The Québécois Art of Living

What these people have is an appreciation for food, drink, love, life and each other that is both fascinating and addictive. It is not about material goods, but good conversation. A cohesiveness, a sense of history, a love of each day as is.

(blu,list) v. to recommend a travel experience. www.lonelyplanet.com/bluelist

BLUELIST.

St-Roch neighborhood (p228.) The show was a full-on hit in Québec City, France and several countries in francophone Africa, but when Olivier tried to get it produced in Montréal she was told 'No' because it focused too much on Québec City.

Robert Lepage is not only Québec City's most famous playwright and director, but is one of the most renowned contemporary directors and writers in the world. Lepage was both born in Québec City in 1957 and got his theatrical training at the city's Conservatoire d'Art Dramatique. He joined the local Théâtre Repère and went on to create one award-winning play after another. He has gone on to stage or direct everything from opera to two of Peter Gabriel's world tours, and was the first North American director ever to do a Shakespeare play at London's Royal National Theatre (1992's *A Midsummer Night's Dream*). He founded his multidisciplinary performing arts Ex Machina company in Québec City in 1993 – amongst his plays he produced the award-winning *La Face Cachée de la Lune* that was later made into a highly praised film.

Most recently, he helped create Cirque du Soleil's *KA*, a permanent show playing in Las Vegas.

Distinctive Québec stop sign outside the historic Château Frontenac (p253)

HISTORY

The first significant settlement that we have knowledge of, on the site of today's Québec City, was an Iroquois village of 500 called 'Stadacona.' The Iroquois were seminomadic, building longhouses, hunting, fishing and cultivating crops until the land got tired, when they moved on.

French explorer Jacques Cartier traveled to the New World in 1534, but barely lasted the winter. By the time May 1536 rolled around Cartier and his remaining crew beat a retreat back to France, kidnapping some of the Iroquois, along with the chief of Stadacona, to taking with them. The Iroquois all died in France but Cartier returned in 1541 to start a post upstream in the New World. Again, he faced a winter of scurvy and disastrous relations with the indigenous population so the plan failed, setting back France's colonial ambitions for 50 years.

Explorer Samuel de Champlain gets the credit for finally founding the city for the French in 1608, calling it Kebec from the Algonquian word meaning 'the river narrows here.'

The English successfully attacked in 1629, but Québec was returned to the French under a treaty three years later and it became the center of New France. Repeated English attacks followed. In 1759 General Wolfe led the British to victory over Montcalm on the Plains of Abraham. One of North America's most famous battles, it virtually ended the long-running conflict between Britain and France. In 1763 the Treaty of Paris gave Canada to Britain. In 1775 the American revolutionaries tried to capture Québec but were promptly pushed back. In 1864 meetings were held in the city that led to the formation of Canada in 1867. Québec City became the provincial capital.

In the 19th century the city lost its status and importance to Montréal. When the Great Depression burst Montréal's bubble in 1929, Québec City regained some stature as a government center. Some business-savvy locals launched the now-famous Winter Carnival in the 1950s to incite a tourism boom.

While the suburbs and outskirts of Québec City kept developing, they sucked the life out of much of the city centre. It left the core poor and run-down until the 1990s when urban renewal projects made places like St-Roch neighborhood livable again.

The changes went hand in hand with diversifying Québec's economy, which started welcoming the high-tech sector, and subsequently saw a flourish downtown in everything from start-ups to research facilities.

In 2001 the city was the site of the Summit of the Americas, which exploded into mass demonstrations against globalization. Images of authorities battling protesters were broadcast around the globe.

Most recently, in 2006, archaeologists made a startling discovery when they uncovered the failed site of Cartier-Roberval (1541–43), one of two forts that were built. Though historic records have long spoken of the site, no one had ever been able to find it. The team who uncovered it did so quite by accident when they were doing perfunctory exploratory work on a site that was slated to be turned into a parkway. Among the items unearthed were porcelain from Italy and Iroquois pottery, both dating from the 1550s. The historians and archaeologists involved believe they may also uncover the bodies of the first settlers who were wiped out by disease. If so, studying the remains will blow the lid off the mystery of early settlement of the colony. Researchers estimate there may be another 15 years of work to do before that happens though. In the meantime, it's expected that part of the site will be open to the public in time for 2008.

Ah, yes, 2008 is shaping up to be a big deal for Québec City. Not only is it celebrating the 400th anniversary of its founding but it will also be hosting the annual summit of francophone countries (La Francophonie).

Hold on tight.

SIGHTS

Québec City is a gorgeous old place whose compact size makes it ideal for walking and exploring. The Old Town is packed with museums, old architecture and fantastic scenery. It's hard to walk more than a few steps without coming across an interesting sight or cobbled street just begging to be explored.

The city itself covers 93 sq km. Part sits atop the cliffs of **Cap Diamant** (Cape Diamond), and part lies below. Quebecers call the upper part the **Haute Ville** (Upper Town) and the lower part **Basse Ville** (Lower Town). Together, the 10 sq km of these historic upper and lower areas, within the stone walls, form the appealing **Vieux-Québec** (Old Town).

The Citadelle, a fort and landmark, stands on the highest point of Cap Diamant. The other major landmark is the splendid, dominating, copper-topped, castle-style Fairmont Le Château Frontenac hotel dating from 1892 (see p252). Behind the château, a large boardwalk called the Terrasse Dufferin edges along the cliff, providing fabulous views across the river. Below Château Frontenac is **Old Lower Town**, the oldest section of the city.

The two main streets heading southwest from **Old Upper Town** are boul René-Lévesque and, to the south, Grande-Allée, which eventually becomes boul Wilfrid-Laurier.

The wider area of Lower Town has the highways leading north, east and west. If you're driving, your plan should be to get to Vieux-Québec, then park the car for the duration of your stay. To the extreme southwest of the city are Pont de Québec or Pont Pierre-Laporte, both bridges leading to the south shore.

To get oriented, **Observatoire de la Capitale** (p227) gives views from 31 floors up.

Lévis, a suburb and a town, is seen directly across the river from Old Town.

The borough of **Ste-Foy-Sillery** is where Université Laval is. The area has a large student population and all the great bars and cheap eats that come with it. But there won't be much here of interest to the average traveler that you wouldn't be able to easily find in and around the Old City, other than enormous box malls that is.

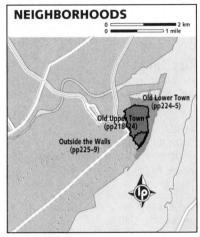

NEIGHBORHOODS

0 ——— 2 km
0 ——— 1 mile

Old Lower Town
(pp224–5)

Old Upper Town
(pp218–24)

Outside the Walls
(pp225–9)

ITINERARIES

Two Days

Start your first day at La Citadelle (p218), making sure you get there in time for the changing of the guard (10am daily June 24 to early September). After that, wander through the rest of Old Upper Town, making sure to stop in at the Basilique-Cathédrale Notre-Dame-de-Québec (p223). Take the funicular down to Old Lower Town (p224) for the *table d'hôte* at one of its fantastic French bistros like L'Échaudé (p237). Spend the afternoon exploring Place-Royale (p224) and taking in one or two of the exhibits at the magnificent Musée de la Civilisation (p225) if you have the time. Once dusk falls, hop on the Lévis ferry for a killer view of Old Québec and watch the sun set on Château Frontenac (p252).

On day two, explore some of the sites outside the walls. Spend the morning exploring Battlefields Park (p222), starting off with Abraham's Bus Tour (p222) to get you oriented before taking in the fabulous exhibitions throughout the park. Don't miss the Discovery Pavilion (p218) and the small but brilliantly conceived Louis S St-Laurent Heritage House (p219). In the afternoon, be awed by Québec art at the Musée National des Beaux-Arts du Québec (p221) before heading to the unselfconsciously cool Café Krieghoff (p238) for dinner or a drink on nearby ave Cartier.

Four Days

As for two days, but add in a day getting to know the parts of Québec City where the locals hang out. Start the day with a trip to the Observatoire de la Capitale (p227) and check out the status of the province's political greats outside the Hôtel du Parlement (p227) – jump on one of their its tours if you can. Afterwards visit the colorful stores and eateries of St-Jean-Baptiste's rue St-Jean (p225) or head down to St-Roch's hip rue St-Joseph (p228) where CEOs rub elbows with squeegee punks and junk shops are just a few short blocks from high-class boutiques. When you're done, head up to Grande-Allée Est for a beer served in thrillingly precarious glasses at Aux Vieux Canons (p239) then around 9pm head down to Les Voûtes de Napoléon (p241) for a rollicking night of québécois folk songs.

ORGANIZED TOURS

Guided walking tours can pack a lot of interest and knowledge into a short time and Québec City has plenty of extremely high-quality tours available. Many of them are specialized, given by people who are passionate about the subject, whether it be literature, history or ghosts.

You'll find popular boat-tour operators moored near Place-Royale and go downriver to Montmorency Falls and on to Île d'Orléans. For city views, you can't beat the cheap Ferry to Lévis (adult/child aged five to 11/senior $2.60/1.80/2.50); boats leave daily every 20 to 60 minutes from 6am to at least midnight.

Hail a *calèche* (horse-drawn carriage) for a fun ride. They can be expensive – $65 for about 40 minutes but drivers do provide some commentary.

Bicycling

Ask for the free cycling map from the Québec City tourism office on rue Ste-Anne.

Boat

CROISIÉRES AML Map p220

☎ 418-692-1159, 800-563-4643; www.croisieres aml.com; Quai Chouinard, Vieux-Port
Offers 2½-hour familial breakfast buffets (adult/child/senior $40/20/38) and four-hour dinner buffet cruises (adult/child/senior $50/25/48).

Québec City skyline over the St Lawrence River

CROISIÉRES LE COUDRIER

Map p220

☎ 418-692-0107, 888-600-5554; www.croisieres coudrier.qc.ca; 180 rue Dalhousie, Bassin Louise, Quai 19, Vieux-Port

Its sight-seeing cruises go for 90 minutes and run all the way to Île d'Orleans (adult/child $27/12). Other offerings include dinner cruises (adult $63) and special three-hour cruises during the Loto-Québec Fireworks Competition (p206).

Bus

DUPONT TOURS

☎ 418-649-9226, 888-558-7668; www.tour dupont.com

This tour operator has a smorgasbord of tours from a basic two-hour city tour (adult/child $30/18) to 6½-hour tours out of town that take in Montmorency Falls and Ste-Anne-de-Beaupré (adult/child $43/23) or Île d'Orléans (adult/child $80/60). Check the website for the full gamut. Not all tours are offered year-round and reservations are a must. There's a free pick-up service and shuttle bus. Family packages are also available.

OLD QUÉBEC TOURS

☎ 418-664-0460, 800-267-8687; www.toursvieux quebec.com

Another great choice with a wide range of local and out of town tours. The classic city tour (adult/child $30/18) covers all the top tourist spots (the Latin Quarter, Château Frontenac, Fortifications, Citadelle etc) and there's also a wide range of tours from a 4½-hour land/cruise-ship combination (adult/child $52/29) to a day-long tour that includes a 2½-hour whale-watching tour (adult/child $100/55). Some tours are seasonal. You'll get the rendez-vous point when you make your reservations.

Walking

GHOST TOURS OF QUÉBEC Map p220

☎ 418-692-9770; www.ghosttoursofquebec.com; 4 1/2 rue d'Auteuil; adult/child age 10 & under/student & senior $17.50/free/15; ☺ tours English/French 8 & 9pm/8:30pm May 1-Oct 31

Local theater actors or storytellers lead you through the streets of the Old Town by lantern recounting the hangings and hauntings of Old Québec. The 90-minute tours are great

fun and usually finish with a visit to the city's most haunted building. Tours leave from the sitting area by 98 rue du Petit-Champlain near boul Champlain in the Old Lower Town. Buy your tickets from the Ghost Tours of Québec office or from the guide 15 minutes before the tour.

In 2007 Ghost Tours is mounting a 1661 witch trial on limited dates throughout the summer, with the audience rendering the verdict at the end. The May and June dates have already sold out. Call for the availability of the performances in July and August.

LA COMPAGNIE DES SIX ASSOCIES

☎ 418-692-3033; walking tours $16

Boasts a great staff and very good walking circuits like the ever-popular 'Vice and Drunkenness,' which creaks open the rusty door on the history of alcohol and prostitution in the city. Other tours, in English and French, focus on epidemics, disasters and crimes. A cheery bunch, they are.

LES TOURS ADLARD

☎ 418-692-2358; 2½hr walking tours $17

Also very well-informed, and can arrange private walks.

LES TOURS VOIR QUÉBEC

Map p220

☎ 418-694-2001; www.toursvoirquebec.com; 12 rue Ste-Anne; adult/child age 8-14/student $17.50/10/15

This group offers some of the best history tours in town. Their specialty is walking tours of Old Québec City. You may end up getting someone like a history professor from Laval University as your guide. Group size is limited to five to six people to make the tours more personal and leave plenty of time and flexibility for questions and exchanges with the guide. Tours last from 90 minutes to two hours. Book by phone or at the counter inside the Centre Infotouriste on rue Ste-Anne.

PAUL GASTON L'ANGLAIS

☎ 418-529-3422; 2hr walking tours $15; ☺ tours English/French 8 & 9pm/8:30pm May 1-Oct 31

Affable archaeologist Paul conducts excellent, novel, thematically diverse walking tours (beer brewing, cemeteries of Old Québec, parks to name a few) when he's not zipping around town doing research on his bike.

OLD UPPER TOWN

The heart of Québec City, the Old Town, is where you will be spending most of your time because it's packed with the city's blockbuster sites and numerous museums on everything from history and the military to religious life in New France. The narrow, winding roads are lined with extraordinary old architecture, with some buildings dating from the 1600s. The grandest military structures, churches and buildings are concentrated in Old Upper Town.

ARTILLERY PARK Map p220

☎ 418-648-4205, 800-463-6769; 2 rue d'Auteuil; admission adult/child age 6-16/senior $4/2/3.50; ⊙ 10am-5pm Apr-Oct; ☐ 3, 7, 11, 28
The French chose this location for their army barracks because of its strategic view of the plateau west of the city and the St Charles River, both of which could feed enemy soldiers into Québec City. English soldiers moved in after the British conquest of New France. The English soldiers left in 1871 and it was changed into an ammunition factory for the Canadian army. The factory operated until 1964 and thousands of Canadians worked there during the World Wars. Now you can visit the Officers' Quarters and the Dauphine Redoubt where guides greet you in character (ie the garrison's cook) and give you the scoop on life in the barracks. There's also a huge model of Québec City in the old Arsenal Foundry.

DISCOVERY PAVILION Map p226

☎ 418-648-4071; 835 ave Wilfrid-Laurier; ☐ 11
The main Québec City tourist office, Centre Infotouriste (p278), is here and this building also houses the wonderful exhibition Canada Odyssey (Level 0; admission adult/child $8/7; ⊙ 10am-5:30pm Jun 24-Sep 4, to 5pm Sep 5-Jun 23). In it, you move from theater to theater where the history of the Plains of Abraham are depicted through clever multimedia presentations and generous dollops of good humor. There's a tremendous exhibit devoted to the French and British colonial military at the end with displays depicting their lives in the New World. The exhibit on their uniforms, which describes the significance of the designs and colors, is extremely well done and has even

nonmilitary buffs lingering and nodding knowingly.

FORTIFICATIONS OF QUÉBEC Map p220

☎ 418-648-7016, 800-463-6769; 100 rue St-Louis; admission to interpretive center adult/child age 6-16/senior $4/2/3.50; ⊙ 10am-5pm May-Oct; ☐ 3, 11
These largely restored old walls are a national historic site. You can walk the complete 4.6km circuit on top of it all around the Old Town for free. From this vantage point, much of the city's history is within easy view. The fortifications' interpretive center is by the Porte St-Louis where you can visit a small but interesting exhibit on the history of the walls as well as an old gunpowder building from 1815. It also offers 90-minute guided walks that include the Old Town (adult/child age six-16/senior $10/5/7.50).

LA CITADELLE Map p220

☎ 418-694-2815; www.lacitadelle.qc.ca; 201 Côte de la Citadelle; admission adult/child age 8-17/student & senior $8/4.50/7; ⊙ 10am-4pm Apr, 9am-5pm May, Jun & Sep, 9am-6pm Jul & Aug, 10am-3pm Oct, to 1:30pm Nov-Mar; ☐ 3, 11
This massive star-shaped fort towers above the St Lawrence River on Cap Diamant. French forces started construction here in the late 1750s leaving a gunpowder building and a redoubt, the beginnings of a defensive structure. But the Citadelle we know today was actually built by the British, who feared two things: an American invasion of the colony and a possible revolt by the local French-speaking population (that's why the cannons point not only at the river, but at Québec City itself). However, by the time the Citadelle was completed (construction began in 1820 and was finished about 30 years later) things were calming down. Twenty years later the Treaty of Washington was signed in 1871 between the United States and the newly minted Dominion of Canada (on behalf of her Majesty the Queen of England of course) ending the threat of American invasion.

The Citadelle now houses about 200 members of the Royal 22e Régiment (the rest live with their families at the nearby Valcartier base). The Vandoos, a nickname taken from the French for 22 (vingt-deux), is the only entirely French-speaking battalion in the Canadian Forces. They have a reputation amongst the Forces as the toughest (ie badass) regiment in the army.

The hour-long guided tours are excellent and will give you the low-down on the spectacular architecture and get you into exhibits on military life from colonial times to today.

The **changing of the guard** ceremony takes place at 10am each day in the summer months. The **beating of the retreat**, which features soldiers banging on their drums at shift's end, happens every Friday at 7pm from July 6 until early September.

The second official residence of the governor general (the Queen of England's representative in Canada) has been located here since 1872 (the other residence is located in Ottawa and called Rideau Hall). There are free one-hour tours of the Citadelle residence.

LOUIS S ST-LAURENT HERITAGE HOUSE Map p226

☎ 418-648-4071; 201 Grande-Allée Est; admission incl with Battlefields Park Day Pass; ⏰ 1-5pm Jun 24-Sep 4; 🚌 11

Louis St-Laurent (1882–1973) was Canada's prime minister from 1948 to 1957. Fluently bilingual due to his Irish mother and Québécois father, he was one of Canada's most distinguished leaders. Under

his watch, Newfoundland joined Canada as its 10th province and important social benefits were established for all Canadians. He spent most of his life in Québec City at this address and the house is 'alive' with his life story. Literally. Each room is hooked up to motion detectors – just walk in and prepare to have family photos start talking to you or phones ring with urgent messages for you to pass on to Mr Laurent. It's all brilliantly done; interactive history at its best.

MARTELLO TOWER 1 Map p226

☎ 418-648-4071; Battlefields Park; admission adult/child $4/3; ⏰ 10am-5pm Jun 24-early Sep; 🚌 11

Like the Citadelle, the British threw up these towers between 1808 and 1812, fearing an invasion by the Americans was in the works. Again, like the Citadelle, the British never got to try the towers out, as the American army was defeated in 1812. Martello Tower 1 is the only one of the original four towers regularly open to the public. For some reason, many visitors balk at having to pay admission here, perhaps put off by its small size. It's too bad because there's heaps of fascinating information packed into the tower's tiny package and it's well worth the money. The interactive exhibitions explore the engineering history of the structures and soldiers living

---

QUÉBEC CITY FOR CHILDREN

With the entire place heaving with history, there is plenty to hold kids' attention. While some of the weightier religious museums and sights won't be of much appeal, kids go giddy over the guides in period costume and are mesmerized by the antique cannons sprinkled everywhere from the **Old Town** (opposite) to **Battlefields Park** (p222).

Much of the accommodation and restaurants are geared to adults, but several of even the poshest French bistros we've listed in our Eating section have children's menus. There are good things to do with younger ones in the central core, while around the edges are other sites fully designed for kids' enjoyment.

In the historic area, walking the **Fortifications** (opposite) suits all ages. **The Citadelle** (opposite) ceremonies, with uniformed soldiers beating the retreat for example, are winners too. **Martello Tower 1** (above) in Battlefields Park has terrific interactive exhibits and parents swear the small size is perfect for children's attention spans. **Terrasse Dufferin** (p215) with its view and abundance of buskers, always delights children. Place d'Armes and Place-Royale are also good for street performers. The cheap ferry to **Lévis** (p216) and any boat cruise always appeals to the whole family as would a slow tour of Old Town in a horse-drawn *calèche* that you'll see in the streets.

For a break from all the history, try the newly overhauled **Parc Aquarium** (Map p205; ☎ 418-659-5264, 866-659-5264; 1675 ave des Hôtels; admission adult/child aged 3-5/child aged 6-12 $15.50/5.50/10.50; ⏰ 10am-5pm May 1-Oct 9, 10am-4pm Oct 10-Apr 30). It focuses on the water life of the St Lawrence River as well as the water-ways and coasts of the rest of Canada. Different family rates are offered depending on the children's ages.

A little further afield, northeast of Québec City on Hwy 138, is honey store and bee museum **Musée de L'Abeille** (Map p205; ☎ 418-824-4411; www.musee-abeille.com; 8862 boul Ste-Anne, Château Richer; admission museum free, bee safari child age 6-13/child over 13 $2.50/4; ⏰ 9am-6pm June 24-early Sep, to 5pm other times except 11am-5pm Mon-Fri & 9am-5pm Sat-Sun Jan & Feb) which gets good reviews from families (kids for the 'safari,' parents for the honey wine!)

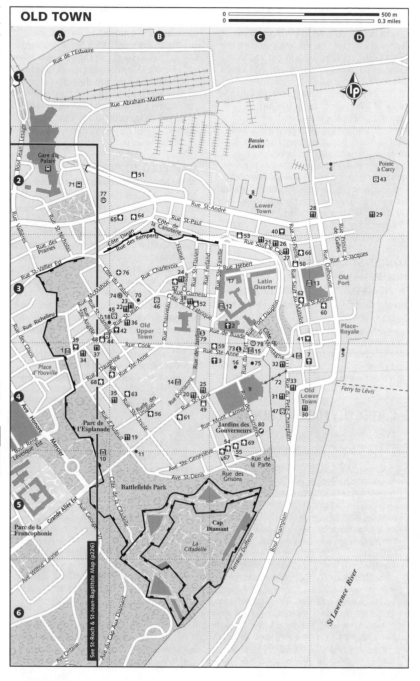

OLD TOWN

conditions in them and children in particular seem to get a real kick out of them.

Martello Tower 2 (Map p226; cnr ave Taché & ave Wilfrid-Laurier, Battlefields Park) is nearby but is not open to the public except during the two dozen or so '1814, council-of-war-style' dinners held each year (adult/child 13-17 & senior $35/32) during which diners must discover who the 'traitor' among them is. It's in French only, but there are translated scripts of the evening available for English speakers who attend can follow along. Call for a schedule. Reservations essential by phone (☎ 418-649-6157) or at **Discovery Pavilion** (p218).

Martello Tower 3 was torn down in 1905 to make way for construction and **Martello Tower 4** is in the St-Jean-Baptiste neighborhood on rue Lavigueur between rue Félix-Gabriel-Marchand and rue Philippe-Dorion.

MUSÉE NATIONAL DES BEAUX-ARTS DU QUÉBEC Map p226

☎ 418-643-2150, 866-220-2150; www.mnba .qc.ca; Battlefields Park; admission adult/child aged under 12/child aged 12-16/student/senior $12/ free/3/5/10; ⌚ 10am-6pm Thu-Tue, 10am-9pm Wed Jun 1-early Sep, 10am-5pm Tue & Thu-Sun, 10am-9pm Wed rest of year; 🚌 11; Ⓟ

Anyone curious about Québec art needs to carve out at least half a day for a visit to this museum, one of the best in the province. There are expert permanent exhibitions that range from art and artists in the early French colonies to Québec's abstract artists. There's also individual halls devoted entirely to the province's artistic giants of the last century.

The do-not-miss permanent exhibitions include one devoted to Jean-Paul Lemieux (1904–90) and the other to Jean-Paul Riopelle (1923–2002) which includes 'L'hommage à Rosa Luxemburg' (Tribute to Rosa Luxemburg; 1986), his largest work ever.

The Brousseau Inuit Art Collection of 2639 pieces spanning 50 years was a personal collection of Inuit art acquired by the museum in 2005.

There are also frequent exhibitions from abroad and elsewhere in Canada.

The museum is spread out through three halls including the Pavilion Charles-Baillairgé, Québec City's former prison.

Québec City

SIGHTS

Rue Ste-Anne in Old Upper Town, Québec City

Audioguides are available for the permanent collections and often for temporary exhibitions as well.

Guides in period getup lead **prison tours** (☎ 418-643-2150; admission adult/youth under 17 $10/5; ☼ 7pm Wed & 2pm Sun Jun 18-Aug 30) during the summer though usually these are in French only. Call ahead for info and reservations.

PARC DES CHAMPS DE BATAILLE (BATTLEFIELDS PARK) Map p220

One of the musts of any trip to Québec City, this park contains the **Plains of Abraham**. This was the stage for the infamous 1759 battle between British General James Wolfe and French General Montcalm that determined the fate of the North American continent. The park, named for Abraham Martin, a Frenchman who was one of the first farmers to settle in the area, is packed with sites, old cannons, monuments and commemorative plaques, so if you're a history buff you could easily spend an entire day just here. **Day passes** (adult/child age under 13/13-17 & senior $10/3/8) are available in the high season summer months and will get you into all the sights for a discounted price. Ask at the Canada Odyssey desk on Level 0 of the Discovery Pavilion.

This park is also a year-round major draw for locals. There's a **nature trail**, **foot paths** and the park is great for **inline skating**. For pavement pounders, there's also a terrific **jogging track** based on a former horse-racing course. In winter, people come here for all the popular winter activities Québec is known for like **snowshoeing**, **cross-country skiing** or a romantic moonlight **sleigh ride**.

The area became an official park in 1908 and has been the site of many modern historical events as well; 'O Canada,' the Canadian national anthem written by Sir Aldophe Routhier with music by Calixa Lavallée, was sung here for the first time on June 24, 1880.

To get your bearings consider the 40-minute **Abraham's Bus Tour** (tickets adult/child $3/free on top of Battlefields Park Day Pass; ☼ 10:30am, noon, 12:45pm, 2pm & 3:30pm early May-early Sep). This fun tour has an actor in period costume motoring you around the park in a tour van telling cheesy jokes and pointing out the park's activities and historical facts. It departs from the Discovery Pavilion.

If you want to explore on your own, pick up the fantastic bilingual tourist map of the park ($3) from the Discovery Pavilion.

Latin Quarter

The **Latin Quarter** refers to a section of the Old Upper Town wedged into the northeast corner. The site of both the Québec Seminary and Laval University, the neighborhood got its name because the religious communities and those at Laval University all conversed in Latin.

BASILIQUE-CATHÉDRALE NOTRE-DAME-DE-QUÉBEC

Map p220

☎ 418-694-0665; 20 rue de Buade; admission free, crypt $1; 🕙 8am-4pm Mon-Fri, 8am-6pm Sat & Sun; 🚌 3, 7, 11

This basilica got its start as a small church in 1647. In the ensuing years, the churches built here suffered everything from frequent fires to battle damage, especially during fighting between British and French armies in 1759. But no matter what, the church was rebuilt and repaired. Each replacement was bigger than the last until it reached the size you see today – a structure completed in 1925. The interior is appropriately grandiose, though most of the basilica's treasures didn't survive the 1922 fire that left behind only the walls and foundations. Everyone from governors of New France to archbishops and cardinals have been laid to rest in the crypt below.

CATHEDRAL OF THE HOLY TRINITY

Map p220

☎ 418-692-2193; 31 rue des Jardins; admission free; 🕙 10am-5pm May 20-Thanksgiving Day (October); 🚌 3, 7, 11

Built from 1800 to 1804, it was designed by two officers from the British army's military engineering corps and modeled on St Martin-in-the-Fields Church in London, England. This elegantly handsome Anglican cathedral was the first ever built outside the British Isles with oak imported from Windsor Castle's 'Royal Forest' just to make the pews. Upon its completion, King George III sent the cathedral a treasure trove of objects, including everything from candlesticks to chalices to silver trays. The elaborateness of the gifts heading towards the New World sent London's chattering classes atwitter. The royal box for the reigning monarch or her representative is located in the upper left balcony if you are facing the altar. (Look out for the royal coat of arms.) The cathedral's bell tower, an impressive 47m-high, competes for attention with the Basilique Notre-Dame located nearby. You will find that a guide is usually around in the summer months and conducts free 10-minute tours of the cathedral.

MUSÉE DE L'AMÉRIQUE FRANÇAISE

Map p220

☎ 418-692-2843; 2 Côte de la Fabrique; adult/child/student/senior $5/2/3/4, free Tue Nov 1-May 31; 🕙 9:30am-5pm Jun 24-early Sep, 10am-5pm Tue-Sun Sep-Jun; 🚌 3, 7, 11

Right on the grounds of the Séminaire de Québec (the Québec Seminary) this excellent museum is purported to be Canada's oldest. (The Musée Scientifique du Séminaire de Québec opened here in 1806). The museum that stands here today has brilliantly atmospheric exhibits on life in the seminary during the colonial era as well as religious artifacts and temporary exhibitions on subjects like endangered species. The priests from the Québec Seminary were avid travelers and collectors and there are some magnificent displays of the scientific objects they brought back with them from Europe, such as old Italian astronomical equipment. The exhibits are capped off by a wonderful short film on New World history from a Quebecer's perspective.

MUSÉE DES URSULINES Map p220

☎ 418-694-0694; 12 rue Donnacona; adult/child age 12-16/student/senior $6/3/4/5; 🕙 10am-noon & 1-5pm Tue-Sat, 1-5pm Sun May-Sep, 1-4:30pm Tue-Sun Oct-Apr; 🚌 3, 7, 11

The fascinating story of the Ursuline nuns' lives and their influence in the 17th and 18th centuries is told in this thoughtful, well set out museum. The sisters established the first girls' school on the continent in 1641 educating both aboriginal and French girls. Marie de l'Incarnation, the founder, was one of the most intriguing figures from the order. Leaving a young son in France after she was widowed, she joined the Ursulines and moved to New France and lived well into old age. She taught herself aboriginal languages and her frequent and eloquent letters to her son back in France are held by historians to be some of the richest and most valuable material available to scholars studying life in the French colony. The Ursulines were also expert embroiderers and many examples of their work are on display. There's a lovely chapel (admission free; 🕙 10am-noon & 1-5pm Tue-Sat, 1-5pm Sun May-Oct) at the same address. It dates from 1902 but retains some interiors from 1723.

MUSÉE DU FORT

Map p220

☎ 418-692-2175; 210 rue Ste-Anne; adult/student/senior $7.50/4.50/5.50; ☽ English shows on the hour 10am-5pm May-Oct, less frequently rest of year; 🚌 3, 7, 11

Not really a museum at all, the Musée du Fort houses a 30-minute multimedia show on the many attempts over the centuries to take Québec City. It's all played out on a model/diorama that lights up in the middle of a mini-theatre. The breathless narration and anaemic smoke puffs that pass for special effects are a bit hokey but it does give a quick, enjoyable, easy-to-grasp audiovisual survey of the city's battles and history, making a good introduction to it.

OLD LOWER TOWN

This is stuffed with more terrific museums as well as numerous plaques and statues. Street performers add to its palpable historic atmosphere.

Teeming **rue du Petit-Champlain** is said to be, along with rue Sous le Cap, the narrowest street in North America, and is also one of the oldest. Look for the incredible wall paintings that feature on the 17th- and 18th-century buildings. There are murals and then there are these!

Place-Royale, the central principal square of Québec City's Lower Town has 400 years of history behind it. When Samuel de Champlain founded Québec, it was this bit of shoreline that was first settled. In 1690 cannons placed here held off the attacks of the English naval commander Phips and his men. Today the name 'Place-Royale' often generally refers to the district.

Built around the old harbor in Old Lower Town northeast of Place-Royale, the **Vieux-Port** (Old Port) is being redeveloped as a multipurpose waterfront area.

From the Upper Town, you can reach the Lower Town in several ways. Walk down Côte de la Canoterie from rue des Remparts to the Old Port or edge down the charming and steep rue Côte de la Montagne. About halfway down on the right there is a shortcut, the Break-Neck Stairs (Escalier Casse-Cou), which leads down to rue du Petit-Champlain. You can also take the **funicular** ($1.50 each way) from Terrasse Dufferin.

CENTRE D'INTERPRETATION DE PLACE-ROYALE

Map p220

☎ 418-646-3167; 27 rue Notre-Dame; adult/child/student/senior $4/2/3.50; ☽ 9:30am-5pm late Jun-early Sep, 10am-5pm Tue-Sun early Sep-late Jun; 🚌 1

This interpretive center touts the area as the cradle of French history. The exhibits focus on the individual people, houses and challenges of setting up on the shores of the St Lawrence River. It goes a bit heavy on the random artifact displays (just how many displays of uncaptioned broken cups and saucers does one visitor need to see at a time?) but otherwise there are slick, worthwhile displays. Children can dress up in costumes on the bottom floor and tours of the Lower Town are offered by guides in period dress during summer.

ÉGLISE NOTRE-DAME-DES-VICTOIRES

Map p220

☎ 418-692-1650; 32 rue Sous-le-Fort; admission free; ☽ 9:30am-4:30pm; 🚌 1

Dating from 1688 Our Lady of Victories Church, a modest house of worship on the square, is the oldest stone church in the USA and Canada. It stands on the very spot where de Champlain set up his 'Habitation,' a small stockade, 80 years prior to the church's arrival. Inside are copies of works by Rubens and Van Dyck. Hanging from the ceiling is a replica of a wooden ship, the *Brézé*, thought to be a good-luck charm for ocean crossings and battles with the Iroquois. The church got its name after British ships were unable to take Québec City in 1690 and again in 1711.

ESPACE 400E/CENTRE D'INTERPRÉTATION DU VIEUX-PORT DE QUÉBEC

Map p220

☎ 418-648-2008; Quai St-André; 🚌 1

This Old Port of Québec interpretation center is being gutted and renamed 'Space 400,' for exhibitions and events during the city's 400th birthday in 2008. When the celebrations are over, Parks Canada will turn it into an exhibition center on immigration and the St Lawrence River.

MUSÉE DE LA CIVILISATION Map p220

☎ 418-643-2158; www.mcq.org; 85 rue Dalhousie; adult/child/student/senior $8/3/5/7, free Tue Nov-May 31; ⏰ 9:30am-6:30pm late Jun-early Sep, 10am-5pm Tue-Sun early Sep-late Jun

The Museum of Civilization wows you even before you have visited the exhibitions. It is a fascinating mix of modern design that incorporates pre-existing buildings with contemporary architecture. The permanent exhibits, like the one on the cultures of Québec's Aboriginals and the one titled People of Québec: Then and Now, are unique and well worth seeing. Many of the exhibits include clever interactive elements. The changing shows are also outstanding and this is really the only museum in town that regularly focuses on contemporary issues and culture. Recent visiting exhibitions included subjects as diverse as Québec's cinematic history and another one about solving murders. This is a big place with lots to see, so you should focus on only one or two exhibitions if you are not planning to make a full day of it. There is free internet in the upstairs caféteria.

OUTSIDE THE WALLS

Québec City's Old Town is undeniably spectacular and one of a kind, but you should spend an afternoon if not an entire day outside the walls, if only to get to know the city's contemporary side and get a more local flavor of the city.

There's fewer significant attractions outside the walls, but that doesn't mean these parts of the city need to be ignored. St-Jean-Baptiste, flanking Old Town to the west, and St-Roch to the northwest of Old Town, are both worth exploring on foot.

St-Jean-Baptiste

The heart of this area is rue St-Jean, which extends from the Old Town. It's got tremendous shops, good restaurants and hip cafés and bars. Near the corner of rue Ste-Augustine is also where you'll find the epicenter of the city's tiny, unofficial gay 'village.' From rue St-Jean, take any side street and walk downhill (northwest) to the narrow residential streets like rue d'Aiguillon, rue Richelieu or rue St-Olivier. Outside staircases are trademarks of Montréal architecture, so are the miniature, scrunched-together houses, some with very nice entrances, typical of Québec City's residential landscape.

ÉGLISE ST-JEAN-BAPTISTE Map p226

☎ 418-688-0350; 400 rue St-Jean; admission free; ⏰ noon-5pm Mon-Sat, 11am-4pm Sun late Jun-early Sep, noon-4pm Mon-Sat, 11am-4pm Sun rest of the year

This colossus completely dominates its area on the southwest end of rue St-Jean.

Old Lower Town, Québec City

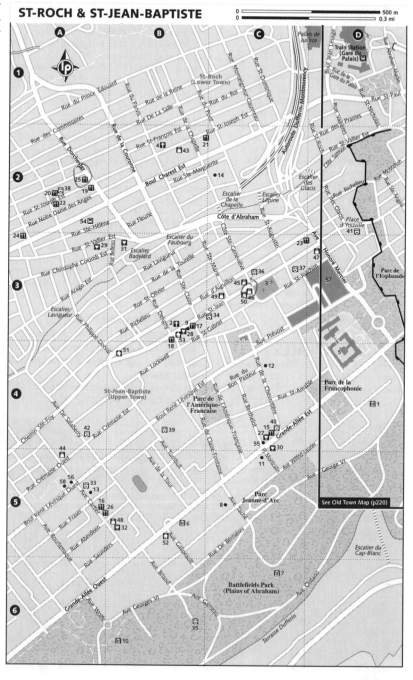

ST-ROCH & ST-JEAN-BAPTISTE

0 _____ 500 m
0 _____ 0.3 mi

The first church was built in 1842 but was destroyed by fire in 1881. It was completely rebuilt by architect Joseph-Ferdinand Peachy and open again for business by 1884. Peachy drew on well-known French churches for inspiration: Notre-Dame-de-Paris for the pillars and Église St-Sulpice for the vaults and Église de la Trinité for the façade. In summer, the church presents modest but well-researched exhibitions on church or neighborhood history.

HÔTEL DU PARLEMENT Map p226

☎ 418-643-7239; cnr ave Honoré-Mercier & Grande-Allée Est; admission free; ⊗ 9am-4:30pm Mon-Fri, 10am-4:30pm Sat & Sun late Jun-Sep (Labour Day), 9am-4:30pm Mon-Fri Sep-late Jun; 🚌 11, 25, 28
The National Assembly building is a Second Empire structure completed in 1886. It's home to the Provincial Legislature. Free tours are given in English and French year round. The 30-minute visits get you into the National Assembly Chamber, the Legislative Council Chamber and the Speakers' Gallery. The facade of the building is decorated with 23 bronze statues of significant provincial historical figures including the iconic former premier René Lévesque (1922–87) and Maurice Duplessis (1890–1959) who kept a stranglehold on the province during his 20-year-long premiership. The grounds here are also used for staging events during Winter Carnival.

NUNAVIK INFORMATION CENTRE
Map p226

☎ 418-522-2224; www.nunavik.ca; 1204 cours du Général-de-Montcalm; admission free; ⊗ 11am-1pm & 2-7pm Jul-Sep, 9am-noon & 1-5pm Mon-Fri Oct-Jun; 🚌 11, 25, 28
Far in Québec's north, Nunavik (not to be confused with Canada's third territory, Nunavut) is almost completely inhabited by Inuit. With no trains or roads into Nunavik, even most Quebecers know little about the Inuit culture or this fascinating region. This modest center was opened mainly to promote tourism to the area's 14 villages, but this is an interesting place for a short stop just to look at the wall pictures or the small craft displays. An incredibly friendly place and the employees are more than willing to shoot the breeze for the genuinely curious, answering questions on anything from the Inuit language to Inuit culture.

OBSERVATOIRE DE LA CAPITALE
Map p226

☎ 418-644-9841, 888-497-4322; 1037 rue de la Chevrotière, Édifice Marie-Guyart; admission adult/student & senior $5/4; ⊗ 10am-5pm Jun 24–mid-Oct, 10am-5pm Tue-Sun rest of year; 🚌 11, 25, 28
Head 221m up to the 31st floor for great views of the Old Town, the St Lawrence

THE REVIVAL OF ST-ROCH

If you spend any time with Québec City locals, it won't be long before they steer you out of the Old Town, pushing you towards '*le nouveau*' St-Roch (New St Roch).

Northwest of the tourist core, St-Roch used to be *location-non-grata* when it came to the provincial capital's urban landscape.

It didn't start out that way.

By the 19th century, St-Roch was a major industrial center crammed with shipyards, shoe factories, tanneries and department stores. The streets teamed with workers. But by the time the 1960s rolled around, people were bleeding into the suburbs leaving St-Roch one of the most run-down and dangerous parts of town. A roof was stuck on top of rue St-Joseph in an effort to create a kind of all-weather mall – it ended up attracting crime and homeless people. However, in the early 1990s the city, led by Mayor Jean-Paul L'Allier, got serious about reviving the place: *Le Jardin de St-Roch* (St Roch Garden) was opened and the roof came off rue St-Joseph.

The neighborhood hasn't been the same since.

Interesting clubs are springing up on rue St-Vallier Est and rue St-Joseph has everything from art galleries and glitzy boutiques to junk shops and fine dining – all drawing a similarly eclectic mix of locals.

Part of what's so cool is just listening to Quebecers talk about it. These days, everyone from university professors to local entrepreneurs to artists seems excited to be able to talk up a dynamic slice of contemporary Québec City for a change, proving there's more to it than just the Old Town.

River and (if it's clear enough) even the Laurentian Mountains. It all helps to get your bearings while the information panels along the way will get you up to speed on some of the local history.

St-Roch

This neighborhood went from a working-class district for factory and naval workers to an abandoned urban wasteland and is now well on its way to being the *it* address in town. Rue St-Joseph is where to head. Though it seems destined for full-on gentrification á la Plateau du Mont-Royal in Montréal, for the moment it's a fascinatingly eclectic place where junk shops and secondhand stores rub against trendy new restaurants and glamorous boutiques. Don't come here for the typical tourist attractions but just to soak up the atmosphere.

ÉGLISE ST-ROCH

Map p226

☎ 418-524-3577; 590 rue St-Joseph; admission free; ☺ 9am-5pm

There are giants and then there is this, the biggest church in Québec City. Measuring over 80m long, 34m wide and 46m high including the steeples, it was built between 1914 and 1923. When the original architects died, this neo-Gothic, neo-Roman structure was finished off by

Louis-Napoléon Audet, the same man who worked on the Ste-Anne-de-Beaupré Basilica. The marble inside the church is from Saskatchewan. See if you can find faint fossil imprints in it. The St-Roch Church hosts the **Festival des Musiques Sacrées de Québec** (the Québec City Festival of Sacred Music; p206), a wonderful time to see it at its best.

Ste-Foy-Sillery

Ste-Foy and Sillery, separate before the municipal mergers, have two distinct characters. Ste-Foy, roughly north of boul Laurier, has a stranglehold on the city's malls but is livened up by the student population at Laval University. Sillery, roughly south of boul Laurier, has leafy streets lined with affluent homes; places like ave Maguire are lined with charming cafés. There's not much here in the way of sights, but if you are in the neighborhood you should make sure to drop by the **Pointe à Puiseaux** located down at the foot of rue d'Église. Here you can take in a gorgeous view of the St Lawrence River.

PARC DU BOIS-DE-COULONGE

Map p205

☎ 418-528-0773, 800-442-0773; 1215 ch St-Louis; admission free; ☺ dawn-dusk; ℗

Not far west of the **Plains of Abraham** (p222) lie the colorful gardens of this park, a paean to the plant world and a welcome respite from downtown. Now open to the public, this wonderful woodland with extensive horticultural displays used to be the private property of a succession of Québec's and Canada's religious and political elite.

Limoilou

Northwest of the Old Town, this borough has only one major historical site. However, if you are in the area it's definitely worth a visit.

CARTIER-BRÉBEUF NATIONAL HISTORIC SITE p205

☎ 418-648-4038, 888-773-8888; 175 rue de l'Espinay; admission adult/youth/senior $4/2/3.50; ⏰ 10am-5pm Mon-Sun early May-early Sep, 1-4pm early Sep-late Sep; Ⓟ
On the St Charles River, north of the central walled section of the city, this **national historic site** marks where Cartier and his men were nursed through the winter of 1535 by First Nations people. There's a full-scale replica of Cartier's ship and a reproduction of an aboriginal longhouse in the park's green (but rather nonauthentic-looking) riverside setting.

Rue du Petit-Champlain, Old Lower Town

WALKING TOUR

This tour will walk you through some of the best-known – as well as the lesser-known – parts of Vieux-Québec and give you a good idea of how the Old Town has changed over the years. Plan to take from two to 3½ hours depending on how often you stop and linger.

See the Old Town section (p218) for more details on some of the sites.

Begin at **Porte St-Louis** (St Louis Gate) 1, first built in 1693. It's gone through several incarnations and the one you're standing under now dates from 1878.

The **Parc de l'Esplanade** 2, which borders the Old Town wall, was a cow pasture before becoming the site of 18th- and 19th-century military exercises, concerts and parades. Proceed along rue St-Louis to see some of the city's oldest surviving houses.

Notice the area around **No 80** 3. This was the site of the town's first City Hall. Look for the French-language plaque with a drawing of what the building looked like way back then.

Moving along, check out the tree at the corner of rue St-Louis and rue du Corps-de-Garde. Supposedly the **cannonball** 4 embedded in its trunk has been lodged there since 1759!

When you reach the corner, have a look at **47 St-Louis** 5, the place where General Montcalm was taken after being shot by the British during the destiny-changing Plains of Abraham Battle on September 13, 1759. He arrived at the fortifications on horseback after being injured and was led through Porte St-Louis by two of his soldiers. Montcalm was taken into a surgeon's office then located at this site. He died here the very next day.

Slightly further on, at 34 St-Louis, you'll see a well-kept home from 1676. It now houses **Aux Anciens Canadiens** 6, a restaurant specializing in Québec fare. The name comes from the title of a novel by Philippe-Aubert de Gaspé, who lived here from 1815 to 1824. Its steeply slanted roof (51.5°) was typical of 17th-century French architecture.

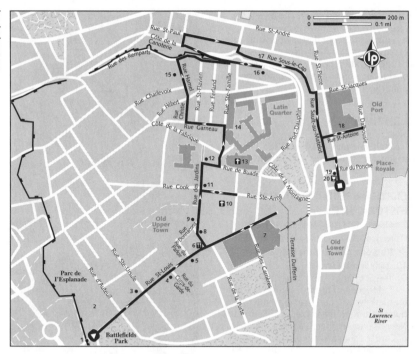

If you like, continue to the end of rue St-Louis and dip into the **Château Frontenac 7** to revel in the luscious interior of sculpted wood, darkened salons and painted ceilings, as well as hoards of tourists and slightly frazzled staff doing their best to dole out Old World service. When you've had enough, come back along rue St-Louis and turn right down rue des Jardins. You'll soon come to *Sans titre* (Untitled), a **sculpture 8** by Jules Lasalle honoring the women from religious orders who came to Québec and educated both French and First Nations girls. The work was created to mark the 325th anniversary of the death of Marie de l'Incarnation, the Founder of the **Ursuline Convent 9** you see in front of you. The feather resting in the woman's hand represents the passing of knowledge from one to another.

For another little detour, turn right onto rue Ste-Anne and you'll see the **Cathedral of the Holy Trinity 10**. It's beautiful inside with wooden floors and soaring windows.

If you are ready for a break, linger for a while on rue Ste-Anne and have your portrait painted by one of the dozen or so artists who show up daily. They specialize in everything from color classic paintings to black-and-white caricature drawings. Alternatively, you can just plunk down at one of the many restaurant terraces and people-watch for a while.

When you're done, continue along rue des Jardins. Notice the awesome **sculpture 11** of a court jester running down a giant ribbon on your right, just past the Caisse Populaire. Titled *Bienvenue* (Welcome), it's by artist Nicole Taillon. Further along, you'll see a park with a brown granite, slightly ostentatious **statue of Taschereau 12**, the first Canadian cardinal. Besides being a renowned scholar, Elzéar-Alexandre Taschereau (1820–98) was one of the founders of the University of Laval.

Hang a right back on rue de Buade and the splendid **Basilique-Cathédrale Notre-Dame-de-Québec 13** is to your left. Enter the grounds of the **Québec Seminary 14** founded in 1663. A place of religious study and education, it's also where American officers were locked up after their capture during the siege of Québec in 1775–76. Today the seminary houses a museum, educational facilities and Laval University's faculty of architecture. Once you enter the courtyard, the largest building opposite you with the sundial on the wall and the inscription *Dies nostri quasi umbra* ('Our days pass like shadows' – in other words 'Time is short, so get on with it') was the grand seminary for older students finishing their theological studies. The whiteness of these walls shows how most of Québec once looked; the brightness kept homes cool in the summer and blended with the snow to protect from distant attack in the winter.

Head down rue Ste-Famille and make a left onto the narrow, very pretty rue Garneau.

Make a right on the third street, rue Christie, which turns into rue Hamel. The tall wall on your left protects the grounds of the 1646 **Augustine monastery 15**, built for the religious sisters who founded a hospital nearby in 1639 – the first European-style medical facility north of Mexico.

At the end of rue Hamel, turn right onto rue des Remparts and follow the wall to the embedded model cannons. Take note of the picturesque houses here, especially **No 14** (c 1900) **16**. It's got Roman and Gothic arches, an Art Nouveau balcony, a renaissance ledge and a medieval château tower.

After you're done, retrace your steps until you reach Côte de la Canoterie, for centuries the main link between the Lower and Upper Towns (and classes). Hope Gate stood at the top of the côte until 1873 to keep the riff-raff from entering the Upper Town uninvited – or from hoping too much.

Make a right onto rue St-Thomas and a right onto rue St-Paul. A block later, at Côte du Colonel-Dambourgès, veer right again and you'll note an alleyway to your left. This is **rue Sous-le-Cap 17**, the narrowest, most cramped and one of the most interesting streets in the city. What today is the back of houses fronting rue St-Paul used to be the front entrances of homes along the waterfront – the river used to creep up all the way to rue St-Paul at high tide. This was also the red-light district. Many of the Upper Town's men made their way to the Lower Town to visit one of the several brothels that used to operate on this street.

Walk the length of rue Sous-le-Cap, looking up at the staircases that shoot up from everywhere, and continue along rue Sault-au-Matelot, which boasts a few low-key art galleries and antique shops. Turn left on **rue St-Antoine 18** where the city has marked the water levels of the St Lawrence River during the history of the settlement right in the

FRENCH-LANGUAGE SCHOOLS

Great as Montréal is, if you are serious about picking up French or improving the French you already have, there is no better place than Québec City. As more than one frustrated French-language student has remarked, once Montréalers realize you're from somewhere else they will do *le switch* into English and you've said good-bye to another chance to road-test your verb conjugations. It's different in Québec City. Though Quebecers grow up learning English like they do in Montréal, because the anglophone minority in Québec is so tiny, they don't hear much of it or get the chance to practice. So as long as you stay away from the tourist-centered businesses, you'll be able to practice away and get plenty of encouragement while you're at it.

If you do decide to come for a language trip, you will be one of hundreds of students who do so regularly. Don't be put off by the Québécois accent; the instructors both teach and speak standard international French.

École de langues de l'Université Laval (☎ 418-656-2321; www.elul.ulaval.ca; bureau 2301 2nd fl, Pavillon Charles-De Koninck, Laval University) is your best bet. It offers 15-week fall and winter courses or five-week spring and summer courses. You can be hook up for accommodation with a Québécois family (from $77/ week with kitchen access to $200/week with full board) or, in the spring and summer sessions, you can stay in residence ($77/week).

However, if you are set on Montréal, your best chance at full French immersion is on the Mountain at Université de Montréal. **Université de Montréal Adult Education Department** (☎ 514-343-6090, 800-363-8876; www.fep .umontreal.ca/langues/; Pavilion 3744, rue Jean-Brillant, 3e étage) has terrific programs that include night or weekend courses, courses in everything from Beginners' French to Québec Culture to advanced courses in written French. This is a very proud French-language campus so people are not prone to making *le switch* so feared by French-language students. Many Americans and South American's attend this program in summer as a kind of study-vacation as it's cheaper than flying to Europe.

OUT & ABOUT

Québec City is surrounded by stunning countryside and there are fantastic attractions for every interest. If you are traveling by car, all the sights below, except for Wendake, can be reached by taking rte 138 northwest of Québec City.

Île d'Orléans

This place is the stunner of the region. It can be visited on a day trip but is easily worth two days or more if you have the time. Cut off from the rest of Québec for centuries (the Taschereau bridge was only built in 1935) the pastoral life-style of the islanders remains very much preserved. One of the first colonies of New France was established here, and thousands of North Americans can trace their roots back to one of the 300 original families that settled here. Divided into six parishes, there is plenty to see here from gorgeous scenery to old churches to 300-year-old stone homes. Local ciders and *produits du terroir* also abound.

Don't miss **Maison Drouin** (☎ 418-829-0330; www.fondationfrancoislamy.org; 4700 ch Royal; admission adult $3; 🕑 10am-6pm mid-Jun–mid-Aug, 1-5pm Sat & Sun mid-Aug–late Sep). This old house was built in 1730 and is one of the most fascinating stops on the island as it was never modernized (ie no electricity, running water) even though it was inhabited until 1984. Guides in period dress give tours of the house in summer. **Éspace Félix-Leclerc** (☎ 418-828-1682; www.felixleclerc.com (in French); 682 ch Royal, St-Pierre; adult/child $6/3.50; 🕑 9am-6pm spring & summer, 9am-5pm fall & winter) highlights the works of one of Québec's most popular singers, whose ancestors were among the original island settlers. At **Parc Maritime de St-Laurent** (☎ 418-828-9672; 120 ch de la Chalouperie, St-Laurent; admission adult/concession $3.50/3; 🕑 10am-5pm late Jun-early Sep) you can learn about the parish's ship-building history.

There's a **tourist office** (☎ 418-828-9411, 866-941-9411; www.iledorleans.com; 490 Côte du Pont, St-Pierre; 🕑 8:30am-7:30pm late Jun-early Sep, 10am-5pm Oct-late Jun) on the island just after you cross the bridge. It's a great place for info and finding accommodation. You can also buy a CD for $22.50 (or rent it for $17.50 plus a $5 deposit) that guides you on a two-hour tour of the island. Île d'Orléans is about a 15-minute drive from Québec City.

Parc de la Chute Montmorency

This waterfall is right by the Taschereau Bridge on the way to Île d'Orléans and is worth a stop if you're in the area. It's 83m high, topping Niagara Falls by about 30m, though it's not nearly as wide. What's cool is walking over the falls on the suspension bridge to see (and hear) them thunder down below. The **park** (☎ 418-663-3330; www.sepaq.com /chutemontmorency; 2490 ave Royale, Beauport; 🕑 year-round) is free but parking ($8.75 per car) and the cable-car (adult/child under 5/youth $8/free/4) can add up over the average 60-minute visit. You can opt to walk the circuit instead of taking the cable car up. This is an interesting stop even in winter. When the spray from the falls freezes, it creates a 30m-high toboggan hill. The falls are about 7km from Québec City.

middle of the street. You may be surprised at how much of today's Lower Town used to be under water!

Nip on back to rue Sault-au-Matelot and follow it to the end. Veer left and turn right onto rue St-Pierre. Just after you pass rue du Porche, you'll see a small, heavily nautical theme park on your right. This is **Parc Unesco 19**, a reminder that everything else you've just seen is part of a Unesco world heritage site. If you feel like kicking back after all the walking, head to **L'Oncle Antoine 20**, a great cellar bar at 29 rue St-Pierre where there's cold local beer and piping-hot pub fare.

EATING

The restaurant scene in Québec City has never been better. The city become a tiny eating mecca all its own. These days, interesting budget eateries share the foodie landscape with some of the most acclaimed restaurants in Canada. It's flipped the city's culinary reputation from overpriced and unvaried to exciting and inviting. Québec City has always excelled at classic French food but excitingly, in the past couple of years, new places are diverging from the regular cozy bistro fare (as great as it is). These new additions to the food scene are going sleek and hip and aren't afraid to take risks. They may not always be completely successful, but it's exciting to see the experimentation none the less.

Wendake

This Huron aboriginal reserve is only about 20 minutes west of Québec City (you'll know you're there when you start seeing the bilingual Huron/French traffic signs). The major attraction here is the **Onhoúa Chetek8e** (☎ 418-842-4308; www.huron-wendat.qc.ca; 575 rue Stanislas-Kosca; admission adult/child/youth $10/5.50/7.50; ☺ 9am-5pm, last tour 4pm; ☐ 72) a reconstructed Huron village (the 'letter' 8 in Huron is pronounced 'oua' like the 'wh' in 'what'). The guides are excellent (one is even a former land-claims negotiator) and take you round the village explaining Huron history, culture and daily life. It may be artificial, but visitors love this place and children go bonkers for the tepee, canoes and bow-and-arrow range. Several guides speak English but call ahead to make sure they aren't already assigned to a tour group or on their day off when you arrive. The onsite **restaurant** (☺ noon-3pm) serves excellent aboriginal food and there's an enormous boutique selling mostly Wendake-made crafts. With activities and shows (at additional costs), you can easily end up spending the whole day here.

If you are coming by car, take Hwy 73 (exit 154). It's very well signed after that.

Ste-Anne-de-Beaupré

Holy Disneyland! If Wal-Mart was running a house of worship, this is what you'd get.

This village is known for the goliath-sized **Basilique Ste-Anne-De-Beaupré** (☎ 418-827-3781; 10018 ave Royale; admission free; ☺ church early-late, information centre (southwest side of basilica) 8:30am-4:30pm) and its role as a shrine.

Churches were built at this location since the mid-1600s but were frequently destroyed by fire. The awe-inspiring basilica of today was constructed after a devastating blaze in 1922 and has been open since 1934.

Ste-Anne's reputation as a shrine started to grow even before the first church had been completed. A crippled Louis Guimont had just started laying stones when he was suddenly cured by 'Good Ste-Anne,' Mary's mother and the patron saint of Québec. Legions of believers swear they have been cured after their pilgrimages here and over 1.5 million people do the trip each year. On July 26, Ste-Anne's feast day, the place goes berserk. The church fills to capacity, the nearby camping grounds are swamped with pilgrims, hotels are booked full and the whole village starts feeling like a kind of religious Woodstock.

You just have to catch a glimpse of the enormous Blessings Office, the first-aid station and what looks like 50-toilet bathrooms to understand the scale that things here can reach.

There's also a **museum** (☎ 418-827-3781 ext 754; admission adult/youth $4/2; ☺ early Jun-early Sep), Magasin Ste-Anne (a store) with shelves of Ste-Anne paraphernalia, religious medals and other souvenirs and the **Cyclorama of Jerusalem** (☎ 418-827-3101), a coliseum-sized, 360° 'panoramic display' produced in Germany in 1882 of Jesus' Crucifixion. It's 14m high and 110m in circumference.

Saturday night masses are a good time to visit. In the middle of the mass, the entire congregation lights lamps and is led out of the church carrying the flames along with their church banners, identifying the congregations they are representing on their pilgrimage. In particular, you'll see many are from New York, Boston and Ontario.

It's about 50km from Québec City.

The buzz it's created has also caused a reverse foodie migration. While before it was always Quebecers heading down to Montréal to eat, these days it's not unusual to see Montréal couples in the Québec City tourist office waving a national magazine or newspaper review in their hand and asking how to get to the latest, greatest resto.

Most of these new additions seem to land in the high range of people's budgets, but often you can get the same food for a much lower price just by going for the *table d'hôte* (set course meal) at lunchtime when meals are cheaper.

The low immigrant population in Québec City means you won't see the range of ethnic restaurants that you do in a place like Montréal, but if you are a lover of French food, Québec City has a wonderful choice of bistros for you to work through.

Opening Hours & Meal Times

Most restaurants in Québec City are open for lunch and dinner in the off season and from about 11am to late in high-season summer. During peak time, many restaurants close when the last customer leaves. Standard lunch hours are 11am to 2:30pm with dinner 5:30pm to 10pm. Note that outside of the Winter Carnival, many restaurants in winter may be closed Sunday and Monday or both. Breakfast cafés open around 7am (9am on Sundays) and close by 3pm. Places really tend to fill up from 8pm onwards in the francophone tradition.

How Much?

Midrange places in Québec City will, on average, charge $18 to $28 for a multicourse meal including a glass of wine. The top end restaurants run upwards of $25; a culinary temple of some renown might charge $60 to $100 or more for a four-course gourmet dinner including wine. Count on $6 to $8 for a glass of drinkable red and $25 to $35 (and up) for a bottle from the house cellar. Taxes amounting to 13.5% apply at all restaurants. Most do not include the taxes in their menu prices, but check the fine print.

Price Guide

$$$ over $25 a meal
$$ $15-$25 a meal
$ under $15 a meal

Booking Tables

If you are in Québec City between May and October or during Winter Carnival, definitely book ahead to dine in one of the finer restaurants. During this peak season popular places can fill up quickly even at odd times like Monday nights.

Tipping

A tip of 15% of the pretax bill is customary in restaurants. Some waiters may add a service charge for large parties; in these cases, no tip should be added unless the service was extraordinary. Leave the tip on the table or hand it directly to staff.

OLD UPPER TOWN

If you are not eating at some of the places we've listed below, be choosy about where you spend your money in the Old Town. Though many have gorgeous settings, and may be great places for coffee, tea or a beer, food at many of them can be disappointing (ie a chicken Caesar salad may turn out to be wilted lettuce with a slice of Spamlike processed chicken slapped on top of it). Your accommodation or the delightfully non-BS tourist office on rue St-Anne in the Upper Town would be great places to ask for recommendations.

Street café, Québec City

Budget

CASSE-CRÊPE BRETON

Map p220   Crêpe $

☎ 418-692-0438; 1136 rue St-Jean; mains under $7; ⏰ 8am-6pm

Tiny and unassuming, this find specializes in hot, fresh crêpes of every kind starting as low as $4. Some diners like to sit at the counter and watch the chef at work.

LE PETIT COIN LATIN

Map p220   Café $

☎ 418-692-2033; 8½ rue Ste-Ursule; mains under $9; ⏰ 7:30am-10:30pm

For a French-style breakfast, try this excellent, very European spot near rue St-Jean for croissants, muffins or eggs. In summer you can eat the low-priced lunch specials out on the patio.

CHEZ ASHTON

Map p220   Québec Fast Food $

☎ 418-692-3055; 54 Côte du Palais; poutine $4; ⏰ 11am-4am Sun-Thu, 11am-4:30am Fri & Sat

You will have to eat at this Québec City fast-food institution at least once. There are dozens of stores all over town all serving up what people from Québec City swear is *the* best *poutine* in the province (Montrealers, of course, usually don't agree). Classic *poutine* is on offer along with Ashton specials like *poutine* with peas or sausage.

PAILLARD CAFÉ-BOULANGERIE

Map p220   Bakery/Sandwiches $

☎ 418-692-1221; 1097 rue St-Jean; sandwich $8; ⏰ 7:30am-7pm

This gorgeous old warehouselike space has high ceilings and huge bay windows looking out onto the street. It's a bit of a madhouse during lunch as people clamor for ham sandwiches with green apples, brie cheese, Dijon mustard and rosemary oil or hot roast beef sandwiches with blue cheese, caramelized onions and horseradish. The kids menu has things like peanut butter and banana sandwiches. There's also an attached bakery.

CHEZ TEMPOREL Map p220   Café $

☎ 418-694-1813; 25 rue Couillard; mains $8; ⏰ 7am-midnight

This no-frills, out-of-sight café on a quiet side street has got heaps of attention from France heavyweights *Voici* and *Guide du Routard* to the *New York Times*. The great breakfast fare is definitely worth the trip in for homemade croissants and to be served up perfect (yes perfect) café au lait. The service is generally disinterested but efficient. The sandwiches, soups and salads served for the rest of the day are good, but not worth a trip in and of themselves.

TIMES CAFÉ

Map p220   Mediterranean $-$$

☎ 418-263-2008; 48 Côte de la Fabrique; mains $10 & up; ⏰ 8am-11pm

Another terrific 'nonstuffy' addition to the Upper Town. This eatery serves Mediterranean food in a beautifully designed space with fire-engine red tables, black-and-white zebra-striped chairs and moody blue lighting. Staff are remarkably friendly given the trendy atmosphere. Pizzas and sandwiches run from $10 to $14 while the veal or seafood dishes can go anywhere from $18 to $30.

Midrange

RÔTISSERIE STE-ANGÈLE

Map p220   Café $

☎ 418-694-3339; 32 rue Ste-Angèle; mains $9-16; ⏰ lunch Mon-Fri, dinner Mon-Sat

Totally charming, particularly the atticlike 2nd floor, this side-street restaurant with a patio features a range of chicken dishes, such as barbecue and coq au vin, but there's also salmon and other meat mains. A kids' menu is available.

ASPARA

Map p220   Asian $$

☎ 418-694-0232; 71 rue d'Auteuil; mains from $13; ⏰ lunch Mon-Fri, dinner daily

I'm in Québec, so why would I want Asian food? Because since 1982 this has been one of the best, tastiest and most consistently good places in town. The mix of Cambodian, Thai and Vietnamese plates utilizing lemongrass, spicy peanut sauces, rice and delicate noodles is outstanding. The upmarket room with soft Oriental music suits the kitchen's high standards. You must try the *poulet oudong* (chicken sautéed in ginger) or the shrimps sautéed in lemongrass.

CONTI CAFFE

Map p220   Mediterranean $$

☎ 418-692-4191; rue St-Louis; mains $14-25;
🕑 11am-'last person gone'

Recently opened on the busy rue St-Louis drag, this is a wonderful addition to the many tourist traps in the area (ie locals come here too). With exposed brick walls and simple white tablecloths, Conti Caffe still manages to look urban and modern but with a terrific warm and welcoming wait-staff. The menu has a great range of prices and dishes such as good pasta (from $14), veal dishes (from $19.50), seafood or game like duck with herbed crust ($21).

Top End

LE SAINT AMOUR

Map p220   French/Québécois $$$

☎ 418-694-0667; 48 rue Ste-Ursule; mains $25-34;
🕑 lunch Mon-Fri, dinner daily

Yes it's expensive, but it's the top-end darling of the provincial capital. There's been an explosion of expensive restaurants in Québec City in recent years, and while they've caused plenty of excitement, none of them inspire the loyalty among locals that Le Saint Amour does. The house specialty is foie gras and it can come seared, as a crème brûlée, as terrine *maison*…you get the idea. There's over 10,000 bottles of wine in the cellar. Service is warm and intelligent and the dining room is flooded with natural light streaming through the pointed glass ceiling. Ps – the lunch *table d'hôte* is often less than $20.

AUX ANCIENS CANADIENS

Map p220   Québécois $$$

☎ 418-692-1627; www.auxancienscanadiens.qc.ca; 34 rue St-Louis; mains $26-49; 🕑 noon-9pm

Housed in the historic Jacquet House which dates from 1676, this place is all about robust country cooking and typical québécois specialties. Here, wait staff in historic garb serve dishes like caribou in blueberry wine sauce ($33), duckling in maple syrup sauce ($30) or Lac St-Jean meat pie served with pheasant and buffalo casserole ($30). Lunch is served noon to 5:45pm and is by far the best deal: $15 gets you a main course, soup, glass of wine or beer and dessert. The restaurant gets its name from the novel *Les Anciens Canadiens* by Philippe-Aubert de

---

TOP 5 QUÉBEC CITY BISTROS

- Café Krieghoff (p238) – for its front and back terraces, coolness and nonstop buzz
- L'Ardoise (opposite) – from food to atmosphere, about as perfect as a bistro can get
- L'Échaudé (opposite) – for its European cool, one place in the Old Town where you'll find plenty of locals
- Le Café du Monde (opposite) – it's the only restaurant in town right on the St-Lawrence River. Need we say more?
- Le Café du Clocher Penché (p240) – for its charming service and bang-on creations

Gaspé, who lived in the house from 1815 to 1824. The original rooms have been left intact, resulting in several small, intimate dining areas.

OLD LOWER TOWN

Rue St-Paul is lined with restaurants. In warm weather, they fling their windows (and walls) wide open and set up outdoor seating on the streets. With the revelry overflowing outdoors there's terrific atmosphere – there's not one terrace that doesn't seem warm and inviting. In winter the streets outside may be deserted, but the revelry packs indoors, and windows positively glow with the warmth and good cheer inside. Many of the best bistros in town are located on this strip. Many can get a little pricey, but do not write them off. Do what the locals do; a carefully chosen *table d'hôte* at lunch time will give you exactly the same food for a more manageable price.

Budget

BUFFET DE L'ANTIQUAIRE

Map p220   Diner $$

☎ 418-692-2661; 95 rue St-Paul; mains $8-10;
🕑 6am-9pm

Tucked in among the bistros and the galleries is this frenetic little diner complete with chefs wearing pointy paper hats and waitresses carrying 'don't-screw-with-me' attitudes while sporting whiskey voices and plenty of swagger. Try to take in the atmosphere while scarfing down the uncomplicated comfort food, including everything from spaghetti to fish fillets on offer daily.

Midrange

LE COCHON DINGUE

Map p220   Café $$

☎ 418-692-2013; 46 boul Champlain; mains around $11; 🕙 8am-1am

Since 1979 this ever-popular people's choice has been serving visitors and locals straight-ahead French standbys. From café au lait *en bôl* to *croque monsieur* ($12), sandwiches, salads, mussels or quiche. It's all good day-to-day food and a kid-friendly place to boot. There's outside seating in warm weather for watching the crowds shuffling by.

LE PETIT COCHON DINGUE

Map p220   Café/Bakery $

☎ 418-694-0303; 24 boul Champlain; mains around $11; 🕙 7:30am-6pm Sun-Wed, 7:30am-9pm Fri & Sat

Just down the street from Le Cochon Dingue, this small, great place to go for coffee, dessert or panini. Staff are lovely and helpful and keep the crowds moving.

L'ÉCHAUDÉ

Map p220   Bistro $$

☎ 418-692-1299; 73 rue Sault-au-Matelot; mains around $11; 🕙 11:30am-2:30pm Mon-Fri, also 6pm-late daily, brunch 10am-2:30pm Sun

A classic little bistro with a refreshingly relaxed and nonstuffy wait staff. This is one of the nicest bistros in the Old Town. Its steak ($22) and salmon ($13) tartares have won a loyal following, making L'Échaudé one of the odd places in the Old Town where locals regularly outnumber the tourists. It has also put together a terrific wine list favoring bottles from France. The lunch *table d'hôte* is often around $15, while the evening *table d'hôte* starts at around $25.

LE LAPIN SAUTÉ

Map p220   French $-$$

☎ 418-692-5325; 52 rue du Petit-Champlain; mains $13-18; 🕙 lunch & dinner

Look for the rabbit-crossing sign as you make your way down the street. This tidy, appealing restaurant specializes in country cooking. Though it's equally adept at salmon, duck and chicken the stars here are the rabbit dishes like rabbit pie $16 and rabbit in maple syrup. There's also a lovely little patio open during warm weather.

LE CAFÉ DU MONDE

Map p220   Bistro $$

☎ 418-692-4455; 84 rue Dalhousie; mains $15-20; 🕙 11am-11pm, brunch 9:30am-2pm Sat, Sun & holidays

This Paris-style bistro is the only restaurant in town directly on the St Lawrence River. Bright, airy and casually elegant it has been a local favorite for years, swearing by bistro classics like *steak frites* and *saucisse de Toulouse*. The menu is authentic and there's a great choice of other dishes like escargot with pernod, *confit de canard* and pasta. The accent is on local Québec products.

L'ARDOISE Map p220   Bistro $$

☎ 418-694-0213; 71 rue St-Paul; mains $13-26 🕙 lunch & dinner

This place just keeps racking up the praise, and it's easy to see why. Not only does it have a mouthwatering bistro menu with beautifully turned-out classics like *confit de canard*, along with tantalizing twists like caribou medallions, horse steak, duck with blueberry sausage or blood sausage grilled with apple. To top if off, the setting itself is stunning; Tiffany-style lamps hang from the ceiling, along with lots of greenery. It's cosy and bright. The kids' menu ($9) has a mini order of *steak frites* (steak and French fries), pasta or chicken strips and includes dessert.

Top End

LE MARIE-CLARISSE Map p220   French $$$

☎ 418-692-0857; 12 rue du Petit-Champlain; mains $23-31; 🕙 11am-'last person gone'

Arguably the best seafood restaurant in town, the wait staff is fantastic, the atmosphere dark and cozy and it's tucked off the climbing stairs on rue du Petit-Champlain. All fish is fresh, and the menu changes daily depending on what seafood is available in the market, but the *marmite* (fish stew) at $31 is the best known, classic dish.

LE PANACHE Map p220   French/Québécois $$$

☎ 418-692-1022; 10 rue St-Antoine; mains $30 & up; 🕙 11:30am-2:30pm Mon-Fri & 6-10pm daily

Dubbed one of Canada's 10 best new restaurants in 2005 by *en Route* magazine, the critics' accolades for this restaurant and chef François Blais's new takes on Québec cuisine haven't stopped. Diners' reactions are sometimes mixed, however. Some love it and say it was worth the trip to Québec City alone, others have said it doesn't live up to either the hype or the price. Despite that, with flavor combos like guinea hen and duck foie gras served with honey emulsion, veal sweetbreads and oyster mushrooms or salmon lobster and baby leek, Le Panache will definitely end up on hard-core foodies' 'must' lists. To cap it off, place Panache's wine list in front of experts – they'll go into raptures. The dining room is best described as 'rustic' upscale Québec, as it is done up like a huge log cabin with luxurious chairs and table settings.

LAURIE RAPHAËL

Map p220   French/Québécois $$$

☎ 418-692-4555; 17 rue Dalhousie; lunch table d'hôte $21, dinner mains $38-44; ⏰ 11:30am-2pm Tue-Fri, 6-10pm Tue-Sun

Laurie Raphaël isn't just a restaurant. It's an experience. The dining room is bright, modern and simple, letting the food take center stage. This is another menu that keeps the focus on *produits du terroir*, or local Québec produce. Chef Daniel Vézina keeps menu descriptions to the minimum, saying he wants to 'leave room for imagination and discovery.' There's also a chef's menu ($56) that's decided at the last minute 'for those that like to be surprised.' The restaurant is named for Vézina's two children.

OUTSIDE THE WALLS

Beyond the walls, there are heaps of terrific eateries of all types and for all budgets.

St-Jean-Baptiste

Here, there's three small but terrific main eating districts: rue St-Jean; ave Cartier between Grande-Allée Ouest and boul René-Lévesque Ouest; and lastly, west along Grande Allée from Old Town where you'll find a popular and lively strip of more than a dozen alfresco, economic, visitor-oriented restaurants complete with touts.

CAFÉ LE SULTAN

Map p226   Lebanese $

☎ 418-525-9449; 467 rue St-Jean; mains $7-11; ⏰ noon-11pm Mon-Thu, noon-midnight Fri, 5pm-midnight Sat

This warm, cozy café is head and shoulders above the normal, soulless Lebanese fast-food restaurant. There are hookah pipes in the windows, music playing in the background, oriental tapestries and petit, tiny tables set up to eat from. The service isn't particularly friendly but the atmosphere is terrific. Try the *mergez* or salad plate.

SOÑAR

Map p226   Tapas $

☎ 418-640-7333; 1147 ave Cartier; tapas $5-9; ⏰ 5-11pm

Done up with a bit of glitz and a bit of slick, this fantastic tapas bar is perfect for light suppers or evening-long grazing. There's a sidewalk terrace out front if it's warm. Skip the main dishes (OK, but not worth the trip in themselves). The reason to come here is the artfully served tapas. There's a huge range from Portobello mushrooms stuffed with feta and dates to fried calamari and tortillas. The ambience is nightclub minimalism. The kitchen closes at 11pm but the bar is open until 3am or there aren't any people left, whichever comes first. Soñar sometimes opens for lunch at around 11:30am if the weather is nice, but call ahead to make sure before making the trip.

CAFÉ KRIEGHOFF

Map p226   Café $

☎ 418-522-3711; 1091 ave Cartier; mains $10-21; ⏰ 7am-11pm

This brilliant little resto is a city classic, with a varied bistro menu and some of the best coffee in town. There's an extensive breakfast menu and you can substitute a veggie pâté for the bacon and sausage in most dishes. If it's warm, you can watch the comings and goings on ave Cartier from a table on the massive front porch, or for quiet and a bit of privacy, go for the sequestered, laid-back terrace out back. Inside, the dining room is decorated with reproductions from the café's namesake painter, Cornelius Krieghoff (1815–72), one of Québec's master painters of the 20th century, who lived just down the street from here on Grande-Allée.

CARTHAGE

Map p226   Tunisian $-$$

☎ 418-529-0576; 399 rue St-Jean; mains from $12; ⏰ noon-3pm & 6-11pm

This BYO Tunisian restaurant offers couscous, meat and vegetarian specials, all lightly spiced. Tables and chairs fill the colorful room while at the tables by the windows patrons kneel on cushions in traditional Middle Eastern style.

LE COMMENSAL

Map p226   Vegetarian $-$$

☎ 418-647-3733; 860 rue St-Jean; $ depends on weight; ☯ 11am-9:30pm

An endless choice of strictly vegetarian food dishes, including vegan and organic options, are served cafeteria-style in this huge and bright location. The food is terrific, and you'll always have interesting pickings to consider; you'll find stews and casseroles with seitan, millet or soy protein, as well as vegetarian twists on Québécois classics like *pâté chinois,* along with soups, salads and desserts. It's all sold by weight, so if you load up the plate the first time around, the final price tag can end up a bit of a shocker. If there's a maple sugar pie on offer the day you're there, be sure to try it. It's a classic! This is a bring your own booze establishment.

VOODOO GRILL

Map p226   Asian Fusion $$

☎ 418-647-2000; 575 Grande-Allée Est; mains $18; ☯ noon-3pm & 5-11pm

Described by the owners as a 'restaurant/ museum,' this place is an experience just to walk through. African and Asian statues peer down at the tables and the dining room is done up in dark, complex colors. The staff all look like they've stepped out of a fashion shoot and on Friday and Saturday nights this place definitely has more of a club feel than a restaurant feel to it. The vast 2nd-floor patio overlooks the fashionable Grande-Allée. Specialties here include wok meals, huge Asian soups and megasalads. A four-service 'surprise' chef's menu goes for $55.

AUX VIEUX CANONS

Map p226   French/Central European $$-$$$

☎ 418-529-9461; 650 Grande-Allée Est; mains $22-50; ☯ 8am-10pm

Calling all beer drinkers! You'll need to make some time for this place. Yes, staff are friendly. Yes, the food is good and the menu spills over with hearty eastern European fare. Yes, it has a terrific location on a bustling section of Grand-Allée. But

are those the reasons to make a bee line to this place. No! The brews are the reason to come, not so much because they are spectacular compared with anything else on offer in the city, but because of the glasses they are served in – yes the glasses. They are so tall, so narrow, so precariously filled, they're served with a wooden brace to support them. You have to see it for yourself. There really is nothing like camping out here with one after a long day of sightseeing.

St-Roch

The rejuvenation of St-Roch means everything from shopping to entertainment has become more exciting – and the eating scene is no exception. What's refreshing here is despite the number of stylish and trendy eateries not a trace of snobbery has entered into the mix (so far). There are some terrific eating experiences to be had here and new places are opening all the time.

LARGO RESTO-CLUB

Map p226   International $$

☎ 418-529-3111; 643 rue St-Joseph Est; mains $9-25; ☯ 11:30am-3pm & 6-11pm

The bouillabaisse ($25) is one of its most popular dishes but the Mediterranean-inspired menu offers up everything from filet mignon and Moroccan dishes to salmon tartare. Besides being an enthusiastic promoter of jazz music (p241) the Largo Resto-Club also does gallery duty, showing off the work of local painters and sculptors.

LE POSTINO

Map p226   Italian $$

☎ 418-647-0000; 296 rue St-Joseph Est; mains $12-17; ☯ 11:30am-10pm Mon-Fri, 8am-10pm Sat & Sun

Prime people-watching real estate at the heart of St-Roch coupled with friendly, unpretentious wait staff make this place a winner and you haven't even eaten yet. There are plenty of classic pasta dishes on the menu for around $10 to $12 as well as a fantastic choice of risottos with genius combinations such as rabbit, roasted parsnips, caramelized shallots and wild mushrooms.

DOWNTOWN

Map p226   Bistro/European $-$$

☎ 418-521-3363; 299 rue St-Joseph Est; mains $13-24; ⏱ 11am-11pm Mon-Fri, 5-11pm Sat & Sun

Fun, relaxed and reasonable, this place is especially popular for lunch during the week. All the usual suspects are featured on the menu including salmon and beef tartare with fries and salads, along with pasta dishes and all-you-can-eat mussels ($16). Inside it is cosy with exposed brick walls, and it does not have the nervous energy of a lot of other bistro-type eateries in town. A children's menu is also available.

L'UTOPIE

Map p226   French $$-$$$

☎ 418-523-7878; www.restaurant-utopie.com; 226½ rue St-Joseph Est; lunch $15-21, dinner from $26; ⏱ lunch & dinner

The loyalty of Québec City locals to Le Saint Amour (p236) seems sometimes to be inviolable, but this new kid on the block is winning their affection slowly but surely. It's got a focused menu highlighting tuna, stag and deer dishes. The wonderful lunch *table d'hôte* includes classics like *confit de canard* and *pavé de saumon*. Everything is served in a bright, open dining room with an exposed wine cellar. Bunches of slender birch trees separate the tables and reach towards the ceiling.

LE CAFÉ DU CLOCHER PENCHÉ

Map p226   French Bistro $-$$

☎ 418-640-0597; 203 rue St-Joseph Est; brunch around $13, mains $23-29; ⏱ 8am-11pm Mon-Fri, 11am-11pm Sat & Sun

This café serves classy, classic bistro fare and proudly shows off local products like Québec cheeses. What sets it apart are the one-of-a-kind weekend brunches. Brioche comes with caramelized pears, homemade crème fraîche, caramel sauce and almonds. An English muffin is served with veggie pâté, poached eggs, cheddar cheese, pesto vinaigrette, roasted potatoes and vegetarian chili. It just gets better and better after that. Brunch reservations strongly recommended.

LE GRAIN DE RIZ Map p226 Asian Fusion $$-$$$

☎ 418-525-2227; 410 rue Saint-Anselme; mains $26-30; ⏱ lunch & dinner

A foodie favorite, this Western-Asian fusion restaurant lies just off rue St-Joseph. There's a range of 'modernized' Vietnamese and Chinese dishes, but it's the chef's inspiration menu where things get interesting. Try the chicken with Earl Grey cream sauce served on couscous ($26) or coconut shrimps with mango salsa ($27). The dining room is cosy without the kind of modern starkness or pretentiousness that often goes with this kind of cuisine. Staff are enthusiastic and approachable and give good tips on navigating the complex menu flavors. The attached store sells imported rice and tea.

French café breakfast

ENTERTAINMENT

Québec City may not have the choice and range of nightlife that you'll find in Montréal but what's here is wonderful; just remember it won't go on as late.

There's no English-language cultural guide in Québec City. *Voir Québec* (published every Thursday) is the free entertainment weekly in town and you'll be able to decipher club and bar listings even if you don't speak French. *Scope* is a glossy monthly that focuses on movies and cinema, again with easy-to-figure-out listings, and *Fugues* is the free gay and lesbian entertainment guide with listings for the entire province of Québec.

Concert Halls & Arenas

AGORA Map p220
☎ 418-692-4672; 120 rue Dalhousie, Vieux-Port
Fantastic open-air rock shows are held here all summer.

COLISÉE PEPSI Map p205
☎ 418-691-7211, 418-525-1212; Parc de l'ExpoCité, 250 boul Wilfrid-Hamel
You are now on hallowed ground…home to the late, great Québec Nordiques (p209). May they RIP. The Nordiques started playing here in 1972 when the venue was known as the Québec Colisée. They played their last game here in 1995 after which the team was moved to Denver, Colorado. Today this 15,000 person arena gets Iron Maiden and Metallica, and hosts games of the Remparts, from the Québec Major Junior Hockey League.

KIOSQUE EDWIN-BÉLANGER Map p226
☎ 418-523-1916; Battlefields Park 418
Thirty-five free concerts are staged each summer in the middle of Battlefields Park. Music covers everything from pop, jazz and world music to blues.

PALAIS MONTCALM Map p226
☎ 418-641-6411 ext 2606; 995 Place d'Youville
This place has slowly been falling off the radar since the Grand Théâtre was built in the 1970s. It was undergoing heavy renovations at the time of research and there's talk the new, improved model is gearing up to carve out its place on the entertainment scene. Keep your eye out, it should be open again by the time you read this.

LIVE MUSIC

CHEZ SON PÈRE Map p220
☎ 418-692-5308; 24 rue St-Stanislas; ☾ 8pm for show at 10pm (9pm Fri & Sat)
One of the city's best-loved *boîte à chansons* (a Québec folk-music club), this spot boasts a great atmosphere and is probably the first place locals will send you if you're interested in seeing this rollicking kind of French folk music. You can catch some newcomers here, plus occasional big-name concerts. The cover charge varies; sometimes it's free.

FOU-BAR
Map p226
☎ 418-522-1987; 525 rue St-Jean ☾ 3pm-3am
Laid-back and with an eclectic mix of bands, this is one of the town's classics for good live music.

GALERIE ROUJE
Map p226
☎ 418-688-4777; 228 rue St-Joseph
This place is a mini cultural heaven. Downstairs is gallery space while upstairs you'll find fantastic gigs ranging from electronic music to DJs.

LARGO RESTO-CLUB
Map p226
☎ 418-529-3111; 643 rue St-Joseph Est; ☾ jazz shows 8pm
Thursday, Friday and Saturday, the music-mad Largo owner lets the jazz club side of this resto shine, bringing in local bands, singers and musicians from as far away as Los Angeles. Upscale, ultrarelaxed, slightly swish vibe.

LES VOÛTES DE NAPOLÉON
Map p226
☎ 418-640-9388; 680A Grande-Allée; ☾ approx 8:30pm-late
Another massively popular *boîte à chansons*. Its impossible-to-find-on-your-own entrance means it will likely be just you and the locals – it's underneath the Restaurant Bonaparte. If you can't find the entrance, just ask a Quebecer to point you the rest of the way.

DRINKING

LE SACRILÈGE
Map p226

☎ 418-649-1985; 447 rue St-Jean; ☺ noon-3am

It's been around for over 10 years, but this watering hole has taken off in a big way recently and most night owls either start or end their revelry here most weekends. Even on Monday night, when neighboring bars are near empty, it's standing-room only at this one. There's a popular terrace out back – get to it through the bar or the tiny brick alley next door. To find Le Sacrilège keep an eye out for the sign with a laughing, dancing monk saucily showing off his knickers.

LES SALONS D'EDGAR Map p226
☎ 418-522-1987; 263 rue St-Vallier Est; ☺ 4:30pm-late Wed-Sun

The unofficial 'official' hangout for the city's theater community, the eavesdropping here is as much fun as the drinking – you'll be privy to conversations on roles lost and roles gained, and can watch new graduates from the drama conservatory mingling awkwardly to build their networks.

L'INOX
Map p220

☎ 418-692-2877; 38 rue St-André; ☺ 11am-1am

In the Old Port area, this brewpub draws beer lovers to its pleasant outdoor patio.

L'ONCLE ANTOINE
Map p220

☎ 418-694-9176; 29 rue St-Pierre; ☺ 11am-1am, until 3am Fri & Sat

Set clandestinely in the stone cave-cellar of one of the city's oldest surviving houses (dating from 1754), this great tavern pours out excellent Québec microbrews (try the Barberie Noir stout or the strong Belgian-style Fin du Monde), several drafts (en fût) and various European beers.

PUB ST-ALEXANDRE
Map p220

☎ 418-694-0015; 1087 rue St-Jean; ☺ 11:30am-around 1am

High ceilings and dark wood house a regular mix of tourists and loyal locals. The pub-grub is fine, though generally unremarkable. It's the atmosphere and the near

encyclopaedic range of suds (250 sorts!) and over three dozen types of single malt that will keep you coming back. Occasional live music (Celtic to jazz) on Friday and Saturday.

SCANNER Map p226
☎ 418-523-1916; 291 St-Vallier Est; ☺ 11am-late Mon-Fri, 3pm-late Sat & Sun

This place is a bit of a mystery. Its interior is unremarkable and the staff of below average enthusiasm, but ask any local between the ages of 18 and 35 to suggest a cool place for a drink and this is one of the first places they'll send you. Come see if you can figure it out. Live rock bands every Saturday from September to May. Terrace outside in summer, babyfoot and pool inside year-round.

TURF Map p226
☎ 418-522-9955; 1179 rue Cartier; ☺ 11am-around 3am Mon-Fri; 9am-3am Sat & Sun

Come in, grab a bowl and walk to the enormous peanut-filled barrel in the middle of the room. Swipe your fill from the barrel and settle in at one of the most popular pubs in the St-Jean-Baptiste neighborhood. Wi-fi is also available if you want to work or surf while you drink. Burgers and pizzas are also on the menu to cushion the blows. Hugely popular with everyone in the 18- to 25-year-old range from the students to the suits.

CLUBBING

CHEZ DAGOBERT Map p226
☎ 418-522-2645; 600 Grande-Allée; ☺ 11am-late Mon-Fri, 3pm-late Sat & Sun

Multifloors, multibars, multiscreens – the capital's classic disco behemoth with everything from live rock to naughty DJs. The music may change; the young, randy crowd stays the same.

MAURICE Map p226
☎ 418-647-2000; 575 Grand Allée Est; ☺ 8pm-3am Wed, 10pm-3am Thu-Sat

Multifloors, multibars, multiscreens. The capital's *other* classic disco behemoth. Set up in a gutted châteaulike mansion and cheekily named after hard-ass former Québec premier Maurice Duplessis, this entertainment complex has three separate partying spaces. There's a **nightclub** where

Québec City   ENTERTAINMENT

LOCAL VOICES: CONFESSIONS OF A QUÉBEC CITY DRAG QUEEN

Québec City has a reputation as a sleepy provincial town, so it may not seem like the best place in the province to launch your drag-queen career. But Réglisse (aka Claude Barabé) begs to differ. He's the undisputable drag star in town. He started in 1996 when he was 29 and has been going ever since. You'll find him most nights at Le Drague (below), either on stage or working the shooter bar. Just keep an eye out for Wonder Woman.

How did you get started?
It was for the first anniversary of one of the gay and lesbian magazines. I did two numbers and it snowballed after that. I've lived this art every since.

Québec's known as a pretty conservative town. Is it?
It's true, we're not a nightlife city where there's always lots of parties, but we prefer the quality of things over quantity.

Does that make a drag career easier or more difficult?
We're so close knit here you can't beat it. Our performances here are to make the public happy, not to make ourselves happy. When we give a show, no matter how much we're paid, or if we're paid at all, we give our very best. We have a tremendous creative team spirit. I'm so proud of that.

You worked for one year in France, what did you miss most about Québec City when you were away?
Poutine of course. That and the solidarity among female impersonators in Québec City.

Every visitor goes to the Old Town first. What would you suggest if they wanted to see a more modern side of the city?
The Parc Aquarium and our bar, Le Drague! Our Musée de la Civilisation is superb also and at the Agora they have open-air rock shows in summer.

Who is your favorite Québécois singer or group?
Usually people are going to answer 'Céline Dion' to this. As for me? Me, I also tell you Céline Dion!

DJs play Latin music on Wednesdays and music from the '80s and '90s on Friday. You'll get the same young, good-looking and randy crowd as Chez Dagobert. There's also a **cigar lounge** with 200 sorts to choose from. The **Charlotte UltraLounge** is also located here but was about to be closed for major renovations when we visited; it will definitely be worth checking out the new digs when you visit.

Gay & Lesbian Venues
The city's gay and lesbian scene is tiny with pretty much everything centered around Le Drague.

L'ALTERNO Map p220
☎ 418-692-2674; 1018 rue St-Jean; ⊗ 4pm-late
Regulars kept telling former Le Drague employee Benoît they wished there was another gay club in town to shake up the scene a little, so finally he just went ahead and opened one, tucked away just inside Porte St-Jean. It's low key during the day with people playing billiards or babyfoot, while it gets wilder at night after 10:30pm

once the DJs come out. It's easy to miss this place – look for the pride flag and go up the stairs.

L'AMOUR SORCIER Map p226
☎ 418-523-3395; 789 Côte Ste-Geneviève; ⊗ 2pm-3am Thu-Sun
The tamer atmosphere at this café-bar is mainly enjoyed by lesbians, but gay men are welcome too. The gay community may be small but the lesbian one is even smaller and this is the only horse in town.

LE DRAGUE Map p226
☎ 418-649-7212; 815 rue Ste-Augustine; ⊗ 10am-late
The star player on the city's tiny gay scene, Le Drague is just off rue St-Jean, located in a little lane which on Thursday and Friday nights becomes a kind of extension of the club. Le Drague is made up of several sections: there's a front outdoor terrace with bar; Zone 1 inside is a two-level disco where the Sunday-night drag shows are held, often starring Réglisse (see above); Zone 2 is a slightly more laid-back space set up like a tavern; and then there's Base

3. The men-only Base 3 is…ummm…well…Let's just say it turns the capital's conservative reputation on its head and has even seen-it-all, done-it-all Montrealers saying 'I didn't know they had *that* in Québec City.'

CINEMAS

At Québec City area multiplex cinemas you'll find québécois, French and American films. English-language films are all dubbed in French. French-language films are not subtitled in English. The city has two fantastic repertory theatres.

CINÉMA CARTIER Map p226

☎ 418-643-8131; 1019 rue Cartier; ☼ 4pm-late
This huge building really was a former movie theatre until it was sliced up with a store on the bottom and retail space up top. The 2nd floor houses an independent video shop with a little movie theatre in the back showing independent films. It's deliciously old world, completely pitch black except for the screen, and set up with big comfy chairs. Subtitles in French only.

LE CLAP Map p205

☎ 418-653-2470 ext 229 (box office); 2360 ch Ste-Foy; ☼ screenings from noon; 🚍 7, 79, 87, 93; 🅿
Located in the Ste-Foy-Sillery borough, Le Clap's mandate is to show off the best of what's going on in the film world. On any given afternoon, you'll find an eclectic mix of films that could include the latest British hit, an old indie French film you've never heard of and probably one American blockbuster thrown into the mix as well. Non–French-language films are almost always dubbed in French instead of subtitled but call ahead to double check – once in a while English-language films here do screen in the original.

THEATER

There are no professional English–language theater companies in Québec City, although an amateur one is sometimes active. If you are interested in seeing a show or finding out what they are up to, ask around at the **Cathedral of the Holy Trinity** (p223) gift shop. All of the theaters listed below stage French-language productions.

LE GRAND THÉÂTRE DE QUÉBEC

Map p226

☎ 418-643-8131, 877-643-8131 (toll-free in Québec only); www.grandtheatre.qc.ca; 269 boul René-Lévesque Est
This is the city's main performing-arts center with a steady diet of top-quality classical concerts, dance and theater. The Opéra de Québec also often performs here.

LES GROS BECS Map p220

☎ 418-522-7880; www.lesgrosbecs.qc.ca; 1143 rue St-Jean; ☼ shows run Sep 1-April 30
Devoted to shows for children and young people, this is a brilliantly creative company. Even its website is stunning, full of animation and cartoons on how to get young people interested in live theatre. (Unfortunately, it's in French only.) All shows listed in its schedules have labels with suggested age limits.

LE THÉÂTRE CAPITOLE

Map p220

☎ 418-694-4444; www.lecapitole.com; 972 rue St-Jean
A terrific, historic old theater that now stages everything from musicals to concerts. Check out the sumptuous attached hotel (p252). This is where Hitchcock held his *I confess* premier (p212).

LE THÉÂTRE DU TRIDENT

Map p226

☎ 418-643-5873; www.letrident.com; 269 boul René-Lévesque Est
Another terrific theater company that regularly stages exciting modern works including plays by the likes of Wajdi Mouawad.

THÉÂTRE PERISCOPE Map p226

☎ 418-529-2183, 418-648-9989; www.theatre periscope.qc.ca; 2 rue Crémazie Est
A terrific place to see creative and cutting-edge contemporary productions.

THÉÂTRE PETIT-CHAMPLAIN

Map p220

☎ 418-692-4744; 68 rue du Petit-Champlain
Theater productions take place here in the summer. The rest of the year this is a great place to see Québec's most popular singing stars like Lynda Lemay.

ACTIVITIES

Outside the Château Frontenac along the riverfront, the 425m-long **Terrasse Dufferin** is perfect for taking a marvelous stroll with dramatic views over the river, perched as it is 60m high on a cliff. It's peppered with quality street performers vying for attention. In 2005 renovation work began on the Terrace and the fortification wall nearby. Part construction site, part archaeological dig, keep your eye out for interpretation panels or upcoming tours of the site. Come for a stroll during winter when the **giant toboggan slide** (11am-11pm) is set up.

OUTDOOR ACTIVITIES

Whether summer or deepest, darkest winter, Québec City locals take to the outdoors.

Cycling & In-Line Skating

There's a huge network of bike paths both inside the city down by the **Vieux-Port** (p224) and out in the surrounding countryside. There's a free bike-route map available at the tourism offices.

For in-line skating in the city, there's a route in **Battlefields Park** (p222). Many swear a cycling trip on Île d'Orléans is an absolute holiday highlight but because there are no bike paths and heaps of traffic in summer, this is not a recommended bike trip to do with children.

CYCLO SERVICE Map p220

☎ 418-692-4052; www.cycloservices.net; 160 Quai St-André; 🚍 1

Inside the farmers market, it rents bikes and organizes excellent bike tours of the city and outskirts to places like **Wendake** (p233) or **La Chute Montmorency** (p232). The knowledgeable and fun guides frequently give tours in English. There are good cycling maps covering the vicinity.

MUSÉOVELO

Map p226

☎ 418-523-9194; 463 rue St-Jean; bike rental per day $20

Located in the St-Jean-Baptiste neighborhood, this place rents, makes and repairs all sorts of bikes. It also has lots of high-quality Canadian-made bike accessories for sale.

SHERPA PLEIN AIR

Map p220

☎ 418-640-7437; www.sherpapleinair.com; 1045 rue St-Jean

These guys operate Navette Shuttle, an excellent, fairly priced service taking people out of the city to sites such as Parc national de la Jacques-Cartier and Cap Tourmente for hiking, bird watching and kayaking. Sherpa even rents and takes bikes, perfect if you want to get out of town and get active.

SOCIÉTÉ PISTE JACQUES-CARTIER/ PORTNEUF

Map p205

☎ 418-337-2900, 800-321-4992; admission season/ day pass $10/5

Formerly a railway linking Saint-Gabriel-de-Valcartier and Rivière-à-Pierre, this trail winds its way through country scenery. In winter it turns into a snowmobile track.

Walking & Jogging

There's a fantastic jogging track at **Battlefields Park** (p222), though die-hard runners training for marathons like to take to the slopes of the Old Town for drills and hill training. Locals also pick this park as the number-one place for summer days or winter night strolls.

RUNNING ROOM

Map p226

☎ 418-522-2345; www.runningroom.com; 1049 ave Cartier; free group runs 6pm Wed, 8:30am Sun

This Alberta-based chain sells running shoes and accessories but also does free group runs led by an employee. Just meet at the store. It also has fantastic route maps that you can download from its site. For Québec City go to www.runningroom .com/hm/inside.

Rafting

VILLAGE VACANCES VALCARTIER

Map p205

☎ 418-844-2200, 800-321-4992; www.raftingval cartier.com; 1860 boul Valcartier; ☼ 8am & 1pm May 6-Aug 1

There are trips down the Jacques Cartier River for beginners and experts, as well as guided trips for families. For the biggest thrills, come in May or June when the water is at its highest. Must reserve at least three days in advance. Canoe rental also available. It's a 20-minute drive from Québec City along Hwy 73 north (exit St-Émile/La Faune).

Ice Skating

The following rinks get set up in winter only, in Old Upper Town.

PATINOIRE DE LA TERRASSE Map p220

☎ 418-829-9898; Terrasse Dufferin; ☼ end Oct–mid-Mar; ☒ 3, 11

A kind of ice-ring gets set up here every winter and is ideal for families and children to putter around on. Skate rentals on site.

PLACE D'YOUVILLE Map p220

☎ 418-641-6256; Porte St-Jean; ☼ end Oct–mid-Mar; ☒ 3, 7, 11, 28

One of the most popular places for ice skating once winter rolls around. You can also rent skates here.

Skiing & Snowboarding

MONT STE-ANNE Map p205

☎ 418-827-4561, 888-827-4579; www.mont -sainte-anne.com; 2000 boul du Beau-Pré

A hugely popular ski resort with 64 ski trails, 17 of which are set aside for night skiing. You'll find all sorts of other winter activities here including snowshoeing, skating and even dogsledding. You can rent skis and snowboards here too.

PARC NATIONAL DE LA JACQUES-CARTIER Map p205

☎ 418-528-8787, 800-665-6527; ☼ winter, roughly Dec-late March

There's a range of snowshoeing and cross-country skiing trails and circuits here from easy to difficult. Those who've done the trails say the winter scenery here is

picture-perfect. The park is about 40km from Québec City along rte 175.

STATION TOURISTIQUE STONEHAM

Map p205

☎ 418-848-2411, 800-463-6888; www.ski-stoneham .com; 1420 ch du Hibou, Stoneham-et-Tewkesbury

Smaller than Mont Ste-Anne and only about 20 minutes from Québec City, there are 32 slopes here for downhill skiing and snowboarding. Night skiing runs are usually open from late November until around mid-March. Take Hwy 73 north until the Stoneham exit.

Swimming

PAVILLON DE L'ÉDUCATION PHYSIQUE ET DES SPORTS Map p205

☎ 418-656-7377; www.peps.ulaval.ca; Pavillon de l'Éducation Physique et des Sports, Laval University; ☒ 7, 11, 13, 18, 87

There's a huge Olympic-sized pool here that's also open to the public. Probably the best bet in town. Call for times.

WATCHING SPORTS

The end of the Nordiques meant the end of professional sport in the city, though the Québec Remparts of the Québec Major Junior Hockey League are quite popular. You can see them at the Colisée Pepsi (p241)

L'HIPPODROME DE QUÉBEC Map p205

☎ 418-524-5283; www.hdeqc.com; 250 boul Wilfrid-Hamel

Where to come to check out the races.

Family sleigh ride through the streets of Québec City

SHOPPING

There's a terrific mix of shopping streets in Québec City despite its small size. And though most people know it just as a mecca for tourist goodies, independent boutiques and shops are all over the place selling one-of-a-kind, only-in-Québec-City made things.

Shopping Areas

Rue du Trésor by the Château Frontenac is claustrophobic and thick with gawkers but nonetheless worth a browse for meeting the (mostly) talented artists and perusing their works, which are surprisingly affordable.

In the Old Lower Town, rue St-Paul is known for antique stores and a handful of interesting galleries.

The part of rue St-Jean in the old city is great for bookstores and magazines while outside the walls, it has everything from soft-core, woman-friendly sex shops to artisanal soaps and interesting clothes stores. In St-Roch, rue St-Joseph has everything from junk shops to high-class boutiques and the only Hugo Boss store in North America besides New York City.

If you are looking for nontouristy goods like a toothbrush, inner soles for your shoes or a fresh pair of athletic socks, you'll probably have to go outside the walls for them. (Within, goods are limited to things like Inuit sculpture, souvenir shirts and maple syrup products.) Ste-Foy-Sillery is home to umpteen malls and box stores, and has the most variety of 'everyday' stuff.

Opening Hours

Most stores open Monday to Wednesday 9:30am or 10am to 6pm; clothing boutiques usually open their doors at 11am. Thursday and Friday retailers have later opening hours, usually until 9pm. Saturday hours are 10am to 5pm and Sunday is afternoon only (noon to 4pm or 5pm). During high season, between May 1 and Labour Day, many stores in Québec City extend their hours well into the night whatever the day, often until 9pm or 10pm. Many stores will stay open as long as people are coming in. Conversely, you'll find several of the smaller, privately owned stores keep more European hours (11am to 4pm Tuesday to Saturday, closed Sunday and Monday) no matter what the season.

OLD UPPER TOWN

Despite its reputation as being overly touristy, there's still plenty of interesting stuff to be had.

EXCALIBOR QUÉBEC

Map p220   Clothing

☎ 418-692-5959; 1055 rue St-Jean; 🕒 10am-9pm

Devoted to all things medieval, this Québec company sells clothes, jewelry and accessories. It also manufactures about 80% of its merchandise. Some of the outfits it stocks are pretty spectacular and they can also be extremely pricey. But there are also plenty of items that have been dialed down a notch and are actually wearable in public. Terrific, good-humored staff are on hand to help you with the sometimes intimidating networks of hooks, eyes and looping ribbons as well as the even more intimidating-looking corsets. This is one of many such stores around the province.

GALERIE ART INUIT Map p220   Art

☎ 418-694-1828; 35 rue St-Louis; 🕒 9:30am-5:30pm

Devoted to Inuit carvings from artists all over arctic Canada, this place is gorgeously set up, elaborately lit with a well-trained staff who knowledgably answer questions. Carvings range from the small to the large and intricate. Be prepared for both steep prices and fantastic quality. It ships internationally.

SIMONS Map p220   Clothing

☎ 418-692-3630; 20 Côte de la Fabrique

One of the city's business success stories, Simons was started by the son of a Scottish immigrant who set up a dry goods store in Québec City. By 1952 his descendents had turned the business into a successful clothing store. It's popular all over Québec for its trendy Twick label and for stocking items that are more cutting edge than those at competing department stores. There's been a Simons at this location since 1870.

OLD LOWER TOWN

A terrific place for browsing, especially rue St-Paul for gallery and antique lovers.

MARCHÉ DU VIEUX-PORT

Map p220   Food

☎ 418-692-2517; 160 Quai St-André; ⏲ 8am-8pm
This is a local market where you can buy fresh fruits and vegetables as well as dozens of local specialties, from Île d'Orléans blackcurrant wine to ciders, honeys, chocolates, herbal handcreams and, of course, maple syrup products. Weekends see huge crowds and more wine tastings than can be considered sensible.

GALERIE D'ESTAMPE PLUS

Map p220   Art

☎ 418-694-1303; 49 rue St-Pierre; ⏲ 11am-5:30pm Mon-Sat, noon-5pm Sun
A terrific gallery specializing in prints by Quebecers. The artists' biographies are pasted on the walls, and there's plenty of postcards and greeting cards if you can't afford the real thing.

VÊTEMENTS 90 DEGRÉS

Map p220   Clothing

☎ 418-694-9914; 141 rue St-Paul; ⏲ usually 11am-6pm
Set up by a Québec City artist who decided to slap simple, strong images and cheeky French text onto T-shirts and tank tops, this store is now going gangbusters. Even non-French speakers are taken with the shirts. The québécois slang can be impenetrable to non-French speakers but the store workers will do their best to try to translate it into English for you. If you still don't get it don't worry, the text may be saucy but it's never vulgar, so feel free to pick something just for the image.

ST-JEAN-BAPTISTE

Rue St-Jean is a terrific shopping street with a nice variety of shops.

BOUTIQUE KETTÖ

Map p226   Ceramics/jewelry

☎ 418-522-3337; 951 ave Cartier; ⏲ 10am-10pm
Illustrator Julie St-Onge-Drouin started up Kettö after her illustrative designs kept finding their way onto ceramic surfaces.

Now at this big, bright and beautifully set-up boutique, they're on everything from plates and mugs to ceramic jewelry. The necklaces in particular are fantastic. Don't be turned off if you find the images too cutesy at first. Plenty of the objects are also done up in bold geometric designs and bright colors that would make great gifts for anyone. Her designs are sold in small boutiques throughout Québec, but here is where you'll find the best selection.

CHOCO-MUSÉE ÉRICO

Map p226   Chocolate

☎ 418-524-2122; www.chocomusee.com; 634 rue St-Jean; ⏲ 10am-5:30pm Mon-Wed, 10am-9pm Thu & Fri, 10am-5:30pm Sat, 11am-5:30pm Sun; open longer in fine weather May-late Sep
The exotic smells and sheer number of flavors here will have a chocolate-lover go into absolute conniptions of joy. Try strawberry-and basil-truffles or the ice cream that comes in orange pekoe tea and beet-and-raspberry flavors. Or go for the chocolate-chip cookie packed with semi-sweet chocolate chunks, dates and black tea. There's a little museum in the back and a window where you can watch the chocolatiers do their work.

JA MOISAN ÉPICIER

Map p226   Food

☎ 418-522-0685; 699 rue St-Jean; ⏲ 9am-10pm
Established in 1871 this is considered the oldest grocery store in North America. The store is beautifully set up and fun just to browse – ever seen black-and-white zebra-striped bow pasta? The products do generally fall on the 'You've got to be kidding!' side of expensive but there will be products here you've never seen before along with heaps of local *produits du terroir*.

KAMA SUTRA

Map p226   Sex Toys

☎ 418-648-6286; 879 rue St-Jean; ⏲ 10am-10pm
This low-key store was started up by a sexologist. Despite being surrounded by all manner of dildos and naughty bits done up in milk chocolate, the fresh-scrubbed friendly staff mingle easily with everyone from students to middle-aged married couples from Toronto in this no-embarrassment environment.

SILLONS

Map p226   CDs

☎ 418-524-8352; 1149 ave Cartier; ☽ 10am-9pm Mon-Fri, 10am-5pm Sat, 11am-5pm Sun

This independent record store has been around for over 15 years and specializes in jazz, world music and music from Québec and France. It's not the best place for metal or hip-hop but other than that this is a great place to come if you want advice on which Jean Leloup or Les Colocs CD you should be adding to your collection.

TAXI

Map p226   Men's Underwear

☎ 418-694-1828; 586 rue St-Jean; ☽ 9:30am-5:30pm

This is a funky little store devoted to one thing and one thing only: men's underwear and lots of it. The T-Shirts and briefs are colorful and cutting edge. Well, as cutting edge as men's cotton underwear can be without raising eyebrows. The company is based in the village of Ste-Anne-de-la-Pérade, about 1½ hours southwest of Québec City. Taxi underwear is 100% Canadian-made.

UN AIR DE FRANCE

Map p226   Homemade Soap

☎ 418-524-5763; 669 rue St-Jean; ☽ 11am-4pm

The owner here isn't necessarily the best ambassador for his products (don't even think about picking up a nontester soap unless you are prepared for the full breadth of his wrath). But he's set up a lovely simple shop devoted to his artisanal soaps and bath products. Animal fats are not used in the soaps and they're kept as 'vegetable based' as possible. The odors are wonderful; rich without smelling fake. The melon and cucumber, green tea or maple syrup soaps are real standouts! There's also a three-hour soap workshop once a month for do-it-yourselfers (in French only). Call for details.

ST-ROCH

Rue St-Joseph is the place to head in this neighborhood. It's a fascinating strip with junk shops and boutiques, high-end cooking stores and secondhand wares and it's changing all the time.

BENJO

Map p226   Toyshop

☎ 418-640-0001; www.benjo.ca; 543 rue St-Joseph Est; ☽ 10am-5:30pm Mon-Wed, 10am-9pm Thu & Fri, 9:30am-5pm Sat, 11am-5pm Sun

This toy shop/children's paradise gives you a glimpse into what the world would be like if adults were overthrown and kids were running things instead. Even the front door is pint-sized (the adult-sized door for us grown-ups is off to the side). There's a train that goes around the store on weekends, and arts and crafts for little ones during the week (usually around $10-15). Evening craft workshops for parents are on Wednesday. Call or check the website for times.

SLEEPING

From old-fashioned B&Bs to hipster boutique hotels, Québec City has heaps of interesting accommodation. Prices rise in the high-season summer months and during Winter Carnival. Competition keeps prices down to a reasonable level the rest of the year. The best choices are the numerous small European-style hotels and Victorian B&Bs scattered around Old Town. They offer character, convenience and a bit of romance. Motels close to town and larger downtown hotels tend to be expensive.

As you'd expect in such a popular city, the top choices are often full so make reservations well in advance, especially for weekends. It's almost impossible to show up in the city on a Saturday morning in summer or during holidays and find a room for the same night.

Budget accommodation also fills up quickly during high season. If you're in a bind, student dorms are available to travelers during the summer at Université Laval (Map p205; ☎ 418-656-5632; www.sres.ulaval.ca; Local 1618, Pavillon Alphonse-Marie Parent). Located in the borough of Ste-Foy-Sillery, about a 15- to 20-minute bus ride away from the Old Town, rooms are clean but very plain and have shared bathrooms.

PRICE GUIDE

$$$ over $160
$$ $60–160
$ under $60

Outlying motels are concentrated primarily in three areas. Beauport is just a 12-minute drive northeast of the city. To get there, go north along ave Dufferin, then take Hwy 440 until the exit for boul Ste-Anne/rte 138. The motels are located on a stretch between the 500 to 1200 blocks. A bike trail from the city passes nearby.

A second area is located west of the center on boul Wilfrid-Hamel (rte 138) – head west on Hwy 440 to the Henri IV exit.

The third area is boul Laurier in the borough of Ste-Foy-Sillery. To get there, follow Grande-Allée west until it turns into boul Laurier.

City buses run to these areas, so whether you have a car or not, they may be the answer if you find everything booked up downtown. The further out you go, the more the prices drop. Prices are generally higher than usual for motels, averaging about $90 to $130 in high season.

OLD UPPER TOWN

This area has the widest choice of accommodation in town, from hostels and familial B&Bs to cheap little hotels and intimate, luxurious inns.

Budget

AUBERGE DE LA PAIX Map p220   Hostel $
☎ 418-694-0735; www.aubergedelapaix.com; 31 rue Couillard; dm incl breakfast $20; 🖳
On a quiet street, this funky hostel has relaxed, welcoming staff and 60 brightly colored rooms outfitted with comfortable wooden furniture. With the cheerfully painted halls and guests lounging in the pleasant garden, it feels less institutional than the official HI hostel nearby. A continental breakfast is served each morning and bedding is provided for $3 per stay.

AUBERGE INTERNATIONALE DE QUÉBEC Map p220   Hostel $
☎ 418-694-0775; www.aubergeinternationale dequebec.com; 19 rue Ste-Ursule; members/ nonmembers dm $22/26, r with shared bathroom $67/71, r with bathroom $77/81; 🖳
Floors are creaky and the frustrating labyrinth of corridors goes on forever, but this lively place positively heaves with energy and bustle all year round. It attracts a great mix of independent travelers, big families with small children and groups. Staff are friendly but usually harried just trying to keep up with all the comings and goings. It's usually full in summer, despite having almost 300 beds, so reserve ahead if you can.

MANOIR LA SALLE Map p220   Guesthouse $
☎ 418-692-9953; 18 rue Ste-Ursule; r with shared bathroom $55-65
Four fat, fluffy cats patrol the halls of this simple, familial accommodation that's clean but unabashedly worn. You may prefer the upstairs rooms to avoid having to go through the lobby to the bathroom, as guests on the ground floor do. Some kitchenettes are available.

Midrange

AU PETIT HÔTEL
Map p220   Hotel $$
☎ 418-694-0965; aupetithotel@sympatico.ca; 3 ruelle des Ursulines; r $65-100
Sitting on a tranquil, dead-end lane and covered in bright awnings and flowers, this place practically beckons you in. The staff aren't exactly the most welcoming (ie if you have an unregistered guest in your room even for a minute expect a flurry of knocks and a scolding from the owner). However, this is a good deal otherwise. The 16 plain, clean rooms are priced by size, each has a private bathroom and the ones across the street in the annex have air-conditioning. The rooms can be quite sparse, but this is a very reasonable option.

HÔTEL ACADIA Map p220   Hotel $$
☎ 418-694-0280, 800-463-0280; www.hotel acadia.com; 43 rue Sate-Ursule; r $69-259, studio apartments from $125; 🅿 🖳
This hotel is spread out over three different houses along this quiet street. Rooms run the gambit from small with shared bathrooms to quite luxurious with fireplaces or whirlpools, which means there's a refreshing cross-section of travelers crowding the lobby clamoring for the free newspapers each morning. Studio apartments with a full kitchen are available too, ideal for extended stays. They're filled with dated furniture and the kind of TVs you probably haven't seen since the 1970s but they are clean and fantastic value. A continental breakfast is available for $7.

AUBERGE ST-LOUIS Map p220   Hotel $$

☎ 418-692-2424, 888-692-4105; www.auberge
stlouis.ca; 48 rue St-Louis; s & d incl breakfast $69-139
Only about a minute or so from the Cita-
delle and the Old Town's main sites, rooms
in this little hotel are clean, wonderfully
kept up, and decorated in shades of light
grey. This wouldn't necessarily be your
first choice (some of the rooms are tiny
or don't get much natural light) but it's a
great place to keep in mind if the nearby
B&Bs are full but you still want to stay in
the Upper Town. The cheaper rooms have
shared bathrooms.

AU CHÂTEAU FLEUR-DE-LYS

Map p220   Hotel $$
☎ 418-694-1884, 877-691-1884; www.quebecweb
.com/cfl; 15 ave Ste-Geneviève; r $80-140; P per
day $12
Set on a quiet street, this towering Victorian
home is just seconds from the Citadelle
and the Dufferin Terrace, yet it feels like it's
far off the beaten track. Old World details
spruce up the rooms without going over-
board. With a laid-back, personable staff this
is an ideal place if you're looking for relaxed
and uncomplicated accommodation. Just
be warned, you may have to access your
private bathroom through a door out in
the hall, rather than from inside your room.
A continental breakfast is included in the

room price. There are 18 rooms but only 12
parking spaces so, if arriving by car, double
check availability when reserving.

MANOIR SUR LE CAP Map p220   Hotel $$

☎ 418-694-1987, 866-694-1987; www.manoir
-sur-le-cap.com; 9 ave Ste-Geneviève; r $85-150; P
A gorgeous place with 14 rooms, some
overlooking Jardin des Gouverneurs, the
Château or the river. It's in a wonderful,
quiet location, well away from the tourist
throngs on rue St-Louis. Rooms are modern, and many have tiny balconies and
attractive stone or brick walls.

LA MARQUISE BASSANO

Map p220   B&B $$
☎ 418-692-0316, 877-692-0316; www.marquise
debassano.com; 15 rue des Grisons; r $85-165;
P per day $14
Young, gregarious owners Veronyc and
Francis have set up a gorgeous home, out-
fitting every room with thoughtful touches
whether it's a canopy bed or a clawfoot
bathtub. Despite being just minutes from
the important sites, this house is located on
a low-traffic street surrounded by period
homes. You'll feel more like a houseguest
staying with friends than just an anony-
mous visitor paying for a bed. The break-
fasts are cold but go on forever with meats,
hard-boiled eggs, cheese, pastries and fruit.

Québec City   SLEEPING

QUÉBEC'S COOLEST HOTEL

Spending hundreds of dollars to sleep on a bed of ice might not sound so great, but North America's first ice hotel has
been a blistering success since opening in 2001.

It's hard to fathom, but everything here is made of ice: the reception desk, the pen you sign the guest book with,
the sink in your room, your bed, even the cocktail glasses, which frequently come in handy…okay, not *everything* is
made of ice. There are no ice toilets for example (heated facilities conveniently located nearby, not to worry!) But once
inside this majestic place, no one feels like nit-picking. Visitors say the bed is not as frigid as it sounds, courtesy of thick
sleeping bags laid on lush deer pelts.

Some 500 tons of ice and 15,000 tons of snow go into the five-week construction of this perishable hotel. One of
the most striking aspects is its size – over 3000 sq meters of frosty splendor. First impressions in the entrance hall are
strangely overwhelming – tall, sculpted columns of ice support a ceiling where a crystal chandelier hangs, and carved
sculptures, tables and chairs line the endless corridors.

Though the structure of the ice hotel remains the same from year to year, everything else changes from the location
of the chapel (at your disposal for cool winter weddings!) to the placement of the lounge.

The hotel is about a half-hour drive from central Québec City at Lac St-Joseph's Station Écotouristique Duchesnay,
giving you easy access to icy activities like skiing, snowshoeing, dog sledding and ice fishing.

The ice hotel offers packages starting at $599 per double including a welcome cocktail and breakfast buffet. If you're
not staying, simply take the tour. It lasts about 30 minutes (adult/child 6-12/senior & student/family $15/7.50/13/42).
For information, contact **Ice Hotel** (Map p205; ☎ 418-875-4522, 877-505-0423; www.icehotel-canada.com; 143 rte
Duchesnay, Ste-Catherine-de-la Jacques-Cartier). It's off exit 295 of Hwy 40, west of Québec City via rte 367.

AU MANOIR STE-GENEVIÈVE

Map p220   Hotel $$

☎ 418-694-1666, 877-692-0316; www.quebecweb
.com/msg; 13 ave Ste-Geneviève; s incl breakfast
$100, d incl breakfast $95-135; Ⓟ per day $11
Gracious staff man this Victorian manor
dating from 1800. Rooms are clean and
classic. The breakfast is continental and
major sites and restaurants are short walks
away. This is ideal for those looking for
slow-paced, old-fashioned accommodation.
All rooms have TVs and private bathrooms
but some don't have air-conditioning so
double check when reserving.

AUBERGE PLACE D'ARMES

Map p220   Inn $$

☎ 418-694-9485, 866-333-9485; www.auberge
placedarmes.com; 24 rue Ste-Anne; r from $115
Overhauled from top to bottom after a
change in ownership, this place now has
some of the smartest looking rooms in
town. Everything from the halls to the
guest rooms are done up in rich crimsons,
navy blues and golds and many of the
rooms have exposed red-brick walls. The
upkeep is immaculate. The inn is located
right across from the Church of the Holy
Trinity and is only a minute away from
the funicular to Lower Town. In summer
months there is a two-day minimum stay
on the weekends. Reception opens from
8am to 11pm.

Top End
L'HÔTEL DU CAPITOLE

Map p220   Hotel $$-$$$

☎ 418-694-4040, 888-363-4040; www.lecapitole
.com; 972 rue St-Jean; r from $135 way up
Right on top of the fabulous Théâtre Capi-
tole, this hotel is one of the city's absolute
gems. Red furniture with sensuous curves
referencing theater dressing rooms of old
are a feature of even the most basic room
and the effect is stunning. But the gold
mine here is the staff. When even the poshest digs in town were losing their patience
on a particularly busy high-season summer
Saturday, the three employees here deftly
handled phone calls, check outs and a
flotilla of particularly demanding check-ins
with such grace, charm and panache you
half felt like giving them a round of ap-
plause when it was all over.

Château Frontenac (right) rises from Terasse Dufferin

FAIRMONT LE CHÂTEAU FRONTENAC

Map p220   Hotel $$$

☎ 418-692-1751, 800-441-1414; www.fairmont
.com; 1 rue des Carrières; r from $230 on up…way,
way up; Ⓟ ⓢ
More than just a hotel, more than just a
landmark, the castlelike Château is the
enduring symbol of Québec City (see
boxed text opposite.) Rooms are sumptu-
ously decorated and come in all shapes
and sizes with a mind-whirring number
of views to choose from. Service here is
professional plus and everyone from the
bellhops to concierges get top marks
from visitors for their finesse in handling
the crowds this place draws on a regular
basis. Even if you aren't staying, the bar is
a wonderful place for a drink while taking
in the spectacular view of the St Law-
rence River. The Kiosk Frontenac out front
houses bus-tour counters and is a popular
rendezvous point.

OLD LOWER TOWN
A cluster of the most tantalizing boutique
hotels in the city are found in this area
along with a handful of hip, small inns.

Budget & Midrange
HÔTEL BELLEY

Map p220   Hotel $$

☎ 418-692-1694; www.oricom.ca/belley; 249
rue St-Paul; r $90-140 high season, $70-100 low
season
A great place for the young and hip who
still like their comfort, this offers spacious,
impeccably decorated though sparse
rooms, with brick walls or wood paneling.
Many rooms include microwave ovens or
small fridges. The wonderful Belley Tavern
is attached to the hotel.

CHÂTEAU FRONTENAC

The Château Frontenac is not only the city's most luxurious hotel, but is so iconic it has become a site in and of itself. Its winding halls and dramatic location have lured everyone from politicians and movie stars to movies and TV shows.

It's probably one of the rare hotels where you can be walking through the lobby and discover the majority of people there aren't even guests but tourists visiting to get close to history, the architecture and see what all the commotion is about (this is the world's most photographed hotel after all).

Designed by New Yorker Bruce Price (father of manners maven Emily Post), the Château was named after the mercurial Count of Frontenac, Louis de Buade, who governed New France in the late 1600s. Completed in 1893 Château Frontenac was one of the Canadian Pacific Railway's series of luxury hotels built across Canada. One part medieval and one part Renaissance, the hotel has had regular extensions over the years, the most recent one being done in 1993.

Its turrets and multiple imposing wings top off its dramatic location on Cap Diamants, atop a cliff that swoops down into the St-Lawrence River. The setting alone is so powerful that Alfred Hitchcock opened his 1953 Québec City–set mystery *I Confess* with that very shot.

During WWII, the Québec Conferences involving British prime minister Winston Churchill, US president Franklin Roosevelt and Canadian prime minister William Lyon Mackenzie King were all held here.

Other illustrious guests have included King George VI, Chiang Kaishek and Princess Grace of Monaco.

More recently, its romantic location caught the attention of American producers who shot an episode of the reality show *The Bachelor* at the hotel.

Guides in period costume give 50-minute **tours** (☎ 418-691-2166; www.tourschateau.ca; adult/child age 6-16/senior $8/5.50/7.25; ☿ 10am-6pm May 1-Oct 15, noon-5pm Sat & Sun Oct 16-April 30) on the hotel's history. Call for reservations.

HÔTEL DES COUTELLIER

Map p220   Hotel $$

☎ 418-692-9696, 888-523-9696; www.hoteldes coutellier.com; 253 rue St-Paul; r from $145

This newly opened hotel is stylish, with friendly service to boot. Refreshingly unpretentious, rooms here are bright and spacious. A mustard-colored bathrobe is draped across the bed when you arrive and every room has a coffee maker. A continental breakfast is packed up in a wicker basket for you every morning and hung outside your door by 7am.

Top End

HÔTEL 71 Map p220   Hotel $$$

☎ 418-692-1171, 888-692-1171; www.hotel71 .com; 71 rue St-Pierre; r from $165

A fabulous addition to the Old Lower Town. This old 19th-century building once housed a bank but now houses a hotel that looks like it's straight out of some architectural magazine. Candles burn in the lobby, sleek black-clad staff drift about their duties and red room numbers smoulder in the dark hallways. Rooms contain modern, minimalist furniture and dramatic bathroom lighting. Heavy red curtains take the place of closet doors. The lobby café serves excellent (and beautifully presented) coffee along with a continental breakfast.

AUBERGE ST-ANTOINE

Map p220   Hotel $$$

☎ 418-692-2211, 888-692-2211; www.saint -antoine.com; 6 rue St-Antoine; r from $169 high season, from $139 low season

Beg, borrow or steal. Just make sure you get the cash to spend at least one night of your life at this genius accommodation. Where to start? The intelligent, mature service? The endless amenities and thoughtful room flourishes? The free, private cinema for guests? A wall clock made of nothing but light and shadow? As if all that wasn't enough, when the neighboring parking lot was dug up to expand the hotel, thousands of historical relics from the French colony were discovered. Hundreds of them are now on display in the lobby, the halls and guest rooms. **Panache Restaurant** (p237), the darling *du jour* of Canada's fine-dining scene, is located just off the hotel's lobby. Auberge St-Antoine has all the elements to one day give the Château Frontenac a serious run for its money when it comes to iconic Québec City accommodation.

HÔTEL DOMINION 1912

Map p220   Boutique Hotel $$$

☎ 418-692-2224, 888-833-5253; www.hotel
dominion.com; 126 rue St-Pierre; r $205-305 high
season, $169-239 low season; ▢

Bathroom sinks glow in the dark, the continental breakfast includes everything from fruit and eggs to rabbit paté, and the concierge will make your dinner reservation as though it was a career highlight. Hotels like this are dangerous – when everything from the atmosphere to the reception staff is this pitch-perfect, it's hard to tear yourself away from your room. Located near the Old Port area, rooms here are quiet and cosy, and guests (understandably) are rabidly loyal.

ST-JEAN-BAPTISTE

Accommodation here means you'll be rubbing elbows with locals more than you would in the Old Town. Delightful B&Bs are scattered throughout the neighborhood. The B&B ban on rue St-Jean has been lifted by the city, so it may be worth a stroll when you arrive to see if anything new and interesting has opened.

AUBERGE CAFÉ KRIEGHOFF

Map p226   Guesthouse $$

☎ 418-522-3711; www.cafekrieghoff.qc.ca;
1091 ave Cartier; r $90-110 high season, $85-95 low
season; ▢

A gem hidden away in the old house above the Café Krieghoff (p238). Spacious rooms are simply decorated but given a little off-beat character with flourishes like antique hat boxes or a hulking, oversized wooden side table. All rooms have private, modern bathrooms and flat-screen TVs but no phones. A common area on the main floor has a phone, umbrellas to borrow and a computer with internet, all free for guests. The best part of the deal is the breakfast voucher for Café Krieghoff each morning. Check-in is at the bar, open 7am to 11pm.

CHÂTEAU DES TOURELLES

Map p226   B&B $$

☎ 418-647-9136; www.chateaudestourelles.qc.ca;
212 rue St-Jean; r $99-119

Located on a great little strip of rue St-Jean, lined with interesting stores and eateries, you'll notice this B&B's soaring turret long

before you get to the door. The lovely owners have done a stunning job with this old house; it's cosy and rustic without straying into kitsch. Named after members of the owners' families, rooms are beautifully decorated and may have exposed red-brick walls or antique sinks. Delightfully lopsided stairs lead up onto a rooftop terrace with a smashing 360° view of, well, just about everything of note in town. Hot breakfasts are included in the room rate.

LE CHÂTEAU DU FAUBOURG

Map p226   B&B $$

☎ 418-524-2902; www.lechateaudufaubourg.com;
429 rue St-Jean; r from $99

Ever thought it might be fun to wake up in an Agatha Christie novel? Good. Once you've stepped through the door of this B&B you'll realize you've finally got your wish. Built by the massively rich Imperial Tobacco family in the 1800s, this place was recently turned into a B&B. The interior is pure British-Lord-of-the-Manor meets French-Marquis style, replete with portraits whose eyes seem to follow you around the room. It's all so creepily cool you half expect the lights to flicker out and find someone thwacked over the head with a candlestick. But never mind. The hosts are the kindest, most good-humored, accommodating people you could hope to meet and their dozen or so pet birds keep the halls filled with happy tweets.

HOTEL RELAIS CHARLES-ALEXANDRE

Map p226   Hotel $$

☎ 418-523-1220; 91 Grande-Allée Est; r high
season $119-129, low season $89-99; ℗ per day $8

This is a small, cozy hotel with a great location near both the Musée National des Beaux-Arts du Québec and Battlefields Park. Rooms here are all different and are best described as low key, rustic and comfortable. They include a CD player and classical disc for ambiance. One of the nicest choices in the area, this hotel is not without its eccentricities. Management schedules some very noisy activities (vacuuming, scraping snow) at some ungodly morning hours and with only a limited number of tables for the morning meal, times must be reserved a day ahead. If you sleep in or are late, good-bye free breakfast.

Excursions

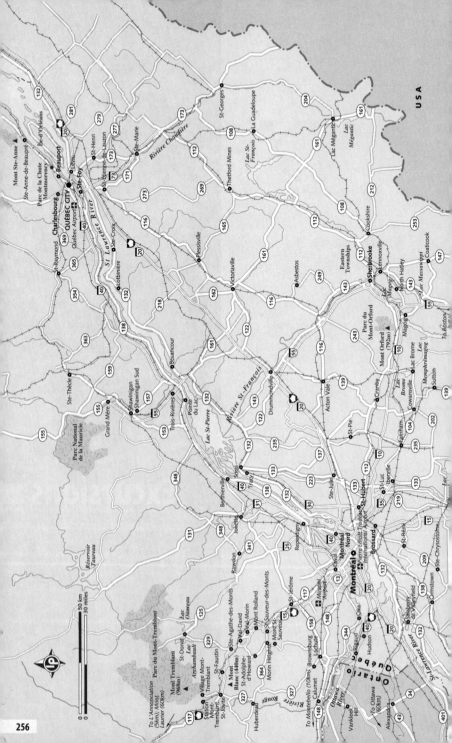

Excursions

As if Montréal and Québec City weren't playgrounds enough, there are literally hundreds of excursions on their doorsteps. Many can be done as pleasant one-day jaunts. If you have a short period of time, a destination in the **Eastern Townships** (p261) is your best bet for its cozy villages and rolling landscapes. For longer jaunts or more outdoorsy pursuits, the **Laurentians** (p258) more than fit the bill offering skiing, hiking and cycling, and golf and tennis at the many resorts. If you've got several days, seek out **Parc du Mont Tremblant** (p258).

Leaving Montréal behind, traveling east on Hwy 138 you begin to get a sense of what small-town Québec is like: stone houses with light-blue trim and tin roofs, silver-spired churches, ubiquitous chip (French fry) wagons, main streets with shops built right to the road. The most picturesque section is from Trois-Rivières onward to the northeast where the villages get ever more charming and the river views get ever more majestic.

TROIS-RIVIÈRES

Trois-Rivières is tiny, tidy and more than 350 years old. Though its glory days as a major industrial player are past, it is still a major pulp and paper center and the largest town between Québec's two main cities. Don't bother looking – there aren't three rivers. The name of the town refers to the way the St-Maurice River divides as it approaches the St Lawrence. The **old town** burned down in 1908 but is still a wonderful place to putter about, with a remarkably sophisticated tourist bureau and infrastructure given its small size—explore it yourself with a brochure from the tourist office or join one of the office's many tours.

TRANSPORTATION

Distance from Montréal 134km
Distance from Québec City 121km
Car Autoroute 40
Bus From the Montréal or Québec City main bus station

Events like the **Festival International de la Poésie**, held in fall, or even one-day events like 'Italian Day' are great times to come. There is a wonderful community atmosphere here and the city turns out in droves to drink it all up.

La Musée Québécois de Culture Populaire is one of the most interesting stops in the area. Its exhibits can touch on anything from the social significance and psychology of garage sales to the history of bikes, set up so museum visitors can learn about them by actually riding them. Also leaving from here, are the do-not-miss tours of the former Trois-Rivières **prison**. When it closed in 1986 it was the oldest continually in-use jail in Canada. The tours are all led by former convicts and cover not only the history of the prison itself but life in Canada's prisons in general. It's fascinating but at times disturbing stuff. Only a couple of the guides know some English, so call ahead to make sure they'll be available when you drop by.

Several old houses on rue des Ursulines are now open to the public as small free museums and serve as excellent examples of period architecture. Cafés and bars are abundant in this lively area. Rue des Ursulines and rue Radisson are also main streets. The **Cathédrale de l'Assomption** is the only Westminster-style church on the continent.

Two-hour cruises along the river aboard the **MV Le Draveur** are available from the dock in Parc Portuaire, at the foot of boul des Forges in the center of the Old Town.

The **Ursuline Museum** has displays relating to the Ursuline Order of nuns who were prominent in the town's development.

La Domaine Joly de Lotbinière, a stately museum between Trois-Rivières and Québec City, was built for Henri-Gustave Joly de Lotbinière (1849–1908), a premier of Québec. This is one of the most impressive manors built during the seigneurial period of Québec and has been preserved in its late 19th-century state. The outbuildings and huge cultivated garden are a treat, and the café serves lunch and afternoon teas.

257

Information

Trois-Rivières tourist office (☎ 819-375-1122; 1457 rue Notre-Dame)

Sights & Activities

Cathédrale de l'Assomption (☎ 819-374-2409; 362 rue Bonaventure; ☯ 9am-6pm)

En Prison (☎ 819-372-0406; 200 rue Laviolette; adult/senior/student $8/6/5; ☯ 10am first tour, last tour 4:45pm June-Labour Day, tours leave 10am-5pm Tue-Sun rest of the year, call for time of last tour)

La Domaine Joly de Lotbinière (☎ 818-926-2462; route de Pointe-Platon, Hwy 132, Ste-Croix; adult/child/student $13.50/8/6; ☯ 10am-5pm beginning May-beginning Oct)

Musée Québécois de Culture Populaire (☎ 819-372-0406; 200 rue Laviolette; adult/senior/student $8/6/5; ☯ 10am-5pm Tue-Sun, to 6pm June-Labour Day)

MV Le Draveur (☎ 819-375-3000; www.croisieres.qc.ca; 1515 rue du Fleuve; adult/child $15.30/7.65)

Ursuline Museum (☎ 819-375-7922; 734 rue des Ursulines; adult/student & senior $3/2; ☯ 9am-5pm Tue-Sun May-Nov, 1-5pm Wed-Sun Mar & Apr, appointment only rest of year)

Sleeping

Auberge Internationale de Trois-Rivières (☎ 819-378-4334; www.hihostels.ca; 497 rue Radisson, Trois-Rivières; dm from $20) Wonderfully clean and friendly youth hostel.

Hôtel Gouverneur (☎ 819-379-4550; www.gouverneur.com; 975 rue Heart, Trois-Rivières; r from $129) Good-quality, business-traveler-type hotel across from the Musée Québécois de Culture Populaire.

Manoir De Blois (☎ 819-373-1090; http://membres.lycos.fr/manoirdeblois; 197 rue Bonaventure, Trois-Rivières; r from $80) A gorgeous family-run hospital. Breakfast is served in this historic home's huge salon set up like a Victorian drawing room.

Transportation

Gare d'Autobus (☎ 819-374-2944; 1075 rue Champflour) This bus station is situated in the old train station. Voyageur Colonial and Orléans Express buses go to Montréal and Québec City. One-way tickets to either city cost the same (adult/child/student $26/16/22) and take from 1¾ to 2½ hours. Some buses to Québec City travel the scenic Highway 138 stopping at villages along the way. This route can take three hours or more.

THE LAURENTIANS (LES LAURENTIDES)

You don't need to be in Montréal long to notice two things: locals who announce a trip to the Laurentians do so with a cat-that-ate-the-canary grin, while their audience lets go with an if-only-us-too sigh.

Once you're here you'll see why.

The region gets its name from the rolling peaks of the Laurentian mountain range. Once as high as the Rockies, they were eroded over centuries to the more modest heights that you see today. Named for their location along the northern side of the St Lawrence River, the Laurentians have become a kind of year-round outdoor playground for Quebecers. In winter, outdoor enthusiasts and nature lovers take to the numerous lakes and forest-sprinkled peaks for everything from skiing, snowshoeing and snowmobiling. Hikers, cyclists, swimmers and campers pick up the slack for the rest of the year.

In between activities travelers linger in the region's villages, many of which offer terrific eating options, some interesting shopping and first rate B&Bs.

The **Laurentians Tourist Association** (Association Touristique des Laurentides) at the **Porte du Nord**, off the highway north of Montréal, has free maps, a reservation service and brochures galore to help you get started.

The region's blockbuster attraction is **Parc National du Mont-Tremblant**. Skiing and its rugged wilderness attracts everyone from families on vacation to Hollywood big-wigs like Catherine Zeta-Jones and Michael Douglas, who own a pied à terre at Lac Desmarais.

TRANSPORTATION

Distance from Montréal 80–150km
Distance from Québec City 295–369km
Car Hwy 15 (Autoroute des Laurentides), or the slower Hwy 117 north
Bus Maheux buses run from Montréal's main bus station to St-Jovite daily (adult $31.50). There's no public transport but in ski season, free shuttles make the 10-minute drive from St-Jovite to Tremblant. There is no direct bus from Québec City.

The name Mont Tremblant comes from the Algonquians, who felt the mountain 'trembled' to punish them. These days the name Tremblant conjures up a different kind of punishment, since several villages in the region were amalgamated into the City of Mont Tremblant and given almost indecipherable variations of the same moniker. With every highway exit now labeled 'Tremblant,' tourists and locals alike play the game of trying to figure out if it's the actual Tremblant where they have their hotel reservations – the best solution is to get detailed directions from your accommodation before heading up.

In any case, the areas of interest to visitors in the City of Mont Tremblant are the Intrawest ski resort known as Station Tremblant, the village of Mont Tremblant now referred to as secteur Village, a low-key area that has a main street lined with good eateries, and secteur St-Jovite, an area worth noting only because you can often find a hotel room here even when accommodation in other regions of the city is full.

Station Tremblant has a chairlift at its base for winter skiing or summer transport up the mountain. There are also walking paths alongside pretty Lac Tremblant and a wonderful tourist cruise around the lake. Shopping, a movie theater, cafés and restaurants dominate the town's core, although they are dwarfed by gleaming accommodations and prices to match. The lower part, by the chairlift, is done up like a miniature fairy-tale village, packed with restaurants and a tourist office, while the upper part is where most of the entertainment is.

Mont Tremblant (968m) itself is the area's highest peak, and a major ski center with more than 60 runs. Its state-of-the-art facilities include golf courses, water sports, cycling and tennis courts. Bicycles and skates can be rented at the ski center for the 10km skating/cycling path that runs through town and up to the mountain's edge.

Opened more than a century ago, the wild, wooded **Parc National du Mont-Tremblant** (1500 sq km) features fantastic hiking and mountain biking trails as well as camping and river routes for canoes. The half-day route from Lac Chat to Mont de la Vache Noire is massively popular. Be sure to reserve a canoe and place on the shuttle bus by calling the **Information Center Parc du Mont-Tremblant** well in advance of your arrival.

The most developed of the park's sectors is the Diable, close to Mont Tremblant and north of pretty **Lac Supérieur**. The information centre here has kayaks, peddle boats and canoes for rent and numerous trails and camp sites in the vicinity.

Nearby in **St-Faustin**, the popular **Cabane à Sucre Millette** is known for both its food and tours.

Another terrific attraction is the **P'tit Train du Nord**, a 200km bike path built on the old Laurentian railway line of the same name. Running between Mont Laurier to St-Jérôme,

Skiing in the Laurentian mountains

B&Bs and bike shops are easily found along the route. Many of the old train stations along the way now house mini-museums, cafés and tourist info offices.

The Laurentian tourist guide available from Tourism Québec has a pull-out guide on the route that will tell you everything you need to know to do the trail. In winter the route is open to cross-country skiers and snowshoers.

Whether you are doing the P'tit Train du Nord or just cruising the Laurentians by car on a day trip from Montréal, there are several villages along the way worth a stop.

St-Sauveur-des-Monts is a small resort town with four nearby ski hills. Its main drag is often clogged on weekends when day-trippers shuffle through the cafés, restaurants and shops.

Mont St-Sauveur is one of the area's main ski centers. Hills are a bit tame but there's night skiing, a huge variety of runs and 100% snow coverage in season, thanks to snow blowers built right into the slopes.

The tiny **Val-David** was a major hippy mecca in the '60s, a hangover still apparent today. The village has two artisanal bakeries, jazz music in its cafés on summer weekends and more than its share of arts and crafts people. For something a bit different, try **Acro-Nature** in nearby **Morin Heights**. It has a three-hour obstacle course for adults, where you can sail from tree to tree on one of the 24 zip lines, and a mini-course for kids.

If you're traveling in summer, stop by **Ste-Adéle** for a meal. There are several interesting eateries across the street from Lac Rond.

Elsewhere, **Ste-Agathe-des-Monts** has a prime location on Lac des Sables. By the beginning of the 1900s, it was well known as a spa town. Later, famous guests included Queen Elizabeth (who took refuge here during WWII) and Jackie Kennedy.

Less than an hour from Montréal, St Jérôme's **Musée d'art contemporain des Laurentides** mounts small but first-rate exhibitions of regional artists' works.

Information

Information Center Parc du Mont-Tremblant (☎ 819-688-2281; www.parcsquebec.com; ch du Lac- Supérior, Lac-Supérieur; ♡ 7am-10pm summer, call for winter hours)

Laurentians Tourist Association (Association Touristique des Laurentides; (☎ 450-224-7007, toll free 180-561-6673; www.laurentides.com; La Porte du Nord, exit 51, Autoroute 15)

Mont Tremblant Tourist Office (☎ 819-425-2434; www.tourismemonttremblant.com; 5080 Montée Ryan; ♡ 8am-7pm Sun-Thu, 8am-10pm Fri & Sat summer, 9am-5pm winter)

Ste-Agathe Tourist Office (☎ 819-326-0457; 24 rue St Paul, Ste-Agathe-des-Monts; ♡ 9am-6pm summer, 9am-5pm winter)

St-Sauveur-des-Monts Tourist Office (☎ 450-229-3729; 605 ch des Frênes, St-Sauveur-des-Monts)

Sights & Activities

Acro-Nature (☎ 450-227-2020; www.mssi.ca; 231 rue Bennett, Morin Heights; adult/youth/child $35/26/21; ♡ 9am-5pm daily, end of Jun-Sep, call for non-summer hours)

Cabane à Sucre Millette (☎ 819-688-2101; 1357 rue St-Faustin, St-Faustin; ♡ 11:30am- 8pm Tue-Sat, 11:30am-7pm Sun Mar-Apr, reservations rest of year)

Musée d'Art Contemporain des Laurentides (☎ 450-432-7171; www.museelaurentides.ca; 101 pl du Curé-Labelle, St-Jérôm; ♡ noon-5pm Tue-Sun; adult $5)

Mont St-Sauveur Ski Centre (☎ 450-227-4671; www .mssi.ca; 350 rue St-Denis, St-Sauveur-des-Monts; ♡ 9am-10:30pm Mon-Sat, 9am-10pm Sun, usually mid-Nov–end of Apr)

Mont Tremblant Ski Centre (☎ 819-681-2000 (general info); www.tremblant.ca; Station Mont-Tremblant; ♡ 8:30am-btw 3:30pm & 4:30pm daily, mid-Nov to mid-Apr)

P'tit Train du Nord (♡ May-Oct for bikes; Dec-Mar for cross-country skiing; daily/season pass bikes $5/15, skiing $7/35, all-season annual pass $45)

Eating

Cigale California (☎ 450-229-1546; 1141 ch du Chante-cler, Ste-Adèle; mains $13-25) Lovely location across from Lac Rond. Exciting menu options include dishes like duck ravioli with coconut-curry sauce.

La Forge Bar & Grill (☎ 819-681-3000; pl St-Bernard, Station Mont-Tremblant; mains bistro $10-20, restaurant $20-30) The best terrace in the whole resort area. The noisy downstairs bistro has good burgers, salads and killer spicy-fried onion chunks; the upstairs restaurant features dishes grilled on maple wood and a noted wine list.

Le Creux du Vent (☎ 819-322-2280; 1430 rue de l'Académie, Val-David; mains $13-24) Tucked in a quiet part of town by the Rivière du Nord, this restaurant has an ever-changing menu inspired by what's in the local markets.

Le Vin à l'Heure (☎ 450-227-2992; 92 rue de la Gare, St-Sauveur-des-Monts; mains $13-18) This bustling little wine bistro is about as perfect as it gets with a oenophile wait staff that's beyond outstanding. The table d'hôte with suggested wines ($52) should be experienced at all costs.

Microbrasserie La Diable (☎ 819-681-4546; Station Mont-Tremblant; mains $10-20) Hugely popular place with six on-site brewed beers sporting names like Devil and Blizzard. European sausages – everything from caribou to Swiss cheese-stuffed varieties – are the perfect accompaniment.

Orange & Pamplemousse (☎ 450-227-4330; rue Principale, St-Sauveur-des-Monts; mains $9-26) It has pasta, meat and chicken dishes and one of the more interesting breakfast menus ($5-12) in town that includes oatmeal pancakes and maple syrup done up with berries and English cream or ricotta cheese.

Sleeping

Auberge de St-Venant (☎ 819 326-7937; www .st-venant.com; 234 St-Venant, Ste-Agathe-des-Monts; r off season $85-130, high season $105-150) There are bright, colorful rooms, enthusiastic owners and plenty of nooks and crannies where you can perch in a deck chair with a beer and take in the sparkling view of Lac des Sables.

Auberge du P'tit Train du Nord (☎ 450-229-2225; www.petit-train-du-nord.com; 3065 rue Rolland, Ste-Adèle; r $99-119) Right next to the bike path, this charming inn has weathered, tidy rooms and staff better at doling out info on the trail than most tourism offices.

Chalet Beaumont (☎ 819-322-1972; www.chalet beaumont.com; 1451 rue Beaumont, Val-David; dm $24, r $55-65) There's great views from this rustic inn/HI hostel perched on a hill above town.

La Belle au Bois Dormant (☎ 819-425-1331; www .belleauboisdormant.com; 108 ch des Bois-Francs, Mont Tremblant (village sector); r $90-110) Its name translates as 'Sleeping Beauty' and this luxurious log cabin which is perched in the woods more than lives up to the fairytale theme.

La Maison de Bavière (☎ 819-322-3528, toll free 1866-322-3528; www.maisondebaviere.com; 1470 ch de la Rivière, Val-David; r $85-140) Done up like a Bavarian lodge, this gîte has a stunning location on the Rivière du Nord, across the street from the P'tit Train du Nord. Breakfasts are prepared with hungry bikers and cross-country skiers in mind.

Manoir Saint-Sauveur (☎ 450-227-1811; 246 ch du Lac-Millette, St-Sauveur; d from $119) A behemoth in the heart of the resort area of St-Sauveur with nice flourishes like poolside singers in summer and computers with internet in the lobby.

Mont Tremblant International Youth Hostel (☎ 819-425-6008; www.hostellingtremblant.com; 2213 ch du Village; dm/r $28/68) Located in the village sector, this hostel has cozy, clean rooms and great staff.

THE EASTERN TOWNSHIPS

Known as the Cantons de l'Est (or l'Estrie in French), the Eastern Townships make for a terrific trip, not only because of the glorious scenery – rolling hills, green farmland, lakes and woodland – but because the region shows a different side of Québec. Once the homeland of Abenaki Indians, the region became a refuge for Loyalists fleeing the USA after the revolution of 1776; Irish and French settlers followed, although the area was mainly English until the 1970s. The region covers 13,100 sq km, beginning 80km southeast of Montréal and stretching to the Vermont and New Hampshire borders.

New Englanders will feel right at home with the covered bridges and round barns – everything from the barns to houses adheres more to British and American architectural styles and flavors than the French influence you'll see most other places in the province. Given its historic mix of Irish and French (see p65), you'll find this one of the most perfectly bilingual areas of Québec, with many locals speaking French and English with such ease it can be hard to tell who's francophone and who's anglophone.

TRANSPORTATION

Distance from Montréal 80-160km
Distance from Québec City 176-228km
Car Autoroute 10 Est (East)

Spring is the season for 'sugaring off': tapping, boiling and preparing maple syrup. Summer brings fishing and swimming in the numerous lakes; in fall the foliage dazzles with drop-dead gorgeous colors, and apple cider is served in local pubs. Skiing is a major winter activity with centers at Mont Orford and Sutton.

Coming from Montréal, stop off at the first **regional tourist office** for events information, though offices are found in most towns including **Coaticook**, **Granby** and **Sherbrooke**.

The Eastern Townships is a great hiking and cycling region, and rentals are available in Sherbrooke and North Hatley among other places. The district also produces some wines, and many of these vineyards are starting to get some serious attention especially for their ice wines (see below). You can pick up a brochure for the self-guided wine tour through the region from any tourist office.

The town of **Granby** is known far and wide in Québec as the home of **Granby Zoo**, with its 1000-plus animals including reptiles, gorillas and kangaroos. One of the most popular spots is at the bottom of the Hippopotamus Pool, where you can watch hippos lumber from the ground before they swim past viewing windows.

South of Autoroute 10, on Hwy 243, is the town of **Lac Brome**, on the lake of the same name and made up of seven former English Loyalist villages. **Knowlton** is certainly one of the most interesting and picturesque: many of the main street's Victorian buildings have been restored, and it's a bit of a tourist center with some fantastic craft and gift shops. A favorite meal in this area is Lac Brome duck, which shows up frequently on the better menus and is celebrated with the town's annual Duck Festival in fall.

Just out of **Magog**, the **Parc du Mont-Orford** is dominated by **Mont Orford** (792m). The park is a skiing center in winter and in summer there are lovely hiking trails, camping and canoe/kayak rental. Each summer the Orford Art Centre presents the **Jeunesses Musicales du Canada** music and art festival. Its **Auberge du Parc Orford** is a comfortable, spacious hotel and hostel with 55 rooms on the wooded grounds of the center.

Lac Memphrémagog is the largest and best-known lake in the Eastern Townships, but most lakefront properties are privately owned. Halfway down the lake is the **Abbaye St-Benoît-du-Lac**; the monks' chants, cider and wide range of expertly made cheeses are famous throughout Québec and people from all over the province descend on the Abby's shop to buy them along with the monks' jams, sweets and jellies. Visitors can also attend services, and there's a hostel for men and another for women nearby at a nunnery.

North Hatley sits at the north end of Lac Massawippi. The village was a popular second home for wealthy US citizens who enjoyed the scenery – and the absence of Prohibition – during the 1920s. Many of these old places are now inns and B&Bs.

ICE WINE

Ice wine was discovered in Germany by accident, when growers found that pressing wine grapes after they froze on the vine left a sweet, highly concentrated juice. Ice wine is what you get when you leave this juice on the vine to ferment, resulting in one of the most coveted dessert wines on the market; it's so expensive because of the amount of grapes that need to be pressed so enough juice can be extracted. Ontario-produced varieties are the out-and-out stars of this luxury sweet-treat, but the Québec-produced kinds are starting to give them a run for their money. If you're doing the winery tour in the Eastern Townships, you'll come across many, fascinating local varieties. But Dunham's Vignoble Orpailleur, with notes of apricot and honey dominating, is by far the best – it's won first or second place in its category at Canadian and international festivals, as well as showing up in restaurants like Toqué! in Montréal (p132).

English-language dramas play at **Piggery Theatre** and there's a choice of galleries as well as antique and craft shops. The town is touristy, but still a gorgeous little place with nice shops, activities and the **Galerie Jeannine Blais**, at the time of research the only gallery in Canada devoted entirely to art naif.

You will need to book as far ahead as possible if you are planning to stay in these parts, especially in summer when B&Bs are often booked solid for several weeks in advance. Be aware that in summer, many B&Bs also have a two-night minimum on weekends.

Sherbrooke is the region's main commercial center with several small museums, a wide selection of restaurants and a pleasant central core lying between two rivers. The 18km walking and cycling path along the Magog River, known as **Réseau Riverain**, makes for an agreeable stroll, beginning at the edge of the Magog River in Blanchard Park. Small but beautifully conceived museums, like the **Musée des Beaux-Arts** and the little known **Société de l'Histoire de Sherbrooke**, are centrally located. The latter in particular is tiny but packs a big punch, with its small, permanent exhibition on the town's history as well as temporary exhibitions; a tour of the city archives which are kept downstairs is included with the ticket price.

The city itself is lovely to take a wander around and has several enormous, outdoor wall murals that are great fun to seek out, while the **Lennoxville** borough is home to Bishop's, the English university, and the Golden Lion Brewing Company, which was Québec's first microbrewery.

Though it doesn't have much in the way of sights, try to make it to the **Coaticook** region. Although it's not on as many visitor's radars as other areas, given its lack of formal sights, it does have the prettiest scenery in the whole region, some wonderful cheese makers (get the cheese-route brochure from the tourist office) and the **Parc de la Gorge de Coaticook**, with the world's longest suspension bridge. Just going for a rambling day-long drive here would be more than worth it.

Cowansville is similar. With no particular sights to speak of, the town has done a bang-up job of identifying its historic homes and buildings with informative interpretation panels.

Information

Magog Tourist Office (☎ 819-843-2744; www.magogquebec.homestead.com; 55 rue Cabana, Magog; 8:30am-7pm summer, 8:30am-5pm winter)

Regional tourist office (☎ 450-375-8774; www.easterntownships.org; Aut 10, exit 68; usually 10am-7pm daily Jun-Sep, 9am-5pm Oct-May)

Sherbrooke tourist office (☎ 819-821-1919; www.tourismesherbrooke.com; 2964 rue King Ouest, Sherbrooke; 9am-7pm Jun 19-Aug 19, 9am-5pm Mon-Sat & 9am-3pm Sun rest of the year)

Sights & Activities

Galerie Jeannine Blais (☎ 819-842-2784; www.galeriejeannineblais.com/galerie/galerie.html; 102 rue Main, North Hatley)

Granby Zoo (☎ 450-372-9113; www.zoodegranby.ca; 525 rue St-Hubert, Granby; adult/child 3-11/child under 3/65 and over $25/16/free/20; 10am-7pm late Jun-late Aug, 10am-5pm late May-late June, 10am-5pm weekends only early Sep-early Oct)

La Société de l'Histoire de Sherbrooke (☎ 819-821-5406; 275 rue Dufferin Granby; adult/child $6/2; 9am-noon & 1-5pm Mon-Fri, 1-5pm Sat & Sun)

Lion d'Or (Golden Lion Brewing Company) (☎ 819-562-4589; www.lionlennoxville.com; 2 rue College, Lennoxville borough, Sherbrooke)

Musée des Beaux-Arts (☎ 819-821-2115; www.mbas.qc.ca; 241 rue Dufferin, Sherbrooke; adult/student & child/senior/child under 6 $7.50/5/6/free; 10am-5pm Tue-Sun Jun 24-Labour Day, noon-5pm Tue-Sun rest of year)

Parc de la Gorge de Coaticook (☎ 819-849-2331; 135 rue Michaud, Coaticook; admission adult/child/concession $6.52/3.91/6.08; 10am-7pm daily summer, call for winter times)

Parc du Mont-Orford (☎ 819-843-9855; www.parksquebec.com; 3321 ch du Parc, Canton d'Orford; adult/child age 6-17/family $3.50/1.50/7; year round; call for times)

Piggery Theatre (☎ 819-842-2431; www.piggery.com; 215 ch Simard, North Hatley)

Vignoble l'Orpailleur (☎ 819-295-2763; www.orpailleur.ca; 1086 rte 202, Dunham; 9am-5pm daily Apr 15-Dec 31, 11am-5pm Sat & Sun, Mon-Fri reservation only Dec 31-Apr 15) Arguably the province's best known wine producer, it's got a terrific little display on the history of alcohol in Québec as well as captions in the vineyards explaining the grape varieties and how they grow. Tours of l'Orpailleur can be arranged – call for information. The on-site restaurant often has shows after dinner – call for times.

Eating

Café Couleur (☎ 450-295-2222; 3819 rue Principale, Dunham; mains from $7.95; ⊗ Apr-Dec) A bright little café right in the centre of town with sandwiches, salads and an interesting selection of hot chocolate and loose teas.

Manoir Hovey (☎ 819-842-2971; 55 rue Principale, North Hatley; table d'hôte $60) A powerhouse of fine Québec cuisine with a monster wine list and expert service. If you are looking for a splurge in the Eastern Townships, this is it. The multi-course discovery menu goes on forever and is inspired by seasonal produce – prices will vary depending on the ingredients.

Sleeping

Au Temps des Mûres (☎ 450-266-1319; www.temps desmures.qc.ca; 2024 ch Vail, Dunham; r $65-80) Cozy without getting caught up in B&B kitsch, this place is helmed by a lovely family on an out-of-the-way dirt road.

Fantastic maple butter and other products from its maple grove appear at breakfast and are for sale.

Le Bocage (☎ 819-835-5653; www.lebocage.qc.ca; 200 ch de Moe's River, Compton; r from $95-225) From the welcome to the antiques, this Victorian gem of a B&B is flawless. A multi-course meal ($48) is served at 7pm and can feature dishes like quail, elk or deer. Reservations essential.

Le Marquis de Montcalm (☎ 819-823-7773; www .marquisdemontcalm.com; 797 rue Montcalm, Sherbrooke; r $89-114) Run by a charming family, this is a bright, airy B&B flooded everywhere with natural light. With sumptuous breakfasts and surprise flourishes in every accommodation – like the ceiling mural in the blue room.

Le Moulin de North Hatley (☎ 819-842-2380; 225 rue Mill, North Hatley; r $90-150) Now filled with rustic, brightly colored rooms, this former grist mill used to sit right next to the town's railroad. It's now run by Belgians who turn out some of the best fries in the region at the restaurant on the ground floor.

Directory

Directory

TRANSPORTATION

Both Montréal and Québec City are well served by major roads, rail lines and airways so are simple to reach. Depending on where you are coming from, if you are going to Québec City, you may have to transfer in Montréal first. Major airlines have links to the major airport, while roads and the public transit into the city centers are regular and efficient. Moving around within Montréal itself is a breeze thanks to its extensive métro and bus networks. Québec City has an extensive public transit system but it does not have a métro or sky train.

AIR

Airlines

In Montréal:
Airport information (☎ 394-7377, 800-465-1213; www.admtl.com; ☺ 6am-10pm) has details on departures and arrivals at Pierre Elliott Trudeau International and Mirabel Airports.

The following is a list of airlines that serve Montréal. Also see 'Air Line Companies' in the English section of the *Yellow Pages*.

Air Canada (☎ 888-247-2262; www.aircanada.ca)

Air France (☎ 800-667-2747; www.airfrance.com)

Air Tango (☎ 800-315-1390; www.flytango.com)

Air Transat (☎ 877-872-6728; www.airtransat.com)

American Airlines (☎ 800-433-7300; www.aa.com)

British Airways (☎ 800-247-9297; www.britishairways.com)

Continental Airlines (☎ 800-231-0856; www.continental.com)

Delta Air Lines (☎ 800-361-1970; www.delta.com)

KLM (☎ 800-225-2525; www.klm.com)

Lufthansa (☎ 800-563-5954; www.lufthansa.com)

Porter Airlines (☎ 888-619-8622; www.flyporter.com) This start-up airline offers direct flights between Montréal and downtown Toronto.

Northwest Airlines (☎ 800-225-2525; www.nwa.com)

Swiss International Air Lines (☎ 877-359-7947; www.swiss.com)

United Airlines (☎ 800-241-6522; www.united.com)

US Airways (☎ 800-432-9768; www.usairways.com)

In Québec City:
Airport information (☎ 418-640-2700; www.aeroportdequebec.com/html/english) has details on departures and arrivals at Aéroport de Québec-Jean Lesage International Airport.

The following is a list of airlines that serve Québec City.

Air Canada (☎ reservation 888-247-2262, general info 888-422-7533; www.aircanada.ca)

Air Canada Jazz (☎ reservation 888-247-2262, general info 888-422-7533; www.flyjazz.ca)

Air Inuit (☎ 800-361-2965; www.airinuit.com)

Air Labrador (☎ 800-563-3062; www.airlabrador.com)

Air Transat (☎ 877-872-6728; www.airtransat.com)

Continental Airlines (☎ 800-537-3444; www.continental.com)

Delta Air Lines (☎ 800-727-2555; www.delta.com)

Northwest Airlines (☎ 800-225-2525; www.nwa.com)

Airports

Montréal is served by **Pierre Elliott Trudeau International Airport** (PET; ☎ 394-7377, 800-465-1213; www.admtl.com), also known as Montréal Trudeau Airport. It's about 21km west of downtown and is the hub of most domestic, US and overseas flights. Mirabel Airport, about 50km northeast of downtown, serves mostly charter flights. PET Airport (coded as YSL) has good connections to the city by car or public bus and métro.

Driving to/from downtown Montréal from PET Airport takes 20 to 30 minutes (allow an hour during peak times). A common route into town is the Autoroute 13 Sud (south) that merges with the Autoroute 20 Est; this in turn takes you into the heart of downtown, along the main Autoroute Ville Marie (the 720).

By public transportation you'll need to catch the bus and switch to the métro.

Outside the arrivals hall at PET Airport, take bus 204 Est and ride to the bus transfer station at Gare Dorval (Dorval Train Station). Here you switch to bus 211 Est; get off at métro station **Lionel-Groulx** (Map pp310–11). Both buses run from 5am to 1am and the entire journey to town should take about an hour. To get to the airport from downtown, reverse the journey ($2.50 one way).

The **Québécois Bus Company** (☎ 931-9002) runs Aérobus shuttles from PET Airport to downtown. It stops at **Station Aérobus** (Map pp310–11, 30 minutes) and **Station Centrale de l'Autobus** (Map p315; 45 minutes). The trip downtown is offered every half-hour from 7am to 11:30pm. One-way/return tickets cost $13/22.75. At Station Aérobus, a shuttle will pick you up and drop you anywhere in downtown free of charge.

Québec City's **Aéroport de Québec-Jean Lesage International Airport** (☎ 418-640-2700; 500 rue Principal) has no shuttle buses or aerobus services to town. A taxi costs a flat fee of $30 to go into the city, around $12 if you're only going to the boroughs surrounding the airport. **Les Amis du Transport Roy & Morin** (☎ 418-622-65660) is a transit service for disabled people.

BICYCLE

Maps of Montréal's city's bicycle paths, including a 12km circuit that runs along the **Canal de Lachine** (p120), are available from the tourist offices and bicycle rental shops. Helmets and padlocks are provided for free.

The same goes in Québec City, where a free color map marks all the routes in down and beyond.

Rental

In Montreal:

Le Grand Cycle (Map pp316–17; ☎ 525-1414; www .velo.qc.ca; 901 rue Cherrier Est; Ⓜ Sherbrooke) Charges 4 hours/daily $20/30.

La Maison des Cyclistes (Map pp316–17; ☎ 521-8356; www.velo.qc.ca; 1251 rue Rachel Est; Ⓜ Mont-Royal) Charges $25 per day for mountain bikes.

Vélo-Tour (Map pp308–9; ☎ 236-8356; 99 rue de la Commune Est; Ⓜ Place-d'Armes)

In Québec City:

Cyclo Services (Map p220; ☎ 418-692-4052; 160 Quai St André) Charges $20 per day for mountain bikes.

Museovelo (Map p226; ☎ 418-523-9194; 463 rue St Jean) Charges $20 per day.

Bicycles on Public Transport

Bicycles can be taken on the métro from 10am to 3pm and after 7pm Monday to Friday, as well as throughout the weekend. Officially cyclists are supposed to board only the first two carriages of the train, but if it's not busy, no one seems to mind much where you board. The water shuttles to Parc Jean-Drapeau take bicycles at no extra charge.

You can't take bikes on buses in Québec City.

BOAT

Cruise vessels ply the St Lawrence River but there are no frequent and affordable passenger services to/from Montréal. Services to/from Québec City include:

AML Cruises (☎ 842-9300; www.croisieresaml.com; admin 530 rue Andre St) Links Montréal and Québec City via a day-long cruise, once a week during the summer. The boat leaves at 8am from Quai King Edward and arrives in Québec City at 5pm, and there is a return trip by bus at 10pm the same night. Tickets include breakfast and lunch and are only slightly cheaper without the return coach. Be sure to reserve ahead.

Canadian Connection Cruises (☎ 800-267-7868; www .stlawrencecruiselines.com; 253 Ontario St, Kingston) Offers four- to six-day luxury cruises between Kingston, Ontario and Québec City, including meals, accommodations and onboard entertainment. Six-night cruises cost $1952 in high season; bank on at least twice that for cruises to/from the US states of New England or New York.

BUS & MÉTRO

Montréal has a modern and convenient bus and métro system which is run by STM (☎ 786-4636 + 8 for English). The métro, the city's subway system, is extensive and aging and delays in recent years have been a fixture for commuters. However, the aging cars are starting to be replaced so things should be much improved by the time you read this. This system is still the best way to get around town. The métro schedule for each line is different. Generally the trains run from 6am to midnight from Sunday to Thursday, but later on Friday and Saturday when they run from 6am to 1:30am.

Tickets have magnetic strips; in the métro stations you must insert them into the turnstiles before you can pass. If you're going through the turnstile next to the ticket booth, put the ticket in the slot by the ticket teller as he or she has to buzz you through.

One ticket can get you anywhere in the city with a connecting bus or métro train. If you're switching between buses, or between bus and métro, you should get a free transfer slip, which is called a *correspondance,* from the driver; on the métro take one from the machines just past the turnstiles

A strip of six tickets (a *lisière* in French) costs $11.50 and single tickets cost $2.50. Buses take tickets or cash but drivers won't give change.

Tourists can buy day passes for $9 or three-day passes for $17, but a weekly card (valid Monday to Sunday) may be better for $18.50.

If you're going to be in town for a calendar month and plan to rely on public transport, buy a monthly pass ($63). It can be shared, as no picture identification is required.

Métro stops are indicated above ground by large blue signs with a white arrow pointing down. A map of the métro network is included at the back of this book (Map p320).

Greyhound (☎ 842-2281; www.greyhound.com) Operates long-distance routes to Ottawa, Toronto, Vancouver and the USA.

Limocar (☎ 450-681-3111; www.limocar.com) A good connection to Mont-Tremblant from Montréal.

Moose Travel (☎ 287-1220; www.moosenetwork .com) Operates a circuit where you jump on and jump off, with pickup points in Montréal, Québec City, Ottawa and Toronto. It also has links to Mont-Tremblant in the Laurentians.

Orléans Express (☎ 888-999-3977; www.orleansexpress .com) Makes the three-hour run between Montréal and Québec City.

Station Centrale d'Autobus (Map p315; ☎ 842-2281; 505 boul de Maisonneuve Est; Ⓜ Berri-UQAM) The main terminal for bus links to Canadian and US destinations. Allow about 45 minutes before departure to buy a ticket; most advance tickets don't guarantee a seat, so arrive early to line up at the counter.

Voyageur (☎ 800-661-8747) Covers the Montréal-Québec City route as well as Montréal–Ottawa. For more info, access them through www.greyhound.ca).

Québec City has a clean, efficient bus system (Réseau de Transport de la Capitale). A bus ticket anywhere in town is $2.25 and a day pass $5.80. A monthly pass goes for $68.

Terminus Gare du Palais (Map p220; ☎ 418-525-3000; 320 rue Abraham-Martin) is the main bus station. If you're coming from Montréal, your bus may stop at **Ste-Foy-Sillery station** (☎ 418-650-0087, 3001 ch des Quatre Bourgeois), so ask first before you get off.

CALÈCHE

These picturesque horse-drawn carriages seen meandering around Old Montréal and on Mont Royal charge about $75 for a tour. They line up at the Old Port and at pl d'Armes. Drivers usually provide running commentary, which can serve as a pretty good historical tour.

In Québec you'll find them just inside the Porte St-Louis.

CAR & MOTORCYCLE
Driving

Fines for traffic violations, from speeding to not wearing a seat belt, are stiff in Québec. You may see few police cars on the roads but radar traps are common. Motorcyclists are required to wear helmets and to drive with their lights on.

Traffic in both directions must stop when school buses stop to let children get off and on. At the white-striped pedestrian crosswalks, cars must stop to allow pedestrians to cross the road. Turning right on red lights is legal everywhere in Québec, including Québec City, but it is illegal in Montréal.

Continental US highways link directly with their Canadian counterparts along the border at numerous points. These roads meet up with the Trans-Canada Highway, which runs directly through Montréal. During the summer and on holiday weekends, waits of several hours are common at major USA–Canada border crossings. If possible avoid Detroit, Michigan; Windsor, Ontario; Fort Erie, Ontario; Buffalo, New York; Niagara Falls on both sides of the border; and Rouse's Point, New York. Smaller crossings are almost always quiet.

If you have difficulty with the French-only signs in Québec, pick up a decent provincial highway map, sold at service stations and usually free at tourist offices.

Visitors with US or British passports are allowed to bring their vehicles into Canada for six months.

Rental

PET Airport has many international car rental firms, and there's a host of smaller operators in Montréal. Whether you're here or in Québec City, rates will swing with demand so it's worth phoning around to see what's on offer. Booking ahead usually gets the best rates, and airport rates are normally better than those in town. A small car might cost $40 to $50 per day with unlimited mileage, taxes and insurance, or $150 to $300 per week plus 7% sales tax.

To rent a car in Québec you must be at least 21 years old and have had a driver's license for at least a year. Drivers 21 to 25 years of age might have to provide a deposit of up to $500. Rentals are cheaper on weekends, although you can snag good weekday deals, too.

In Montréal:

Avis (Map pp310–11; ☎ 800-321-3652; 1225 rue Metcalfe; ☽ 7am-7pm Mon-Wed, 7am-9pm Thu-Fri, 7am-5pm Sat, 8am-7pm Sun; Ⓜ Peel)

Budget (Map pp310–11; ☎ 866-7675; www.budget .com; 95 rue de la Gauchetière Ouest, in Gare Centrale; ☽ 7:30am-6pm Mon-Fri, 9am-5pm Sat & Sun; Ⓜ Bonaventure)

Discount Car (Map pp310–11; ☎ 286-1929, 800-263-2355; www.discountcar.com; 607 boul de Maisonneuve Ouest; ☽ 7:30am-7pm Mon, 7:30am-6pm Tue-Thu, 7:30am-8pm Fri, 8am-5pm Sat & 9am-5pm Sun; Ⓜ McGill)

Hertz (Map pp310–11; ☎ 938-1717, 800-263-0678; www.hertz.com; 1073 rue Drummond; ☽ 7am-9pm Mon-Fri, 7am-7pm Sat, 8am-9pm Sun; Ⓜ Lucien-L'Allier)

Rent-a-Wreck (Map pp308–9; ☎ 866-979-5500, 343-5500; www.rentawreck.ca; 7146 Côte-des-Neiges; ☽ 8am-5pm Mon-Fri, 8am-4pm Sat; Ⓜ Côte-des-Neiges)

Zap World Scooters (Map p314; ☎ 289-9927; near Quai Alexandra, Old Port; ☽ 10am-9pm daily late June-early Sep; adult/child per 30 min $18/12; inline skates per hr from $9.50) Whiz around the Old Port on a miniscooter – 'the future of transportation.' Safety helmets are included.

In Québec:

Budget (Map p220; ☎ 866-7675; www.budget.com; 29 Côte-du-Palais)

Hertz (Map p226; ☎ 418-647-4949; 580 Grande-Allée Est; ☽ 7:30am-6pm Mon-Fri, 8am-5pm Sat & Sun)

TAXI

Flag fall is a standard $2.75 plus another $1.30 per kilometer. From PET Airport to downtown Montréal the fare is a flat $31, and from Mirabel Airport it's $69. Prices are posted on the windows inside taxi-cabs. Try **Taxi Diamond** (☎ 273-6331) or **Taxi Co-Op** (☎ 636-6666). In Québec City the biggest company is **Taxi Coop Quebec** (☎ 525-5191)

TRAIN

Canada's trains are arguably the most enjoyable and romantic way to travel the country. Long-distance trips are quite a bit more expensive than those by bus however, and reservations are crucial for weekend and holiday travel. A few days' notice can cut fares a lot.

Montréal's **Gare Centrale** (Central Station; Map pp310–11) is the local hub of **VIA Rail** (☎ 989-2626, 800-361-5390; www.viarail .ca) and in Québec it's **Gare du Palais** (Map p220; ☎ 989-2626; 450 rue de la Gare-du-Palais).

Service is very good along the so-called Québec City–Windsor corridor that connects Montréal with Ottawa, Kingston, Toronto and Niagara Falls. Drinks and snacks are served from aisle carts, and some trains have a dining and bar car.

AMT commuter trains (☎ 869-3200; www .amt.qc.ca) serves the suburbs of Montréal. Services from Gare Centrale are fast but infrequent, with two-hour waits between some trains. Gare Windsor is used for just a few commuter trains.

TRAVEL AGENTS

In Montréal:

American Express (Map pp310–11; ☎ 284-3300, 800-668-2639; 1141 boul de Maisonneuve; ☽ 9am-5pm Mon-Fri; Ⓜ Peel) Standard Amex travel and banking services: plane tickets, traveler's checks, travel insurance.

Boutique Tourisme Jeunesse (Map pp316–17; ☎ 844-0287, 866-461-8585; 205 ave Mont-Royal; ☽ 10am-6pm

Mon-Wed, 10am-9pm Thu & Fri, noon-5pm Sat, 10am-5:30pm Sun; Ⓜ Mont Royal) This well-stocked youth-travel boutique sells books, maps, travel insurance, student ID cards and plane tickets.

Voyages Campus (Map p315; ☎ 843-8511, 866-246-9762; www.travelcuts.ca; 1613 rue St-Denis; ⏱ 9am-5pm Mon-Tue, 9:30am-5pm Thu & Fri; 10am-3pm Sat; Ⓜ Berri-UQAM) Eight locations in Montréal. Sells student ID cards and air tickets, and has details of working holidays and language courses. Known as Travel CUTS outside Québec.

In Québec City:

American Express (Map p205; ☎ 658-8820, 800-668-2639; pl Laurier)

Boutique Tourisme Jeunesse (Map p226; ☎ 522-2552, 866-461-8585; 94 boul René-Levesque)

Voyages Campus (Map p205; ☎ 654-0224, 866-246-9762; www.travelcuts.ca; Pavilion Maurice-Pollack, Local 1258, Université Laval; ⏱ 9am-5pm Mon-Fri)

PRACTICALITIES

The flow of visitor information in Montréal and Québéc City is astonishingly good.

ACCOMMODATIONS

In Montréal the average room rate is about $130 with seasonal variations. The lowest period is from January to March and the highest period is from mid-June to August, when tourist travel is at its peak. However, the weakness of the American dollar lately (or strength of the Canadian dollar) has had an impact on tourism to Montréal, so if this is still the case when you visit you may find room rates somewhat lower. Rates for the business hotels drop on weekends, while the rates for the tourist hotels tend to rise. You can book a hotel room through Montréal's main tourist office, the **Centre Infotouriste** (p278), and a variety of booking services. See p190 for more information on the price ranges used in this book. Accommodations are organised in the Sleeping chapter under neighborhood headings and are then listed in budget order.

In Québec the average hotel room rate will be somewhat higher in summer and during winter carnival, generally around $150. You can book rooms at the **Bureau d'Information Touristique du Vieux-Québec** (Map p220). Note that some hotels include taxes in their quoted prices – 6% GST, 7.5% provincial sales tax plus a 'hospitality tax' of anywhere from 2% to 4% per person per night – while others don't.

BUSINESS HOURS

Most banks in Montréal and Québec City are open 10am to 3pm Monday to Wednesday and Friday, and 10am to 7pm Thursday. Government offices generally open 9am to 5pm weekdays. Post offices are open 8am to 5pm Monday to Friday. More and more drugstores are adding postal franchises in their stores however and may offer limited postal services on weekends.

Hours for museums vary but most open at 10am or 11am and close by 6pm. Most are closed Monday but stay open late on Wednesday.

Restaurants typically open 11am to 2:30pm and 5:30pm to 11pm; cafés serving breakfast may open at 8am or 9am. Many bars and pubs open 11am till midnight or longer; don't expect slicker places to open before 5pm or so.

Some attractions outside Montréal shut down completely or operate sporadic hours in winter (May to September). In Québec City, some attractions close down completely outside of peak periods.

CHILDREN

Montréal is a kid-friendly town. There's no time to be bored.

The **Tour De La Ronde Amusement Park** (p82) in Parc Jean-Drapeau will keep the little ones entertained all day in summer. Another good bet is the **Montréal Planetarium** (p86) or the creepy-crawlies at the **Insectarium** (p97) in the Jardin Botanique. The Old Port area offers a number of popular options, such as the interactive **Centre de Sciences** and the **IMAX Cinema** (p80). The abundance of bicycle paths that weave through green surrounds offers a great diversion for kids, especially along the **Canal de Lachine** (p120) from the Old Port.

Québec City, with its old architecture, guides dressed in period costume and military attractions, is also packed with activities of interest to kids. See p219 for more ideas on travel with kids in the provincial capital.

Lonely Planet's *Travel with Children* also has some valuable tips.

Babysitting

Many hotels can provide referrals to reliable, qualified babysitting services. Some well-known services include **Denise Miller** (☎ 365-3111) and **Domesti-Serv** (☎ 426-7277). Going rates are $12 an hour for one to two children and $15 for three to four children, with a surcharge applying after midnight.

In Québec City, you may have difficulty finding an English-speaking babysitter through the agencies. Your best bet is to inquire at your accommodation, as most hotels have a list of English-speaking child carers for guests.

CLIMATE

Even the earliest European explorers were surprised by the seasonal extremes of Montréal. Summer arrives late in Montréal, with temperatures still very changeable into early June. From July it can get brutally hot and steamy, and highs of 25°C or 30°C keep people wearing shorts until late August, but the nights soon turn chilly. Fall comes in a burst of color in late September.

Global warming has dulled winter's edge to daytime temps of -20°C to -6°C, but unfortunately not the frigid razor-blasts of air that can pop the wind-chill factor to -30°C or lower. Snow arrives in November and can pile high in some areas till mid-March. Blasts of wind down the St Lawrence River valley bring a cold damp that seems to creep into your bones and makes Montréal's underground city an attractive refuge.

Winters in Québec City are a few degrees colder than Montréal. In the height of the season in mid January, many people don snowsuits while doing their errands.

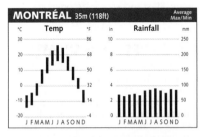

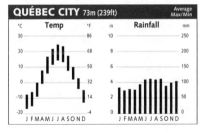

COURSES

Montréal has a bewildering number of courses available, from one-day evening workshops to full-blown instruction lasting several months. Options for short-term visitors tend to be limited, but be sure to check the classifieds in free weeklies like *Mirror* or *Hour* for what's on.

Québec City also has a fantastic range of courses, but nothing in English.

Cooking

For an overview of what's on offer, go to www.montrealfood.com/cookclass.html. Most French cooking courses are offered in French only; Italian and other cuisine courses are available in English.

Académie Culinaire du Québec (Map p314; ☎ 393-8111; 360 Champ de Mars; **M** Champ-de-Mars) This esteemed cooking academy conducts regular cooking workshops and short courses (in French) starting at $40 for a two-hour class.

Mezza Luna Cooking School (Map p318; ☎ 271-2057; 6851 rue St-Dominique; **M** De Castelnau) Single sessions on Italian cooking (in French, English and Italian) known far beyond Montréal's borders ($40 per class). Elena Faita gives free demonstrations on pasta-making every Saturday at 2pm at the Quincaillerie Dante (same address).

Language

For courses in Québec City, see p231.

As a French-English university town, Montréal is a popular place to learn a foreign language. University courses and language schools abound.

Concordia University (Map pp308–9; ☎ 848-2424; 1455 boul de Maisonneuve; **M** Guy-Concordia) Runs 10-week French courses in spring and fall, from $215.

McGill University (Map pp310–11; ☎ 398-6160; www.mc gill.ca; 688 rue Sherbrooke Ouest; **M** McGill) Year-round, accredited intensive and part-time courses in French.

Montréal International Language Centre (Map pp310–11; ☎ 939-2056; www.cilm.qc.ca; 2000 rue Ste-Catherine Ouest; Ⓜ Atwater) Tailor-made language courses at this offshoot of LaSalle University.

YMCA (Map pp310–11; ☎ 849-8393; www.ymca.ca; 1450 rue Stanley; Ⓜ Peel) Offers day and evening French courses, four to six weeks, along with courses in Spanish and Italian.

CUSTOMS

For the latest customs information, contact the Canadian embassy or consulate at home. Don't get caught bringing in illegal drugs as sentences can be harsh. Mace, pepper spray, pistols and firearms (except hunting rifles) are also prohibited. Most fruit, vegetables and plants can be confiscated, so avoid or ask ahead.

Visitors to Canada aged 18 and older can bring up to 1.14L (40oz) of liquor or 24 12oz cans of beer or ale, and up to 50 cigars, 200 cigarettes, 200g of tobacco and 400 tobacco sticks into Canada – but all these items are cheaper in the USA. The value of alcohol and tobacco is limited to $200 within 48 hours and $750 within seven days. You can also bring in gifts valued up to $60 plus a 'reasonable amount' (up to the agent's discretion) of personal effects.

Visitors returning to the USA can bring home US$800 worth of foreign goods duty-free within a 48-hour period. The allowance drops to US$200 for shorter periods. US residents aged 21 and older may bring back 1L of alcohol, and people of all ages are allowed 200 cigarettes and 100 non-Cuban cigars.

Duty-free limits for the UK are 200 cigarettes or 50 cigars, 1L of spirits or 2L of fortified or sparkling wine, 2L of still table wine, 60ml of perfume, 250ml of toilet water plus $145 worth of other goods and souvenirs.

Australian residents aged 18 and up can bring home A$900 of gifts and souvenirs, 250 cigarettes or tobacco and 2.25L of alcohol. Residents aged under 18 may bring back $450 worth of goods.

DISCOUNT CARDS

The Montréal Museums Pass allows free access to 32 museums for three days plus a three-day bus pass. It's available from the city's tourist offices ($45). You can also get it without the bus card for $35.

An International Student Identity Card (ISIC) can pay for itself through half-price admissions, discounted air and ferry tickets and cheap meals in student caféterias. In Montréal, ISIC cards are issued by Voyages Campus (www.travelcuts.com) and other student travel agencies. The price will depend on what country you buy it in. The International Student Travel Confederation (www.istc.org) is another good source for ISIC cards.

In Québec City, the Québec City Museum Card is $40 and you get free access for three consecutive days to 24 sights and activities including the major museums and the Lévis ferry. Also included is a stack of coupons for discounts at other attractions and two free day-passes for public transit. Buy it at participating museums or at the tourist office.

ELECTRICITY

Canada, like the USA, operates on 110V, 60-cycle electric power. Non–North American visitors should bring a plug adapter for their own small appliances. Note that any gadgets like hair dryers built for higher voltage and cycles (such as 220/240V, 50-cycle appliances from Europe) will probably run more slowly.

Canadian electrical goods have a plug with two flat, vertical prongs (the same as the USA and Mexico) or sometimes a three-pronger with the added ground prong. Most sockets can accommodate both types.

EMBASSIES & CONSULATES

All foreign embassies are located in Ottawa, but Montréal has fairly good consular services. Only the main consulates are listed here; check the *Yellow Pages* for a detailed list. Australian citizens should call the Australian High Commission (☎ 613-236-0841; 710-50 O'Connor St, Ottawa).

In Montreal:

Denmark (Map pp310–11; ☎ 877-3060; 1 pl Ville-Marie; www.danish-embassy-canada.com; ☾ 9am-5pm Mon-Fri)

France (Map pp310–11; ☎ 878-4385; www.consulfrance-montreal.org; 1 pl Ville Marie; ☾ 8:30am-noon Mon-Fri)

Germany (Map pp310–11; ☎ 931-2277; www.montreal.diplo.de; 1250 boul René-Lévesque Ouest; ☾ 9am-noon Mon-Fri)

Italy (Map pp310–11; ☎ 849-8351; www.italconsul.mon treal.qc.ca; 3489 rue Drummond; ☽ 10am-4pm Mon-Fri)

Japan (Map pp310–11; ☎ 866-3429; www.montreal .ca.emb-japan.go.jp; 600 rue de la Gauchetière Ouest; ☽ 9am-noon & 2-5pm Mon-Fri)

Netherlands (Map pp310–11; ☎ 849-4247; www .dutchconsulatemontreal.org; 1002 rue Sherbrooke Ouest, ste 2201; ☽ 8:30am-1:15pm & 2-5:15pm Mon-Fri)

Switzerland (Map pp310–11; ☎ 932-7181; www.eda .admin.ch; 1572 ave Docteur-Penfield; ☽ 10am-1pm Mon-Fri)

UK (Map pp310–11; ☎ 866-5863; www.britishhigh commission.gov.uk; 1000 rue de la Gauchetière Ouest; ☽ 8:30am-noon & 1-5pm Mon-Fri)

USA (Map pp310–11; ☎ 398-9695; www.usembassycanada .gov; 1155 rue St-Alexandre; ☽ 8:30am-noon Mon-Fri)

In Québec City:

France (Map p205; ☎ 694-2294; www.consulfrance -quebec.org; 25 rue St-Louis)

Italy (Map p205; ☎ 529-9801; 355 23e rue; ☽ 10am-4pm Mon-Fri)

Netherlands (Map p205; ☎ 525-8334; 1040 ave Belvédère, Ste-Foy-Sillery)

USA (Map p220; ☎ 692-2095; www.usembassycanada .gov; 2 pl Terrasse Dufferin; ☽ 8:30am-noon Mon-Fri)

EMERGENCY

When in doubt, call ☎ 0 and ask the operator for assistance.

Poison Centre	☎ 1800-463-5060
Police, ambulance, fire	☎ 911
Police (less urgent)	☎ 280-2222

GAY & LESBIAN TRAVELERS

Fugues is the free, French-language, authoritative monthly guide to the gay and lesbian scene for the entire province of Québec. It's an excellent place to find out about the latest and greatest naughty club or gay-friendly accommodation.

Montréal's sexual enlightenment makes the city a popular getaway for lesbian, gay and bisexual travelers. The gay community is focused in the Village, and it's huge business. Gay Pride Week attracts hundreds of thousands in early August, and the Black & Blue Festival fills the Olympic Stadium for a mega-fest in early October.

Gays and lesbians are well integrated into the community – in the Plateau, two men holding hands in public will get little more than a quick look of curiosity, though in other areas of the city (outside of the Village of course) it may attract a lot of attention.

In Montréal:

Centre d'Information Gay Touristique du Village (Map p315; ☎ 888-595-8110; www.infogayvillage.com; 1260 rue Ste-Catherine Est, Bureau 209) The Village's gay business-information source, with scads of tourist maps, brochures and referrals to local hotels, restaurants and saunas.

Gay Line (☎ 866-5090; www.gayline.qc.ca; ☽ 7-11pm) Provides information, counseling and referrals to organizations within the gay community.

In Québec City:

Québec City is a conservative town with a more village feel to it – open displays of affection between same-sex couples will attract a lot of attention. There's a tiny but close-knit gay community centered around the club action at **Le Drague** (p243).

HOLIDAYS

Banks, schools and government offices close on Canadian public holidays, while museums and other services go on a restricted schedule. A rising tide of buses, trains and cars flood the transport routes on the days either side, and the Laurentian resorts get very busy with day-trippers from Montréal.

While not an official holiday, National Aboriginal Day falls on June 21 when Canada's heritage of First Nations, Inuit and Métis cultures is celebrated at public and private institutions.

Residential leases in Montréal traditionally end on June 30, so the roads are always clogged on July 1 as tenants move to their new homes.

The main public holidays are:

New Year's Day January 1

Good Friday & Easter Monday late March to mid-April

Victoria Day May 24 or nearest Monday

Jean-Baptiste Day June 24

Canada Day July 1

Labour Day first Monday in September

Canadian Thanksgiving second Monday in October

Remembrance Day November 11

Christmas Day December 25

Boxing Day December 26

INSURANCE

A policy covering theft, medical expenses, and compensation for cancellation or delays in your travel arrangements is highly recommended. If any items are lost or stolen, make sure you get a police report right away or your insurer might not pay up.

The travel policies handled by **Voyages Campus** (p269) or other student organizations are usually good value. The largest seller of medical insurance to visitors to Canada is **Trent Health** (☎ 800-216-3588; www.travelinsurance.ca), which offers policies from seven days to one year.

INTERNET ACCESS

Internet providers big and small have local dial-up numbers in Montréal and Québec City. MSN has given up providing access in Canada but you can access **AOL** (☎ 807-8185) and **Earthlink** (☎ 876-1183). Good local providers include **Videotron** (☎ 599-2743) and **Inter.net** (☎ 599-2743).

Battlenet 24 (Map pp310–11; ☎ 846-3333; 1407 rue du Fort; per hr $3.50; ☺ 24hr; Ⓜ Guy-Concordia)

Chapters (Map pp310–11; ☎ 849-8825; 1171 rue Ste-Catherine Ouest; $2 per 20 min; ☺ 9am-11pm; Ⓜ Peel)

Intertainment Café (Map pp310-11; ☎ 788-8008; 1425 boul René-Lévesque; per 30/60 min $2.25/3.50; ☺ 8am-midnight Mon-Thu, 8pm-2am Fri, noon-2am Sat, noon-midnight Sun; Ⓜ Lucien-L'Allier)

Net.24 (Map pp310–11; ☎ 845-9634; 2157 rue Mackay; per hr $4; ☺ 24 hr; Ⓜ McGill)

Tribune Café (Map p315; ☎ 840-0915; 1567 rue St-Denis; per 30 min $2.88; ☺ 7:30am-10:30pm Mon-Fri, 7:30am-11:30pm Sat & Sun; Ⓜ Sherbrooke)

In Québec City, internet cafés aren't as ubiquitous. However, many hotels, inns and guesthouses have a computer with free internet in their lobbies for guests.

Centre Internet (Map p220; ☎ 692-3359; 52 Côte-du-Palais; per hour $6.50; ☺ 9:30am-9.30pm) Centrally located in the Old Town, this is the best place with the fastest connections.

LEGAL MATTERS

If you're charged with an offense, you have the right to public counsel if you can't afford a lawyer. In that case see our listings, following.

The blood-alcohol limit while driving is 0.08%. Driving motorized vehicles including boats and snowmobiles under the influence of alcohol is a serious offense in Canada. You could land in jail with a court date, heavy fine and a suspended license. The minimum drinking age is 18 – this is the same age as for obtaining a driving license.

It's an offense to consume alcohol anywhere other than at a residence or licensed premises, which technically puts parks, beaches and the rest of the great outdoors off-limits.

If you need English-language legal help in Québec City, contact the Québec Law Network (below) for help finding an English-speaking lawyer.

McGill Legal Information Clinic (Map pp310–11; ☎ 398-6792; www.mlic.mcgill.ca/; 3480 rue McTavish; ☺ 9am-5pm Mon-Fri) Staffed by law students who dispense free information and suggestions for whatever bind you're in.

Québec Law Network (Map pp310–11; ☎ 722-9944; www.avocat.qc.ca; 4841 Elmview, Bureau 100) A professional legal service for the general public on a call or walk-in basis (its office is in the suburb Dollard Des Ormeaux, on the anglo-western part of Montréal island). A telephone appointment costs $44.95.

MAPS

If you're going to explore the cities in detail, the hands-down best maps are published by Mapart – indeed, some local bookstores don't stock anything else. The yellow-covered *Montréal Urban Community* takes in the entire island, while the larger-scale *Montréal Explorateur* focuses on downtown. Both versions highlight a wealth of tourist attractions in easy-to-read colors. If you are planning to do some traveling around, Mapart's *Deluxe Road Atlas of Québec* ($29.95) is fantastic. Along with road maps for the entire province, it features blown-up maps of the central districts of Montréal, Québec City and Trois-Rivières, among dozens of other smaller towns which are included at the back of the book.

Rand McNally's *Montréal & Québec City* gives a clear overview of both cities but without Mapart's depth of detail.

Rental-car firms offer maps as well, sometimes for free.

MEDICAL SERVICES

Canadian healthcare is excellent but it's not free to visitors, so be sure to get travel insurance before you leave home. Canada has no reciprocal healthcare with other countries and nonresidents will have to pay up front for treatment and wait for the insurance payback.

Medical treatment is expensive: a standard city hospital bed will cost around $600 a day and can rocket to $2500 a day for nonresidents. Healthcare cutbacks mean that you might end up having to wait several hours in a Montréal emergency room if your condition isn't labeled as being 'urgent.'

Clinics

For minor ailments, visit the CLSC (Community health center; Map pp310–11; ☎ 934-0354; 1801 boul de Maisonneuve) downtown or call ☎ 527-2361 for the address of the closest one. Expect to pay cash up front, as checks and credit cards are usually not accepted. You should contact your travel-insurance agency first for referrals, if you intend to make a claim later. Your consulate (see p272) should also have a list of specialists in the Montréal area.

Emergency Rooms

In Montréal:

Montréal General Hospital (Map pp310–11; ☎ 934-1934 ext 42190; 1650 ave Cedar; Ⓜ Guy-Concordia)

Royal Victoria Hospital (Map pp310-11; ☎ 934-1934 ext 31557; 687 ave des Pins Ouest; Ⓜ McGill)

In Québec City:

Hôpital Laval (Map p205; ☎ 656-8711; 2725 ch Ste-Foy)

METRIC SYSTEM

Canada changed from imperial measurement to the metric system in the 1970s.

All speed limits are in kilometers per hour and gasoline is sold in liters. Radio stations straddle the fence, often giving temperatures in both degrees Celsius and Fahrenheit.

Measurements in this book are given in metric units.

MONEY

Prices quoted in this book are in Canadian dollars ($) unless stated otherwise. Canadian coins come in one-cent (penny), five-cent (nickel), 10-cent (dime), 25-cent (quarter), $1 (loonie) and $2 (toonie) pieces. Amounts less than $1 are shown in cents with a ¢ symbol following the amount (eg 25 cents is 25¢). The gold-colored 'loonie' features the loon, a common water bird.

Paper currency comes in $5 (blue), $10 (purple), $20 (green) and $50 (red) denominations. The $100 (brown) and larger bills are less common. Given rampant counterfeiting many stores flat-out refuse to take $100 and even sometimes $50 bills. This is not really legally allowed, unless there is some real reason to believe the bills are fake, but many stores insist on such a policy.

ATMs

Montréal has droves of ATMs linked to the international Cirrus, Plus and Maestro networks – not only in banks, but also in pubs, convenience stores and hotels. Many charge a small fee per use, and your own bank may levy an extra fee – check before leaving home.

Currency & Exchange Rates

There's a handy currency converter at www.oanda.com.

Changing Money

Change a little money before you arrive. The main shopping streets, including rue Ste-Catherine, boul St-Laurent and rue St-Denis, have plenty of banks, indicated by the $ symbol on the maps in the back of this book. There are also foreign-exchange desks in the departures and arrivals sections of PET Airport and Aéroport de Québec-Jean Lesage International Airport.

In Montréal:

American Express (Map pp310–11; ☎ 284-3300, 800-668-2639; 1141 boul de Maisonneuve; ☉ 9am-5pm Mon-Fri; Ⓜ Peel)

Thomas Cook (Map pp310–11; ☎ 284-7388; Centre Eaton, 705 rue Ste-Catherine Ouest)

In Québec City:

Transchange International (Map p220; ☎ 694-6906; 43 rue de Baude)

Credit Cards

Call these numbers to report lost/stolen cards:

American Express	☎ 800-528-4800
Diner's Club	☎ 800-234-6377
Discover	☎ 800-347-2683
MasterCard	☎ 800-307-7309
Visa	☎ 800-336-8472

Traveler's Checks

In Canada, traveler's checks are as good as cash. Many establishments, not just banks, will accept them like cash, provided they're in Canadian dollars. The major advantage of traveler's checks over cash is that they can be replaced if lost or stolen. They offer good exchange rates but not necessarily better than those from ATMs.

If your traveler's checks are lost or stolen, call the appropriate toll-free numbers: **American Express** (☎ 1-800-221-7282), **Thomas Cook** (☎ 1-800-223-7373), **Visa** (☎ 1-800-227-6811). Keeping a record of the check numbers will help you to get a swift refund.

NEWSPAPERS & MAGAZINES

In Montréal, the *Montreal Gazette* is the only English-language daily and covers national affairs, politics and arts. The Friday and Saturday editions are packed with entertainment listings. Alternative weeklies *Mirror* and *Hour* contain local news and entertainment.

The national newspapers are the *Globe and Mail* and *National Post*, both published in Toronto, and both with arts sections that cover events across the country.

Readers of French can pick up the federalist *La Presse,* as well as the separatist-leaning *Le Devoir*, which does wonderful features on Québec's francophone movers and shakers. *Le Journal de Montréal* is a tabloid and the biggest circulation French daily in Canada. Check *Voir* and *Ici* for entertainment info in French.

Maclean's and *Saturday Night* are Canada's chief general-interest magazines. *Canadian Geographic* has excellent articles and photography on a range of (primarily Canadian) topics. *L'actualité* is the Québec monthly news magazine.

PHARMACIES

The big chains are Pharmaprix and Jean Coutu. Many stores are large and well stocked, and some branches are open late.

In Montréal:

Jean Coutu (Map pp310–11; ☎ 866-7791; 974 rue Ste-Catherine Ouest; ⊗ 8am-10pm Mon-Fri, 9am-10pm Sat, 10am-8pm Sun)

Pharmaprix (Map pp310–11; ☎ 933-4744; 1500 rue Ste-Catherine Ouest; ⊗ 8am-midnight daily) Also has a 24-hour location near **Mont Royal** (Map pp308–9; ☎ 738-8464; 5122 ch de la Côtes-des-Neiges).

In Québec:

Jean Coutu (Map p226; ☎ 418- 522-1235; 110 boul René-Lévesque Ouest; ⊗ 9am-9pm Mon-Sat, 10am-9pm Sun)

POST

Montréal's **Main Post Office** (Map pp310–11; 1250 rue University) is the largest but there are many convenient locations around town. Poste restante (general delivery) is available at **Station pl-d'Armes** (Map p314; 435 rue St-Antoine, Montréal H2Z 1H0) – mail is kept for two weeks and then gets returned to the sender. The main **Canada Post/Postes Canada** (☎ 800-267-1177) number handles queries for all offices.

In Québec City the **post office** (Map p220; 5 rue du Fort) in the Upper Town offers the biggest selection of postal services.

Postal Rates

Stamps are available at post offices but also at newspaper shops, convenience stores and hotels. The national mail service, Canada Post/Postes Canada, is neither quick nor cheap but it's reliable. Standard 1st-class airmail letters or postcards cost 51¢ to Canadian destinations and 89¢ to the USA (both are limited to 30g). Those to other destinations cost $1.49 (their limit is also 30g).

RADIO

In Montreal:

CBC 2 (93.5 FM, streaming) Classical and jazz.

CBC Montréal 1 (88.5 FM, streaming) Chief channel for news, educational and cultural programs in English.

CHOM (97.7 FM) Rock and alternative.

CISM (89.3) Université de Montréal station, indie francophone music.

CJAD (800AM) Talk radio.

CJFM (95.9 FM) Pop and easy listening.

CKGM (990AM) Oldies.

Q92 (92.5 FM, streaming) Soft rock and oldies.

Radio Canada (95.3FM) French equivalent of CBC Montréal 1.

In Québec City:

CBC Québec 1 (104.7 FM, streaming) Chief channel for news, educational and cultural programs in English.

CFOM (102.9FM) French-language oldies.

CHIK (98.9) Pop, francophone music; French language.

CHRC (80FM) French-language news.

CHYZ (94.3FM) French-language student radio from Université Laval.

Radio-Canada (106.3 FM) French-language news, talk, culture.

Rock Détente (107.3) Rock music; French language.

SAFETY

Violent crime is rare (especially involving foreigners) but petty theft is more common. Watch out for pickpockets in crowded markets and public transit places, and use hotel safes where available.

Cars with foreign registration are popular targets for smash-and-grab theft. Don't leave valuables in the car, and remove registration and ID papers.

Take special care at pedestrian crosswalks in Montréal: drivers don't take them seriously.

TELEPHONE

Bell Canada, the public phone giant, serves all of Québec. Local calls from a pay phone cost 25¢. With the popularity of cell phones, public phones are getting harder and harder to find. When you do find them they will generally be coin-operated but many also accept phone cards and credit cards.

The area code for the entire Island of Montréal is ☎ 514. The immediate region around the island is ☎ 450, while Québec City's area code is ☎ 418. Both cities are slowly converting over to 10-digit phone numbers from seven. That means that when you dial your seven digit number,

you will increasingly be asked to punch in the area code as well. This may apply even if you are dialing from the same area code as where you want to call.

Toll-free numbers begin with ☎ 800, ☎ 888, ☎ 877 or ☎ 777 and must be preceded with 1. Some numbers are good throughout North America, others only within Canada and still others in just one province.

Dialing the operator (☎ 0), directory assistance (☎ 411) or the emergency number (☎ 911) is free of charge from both public and private phones. If you require long-distance directory assistance, you need to dial ☎ 1 + area code + 555-1212. This phone service is also free of charge.

Cell Phones

The GSM/GPRS network in Québec is sparse – outside the urban areas reception may be poor.

Consumer electronics stores like Future Shop (p182) sell wireless and prepaid deals of use to travelers.

In Montréal:

Espace Bell (Map pp310–11; ☎ 843-8488; www.bell.ca; 677 rue Ste-Catherine Ouest)

Rogers AT&T (Map pp310–11; ☎ 830-2532; www.rogers.com; 1104 rue Ste-Catherine Ouest)

Telus (☎ 830-2532; www.telusmobility.com)

In Québec City:

Espace Bell (Map p205; ☎ 658-8678; www.bell.ca; 677 pl Laurier, Ste-Foy-Sillery)

Phone Cards

Bell Canada's prepaid Quick Change card, in denominations of $5, $10 and $20, works from public and private phones. It's available from post offices and vending machines.

Many local phone cards offer better rates than Bell's. Sold at convenience stores and newsstands, the cards have catchy names such as Mango, Big Time, Giant and Lucky.

The Phone Card Store (www.phonecardstore.ca) sells virtual phone cards online and can tell you precisely which card is cheapest for the country you want to call – they simply email you a dial-up number and an account PIN.

TELEVISION

The main public-radio and TV stations are run by the Canadian Broadcasting Corporation (CBC is the English-language service, and Radio-Canada is French-language). It's the flagship of Canadian content in music and information, much like the BBC is in Britain.

The other major English-language national TV network is the Canadian TV Network (CTV, channel 11), the chief English-language commercial channel. It broadcasts a mix of Canadian and US programs as well as popular national news every night.

In Québec the major French-language commercial channels are Télé-Québec (TVA) and Télévision Quatre-Saisons (TQS). These channels are where you will find news, Québec drama and comedy shows, movies from France and US shows dubbed into French.

TIME

Montréal is on Eastern Time (EST/EDT), as is New York City and Toronto. Noon in Montréal is 9am in Vancouver and Los Angeles, 1pm in Halifax, 5pm in London and 6pm in Paris, 2am the next day in Tokyo and 3am the next day in Sydney.

Canada switches to daylight-saving time (one hour later than Standard Time) on the last Sunday in April, making the days seem deliciously long. Clocks are turned back to Standard Time on the last Sunday in October.

Train schedules, film screenings and schedules in French use the 24-hour clock, also known as military time (eg 6:30pm becomes 18:30) while English schedules use the 12-hour clock.

TIPPING

A tip of 15% of the pretax bill is customary in restaurants. A few restaurants may include a service charge on the bill for large parties. No tip should be added in this case, unless you feel the service was extraordinary and deserving of even more. It is acceptable to hand the tip directly to a member of staff or to discreetly leave it behind on the table as you leave. You are expected to tip when you receive bar service too, and it especially helps to give a nice fat tip at the time of ordering your first drink – this way, you won't go thirsty all night.

Tips of 10% to 15% are also given to taxi drivers, hairdressers and barbers. Hotel bellhops and redcaps (porters) at airports and train stations should get a dollar or two per item minimum.

TOURIST INFORMATION

Montréal and Québec province share two central phone numbers for **tourist information offices** (☎ 514-873-2015, 877-266-5687; www.tourism-montreal.org). The airports have information kiosks that open year-round.

Centre Infotouriste (Map pp310–11; 1001 rue Square-Dorchester; ☯ 7am-8pm Jun-Labour Day, 9am-6pm rest of year; Ⓜ Peel) Teems with information on all areas of Montréal and Québec. The center also has a bookstore and currency-exchange counter, and staff can arrange guided tours and car rentals. Hotel reservations are provided free of charge.

Old Montréal Tourist Office (Map p314; 174 rue Notre-Dame Est; ☯ 9am-7pm late Jun-early Oct, 9am-5pm rest of year; Ⓜ Champ-de-Mars) Just off bustling pl Jacques-Cartier, this little office is always humming but staff are extremely helpful.

Old Port Tourist Kiosk (Map p314; IMAX/Centre de Sciences, Old Port; ☯ 10am-7pm Jun-Labour Day) At the entrance to the IMAX/Centre de Sciences complex.

In Québec City:

Centre Infotouriste (Map p220; ☎ 649-2608, 800-363-7777; 12 rue Ste-Anne; ☯ 8:30am-7:30pm late Jun-early Oct, 9am-5pm rest of year) Central location in Old Town.

Centre Infotouriste (Map p205; ☎ 641-6290, 800-266-5687, ext 798; 835 ave Wilfrid-Laurier; ☯ 8:30am-7:30pm Jun-early Oct, 9am-5pm Mon-Thu & Sat, 9am-6pm Fri, 10am-4pm Sun rest of year) In Battlefields Park.

TRAVELERS WITH DISABILITIES

Most public buildings in Montréal – including tourist offices, major museums and attractions – are wheelchair accessible, and many restaurants and hotels also have facilities for the mobility-impaired. Métro stations are not wheelchair accessible. However, almost all major bus routes are now serviced by NOVA LFS buses adapted for wheelchairs. It's recommended that you consult the bus service's website (www.stm.info/English/bus/a-usager-aps.htm) if you are a first-time user, to check availability on your route and become familiar with the boarding procedure on the adapted buses. **Access to Travel** (www.accesstotravel.gc.ca) provides details of accessible transportation across Canada.

Kéroul (Map pp308–9; ☎ 252-3104; www.keroul.qc.ca; 4545 ave Pierre-de-Coubertin; Ⓜ Pie-IX) Publishes *Québec Accessible* ($15), listing 1800-plus hotels, restaurants and attractions in the province rated by accessibility. It also offers packages for disabled travelers going to Québec and Ontario.

VIA Rail (Map pp310–11; ☎ 871-6000, 888-842-7733; www.viarail.com) Accommodates people in wheelchairs in 48 hours notice. Details are available at Via Rail offices at the Gare Centrale, Québec City's Gare du Palais and other Canadian train stations.

Buses in Québec City's public transit are not wheelchair accessible, though there are other services available for travelers with disablities.

Transport Adapté du Québec Métro inc (☎ 687-2641) Has 20 wheelchair adapted minibuses that zip around Québec. Make reservations from 7am to noon.

Transport Accessible du Québec (☎ 641-8294) Wheechair-adapted vans available. Make reservations 24 hours in advance.

VISAS

Visas are not required for visitors from nearly all Western countries. You will need to get a visa if you are from South Africa, Taiwan, developing countries or certain parts of Eastern Europe. Visa requirements change frequently so it would be a good idea to check with the **Citizen and Immigration Canada call center** (☎ 888-242-2100; www.cic.gc.ca), or to touch base with your Canadian consulate.

Single-entry visitor visas ($75) are valid for six months, while multiple-entry visas ($150) can be used over two years, provided that no single stay exceeds six months. Extensions cost the same price as the original and must be applied for at a Canadian Immigration Center one month before the current visa expires. A separate visa is required if you intend to work in Canada.

A passport and/or visa does not guarantee entry. The admission and duration of a permitted stay is based on a number of factors, including being of good health, being law abiding, having sufficient money and, possibly, having a return ticket out of the country.

If you are refused entry but have a visa, you have the right of appeal to the Immigration Appeal Board at the port of entry. People aged under 18 years should have a letter from a parent or guardian.

WOMEN TRAVELERS

Montréal holds high standards for women's safety, especially when compared to major US cities. Still, the usual advice applies: women should avoid walking alone late at night or in poorly lit areas, like Parc du Mont-Royal.

It is illegal in Canada to carry pepper spray or mace. Instead, some women recommend carrying a whistle to deal with attackers or potential dangers. If you are sexually assaulted call ☎ 911 or the **Sexual Assault Center** (☎ 934-4504) in Montréal for referrals to hospitals that have sexual-assault care centers in Montréal or Québec City.

WORK

It is difficult to get a work permit in Canada as employment opportunities go to Canadians first. You will need to provide proof of a valid job offer from a specific employer to your local Canadian consulate or embassy.

Employers hiring casual workers often don't ask for a permit, but visitors working legally in the country have Social Insurance numbers. If you don't have one and get caught, you will be told to leave the country.

One-year working-holiday visas are made available to 5500 Australians and 800 New Zealanders between the ages of 18 and 30 every year. Apply as early as possible and allow 12 weeks for processing. Application forms are available through the Canadian consulate (www.canada.org.au) in Sydney.

The Student Work Abroad Program (SWAP) offers 3500 working holidays every year for people 18 to 25 years of age in nearly 20 countries, including Australia, Britain, France, Ireland, Japan, South Africa, the USA and New Zealand. Participants are issued with a one-year, nonextendable visa to work anywhere in Canada. Most 'Swappers' find jobs in the service industry as waiters, hotel porters, bar attendants or farmhands. SWAP Canada (via www.travel cuts.com) and student travel agencies can provide details.

Business Centers

Compared to Toronto and other Canadian cities, Montréal is attractive for its well priced office rents, skilled labor and business facilities.

HQ Global Workplaces (Map pp310–11; ☎ 934-5518; www.hq.com; 1250 boul René-Lévesque Ouest) Provides turnkey office facilities, conference rooms, and secretarial and administrative support for the short and long term.

Montréal International (Map p314; ☎ 987-8191; www.montreal-intl.com; 380 rue St-Antoine Ouest, Centre de Commerce Mondial) Organizes conferences and access to rented offices, project counseling and relocation services.

In Québec City, you will have difficulty finding business centers offering services in English. Given the tiny English minority in town, you can't count on easily finding English-language secretarial services or administrative support at the last minute if at all. Your best bet is to inquire at the business center of your hotel for contacts or recommendations and make your inquiries as far ahead of time as possible. For larger events, however, there is an excellent convention center near Old Town:

Centre de Congrès de Québec (Map p226; ☎ 644-4000; 888-679-4000; www.convention.qc.ca; administration 900 boul René-Lévesque Est, convention center 1000 boul René-Lévesque Est)

Language

Language

It's true – anyone can speak another language. Don't worry if you haven't studied languages before or that you studied a language at school for years and can't remember any of it. It doesn't even matter if you failed English grammar. After all, that's never affected your ability to speak English! And this is the key to picking up a language in another country. You just need to start speaking.

Learn a few key phrases before you go. Write them on pieces of paper and stick them on the fridge, by the bed or even on the computer – anywhere that you'll see them often.

You'll find that Quebecers appreciate travelers trying their language, no matter how muddled you may think you sound. So don't just stand there, say something! If you want to learn more French than we've included here, pick up a copy of Lonely Planet's comprehensive but user-friendly *French Phrasebook*.

CANADIAN FRENCH

The French spoken in Canada is essentially the same as what you'd hear in France. There are differences, however, just as there are between the English of New Zealand and the English of Australia. Although many English (and most French) students in Québec are still taught the French of France, the local tongue is known as 'Québécois' or *joual*. While many around the world schooled in Parisian French would say *Quelle heure est-il?* for 'What time is it?,' on the streets of Québec you're likely to hear *Y'est quelle heure?* Québécois people will have no problem understanding more formal French.

Other differences between European French and the Québec version worth remembering (because you don't want to go hungry!) are the terms for breakfast, lunch and dinner. Rather than *petit déjeuner*, *déjeuner* and *dîner* you're likely to see and hear *déjeuner*, *dîner* and *souper*.

If you have any car trouble, you'll be happy to know that English terms are generally used for parts. Indeed, the word *char* (pronounced 'shar') for car may be heard. Hitchhiking is known not as *auto stop* but as *le pousse* (the thumb).

Announcers and broadcasters on Québec TV and radio tend to speak a more refined, European style of French, as does the upper class. Visitors to the country without much everyday French-speaking experience will have the most luck understanding them.

Despite all this, the preservation of French in Québec is a primary concern and fuels the separatist movement.

New Brunswick is, perhaps surprisingly, the only officially bilingual province. French is widely spoken, particularly in the north and east. Again, it is somewhat different from the French of Québec. Nova Scotia and Manitoba also have significant French-speaking populations, and there are pockets in most other provinces.

The following is a short guide to some French words and phrases that may be useful for the traveler. Québec French employs a lot of English words; this may make understanding and speaking the language a little easier.

For words and phrases related to food and dining, see p000. For a far more comprehensive guide to the language, get a copy of Lonely Planet's *French Phrasebook*.

SOCIAL
Be Polite!

Politeness pays dividends and the easiest way to make a good impression on people you encounter is always to say *Bonjour Monsieur/Madame/Mademoiselle* when you enter a shop, and *Merci Monsieur/Madame /Mademoiselle, au revoir* when you leave. *Monsieur* means 'sir' and can be used with any adult male. *Madame* is used where 'Mrs' or 'Ma'am' would apply in English. Officially, *Mademoiselle* (Miss) relates to unmarried women, but it's much more common to use *Madame* – unless of course you know the person's marital status! Similarly, if you want help or need to interrupt someone, approach them with *Excusez-moi, Monsieur/Madame/Mademoiselle.*

Meeting People

Hello.
Bonjour/Salut. (polite/informal)
Goodbye.
Au revoir/Salut. (polite/informal)
Please.
S'il vous plaît.
Thank you (very much).
Merci (beaucoup).
You're welcome. (don't mention it)
Je vous en prie.
Yes/No.
Oui/Non.
Do you speak English?
Parlez-vous anglais?
Do you understand (me)?
Est-ce que vous (me) comprenez?
Yes, I understand.
Oui, je comprends.
No, I don't understand.
Non, je ne comprends pas.

Could you please ...?
Pourriez-vous ..., s'il vous plaît?

repeat that	répéter
speak more slowly	parler plus lentement
write it down	l'écrire

Going Out

What's on ...?
Qu'est-ce qu'il y a comme spectacles ...?

locally	dans le coin
this weekend	en fin de semaine
today	aujourd'hui
tonight	ce soir

Where are the ...?
Où sont les ...?

clubs	clubs/boîtes
gay venues	bars gais
places to eat	restaurants
pubs	pubs

Is there a free entertainment weekly?
Est-ce qu'il y a un journal gratuit avec les horaires des spectacles?

PRACTICAL
Question Words

Who?	Qui?
Which?	Quel/Quelle? (m/f)
When?	Quand?
Where?	Où?
How?	Comment?

Numbers & Amounts

0	zéro
1	un
2	deux
3	trois
4	quatre
5	cinq
6	six
7	sept
8	huit
9	neuf
10	dix
11	onze
12	douze
13	treize
14	quatorze
15	quinze
16	seize
17	dix-sept
18	dix-huit
19	dix-neuf
20	vingt
21/22	vingt et un/vingt deux
30	trente
40	quarante
50	cinquante
60	soixante
70	soixante-dix
80	quatre-vingts
90	quatre-vingt-dix
100/200	cent/deux cent
1000/2000	mille/deux mille

Days

Monday	lundi
Tuesday	mardi
Wednesday	mercredi
Thursday	jeudi
Friday	vendredi
Saturday	samedi
Sunday	dimanche

Where's the nearest ...?
Où est ... le plus proche?

ATM	le guichet automatique
foreign exchange office	le bureau de change

Banking

I'd like to ...
Je voudrais ...

cash a cheque	encaisser un chèque
change money	changer de l'argent
change some traveler's cheques	changer des chèques de voyage

Post

Where is the post office?
Où est le bureau de poste?

I want to send a ...
Je voudrais envoyer ...

letter	une lettre
parcel	un paquet
postcard	une carte postale

I want to buy ...
Je voudrais acheter ...

an aerogram	un aérogramme
an envelope	une enveloppe
a stamp	un timbre

Phones & Mobiles

I want to buy a phone card.
Je voudrais acheter une carte téléphonique.
I want to make a call (to Australia/to).
Je veux téléphoner (en Australie).
I want to make a reverse-charge/collect call.
Je veux téléphoner à frais virés.

Where can I find a/an ...?
Où est-ce quee je peux trouver ...?
I'd like a/an ...
Je voudrais ...

adaptor plug	une prise multiple
charger for my phone	un chargeur pour mon cellulaire
mobile/cell phone for hire	louer un cellulaire
prepaid mobile/ cell phone	un cellulaire à carte pré-payée
SIM card for your network	une carte SIM pour le réseau

Internet

Where's the local internet café?
Est-ce qu'il y a un café Internet dans le coin?

I'd like to ...
Je voudrais ...

check my email	consulter mon courrier électronique
get online	me connecter à l'internet

Transportation

What time does the ... leave?
À quelle heure part ...?

bus	le bus
ferry	le bateau
plane	l'avion
train	le train

What time's the ... bus?
Le ... bus passe à quelle heure?

first	premier
last	dernier
next	prochain

Are you free? (taxi)
Vous êtes libre?
Please put the meter on.
S'il vous plaît, pouvez-vous partir le compteur?
How much is it to ...?
C'est combien pour aller à ...?
Please take me to (this address).
Conduisez-moi à (cette adresse), s'il vous plaît.

FOOD

breakfast	le petit déjeuner
lunch	le dîner
dinner	le souper
snack	un casse-croûte
eat	manger
drink	boire

Can you recommend a ...
Est-ce que vous pouvez me conseiller un ...

bar/pub	bar/pub
café	café
restaurant	un restaurant

Is service/cover charge included in the bill?
Le service est compris?

For more detailed information on food and dining out, see pp28-32.

EMERGENCIES

It's an emergency!
C'est urgent!
Could you please help me/us?
Este-ce que vous pourriez m'aider/nous aider, s'il vous plaît?
Call the police/a doctor/an ambulance!
Appelez la police/un médecin/ une ambulance!

Where's the police station?	I need a doctor (who speaks English).
Où est le poste de police?	J'ai besoin d'un médecin (qui parle anglais).

HEALTH

Where's the nearest ...?
Où est ... le/la plus prochain/e? (m/f)

chemist (night)	la pharmacie (de nuit)
dentist	le dentiste
doctor	le médecin
hospital	l'hôpital (m)

Symptoms

I have (a) ...
J'ai ...

diarrhoea	la diarrhée
fever	de la fièvre
headache	mal à la tête
pain	une douleur

GLOSSARY

allophone – a person whose mother tongue is neither French nor English

anglophone – a person whose monther tongue is English

Automatistes – group of French-Canadian dissident artists founded by Paul-Émile Borduas in the early 1940s

beaux arts – architectural style popular in France and Québec in the late 19th century, incorporating elements that are massive, elaborate and often ostentatious

Bill 101 – law that asserts the primacy of the French language in Québec, notably on signage

boîte à chanson – club devoted to *chanson française*, folk music from Québec or France

boreal – refers to the Canadian north and its character, as in the boreal forest or the boreal wind

brochette – kebab

cabane à sucre – the place where the collected maple sap is distilled in large kettles and boiled as part of the production of maple syrup

calèche – horse-drawn carriage that can be taken around parts of Montréal and Québec City

Canadian Shield – also known as the Precambrian or Laurentian Shield, this is a plateau of rock that was formed 2½ billion years ago and covers much of the northern region of the country

Cantons de l'Est – Eastern Townships, a former Loyalist region southeast of Montréal toward the US border

CLSC – Centre Local de Santé Communautaire, or local community health center, marked with green-and-white CLSC signs

correspondance – a transfer slip like those used between the metro and bus networks in Montréal

côte – a hill, as in Côte du Beaver Hall

dépanneur – called 'dep' for short, this is a Québec term for a convenience store

Estrie – a more recent term for Cantons de l'Est (see above) but that refers to the same thing

First Nations – a term used to denote Canada's indigenous peoples, sometime used instead of Native Indians or Amerindians

francophone – a person whose mother tongue is French

Front de Libération du Québec (FLQ) – a radical, violent political group active in the 1970s that advocated Québec's separation from Canada

gîte (du passant) – French term for B&B or similar lodging

Group of Seven – a group of celebrated Canadian painters from the 1920s

Hochelaga – name of early Iroquois settlement on the site of present-day Montréal

Hudson Bay Company – an English enterprise created in 1670 to exploit the commercial potential of the Hudson Bay and its waterways. The Bay (La Baie) department store is the last vestige of Canada's oldest firm.

Je me souviens – this Québec motto with a nationalist ring ('I remember') appears on license plates across the province

loonie – Canada's one-dollar coin, so named for the loon stamped on one side

Mounties – Royal Canadian Mounted Police (RCMP)

portage – old process of transporting boats and supplies overland between navigable waterways. Also the overland route used for such a purpose.

poutine – French fries served with gravy and cheese curds. Also comes in several other varieties

Québécois – the French spoken in Québec, someone from the province of Québec, someone from Québec City

Quiet Revolution – period of intense change in Québec during the 1960s marked by state intervention, educational reform, secularization of society and an increased awareness of national identity among Québecers

Refus Global – the radical manifest of a group of Québec artists and intellectuals during the Duplessis era (1944–59)

ringuette – a sport played on ice, similar to hockey but with a ring instead of a puck and a straight stick with no flat or angled end

SAQ – Société des Alcools du Québec, a state-run agency whose branches sell wines, spirits, beer etc

seigneury – land in Québec originally held by grant from the King of France. A seigneur is thus a holder of a seigneury.

stimés – hotdog with a steamed bun
Sulpicians – society of Catholic priests founded in Paris in 1641

table d'hôte – fixed-price meal (of the day)
téléroman – a type of Québec TV program that's a cross between soap opera and prime-time drama, in French
toastés – hotdog with a toasted bun

toonie – also spelled 'twonie,' a Canadian two-dollar coin introduced after the '*loonie*,' or one-dollar coin
tourtière – Québec meat pie usually made of pork and beef or veal, sometimes with game meat

voyageur – a boatman (or woodsman, guide, trapper or explorer) employed by one of the early fur-trading companies

Behind the Scenes

THE LONELY PLANET STORY

The story begins with a classic travel adventure: Tony and Maureen Wheeler's 1972 journey across Europe and Asia to Australia. There was no useful information about the overland trail then, so Tony and Maureen published the first Lonely Planet guidebook to meet a growing need.

From a kitchen table, Lonely Planet has grown to become the largest independent travel publisher in the world, with offices in Melbourne (Australia), Oakland (USA) and London (UK). Today Lonely Planet guidebooks cover the globe. There is an ever-growing list of books and information in a variety of media. Some things haven't changed. The main aim is still to make it possible for adventurous travellers to get out there – to explore and better understand the world.

At Lonely Planet we believe travellers can make a positive contribution to the countries they visit – if they respect their host communities and spend their money wisely. Every year 5% of company profit is donated to charities around the world.

THIS BOOK

This first edition of *Montréal & Québec City* was written by Eilís Quinn. This guidebook was commissioned in Lonely Planet's Oakland office, and produced by the following:

Commissioning Editor Emily K Wolman

Coordinating Editor Alison Ridgway

Coordinating Cartographer Anthony Phelan

Coordinating Layout Designer Jessica Rose

Managing Editors Barbara Delissen & Geoff Howard

Managing Cartographer Alison Lyall

Assisting Editors Emma Gilmour, Charlotte Harrison, Jocelyn Harewood, Shawn Low, Kate McLeod, Simon Sellars

Assisting Cartographers Owen Eszeki

Assisting Layout Designers Jim Hsu, David Kemp, Wibowo Rusli, Jacqui Saunders, Cara Smith

Cover Designer Jane Hart

Color Designer Jessica Rose

Indexer Alison Ridgway

Project Manager Nancy Ianni

Language Content Coordinator Quentin Frayne

Thanks to
Piotr Czajkowski, Sally Darmody, Jennifer Garrett, Darren O'Connell, Lachlan Ross, Celia Wood

Cover photographs Montreal's Olympic Stadium, Montréal, Quebéc Tibor Bognar/APLCorbis (top), Brightly coloured convention center, Chris Cheadle/Getty Images (bottom) Ray Laskowitz/Lonely Planet Images, (back).

Internal photographs by Ray Laskowitz/Lonely Planet Images except for the following: p70 Eddie Brady; p7 (#3), p9 (#2), p10 (#1 & #3), p12 (#2), p51, p64, p117, p129, p200, p209, p214, p229 p252 Chris Cheadle/Getty Images; p11 (#3), p13 (#1), p16 Richard Cummins/Lonely Planet Images; p15 (#1) Alain Evrard/ Lonely Planet Images; p7 (#2) Rick Gerharter/Lonely Planet Images; p12 (#1), p14 (#1) Kevin Levesque/Lonely Planet Images; p5 (#1), p6 (#3), p9 (#4) & p11 (#2) Abbott Low Moffat III/ freelance; p13 (#2) Stephen Saks/Lonely Planet Images; p8 (#1), p6 (#2) Neil Setchfield/Lonely Planet Images; p12 (#3), p14 (#2 & #3) p216, p222, p225 Mario Tama/Getty Images; p15 (#2) & p259 Glenn van der Knijff/Lonely Planet Images

Thanks to www.tourisme-montreal.org for p4 (#2) Jean-Marc Ayral/Productions de l'Œil; p4 (#1) Caroline Hayeur; p20 Gilles Mingasson/Productions de l'Œil, p5 (#3), p10 (#2), p38 p54, p78, p80, p111, p121, p136, p141, p158, p182 Stéphan Poulin; p106 Pierre St-Jacques/Canadian Tourism Commission; p4 (#4) Linda Turgeon; p23 Just for Laughs Festival; p75 Tourisme Québec

Thanks to Hugo at www.montrealjazzfest.com for supplying images p3 Denis Alix/Montréal Jazz festival & p57 Victor Diaz Lamich/Montréal Jazz festival.

Thanks for Local Voices Photos: p26 Pascale Prinsen-Geerligs & p58 Melvin Fossett by Eilís Quinn; p30 Normand Laprise by Louis Prud'homme; p37 Benoît Labonté, supplied by Montréal City Hall; p39 Karim Benzaïd, by Michel Pinault; p58 Vic Vogel, supplied by Bob Pover; p169 Chantal Petitclerc, supplied by Guy Ménard; p243 Réglisse aka Claude Barabé

All images are copyright of the photographer unless otherwise indicated. Many of the images in this guide are available for licensing from Lonely Planet Images: lonelyplanetimages.com.

THANKS
EILÍS QUINN

Mille mercis, 'a thousand thank yous', and probably a hell of a lot more are due to Céline Côté, Robert Gillet, Mathieu at Mille Grains, the staff of the Cinéma Cartier in Québec City and to Marc-Alex and Gabriel at HMV Montréal for turning me on to Karkwa and Fred Fortin, you guys are walking musical encyclopedias, amazing! Also in Québec City mille mercis are due Hélène Morin and M Robitaille at the Union des Artistes and to Patrick Ouellet and David Desjardins at *Voir Québec*. All went above and beyond with their time, generosity and enthusiasm. Each of you has a beer on me if you're ever in Montréal.

Je tiens aussi á souligner l'aimable collaboration de Karim Benzaïd, Melvin Fossett Benoît Labonté, Normand Laprise, Chantal Petiticlerc, Pascale Prinsen-Geerligs, Vic Vogel et Réglisse. My profound thanks to you all for making time in your days for our long chats.

And last, but totally not least, to all of the incredible artists, actors, musicians, performers, writers and filmmakers in this wild and wacky province. No matter how often, or where I've tried to pick up and move to, you guys keep me anchored to Québec and have made it impossible to ever leave.

SEND US YOUR FEEDBACK

OUR READERS

Many thanks to the travelers who used the last edition and wrote to us with helpful hints, useful advice and interesting anecdotes:

Scott Ahearn, John Annabell, Denise Arnold, Pascale Aucoin, Katherine Austin, Idelberto Badell, Martine Baldassi, John Barthelme, Yvon Beauchamp, Pierre Bellavance, Melanie Benoit, Andrea Berreth, Alison Bibra, Mariette Bliekendaal, Nico Bohr, Stephanie Bolduc, James Bown, Willard Bradley, Peter Brereton, Paul Burton, Donna Buxton, Kelly Byrnes, Mark Canning, Thierry Carquet, Ajittt Chauhan, Kaity Cheng, Eve Chenu, K M Chow, Phil Clark, Neville Clarke, Roger Cloutier, Thea Collin, Lenior Corbeau, Mario Cordina, Kevin Crampton, Brenda Crnkovic, Kirk Dale, Steffen Daniel, Janet David, R Laurence Davis, James Derry, Dominique Devoucoux, Myriam Dulude, Geoffroy Faribault, Gabriele Faust, Richard Foltz, Maggie Fox, Constantin Friedman, Laraine Frilay, Boris Funke, Bruce Gilsen, Eddie Glennon, Heiko Glessmann, Colin Godfrey, George Goracz, Lynda Graham, Parveen Grewal, Sabine Groener, Jean-Lou Hamelin, Sarah Harmer, Lindsay Harris, Derek Henderson, Carol Hobden, Barbara Hopkins, Jim Hulme, Alan Humphries, Christopher James, Jocelyn Jouan, Junko Kajino, Cheri Kalvort, P Keene, Ian Kilroy, Jasmine Kinjo, Tobias Krause, Celeste Kroll, Peter Kubalek, Kim Latendresse, Kimberlee Lauer, Sylvie Laurenty, Caroll Leduc, Scott Lehmann, Leen Maes, Abi Mansley, Mike Mannion, Hilary Marrinan, Donna Martin, Kathleen McCarthy, Hugh McGuire, Lynnell Mickelsen, Andy & Maureen Mills, Birgit Nepl, Hiroki Ochiai, Sabrina Olender, Wendy Persoon, Sara Pines, Sally T Ringe, Adolfo Rodriguez, Hans-Peter Roggensack, Michael Rowe, Sandrine Ruaux, Matteo Ruggeri, Maik G Seewald, Richard Seguin, Stuart Sharp, Massimo Simoncini, Jocelyne Simoneau, Barney Smith, Allan & Leah Soroko, Tina Spangler, Maxime St-Laurent, Gannon Sugimura, Michel Tanguay, Laurie Thatcher, Suzi Thomson, Betsy Treadway, Frederic Tremblay, Amanda Trombley, Isabel Heim Vadis, Ferenc Vanhoutte, Salvatore Vespa, Janet Wagner, Virginia Wan, Pauline Watson, Patrick Weeding, Kellie Williams, Alison Wilson, Ann Yonetani

ACKNOWLEDGMENTS

Many thanks to the following for the use of their content: Montréal Metro © 2006 Société de transport de Montréal

Notes

Notes

Notes

Notes

Index

See also separate indexes for Eating (pp300-1), Entertainment (pp301-2), Shopping (p302) and Sleeping (pp302-3).

Index

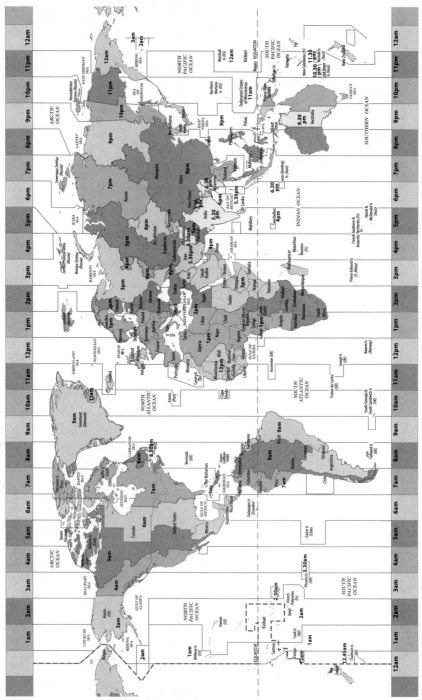

304

MAP LEGEND

ROUTES

Tollway	One-Way Street
Freeway	Mall/Steps
Primary Road	Tunnel
Secondary Road	Walking Tour
Tertiary Road	Walking Tour Detour
Lane	Walking Trail
Under Construction	Walking Path
Track	Pedestrian Overpass
Unsealed Road	

TRANSPORT

Ferry	Rail
Metro	Tram
Monorail	Cable Car, Funicular

HYDROGRAPHY

River, Creek	Canal
Swamp	Water

BOUNDARIES

International	Ancient Wall
State, Provincial	Cliff

AREA FEATURES

Airport	Forest
Area of Interest	Land
Building, Featured	Mall
Building, Information	Park
Building, Other	Reservation
Building, Transport	Rocks
Cemetery, Christian	Sports

POPULATION

✪ CAPITAL (NATIONAL)	◉ CAPITAL (STATE)
● Large City	● Medium City
● Small City	○ Town, Village

SYMBOLS

Sights/Activities	Drinking	Information
Beach	Drinking	Bank, ATM
Castle, Fortress	Café	Consulate
Christian	**Entertainment**	Hospital, Medical
Monument	Entertainment	Information
Museum, Gallery	**Shopping**	Internet Facilities
Other Site	Shopping	Police Station
Ruin	**Sleeping**	Post Office
Swimming Pool	Sleeping	Telephone
Zoo	**Transport**	Toilets
Eating	Airport	**Geographic**
Eating	Bus Station	Lookout
	Parking Area	Mountain
	Petrol Station	National Park
	Taxi Rank	Pass
		Waterfall

Maps

ISLAND OF MONTRÉAL

A · **B** · **C** · **D**

To Oka
(8km)

Ste-Marthe-
Sur-le-Lac

640

Deux-
Montagnes

St-Eustache

Chemin de la Grande Côte

Rivière des Milles Îles

Boul Ste-Rose

Boul Dagenais

Lac des Deux
Montagnes

Chemin Bord du Lac

Rue les Érables

Parc Nature
du Cap
St-Jacques

Montée Wilson

Chemin Cherrier

Montée de l'Église

Île Bizard

Chemin
du Tour

148

Montée Champagne

13

Boul Gouin

To Sucrerie de la
Montagne (40km),
Ottawa (155km)

Morgan
Arboretum

Senneville

Ste-Anne
de Bellevue

Île Bizard

Chemin du Bord de l'Eau

440

Boul Cleroux

Chemin Ste-Marie

Ste-Geneviève

Baie d'Urfé

Pierrefonds

Boul Pierrefonds

8

Roxboro

Chemin du Souvenir

Autoroute Chomedey

117

Île Perrot

20

Kirkland

Boul Beaconsfield

Boul St-Charles

Boul St-Jean

Dollard des
Ormeaux

Boul des Sources

Rivière des Prairies

Boul Samson

Boul Gouin Ouest

Boul Perrot

Beaconsfield

Chemin Lakeshore

Boul Hymus

Boul Brunswick
Voie de Service Nord

Parc Nature
du Bois
de Liesse

Boul Henri Bourassa

Pointe Claire

Golf
Dorval
3

Pointe du
Moulin

Biae de
Valois

Lac St-Louis

Chemin Bord du Lac

Airport International
de Montréal
(Pierre Elliott Trudeau
International Aitport)

40

Boul Marcel Laurin

Dorval

Ave Dorval

Chemin de la Côte Vertu

St-Laurent

117

Île Dorval

Autoroute de la Côte de Liesse

13

520

15

Chemin St-Bernard

Île des
Soeurs
Grises

Principale

Boul St-François

Boul St-Joseph

Côte St-Luc

Autoroute Décarie

132

Châteauguay

Rivière Haute

Boul St-Francis

Kahnawake

Lachine

Hampstead

Rivière Châteauguay

Boul Salaberry

Boul d'Anjou

138

132

St-Pierre

Montréal
Ouest

138

20

138

Boul René Lévesque

138

Boul Ste-Marguerite

Boul Industrie

Kahnawake
Indian Reserve

207

Pont
Honoré
Mercier

Rue Airlie

Boul Newman

Boul des Trembles

Ste-Marguerite

30

Chemin St-Isidore

Rivière Suzanne

Parc
Angrignon

La Salle

Boul LaSalle

Verdun

Rue St-Jacques

Rapides de Lachine

Île au
Chèvres

Île au
Diable

Île aux Hérons

See City of Montreal Map (pp308–9)

Rivière St-Régis

Rang St-Régis Nord
Rang St-Régis Sud

Montée Ste-Catherine

Ste-Catherine

132

St Lawrence River

Rue Marie-Victorin

Rue Principale

Chemin St-Rémi

209

Rue St-Pierre

Rivière St-Pierre

St-Constant

4

0 _____ 5 km
0 _____ 3 miles

E **F** **G** **H**

640
To Mirabel
Airport (22km)   Ste-Thérèse   **1**
Parc
Milles Îles   Montée Lesage
Boisbriand   Chemin Gascon
344   15   Rosemère   Lorraine
6   117   Bois-des-Filion   640
Chemin de la Grande-Côte   Côte Terrebonne
Boul Ste-Rose   337
Boul Curé-Labelle   Boul des Terrasses   Boul des Mille Îles
Boul Ste-Rose   344   To St-Donat
Rang de l'Équerre   Ave des Perron   (130km)   **2**
Boul Bellerose   Boul Ste-Marie   125
15   Mtée St-Aubin   Île de Jésus   Terrebonne   25
Laval   Boul St-Élzear Ouest   Boul des Laurentides   To Joliette
Boul Chomedey   Boul St-Martin   Rang Bas   (37.5km)
2   Boul René   St-François   125
Boul Daniel-Johnson   Laennec   Montée St-François   Rivière des Mille Îles   640
Boul Industriel   148   440   125
Boul de la Concorde   335   19   Boul 440   **3**
Boul Cartier   25   Montée du Moulin   Lachenaie
15   Boul Lévesque   Rivière des Prairies   Boul des Mille Îles
Autoroute des Laurentides   Boul Henri Bourassa Est   Boul Léger   344
Boul Henri   19   **Montréal**   Boul Lacordaire   **Rivière-des-**   Boul Lévesque
Bourassa Ouest   **Nord**   Boul Langelier   **Prairies**
Rue Sauvé   Boul Amand-Bombardier   Parc Nature
Ave Papineau   Boul St-Michel   Boul Henri Bourassa Est   de la Pointe-
aux-Prairies
40   15   125   **St-Léonard**   Autoroute Métropolitaine   40   138   To Trois-
Mont-   Parc   25   Rue Jarry Est   Boul Roi-René   138   **Pointe-aux-Trembles**   Rivières
Royal   Jarry   40   25   **Anjou**   Ave St-Donat   Rue Sherbrooke Est   (100km)   **4**
335   Boul Pie IX   Cimetière   Rue Notre-Dame Est
Rue St-Denis   Parc   Repos   138   Île Ste-
Outremont   Maisonneuve   St-François   Ave St-Georges V   **Montréal Est**   Thérèse
Boul Langelier   d'Assise   25   St Lawrence River
Parc du   138   Rue Dickson   Île de
Mont-Royal   Parc   Rue Sherbrooke Est   Île Ste-   la Commune   Île
Westmount   LaFontaine   Rue Hochelaga   Marguerite   Parc des Îles   Grosbois
Rue Sherbrooke Ouest   **Montréal**   1   Rue Ontario Est   de Boucherville   **5**
Île Ste-   Rue Notre-Dame Est   Boul Marie Victorin
Hélène   **Longueuil**   20   132   **Boucherville**   132
10   Parc Jean-   134
20   Drapeau   Boul Fernand-Lafontaine   Boul de Mortagne
Pont Victoria
Île des   **St-Lambert**   Boul Jean-Vincent
Soeurs   Hippolyte-Lafontaine   Boul de Montarville
Boul Roland-Therrien   Boul Jacques-Cartier   Rue Montbrun   **6**
20   112   Chemin du Tremblay
Bassin de   **Greenfield**
la Prairie   **Park**   116   Rue de Touraine
7   Boul Tachereau
10   Boul Grande-Allée
132   Boul St-Wilfrid Laurier   Chemin de la Savane-de-Bretagne   To Québec City   30
15   132   134   To USA (48km); Granby Zoo (50km);   Aéroport   20   (230km)
Eastern Townships (80km)   de St-Hubert

307

CITY OF MONTRÉAL

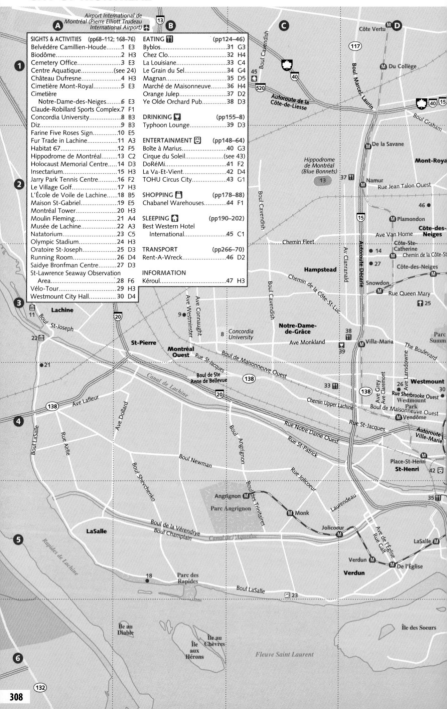

DOWNTOWN

Parc Summit

Chemin Remembrance

Lac des Castors (Beaver Lake)

Parc du Mont-Royal

Chemin Trafalgar
Ave Highland
Ave Travalgar
Chemin de la Côte-des-Neiges
Chemin Hill Park Cir
Chemin Hill Park

Redpath Cres

The Boulevard

Ave Cedar
Ave Mt-Pleasant
Ave Montrose
Ave de Ramezay
Chemin Daulac
Ave Cedar
Chemin McDougall
Chemin Ramezay
Ave Severn
Rosemount C

Ave Cedar

Redpath Cres

Chemin St-Sulpice
Chemin de la Vigne
Ave Holton
Chemin Piquet
Ave des Pins Ouest
Parc Percy Walters

Ave Mountain
Ave Rosemount
Rue Mt-Pleasant
Ave Elm
Ave Wood
Chemin de Casson
Chemin Barat
Chemin Bresby
Ave Docteur-Penfield

Rue Simpson
Rue Redpath
Ave du Musée
Rue de la Montagne

Ave Oliver
Ave Greene
Rue Sherbrooke Ouest
Ave Atwater
Ave Summerhill
Chemin de la Côte-des-Neiges
Rue Sherbrooke Ouest

Boul de Maisonneuve Ouest
Atwater
Ave Lincoln
Ave Lambert Closse
Ave Chomedey
Boul de Maisonneuve Ouest

Guy-Concordia

Square Cabot
Rue Ste-Catherine Ouest
Rue Towers
Rue Pierce
Rue Bishop
Rue Crescent
Rue Mackay
Rue Guy

Boul Dorchester
Rue Staynor
Ave Clandeboye
Rue Prospect
Rue Selby
Rue Sussex
Rue Seymour
Rue du Fort
Rue Baile
Rue St-Marc
Rue St-Mathieu
Rue Tupper

Ave Bruce
Ave Columbia
Ave Souvenir
Ave Hawarden
Boul René-Lévesque Ouest

Autoroute Ville-Marie
Georges-Vanier

Ave Bel Air
Ave Brewster
Ave Walker
Ave Marin
Rue St-Antoine Ouest
Ave Overdale
Lucien-L'Allier
Gare Windsor

Rue Coursol
Rue St-Martin
Rue St-Antoine Ouest
Rue Lusignan
Rue Versailles
Rue Lucien-L'Allier
Ave Atwater
Rue Quesnel
Parc Campbell-Centre
Lionel Groulx
Rue St-Jacques

Rue Delisle
Rue Workman
Parc Vinet
Ave Lionel Groulx
Boul Georges-Vanier
Petite Bourgogne
Rue St-Jacques
Rue Richmond
Rue Guy
Pl Victor Hugo

Rue Notre-Dame Ouest
Rue Duvernay
Rue Ste-Émilie
Rue Vinet
Rue Dominion
Rue Chatham
Rue des Seigneurs
Parc Herb-Trawick
Rue Paxton

Rue Ste-Cunégonde
Rue Barré
Rue Notre-Dame Ouest

DOWNTOWN (pp310–11)

OLD MONTRÉAL & CHINATOWN (p314)

OLD MONTRÉAL & CHINATOWN

0 — 400 m
0 — 0.2 miles

0 ———————— 400 m
0 ———————— 0.2 miles

Rue Sherbrooke Est
Carré St-Louis
Rue St-Denis
Rue de Malines
Rue de Rigaud
Rue Berri
Quartier Latin
Terr St-Denis
Ave Otario Est
Ave Joly
Ave Emery
Rue Cherrier
Rue Berri
Marché St-Jacques
Rue Wolfe
Rue Montcalm
Rue Amherst
Rue St-André
Rue St-Christophe
Rue St-Hubert
Rlle de la Providence
Ave de L'Esplanade
Place Émile Gamelin
Pl Pasteur
Berri-UQAM
Rue Ste-Catherine Est
Rue Sanguinet
Rue Labrecque
Rue St-Timothée
Rue Mercure
Émilie Gamelin
Rue Larivière
Rue Berthier
Rue Beaudry
Rue Robin
Boul de Maisonneuve Est
Rue de la Visitation
Rue Panet
Rue Logan
Rue Plessis
Rue Alexandre de Sève
Rue La Fontaine
Rue de Champlain
Ave Papineau
Parc Persillier-Lachapelle
Beaudry
Boul René-Lévesque Est
Rue Dalcourt
Rue Martineau
Rue Jeannotte
Rue Ste-Rose
Rue Cartier
Rue Danseau
Rue de Champlain
Rue Ste-Catherine Est
Rue Donon
Rue Tansley
Ave de Lorimier
Rue Labelle
Rue Roullier
Rue de La Gauchetière Est
Rue St-André
Rue Bernadette
Rue Notre-Dame de Grâce

315

PLATEAU DU MONT ROYAL

SIGHTS & ACTIVITIES (pp68–112; 168–76)
Altitude Sports Plein Air................1 C4
Armoury of the Mount Royal
  Fusiliers...2 C5
Coupe Bizzarre.................................3 B5
Église St-Jean-Baptiste...................4 C4
George Étienne Cartier
  Monument.......................................5 A4
Institut des Sourdes-Muettes........6 D5
La Maison des Cyclistes..................7 F4
Le Grand Cycle................................8 D6
Palestre Nationale...................(see 53)
Piscine Schubert..............................9 B4
Place Roy.......................................10 D5
Terra Spa.......................................11 B5
Tonic..12 B4

EATING 🍴 (pp124–46)
Au Pain Doré..................................13 B6
Au Pied de Cochon.........................14 D4
Beauty's...15 B2
Bières & Compagnie......................16 C3
Boulangerie Mr Pinchot.................17 E3
Brûlerie St Denis............................18 D4
Café Cherrier..................................19 D6
Café Fruits Folie.............................20 D5
Café Santropol...............................21 B4
Chez Cora......................................22 F3
Coco Rico.......................................23 B5
Euro Deli..24 B6
Jano...25 B5
L'Avenue..26 D3
L'Express..27 D5
La Binerie Mont-Royal...................28 C2
Le Nil Bleu.....................................29 C6
Le Poisson Rouge...........................30 E4
Ma-am-m Bolduc...........................31 H3
Maestro SVP...................................32 B6
Mazurka...33 B6
Misto..34 D2
Moishe's...35 B5
Ouzeri...36 C2
Patati Patata...................................37 B4
Provigo Supermarket.....................38 B3
Restaurant Rapido du Plateau.......39 C3
Schwartz's......................................40 B5
St-Viateur Bagel & Cie...................41 E2
Tampopo..42 E3
Vents du Sud..................................43 C5

DRINKING 🍷 (pp155–8)
Barouf..44 D4
Blizzarts...45 B4
Edgar Hypertavern.........................46 F3
Else's..47 C5
Go-Go Lounge................................48 B6
La Sala Rosa...................................49 B1
Le Swimming..................................50 B6
Les Folies.......................................51 D2
Sofa..52 D4

ENTERTAINMENT 🎭 (pp148–64)
Agora de la Danse.........................53 D6
Barfly...54 B4
Belmont...55 B3
Bily Kun...56 C3
Cactus..57 D3
Café Campus..................................58 B6
Casa del Popolo.............................59 B2
L'Academie de Tango Argentin......60 B3
L'Escogriffe............................(see 57)
Laïka...61 B4
Le Ballatou.....................................62 B3
Le Divan Orange............................63 B3
Le Saloni Daomé............................64 C2
Les Bobards....................................65 B3
Passeport..66 C4
Quai Des Brumes...........................67 D3
Théâtre de Quat' Sous...................68 C5
Théâtre de Verdure........................69 E4
Théâtre du Rideau Vert..................70 C2

SHOPPING 🛍 (pp178–88)
Au Tourne-Livre.............................71 D2
Cruella...72 B2
Friperie St-Laurent.........................73 B4
Kanuk...74 D4
Les Disques Beatnick.....................75 C5
Librairie Michel Fortin...................76 C5
Marché du Disque..........................77 D2
Revenge...78 C5
Scandale...79 B6
Schreter..80 B3
Twist Encore............................(see 73)
U&I...81 B6

SLEEPING 🛏 (pp190–202)
Á la Bonne Heure...........................82 D3
Anne ma Soeur Anne.....................83 D4
Au Piano Blanc...............................84 D3
Auberge de Jeunesse Maeva..........85 D1
Auberge de la Fontaine..................86 F4
Couette et Café Cherrier................87 D6
Downtown B&B Network...............88 C6
Hôtel de l'Institut...........................89 D6
Le Rayon Vert................................90 D3
Mini Hotel B&B Les Pins................91 B5
Pierre et Dominique B&B...............92 C6
Relais Montréal Hospitalité............93 C5
Shézelles..94 D3

TRANSPORT (pp266–70)
Vélo Québec............................(see 99)

INFORMATION
Banque Desjardins..........................95 D2
Banque Laurentienne.....................96 G2
Banque Laurentienne.....................97 B5
Boutique Tourisme Jeunesse..........98 C2
Mont-Royal Information Booth.......99 D3

Rue de Mentana

🍴 41

42
🍴

Rue Boyer
Ave Christophe Colomb
Rue de la Roche
Rue de Brébeuf
Rue Chambord
Rue de Lanaudière
Rue Garnier
Rue Fabre
Rue Marquette
Ave Papineau
Rue Cartier
Rue de Bordeaux
Ave de Lorimier

22 🍴
🚻 46
Ave du Mont-Royal Est
🚻 96

17 🍴

Rue Marie-Anne Est
🍴 31

🍴 30
● 7 🚻 86
Ave Bureau
Rue Rachel Est

69 🏛

Parc
LaFontaine

Rue de Mentana
Rue Napoléon
Ave du Parc La Fontaine
Ave Calixa Lavallée

Rue Sherbrooke Est

Rue Amherst
Rue Wolfe
Rue Montcalm
Rue Beaudry
Rue Plessis

Hospital
Notre-
Dame

Parc
Persillier-
Lachapelle

LITTLE ITALY, MILE END & OUTREMONT

SIGHTS & ACTIVITIES	(pp68–112; 168–76)
Église Madonna della Difesa	1 D2
Église St-Viateur	2 A6
Marché Jean Talon	3 C2
Ovarium	4 D3
St Michael & St Anthony's Church	5 B5

EATING	(pp124–46)
Café l'Esperanza	
(Café la Pharmacie)	6 C5
Caffé Italia	7 C2
Chez Lévêque	8 A6
Fairmount Bagel	9 C6
Il Molino	10 C3
La Maison du Bagel	11 B5
La Moulerie	12 A4
Le Petit Alep	13 C1
Lester's	14 A4
Milano Supermarket	15 C2
Milos	16 B5
Pizzeria Napoletana	17 C2
Restaurant Berlin	18 B6
Senzala	19 B4
Wilensky's Light Lunch	20 C6

DRINKING	(pp155–8)
Dieu du Ciel	21 C6
Mile End	22 C5

ENTERTAINMENT	(pp148–64)
Kola Note	23 B5
Main Hall	24 C5
Théâtre Outremont	25 A4

SHOPPING	(pp178–88)
Au Papier Japonnais	26 C6
Bodybag by Jude	27 C4
General 54	28 C5
Jet-Setter	29 C6
Le Marché des Saveurs	30 D2
Local 23	31 C4
Quincaillerie Dante	32 C2
Un Amour des Thes	33 A4

INFORMATION	
Banque Laurentienne	34 C1
Banque Nationale	35 B6
Laundry	36 C6
Mezza Luna Cooking School	(see 32)